Consensus, Conflict, and American Historians

BERNARD STERNSHER

Consensus, Conflict, and American Historians

INDIANA UNIVERSITY PRESS: BLOOMINGTON & LONDON

Published in Canada by Fitzhenry & Whiteside Limited,
Don Mills, Ontario

Manufactured in the United States of America

Library of Congress Cataloging in Publication Data

Sternsher, Bernard, 1925–
    Consensus, conflict, and American historians.

    Includes bibliographical references.
    1. United States—Historiography.   2. Historians—
United States.   I. Title.
E175.S74   973'.07'2   73-16531
ISBN 0-253-31410-0   75 76 77   1 2 3 4

To my mother Eleanor Bernard Sternsher

Contents

vii

III. Departure from Consensus

IV. Departure from the Consensus View

Preface

Studies relevant to this one have appeared continuously during the course of this inquiry and since its completion. Several articles which were published, or which I learned about, too late for consideration ought to be mentioned. Samuel P. Huntington, "Paradigms of American Politics: Beyond the One, the Two, and the Many," *Political Science Quarterly*, 89 (March 1974), 1–26, is pertinent to chapter 3. James F. Ward, "Toward a Sixth Party System? Partisanship and Political Realignment," *Western Political Quarterly*, 26 (September 1973), 385–413, disagrees with the views of Walter Dean Burnham presented in chapter 6. Howard J. Wiarda, "Toward a Framework for the Study of Political Change in the Iberic-Latin Tradition: The Corporative Model," *World Politics*, 25 (January 1973), 206–35, and James Holt, "Louis Hartz's Fragment Thesis," *New Zealand Journal of History*, 7 (April 1973), 3–11, are assessments of Hartz's fragmentation theory in regard to areas other than the United States—the kind of appraisal called for in chapter 8. Also relevant is James L. Sundquist's *Dynamics of the Party System: Alignment and Realignment of Political Parties in the United States* (Washington, D.C., Brookings Institution, 1973). Unlike Burnham, Sundquist foresees a reversal of the present ticket-splitting and a revival of party loyalties like those of the New Deal era.

History colleagues at Bowling Green State University to whom I am indebted are Lawrence Friedman, Gary Hess, James Graham, and John Resch, who criticized an earlier version of the manuscript, and Stuart Givens and William Rock, former chairmen, who provided constant encouragement. I wish to thank the students in my graduate seminar in American historiography for their fruitful discussions of much of this material as well as their identifying a number of useful sources. I should also like to express my gratitude to the Faculty Research Committee for a grant which enabled me to finish this study in the summer of 1973.

Consensus, Conflict, and American Historians

PART ONE

The Consensus View

and Its Critics

Chapter One
The Consensus View: Ideology and Politics

Point of Entry

In *American Historical Explanations: A Strategy for Grounded Inquiry*, Gene Wise analyzes three approaches that American historians have taken to their subject in the twentieth century: the Progressive, the counter-Progressive, and the New Left (sometimes called neo-Progressive).[1] From about 1910 to about 1950 the Progressive interpretation dominated the field. From about 1950 to about 1965 the counter-Progressive explanation was more widespread. It has been called consensus history, but the theme of consensus and continuity is only one aspect of the counter-Progressive view.

Wise shows how the Progressives and counter-Progressives differed on the question of historical change: the chances of bringing it about, its causes, and its nature. The Progressives believed in the effectiveness of political effort, while the counter-Progressives were "not much for political action." They felt that "those things which really were quite bad couldn't be righted easily or quickly; panaceas, they contended, often made things worse." The Progressives' main concerns were politics and economics, and they were partly environmentalists regarding the causes of change: some ideas, bad or regressive ones, they maintained, reflected dominant groups' self-interest and held back progress. At the same time, other ideas, good or progressive ones, were self-generating and transcended interests, and the idea of progress could serve as "a lever to right the system." The counter-Progressives "inclined away from environmental explanations of people's behavior and were given to exploring the motive forces of history inside the minds and psyches of men." They did not share the Progressives' concern with economics and politics. They derived their perspectives instead from psychology, art, literature, and philosophy. They focused on "people's pictures of reality as embodied through images, myths, and symbols and dramatized in those psychic quests which take men's inner compulsions and project them outward." For the Progressives ideas either connected directly to reality or they did not, but the counter-Progressives saw "even the most blatant falsehoods shaping the behavior of men. They felt these 'myths' had a reality which couldn't be explained away simply by proving them untrue." While the Progressives assumed that most people were ruled by economic motives, the counter-Progressives believed that men are impelled to behave the way they do by psychic quests like the drive for status or the desire to recover some lost innocence. "Where Progressives tried unmasking ideas to see the real driving things below, counter-Progressives tried unmasking things to see the real driving ideas below."[2]

With respect to the nature of change, Wise says the "single master key" to the counter-Progressive form might be its "sense of ambiguity about change." Unlike the Progressives, who found reality directly observable, the counter-Progressives probed myths, symbols, images, nuances, and incongruities, and they uncovered paradox, irony, perversity, and ambiguity. While the Progressives judged everything in experience true or false, the counter-Progressives reflected on the "existential uncertainty of it all." The ideas and motives which drove men, the counter-Progressives believed, were "situation specific," and situations were always shifting. The Progressives insisted that "bad things come from bad ideas, and bad men . . . good things come from good ideas and good men" but counter-Progressives found "good men doing bad things, and through good ideas." Ideas were complex, powerful, and perverse, often producing gains and losses simultaneously. Thus there was no consensus among counter-Progressives on "how one judges whether a change is congenial to justice or not."[3]

The ambiguity which the counter-Progressives stressed over all other ambiguities was the ambiguity of progress. While the Progressives saw progressive change as a "straightforward victory of enlightened reason over inertia," the counter-Progressives, Wise writes, found people sometimes "backing forward into good things" or "backing into their futures" and, ironically, achieving the opposite of what they had intended. Ideas sometimes pointed forward and backward at the same time, and all human actions were a "complicated blend of good and bad and reasonable and unreasonable." Unlike the Progressives, who used a straight-line logic (B follows from A) or a dualistic, either/or logic (A and B are opposed), the counter-Progressives employed a dialectic or both/and logic: things frequently move in a circle, and opposites often merge psychologically in counterpoised tension or in a dialogue which yields a third alternative. Progress was not "all of a piece." Shot through with "reactionary and primitive counterstrains," it was an "over-simplified kind of commitment." Finally, the counter-Progressives' view of progress was evident in their choice of heroes. While Progressives found their idols in Williams, Paine, Jefferson, Jackson, and Wilson, counter-Progressives revealed ambiguities in these Progressive favorites. They also looked with sympathy on the Progressives' villains—conservatives like Winthrop, Hamilton, and businessmen—and they discovered their own identity in figures who shared their sense of ambiguity: Edwards, Melville, Hawthorne, Horace Bushnell, and Henry Adams. If there was an "overarching strategy" in counter-Progressive writings, Wise declares, it was the "drive to break through the progress form."[4]

The counter-Progressives rejected the Progressives' dualisms of haves versus have-nots, in part, Wise notes, because they did not think that have-nots were as desperate in America as elsewhere. This rejection followed from their emphasis on unities—ideas holding Americans together—over conflicts —things dividing Americans. The "most basic public reality" in the counter-Progressive view was culture, a unifying agent, rather than class, a divisive factor and the main feature of the Progressive portrayal of American society. Thus critics of counter-Progressive writings labeled them "consensus." Wise identifies Louis Hartz, Daniel J. Boorstin, Clinton Rossiter, and John William Ward as counter-Progressives whose quest for culture resulted in a "rather homogeneous" picture of America. Hartz, Boorstin, and Richard Hofstadter are the leading generalizers of consensus as a principle for interpreting American history, and in the following pages Hartz and Boorstin receive far more attention than any other counter-Progressives. But Hartz's and Boorstin's interpretations are quite different. Hartz, as Wise points out, is one of the counter-Progressives who "tried unmasking things to see the real driving ideas below"—the symbol-myth-image writers like Henry Nash Smith, Leo Marx, Ward, Alan Trachtenberg, Charles Sanford, Hofstadter, Marvin Meyers, R.W.B. Lewis, Perry Miller, David Noble, and Merrill Peterson. Boorstin—along with Rossiter, Stanley Elkins, and David M. Potter—in some important ways does not fit into the myth-image-symbol group. He is, Wise observes, "the most noted spokesman for this other [experiential] strain in counter-Progressive thinking." Like Rossiter and Elkins, he is committed to the organic continuity of the American experience: "with Boorstin, it was experience, not ideas, which captured the meaning of America."[5]

In his brilliant study, one of the most provocative works in the history of American history, Wise's basic aim is not to present the content of different approaches but to suggest ways of analyzing the process of change from one form to another. Applying his strategy of inquiry in case studies, Wise focuses on Frederick Jackson Turner, Vernon Louis Parrington, Lionel Trilling, Reinhold Niebuhr, Lewis, and Miller, and he writes as an intellectual historian. I am interested not only in the idea of consensus but also in the question whether the idea is empirically true. That is why I distinguish between the consensus view and the fact of consensus, and why I depart at various points from written history to history itself, as well as to sociology, economics, and especially political science. Undoubtedly I shall miss some points that a specialist in intellectual history would see, but I hope that my interest in political history and the social sciences will enable me to point out at least a few things that such a specialist might overlook.

Conformity: Uni-Ideological and Non-Ideological

Consensus writings contain two principal, opposing views of the role of ideology in America. Robert A. Dahl and Louis Hartz express one: Americans, Dahl remarks, "are a highly ideological people. It is only that one ordinarily does not notice their ideology because they are, to an astounding extent, all agreed on the same ideology."[1] Hartz agrees: "We have only had the American Way of Life, a nationalist articulation of Locke which usually does not know that Locke himself is involved. . . ."[2] Arthur Mann paraphrases Hartz: "America was barren of ideologies because it was itself an ideology. . .only this country has enjoyed a 350-year-old consensus of private property, the atomistic society, popular sovereignty, and natural rights."[3] Consensus writers who stress ideology reduce Mann's synthesis to two components: *capitalism* (private property and the atomistic or unplanned economy—although "atomism" connotes the absence of regimentation in general) and *democracy* (popular sovereignty and natural rights).

Daniel J. Boorstin expresses the other view of the role of ideology in America, stressing Americans' belief that "the earliest settlers or the Founding Fathers equipped our nation at birth with a perfect and complete political theory, adequate to all our future needs."[4] Unlike Hartz, Boorstin sees conformity not as the result of universal adherence to a definite ideology but as the consequence of the actual absence of ideology. As Irving Kristol comments, Hartz emphasizes the *uni*-ideological character of American democracy—consensus around the liberal democratic idea consisting of a few Lockean dogmas—while Boorstin stresses America's *non*-ideological character, which reflects a "pragmatic" adaptation to life on the American continent.[5]

Actually, it is necessary to travel a somewhat complicated route to reach a conclusion like Kristol's. Boorstin sees conformity as the result of "givenness," the "belief that an explicit political theory is superfluous precisely because we already somehow possess a satisfactory equivalent."[6] "It is not perfectly clear," J.R. Pole observes, whether Boorstin's "principal assertion is that Americans have repudiated political theory, or rather that they have shared a common theory presented to them as part of the deed of gift that went with the continent, a gift that rendered all further speculation needless."[7] With careful analysis, it becomes evident that in Boorstin's view Americans have repudiated political theory, although this rejection is not a simple matter, taking, as it does, two forms. Consciously, Americans have repudiated theory in that, possessing the Founding Fathers' legacy, they have felt no need for any additional or alternative theory. Unconsciously, they have discarded theory in that what they possess and share—the legacy they consider a theory—is *not* a theory. As Pole points out, Boorstin describes "not the existence of a theory but only the *belief* in the existence of a theory. . . ."[8] The description of a belief, by itself, leaves a question to be answered, for, as Pole notes, "either the belief is correct, and a theory did exist, or the belief is incorrect, and no such theory existed."[9] In other words, if Americans believed they possessed a theory, and they did, they would be *uni*-ideological; if they believed they possessed a theory, and they did not, they would be *non*-ideological. Since Boorstin holds that what they believed was a theory—was not,[10] he is consistent in presenting his thesis. Consistency, to be sure, is not necessarily validity. Pole himself concludes that what Americans believed was a theory—*was* a theory, and, as we shall see in chapters 2 and 3, this conclusion is central in his criticism of Boorstin's consensus view.

Unlike Hartz, Boorstin minimizes the influence of Locke and other natural-rights theorists. The achievement of the Founding Fathers was the "affirmation of the tradition of British institutions" rather than the "affirmation of a theory."[11] Not only does Boorstin note the "poverty of our later theorizing"[12] and maintain that the Founding Fathers were not inclined to theorize about politics, but, extending his thesis back to 1620 or 1607, he also claims that Americans have always been nonideological. Many historians reject this claim and Boorstin's characterization of a "Revolution without Dogma" in chapter 3 of *The Genius of American Politics*. John R. Howe, Jr., cites the work of Bernard Bailyn, Cecelia Kenyon, and others in arguing that the "revolutionary generation was profoundly dogmatic, was deeply fascinated with political ideology—the ideology of Republicanism."[13]

One ought not to ascribe to Boorstin the generalizations that any society which is not interested in political theory will necessarily be conformist and devoid of violent conflict, or that any society which is intensely interested in political theory will necessarily experience violent conflict. Although these axioms could conceivably be deduced from the possible implications of occasional statements by Boorstin, to do so would be to move beyond the scope of his concern—the American experience. In Boorstin's work, Pole explains, Europe "stands in contrast, a backcloth against which America is staged," and he "seldom loses sight of the alternatives it could propose."[14] Despite his occasional brief references to Europe, however, Boorstin shuns Hartz's direct, detailed comparative approach. Thus, in Boorstin's argument, as David W. Noble shows, there is no contradiction between the assertion that through their Revolution Americans affirmed their faith in ancient British institutions and the claim that they had stepped out of European history into a state of nature, for ancient British institutions were incorporated in the state of nature that was the foundation and thus the essence of the utopian American experience. Americans were the inheritors of European laws, culture, and institutions, but they had been so situated as to be able to start life anew. They had used European traditions and institutions to adjust to physical nature and, without a plan, to make a new society. They therefore had no enthusiasm for plans to make society over or for attempts to clothe their political ideas and institutions —which had developed organically from the nation's origin in a state of nature—with theory. They could concentrate on the means of improving society because they agreed on ends.[15] In sum, the European inheritance was merely a reactive phenomenon, one element in the process of nonideological adjustment to the environment. This virtual exclusion by Boorstin of European ideology as an active causal force from American development and Hartz's elevation of Lockean liberalism to the status of ultimate explanatory factor derive from two fundamentally different concepts of the cause, but not the content, of consensus in America.

External and Internal Pressures on Historians

Why did the consensus approach to American history become prominent after the Second World War? The rise of the consensus historians in the postwar period, Gerald N. Grob and George Athan Billias maintain, was partly the result of external and internal pressures on the historical profession. Because of the Cold War some scholars desired, consciously or unconsciously, "to present an image to the rest of the world of a nation that had been strong and united throughout most of its history." Within the historical profession an inevitable reaction to Progressive history, which emphasized polarized conflict and cyclical discontinuity, set in. Grob and Billias also characterize the consensus historians as "neo-conservative" because "they seemed to hark back to the conservative historical position that had prevailed prior to the advent of the Progressive scholars." This designation, however, involves more than historiographical trends. The consensus historians showed their "inherent conservatism" and usually rejected the idea of progress as an article of faith.[1]

Other scholars have related consensus history to world affairs. Thomas L. Hartshorne identifies two main responses by American intellectuals to the Cold War: a negative kind of thinking which focuses on America's shortcomings, and a positive approach which "would make 'Americanism' more explicit."[2] Hartshorne places the writings of Hartz, Boorstin, and Clinton Rossiter in the positive category while pointing out that they shared to some extent the negative critics' conclusion that in international relations Americans were "incapacitated by their own moral inflexibility."[3] Hofstadter recognizes both external and internal pressures on historians, conceding that "the Cold War brought a certain closing of the ranks, a disposition to stress common objectives. . . . But the change in historical mood was not simply a response to the new political environment. Ideas have an inner dialectic of their own." Progressive historiography had pushed polarized conflict as an interpretive principle to the point where it verged on self-caricature, and "the pendulum had to swing in the opposite direction if we were to have any new insight into American history."[4]

It appears that Samuel Eliot Morison responded to rather than caused a swing in the pendulum when he said in his presidential address to the American Historical Association in 1950 that the Jefferson—Jackson—F. D. Roosevelt line—to which he himself subscribed—had too long prevailed, that "We need a United States history written from a sanely conservative point of view."[5] Other scholars have associated the consensus history that appeared in the next decade with conservatism. William J. Newman describes Boorstin's and Hartz's views as an expression of the "Conservative Mood" of the 1950s, an attempt to get rid of conflict and to "grasp that shiny essence that stands above and beyond conflict."[6]

That the external and internal pressures which Grob and Billias specify had much to do with the emergence of consensus history is undeniable, but the sources of this development will not fit into a tidy formula. Expressions and origins of the consensus view can be traced to the pre−Cold War period; in reacting to Progressive historiography, various writers moved in different directions; and some historians did not approve of the consensus they described. Nor could certain consensus historians be correctly called "conservatives."

Writers on consensus historiography, who almost invariably refer to the works of Hofstadter (1948), Boorstin (1953), and Hartz (1955), and particularly those who emphasize the response to external threats to American values, ought not to overlook Ralph Gabriel's *The Course of American Democratic Thought* (1940). Gabriel stressed unity and continuity, asserting that most Americans had assumed that basic principles governed human affairs, that the dignity and worth of the free individual were paramount, that the United States had a mission to foster its way of life domestically and internationally. Gabriel's work was undoubtedly affected by the emergence of an external threat—not Communist but Fascist and pre-Cold War.[7]

In 1968 Hofstadter wrote, "My own assertion of consensus history in 1948 had its sources in the Marxism of the 1930s."[8] Portraying American culture, in *The American Political Tradition*, as "fiercely individualistic and capitalistic," he asserted that American reform movements had not been of fundamental importance because they had essentially been struggles of little capitalists against big capitalists.[9] Lincoln Steffens and John Chamberlain, who also wrote from the standpoint of the far left sector of the political spectrum, had made this assertion nearly two decades earlier.[10] It was an expression of what later came to be called the "entrepreneurial" thesis, which is an important aspect of consensus history. Whether an exponent of the entrepreneurial thesis sees the struggles among capitalists as essentially meaningless or genuinely consequential, however, determines the qualifications with which he applies the consensus thesis to American history. That reformers themselves thought their struggles were significant is suggested by the Progressive Brand Whitlock's comment on the dissection of the Progressive mind in *Farewell to Reform:* "We weren't such damn fools as Chamberlain seems to think us."[11]

"It should be clear," James P. Young states, "that the Hartz and Hofstadter theses are complementary,"[12] and it seems appropriate at this point briefly to elaborate the entrepreneurial interpretation. In chapter 3 of *The American Political Tradition*, "Andrew Jackson and the Rise of Liberal Capitalism," Hofstadter links the democratic upsurge of the Jacksonian era to the ambitions of the "small" or "expectant" or (one may add, since Hofstadter mentions the aspirations of the skilled craftsman) "would-be" capitalist: "a hardworking, ambitious person for whom enterprise was a kind of religion, and everywhere he found conditions that encouraged him to extend himself." These rising entrepreneurs saw the granting of economic privileges by government—through the states' method of granting corporate charters, for example—as confining competition, barring new men from engaging in enterprise, and threatening popular government. The Jacksonian movement was essentially a laissez-faire attempt to increase already expanding opportunities by eliminating restrictions and privileges imposed or granted by government. It was a "phase in the expansion of liberated capitalism."[13]

When Hofstadter wrote that small businessmen and workingmen believed banks enjoyed government-bestowed privileges which stifled competition and the entrepreneurial impulse,[14] he echoed the conclusion Bray Hammond had presented in articles, published in 1946 and 1947, on the struggle between Jackson and Biddle over the Second Bank of the United States.[15] In an article which appeared in 1949, Joseph Dorfman also took an entrepreneurial approach to the Jacksonian era.[16] Although Hofstadter, Hammond, and Dorfman all dissented from Arthur M. Schlesinger, Jr.'s identification of the main theme of *The Age of Jackson* (1945) as the conflict between the business community and the rest of society, Hammond and Dorfman, unlike Hofstadter, did not argue for the consensus idea as a theory of American history. Hammond and Dorfman also differed from Hofstadter in ascribing real significance to the entrepreneurs' battles to democratize business.

There are other appraisals of the Jacksonian era, needless to say, besides the entrepreneurial and the Progressive or Schlesinger assessments. Frank Otto Gatell's conclusion concerning the Bank War in New York City emphasizes nonideological politics: "Many Jackson party leaders in New York City had no trouble living with Biddle's monster during the 1820's, and some of them served the monster effectively and enthusiastically. Their subsequent political hostility to the Bank of the United States resulted from the call for party discipline following the declaration of the Bank War."[17] Robert V. Remini holds that the "Bank War was essentially a political struggle, with the President calling the shots, and only secondarily an economic battle among various 'men on the make.' "[18] Lee Benson, in his study of *ante bellum* New York state politics, rejects both the entrepreneurial and Progressive interpretations, stressing value conflicts among competing ethnocultural and religious groups rather than issues of political economy.[19]

Some historians apply the entrepreneurial thesis, or a variant of it, to later reform movements. In Walter T.K. Nugent's *The Tolerant Populists* the protesters appear as small businessmen-farmers who organized to obtain better prices and marketing conditions.[20] The Progressive movement, Otis L. Graham, Jr., notes, "takes on the aspect of a counterattack by business interests against other business interests—big business versus little business rather than vice versa—in Samuel P. Hays, *The Response to Industrialism: 1885−1914* (1957), Robert Wiebe, *Businessmen and Reform: A Study of the Progressive Movement* (1962), and Gabriel Kolko, *The Triumph of Conservatism: A Reinterpretation of American History, 1900−1916* (1963).[21] The descriptive formula for this counterattack—big business versus little business—is not interchangeable with its converse—little business versus big business—as simply another way of characterizing the same entrepreneurial interpretation. Although many historians do depict Progressivism as anti-big business,[22] Kolko, in particular, considers Progressivism a pro-big business movement.

Increasing competition and decentralization, not growing monopoly, Kolko insists, were the main trends in the American economy at the start of the twentieth century. Big businesses, having failed to exclude new competitors through such means as pools, trusts, holding companies, and mergers, and becoming less efficient than many smaller enterprises, engineered much progressive federal legislation in order to assure their control over the economy.[23] Big business was successful in its conservative attempt to maintain existing social and power relations in a new economic context—its effort politically to rationalize the economy by arranging for the regulation of the regulators by the regulated—because both major political parties subscribed to the ideology of "political capitalism." This ideology "operated on the assumption that the general welfare of the community could best be served by satisfying the concrete needs of business." It embodied "the nearly universal belief among political leaders in the basic justice of private property relations as they essentially existed, a belief that set the ultimate limits on the leaders' political actions."[24] Although Kolko stresses the initiative of big rather than small capitalists, he does describe a fiercely capitalistic culture, and his variant of the entrepreneurial thesis, as he himself characterizes it, stresses consensus.[25] His interpretation of Progressivism, as we shall see in chapter 7, is an expression of the consensus aspect of New Left history.

Although the sources of Gabriel's and Hofstadter's consensus views antedate the post–Second World War confrontation of the superpowers, the contributions to consensus historiography of political scientist Clinton Rossiter appear to be, at least in part, a response to the Cold War. The American consensus, Rossiter asserts, means "the unwritten laws of American politics demand that the parties overlap substantially in principle, policy, character, appeal, and purpose—or cease to be parties with any hope of winning national elections."[26] Rossiter served as general editor of and contributed a volume to the Harcourt, Brace and World series, "Communism in American Life," to some extent a Cold War scholarly enterprise.[27] He is also often referred to as a spokesman for the New Conservatism,[28] but it is difficult to pinpoint his precise position on the political spectrum. Rossiter himself says that his having written a nonpejorative book on American conservatism does not make him a conservative. He describes himself as "a man who is at once the most liberal of conservatives and the most conservative of liberals."[29] In any event, in his *Conservatism in America: The Thankless Persuasion*, published in 1955, the year in which Hartz's *The Liberal Tradition in America* also appeared, he discovered a conservatism in America so liberal that his and Hartz's basic conclusions are similar. Rossiter criticized American conservatism, as Hartshorne notes, because "it had been so profoundly influenced by the liberal ideology that it did not constitute an effective alternative. His call for a refurbished, responsible American conservatism was not a rejection of liberalism."[30]

Nor does the label "neo-conservative" nicely fit *both* Hartz and Boorstin, understandably the only consensus historians whom Grob and Billias name and whose work they discuss in a brief survey of the history of American history (although they do devote a paragraph to a description of the themes presented in specialized studies by other "neo-conservative" scholars[31]). Hartz, it is true, like Hofstadter and Boorstin, was influenced in the thirties by Marxism,[32] and he sees the Cold War as bringing "into the plainest view" the American consensus.[33] This does not mean, however, that a combination of his experience of the 1930s and the "Mood of the 1950s" fully or even substantially accounts for his analytical approach, which derives from his training in comparative political theory under Benjamin F. Wright, who published studies of natural-law doctrines in America and "American Democracy and the Frontier"[34]—subjects of central concern to Hartz. As for Hartz's assessment of American political thought, it is apparent that he is a liberal, disturbed by the soporific implications of the Lockean consensus he finds.[35] Discussing the descriptive task of the historian, Hofstadter points out that "the idea of consensus is not intrinsically linked to ideological conservatism" and the historian "is not required to endorse what he finds."[36] This comment applies to Hartz and to Hofstadter himself, who, having abandoned the Marxist perspective, designated himself a liberal[37] but harshly criticized the reform tradition. In the case of Boorstin, there is good reason to consider his consensus writings a response to the Cold War on the part of a former Marxist who is now a neo-conservative and approves of what he finds. He has himself referred to his "attempt to discover the unique virtues of American democracy" as an expression of his opposition to the Communist Party.[38] Boorstin's "repudiation of the Communist Party is long since behind him," Kenneth S. Lynn observes, but "no other American historian of our time is so ridden—so imaginatively dominated—by memories of the 1930s."[39] Newman remarks that although Boorstin "would not have us confuse him with conservatives . . . it is a fine line that he wants us to draw."[40]

It appears that the conservative Conyers Read, in his presidential address to the American Historical Association in 1949, like Morison in his presidential address of the following year, reacted to rather than initiated a trend among historians. Read attempted to enlist historians in the Cold War, urging them to "recognize certain values as beyond dispute" and to defend them against "all assaults, historical and otherwise."[41] The response to this exhortation by historians who had not been caught up in the trend which Read hoped to enhance was less than unanimous. In his presidential address to the Mississippi Valley Historical Association in 1952, Merle Curti dissented from the consensus approach in general and Read's counsel in particular: "Any position that calls for suppressing 'pathological' episodes in our past and for using our craft to support a currently held policy, should give us pause."[42]

The Historian as Individual: Daniel J. Boorstin

It should be apparent by now that to refer to schools of historians is to "ignore the special, personal quality of each particular historian. Not only does he think and speak for himself; also his working life may extend over half a century. Historians, like other men, are apt to modulate from one point of view to another, to change their minds."[1] We can see that Hofstadter, Boorstin, and Hartz all moved during their careers from left to right on an intellectual-political track; but Hofstadter and Hartz got off before Boorstin did. That is, Boorstin traveled further toward the right (or conservative) terminal on this route, suggesting that the Marxist influence on him may have been greater than it was on Hofstadter and Hartz—if the degree of later rejection reflects the depth of earlier commitment.

Boorstin's is obviously not the only such case relevant to this inquiry, but it will be illustrative to consider it here since the consensus theme has been central in his writings over a considerable period of time. Moreover, as John P. Diggins asserts, the "consensus versus conflict" school of thought "flowered in large part as a response to Boorstin's work."[2] The same may be said of Hartz's work, and we shall have occasion, particularly in chapters 2 and 8, to discuss the development of his historical concepts in the decade after the the the appearance of *The Liberal Tradition in America*.

The evolution of Boorstin's thought, incorporating anti-Progressive or anti-Beard elements as well as a left-to-right course of development undoubtedly accelerated by the Cold War, has embodied an inner dialectic of its own. Perhaps a way of portraying this dialectic concisely but adequately for present purposes is to summarize Noble's step-by-step analysis of the unfolding of Boorstin's thought:

1. Advocacy in the 1930s of sweeping reform to destroy the power of the irresponsible business aristocracy.

2. Analysis in *The Mysterious Science of the Law* (1941) of the chief support of a reactionary status quo, the common law tradition, which showed that the most influential statement of this tradition, Blackstone's *Commentaries*, drew on the prestige of natural law to provide an ideological rationalization for the property rights of the capitalist class of eighteenth-century England.

3. Insistence at the end of the study of Blackstone that, having seen the objective of Blackstone's ideology, one must be aware of what one's reason serves—one's values and the preconceived and desired objective that derives from them—to be certain that one's reason serves a moral end.

4. During the Second World War, loss of faith that progress would bring about the demise of the business aristocracy, a consequent loss of a moral end to support, and a desire to escape from ideological commitment and conflict.

5. Discovery of a position in Jefferson's views, set out in *The Lost World of Thomas Jefferson* (1948). Ideological commitment was

unnecessary since Jefferson's outlook was not ultimately related to values but was built on his experience with the facts of nature; Boorstin held that Americans, unlike Europeans, lived by the Jeffersonian covenant—outside of culture in harmony with nature.

6. Misgivings concerning this escape from ideology, doubts which produced the conclusion that the world of Jefferson was lost to twentieth-century Americans as a consequence of the nineteenth-century industrial revolution, which had separated them from nature and led them to believe, with un-Jeffersonian arrogance, that they possessed the "energy, craftsmanship, and power" of their creator and could build their own social universe.

7. Misgivings concerning these misgivings yielding the conclusion that Americans had not arrogantly abandoned the Jeffersonian covenant despite increasing institutional complexity because the source of their values was still nature—institutions were used only as tools of adjustment to nature, thereby making institutional and social complexity itself natural.

8. Persistent misgivings, nevertheless, that, if not institutional complexity, then something had subverted Jefferson's America, separating the people from nature and plaguing them with ideological difficulties; the culprit was not Beard's business aristocracy but an artificial elite of intellectuals who, failing to see that American society was built on eternal, immutable natural principles, imagined it trapped by institutions that were part of the European historical environment with its irrational, tragic qualities. They had adopted the European heresy that men must transcend their social environment to create a good society.

9. An appeal in *The Genius of American Politics* (1953) to American intellectuals, who mistakenly applied European ideology to their country, to repent the errors that had made them critics of the status quo and to return to the Jeffersonian covenant by exercising their only freedom, which was to conserve God's gift, discoverable not in abstract reason but in the details of life.

10. An objective demonstration in *The Americans: The Colonial Experience* (1958) and *The Americans: The National Experience* (1965) of the affirmations of *The Genius of American Politics*.

11. The discovery, announced in *The Image: A Guide to Pseudo-Events in America* (1962), of a more fearful threat to America's innocence than Beard's business aristocracy or the

artificial elite of intellectuals—corruption within the "people," who, displaying a consuming interest in the appearance of things, had abandoned the Jeffersonian covenant and the metaphysical reality of American simplicity for the European idea of material progress and for artificial complexity.[3]

In *The Image*, Noble writes, Boorstin "seemed to deny much of the intellectual position he had constructed over the last decade."[4] He did not depart from his view that Americans' direct experience with nature was the source of "givenness" and the key to understanding their history, but he discerned, as Pole puts it, "the decline in the immediacy of experience. Increasingly, we see, hear, and know things at second hand, and increasingly, he suggests, our experience comes preselected, arranged by various sorts of advertiser, editor, or impresario, prepackaged and predigested."[5] Thus, Boorstin declares, "We are haunted not by reality, but by those images we have put in place of reality."[6] Insofar as experience was the touchstone of his interpretation, Boorstin did not change the basis of his analysis of American history. His judgment in *The Image*, however, was one that his previous interpretation (intellectuals' only freedom was to conserve God's gift) had not allowed to the analyst. As Noble explains, Boorstin

> had argued that man should endeavor to follow the natural laws one discovered by commonsense experience in society, that one could not discover first principles through the use of abstract reason, and that the ought and the is were organically unified in the current society. Like Blackstone he had denied the possibility of standing outside the *status quo* and criticizing it.
>
> But now Boorstin was standing outside his society and criticizing its forms.[7]

When Boorstin criticized the people's acceptance of a democratic philosophy of education devoid of fixed standards of values, when he asserted that the American pragmatic tradition had always displayed a consuming interest in the appearance of things, he cast doubt on popular culture and questioned the people's values. He deprived himself of his purpose—saving

America from the temptation of foreign ideology—for the sources of the new corruption such as advertising and the *Reader's Digest* could not be identified with alien ideology.[8] Accordingly, Noble concludes,

> Boorstin has sundered the organic unity of the is and the ought, the real and the ideal, that had marked America's philosophy of history. He has placed the moral drama of a threat to the Jeffersonian covenant within the community itself. And he provides little assurance that the people will cease to wander along strange paths away from the ark of the covenant of arcadian simplicity.[9]

In an article appearing six years after the publication of Noble's *Historians against History*, Diggins observes that the Boorstinian edifice "seems to have suffered erosion in *The Image* . . . from 'givenness' to 'nothingness' is a peculiarly American pathos that cannot be attributed to the intrusion of alien ideas."[10] Diggins also notes that Boorstin's interpretation of the Civil War in *The National Experience* attributes to Southerners an unrealistic political theory or "metaphysical politics" which was explicitly and emphatically excluded from his treatment in *The Genius of American Politics* of the Civil War as a nonideological clash between two descriptive sociologies and two constitutional orthodoxies.[11] In any event, Boorstin's analysis of the collapse of the Union in *The National Experience* does not mean that the volume as a whole represents a departure from the main nonideological theme of *The Genius of American Politics*. In writing about the young radicals of the 1960s, however, in an article and a book which appeared after Noble's study and too late for Pole to consider, Boorstin, as Diggins shows, departed in a basic way from his advice to intellectuals in *The Genius of American Politics*. In "The New Barbarians," published in *Esquire* in October 1968,

> Boorstin dismisses the unquiet desperation of radical students as the barbaric thirst for sensation. Whatever one thinks of Boorstin's description of the phenomenon, there is cold irony here: he is now asking the militant young to do what he previously believed to be alien to the American character: to give philosophical content to their thoughts, to go to the root of

matters by posing questions of ultimate knowledge and value, to "search for meaning"; in short, to become speculative theorists rather than mindless activists.[12]

In *The Decline of Radicalism: Reflections on America Today* (1969),

Boorstin maintains that the Old Left of his generation was truly radical, whereas the New Left is "closer to dyspepsia than to an ideology; the New Barbarism has tried to generalize its stomach aches but it has been unable to cast them into a philosophy." The unpardonable sin of the New Left, it would seem, is that it learned all too well America's genius for dismissing all problems of ideology and philosophy as superfluous.[13]

But whatever the later developments in Boorstin's thought, his interpretation of consensus remains of lasting interest. Pole, who has evaluated Boorstin's work through *The Americans: The National Experience*, observes, "The justification for reviewing his achievement at this stage is that it would continue to exert a profound influence over American historical thought even if he were now to make an entirely new departure."[14] In fact, although the first two volumes of *The Americans* can be considered an attempt at an objective demonstration of the affirmations of *The Genius of American Politics*, to anyone unfamiliar with *The Genius* they might well appear to be a special kind of social history. In any event, *The Genius*, as Pole says, is a "landmark in his thought and influence."[15] It contains some contemporary criticism, but its central observations are "so significant and far-reaching that they are likely to have lasting influence even after they are separated from the didactic theories which they are intended to sustain."[16]

The Similarity of the Major Parties

The general view expressed in the consensus approach to American history takes on a more particular form when it focuses on politics. A main theme in consensus historiography is that essential ideological conformity emerged in American politics sometime between 1776 and 1840, and that the development of widespread conformity in political thought soon became evident in political behavior. "American democracy," Charles G. Sellers,

Jr., writes, "emerged victorious on the plane of political ideology around 1776 or 1800 and on the plane of political practice around 1828."[1]

A frequently cited sign of conformity in politics is the similarity of the major parties in ideology and policy, and, to a lesser extent, in membership or composition. Walter Adams sees this similarity "beginning with the Revolutionary War."[2] Sellers reference to the triumph of democracy as an ideology around 1776 (as an alternative to 1800) and Adams' unqualified attribution of pragmatism and empiricism to the major political movements before 1800 clash with Howe's assertion that the revolutionary generation was steeped in political ideology and engaged in heated ideological combat. Van Beck Hall's findings in his recent study of politics in Massachusetts in the period 1780–1791 are in basic accord with Howe's claim, while Richard R. Beeman, in his 1972 study of politics in Virginia in the years 1788–1801, describes both conflict and consensus: interparty strife over the role of the national government, along with the continued dominance of a closed oligarchic system which rarely clashed with the new system of party politics.[3]

Sellers' and Adams' chronology minimizes the contention between the Federalists in power and the Jeffersonians which Howe and others stress. Indeed, Richard S. Buel holds that the ideological division of the politics of the 1790s, which arose from deep disagreement over ways of fulfilling the promise of the Revolution, persisted for more than a decade into the nineteenth century.[4]

Most historians who discuss the emergence of consensus in American politics date this development as having occurred in 1800 or later. After Jefferson took power, Hofstadter writes, "before long the two parties were indistinguishable."[5] Analyzing the mixed public-private nature of the early national economy, E.A.J. Johnson asserts that "it is only meretricious to contrast Hamiltonian with Jeffersonian policy."[6] William D. Grampp makes this point concerning Jefferson's thought, as well as his practice, concluding that "after 1805, he proposed measures that were consistent with the objectives established by Hamilton, though his methods differed from those of Hamilton in revealing a greater concern with constitutional legitimacy."[7]

In regard to the Federalists, out of power, David Hackett Fischer holds that a generation of younger Federalists copied Jeffersonian techniques in competing for the votes of the plain people.[8] Charles M. Wiltse declares that when the Federalists countered Jefferson's and Madison's use of federal power with the Jeffersonian doctrine of state sovereignty, "the last ideological differences between the parties were gone."[9] Although in theory two principled opposing parties could exchange doctrines and remain in principled conflict over them, Wiltse implies that the readiness of both parties to alter their views in response to changes in their political situations spelled the end of their capacity for sustained commitment to and combat in behalf of any specific basic tenet about government, and that subsequent conflict between parties involved something less than deep-seated adherence to fundamental principles. James M. Banner also notes that the Federalists employed "constitutional arguments sharply reminiscent of the Kentucky and Virginia Resolutions which they had only a few years earlier rejected. . . ." Banner points out that the Federalists' argument stemmed "from a concern for the state of the union itself [as well as] from a simple concern for their own place in it." One might maintain that their argument was a principled one: if the union could not be made lovable (admittedly through remedies they had previously scorned), they would leave it. Federalist activists, however, were not prepared to pursue the principle of a perfect union that far, for "one group above all—the leaders of the party organization—steadfastly resisted the mounting call for separate state action and remained resolutely opposed to disunion." When a New England Convention appeared imminent in 1814, they yielded to the clamor only to the point of supporting interposition rather than secession, and "primarily in their own defense, not New England's."[10] One might argue that the Federalist activists believed in the preservation of the union, however imperfect, and compromise as general principles—and it would surely be unsound to ascribe to them only a single motive—but the implicit burden of these comments by Wiltse and Banner is that both parties subordinated ideology to political ambition, thereby becoming essentially consensual.

Still, the first two decades of the nineteenth century were

not an era of swift, smooth transition to psychological and philosophical serenity and placid politics. "Half Federalist and half Republican, Monroe," Wiltse writes, "faced only local opposition in 1816 and in 1820 had been unopposed."[11] But Marcus Cunliffe cautions against investing the period 1789–1837 "with a false aura of tranquility. In some respects, especially up to 1815, it was a time of prolonged crisis, full of regret and foreboding, hostility and confusion."[12] Banner and Linda K. Kerber vividly demonstrate that for the Federalists the period from Jefferson's election to Madison's was a time of difficult adjustment to the triumph of the Democratic-Republicans.[13] Norman L. Stamps shows in his study of the major parties in Connecticut in the years 1800–1816 that both the Federalists and the Jeffersonians built efficient political and governmental organizations, campaigned vigorously, and consistently voted along party lines on nearly all issues which came before the legislature.[14] Even the recent studies of the Jeffersonian Republicans in New Jersey by Carl E. Prince and in Massachusetts by Paul Goodman, both of which reject the emphasis in earlier party histories on duality in composition and ideology as the source of conflict between the parties, describe considerable interparty strife resulting from the clash of establishment and anti-establishment interests. In a later study in which he compares the leadership cadres of the Jeffersonians and Federalists in New Jersey, Prince concludes that "the Federalist leadership by and large derived from a long-standing but narrowly based New Jersey elite while the Republicans for the most part came out of an upwardly mobile, much more broadly based middle class . . . to deny the existence of meaningful class distinctions in the politics of New Jersey is to ignore a pertinent portion of the available historical record."[15]

Moving further into the nineteenth century, it seems that, like Sellers, other leading students of voter and party behavior in the age of Jackson depreciate the importance of ideological conflict in that era. Benson concludes that in New York State the Whigs and most other parties, as well as the Jacksonians, at least preached the gospel of democracy.[16] Richard P. McCormick maintains that as the franchise was liberalized the new, less-privileged voters in New York and North Carolina did not ascribe conflicting ideologies to the major parties, dividing evenly between the Whigs and Democrats and thereby undermining the economic-class interpretation of political behavior.[17] McCormick has also made a full-length presentation of the thesis that winning elections rather than promoting ideologies was the objective of political parties in the years 1824–1854.[18] Lynn L. Marshall, a student of the Whigs whose views on party formation differ from McCormick's, also emphasizes the relative insignificance in the Jacksonian period of "elevated political ideology."[19] Michael Wallace delineates the development of attitudes toward the existence and competition of political parties that paved the way for the emergence in the age of Jackson of the second party system, which will be discussed in chapter 4, with its balanced parties in every section and nearly every state. Like McCormick and Marshall, Wallace concludes, "Because their goal was the preservation of the party, the politicians lost interest in other, more ideological objectives."[20] (Wallace uses the term *consensus* frequently and consistently to denote the belief in the virtue of the absence of political parties, not, as in this inquiry, to signify the ideological similarity of different parties.[21])

A survey of consensus historiography indicates that the year 1840 may safely be taken as the later limit of the era of the emergence of ideological conformity and the attraction to the opposing major parties, through similar appeals, of greater numbers of similar voters. Analyzing voter participation in presidential elections from 1800 to 1844, McCormick declares that "in 1840 the 'new democracy' made its appearance with explosive suddenness."[22] In this situation, Hartz comments, "the Whigs themselves have become log-cabin democrats. . . ."[23] Henry Bamford Parkes remarks:

> the 1840 election meant that both parties had fully accepted democracy and were competing with each other for the votes of the plain people. In the future there were no obvious class differences between them, nor were there any clearly defined differences of principle. . . . It was at this period that the American party system acquired that independence of economic and class divisions that all Europeans and many Americans have always found so anomalous and bewildering.[24]

Although scholars, both liberal and conservative, describe an American consensus, they do not agree as to whether it is, as Rossiter holds, a "blessed fact."[25] They "disagree widely," Higham notes "on the worth and durability of such homogeneity as they perceive."[26] This discord is especially apparent in regard to the similarity of the major parties, the subject of a number of studies in the 1950s beginning with the publication in 1950, by the American Political Science Association's Committee on Political Parties, of *Toward a More Responsible Two-Party System*.[27] Statements of this view, and its opposite, have continued to appear down to the present.

Boorstin believes that "our national well-being is in inverse proportion to the sharpness and extent of the theoretical differences between our political parties."[28] Andrew Hacker, on the other hand, doubts that our nonideological politics is adequate to meet the challenges of the future,[29] and Marshall Dimock appeals for the formation of ideologically distinct parties.[30] Paul W. Glad, in his volume on the McKinley-Bryan contest, concisely characterizes the opposing positions:

> To conservatives, then, the election of 1896 provides an outstanding example of what one of them has called the "genius of American politics." This "genius" involves nothing less than a capacity to consider and dispose of concrete issues without resorting to doctrinaire and revolutionary extremes. . . . To those of more radical temperament, the election demonstrates what they feel is becoming increasingly obvious in the second half of the twentieth century: that parties and political institutions are structurally inadequate and that they are incapable of responding to changing social and economic needs.[31]

Another historian of the politics of the Gilded Age, Richard Jensen, presents the conservative view:

> Did the political system of the 1890's work? The answer depends on one's views of current events. My answer is yes, if one is asking whether a satisfactory state of stability was reached that won the active support of the majority of the people. I have too deep a commitment to pluralistic democracy and to full political participation to approve of any alternative to them.[32]

Nor should we overlook the views of neoconservative intellectuals and Goldwater conservatives. In the first issue of William F. Buckley, Jr.'s *National Review* the editors identified as the most immediate threat to the American political system Fabian reformers' efforts to win control of both the Democratic and Republican parties.[33] Goldwater conservatives also deplore consensus or "me-tooism." They desire to effect a realignment of the parties which will enable voters to choose between two clearly opposing alternatives. James MacGregor Burns observes that, unlike other advocates of ideologically distinct parties, the Goldwaterites want to bring about a party realignment and gain control of the government in order to turn the clock back, "to exorcise the twentieth-century problems that bewilder them."[34] The Goldwaterites have thus been called "restorationists" and representatives of the "radical right." Burns, who has written at length about the overlapping of the two major parties, judges the "kind of party realignment planned by the [Goldwater] conservatives . . . undesirable and impossible." Burns himself takes an in-between position, calling for "a different kind of party realignment . . . which would not confront the nation with a cruel choice between extremes" but would give voters "a clear choice between a *responsibly liberal* Democratic party and a somewhat right-of-center Republican Party."[35]

Burns expressed this opinion shortly before the elections of 1964, the results of which might have prompted many Republicans to ask, "What's wrong with me-tooism?" In any event, contemporary commentaries on the presidential contest did not interpret the massive movement by Republican voters away from their party's candidate as anything more than a temporary defection. The Survey Research Center at the University of Michigan, however, did point out that beneath the national Democratic tide the Goldwater Republicans' "Southern strategy" had the greatest impact, among "short-term" forces, on geographical voting returns. An electoral map constructed by entering state by state or region by region the departure of the presidential vote in a more Republican or more Democratic direction than the normal voting of the area involved, with pro-Goldwater deviations considered "high ground," would show one primary "tilt" or gradient across the nation. The very lowest ground would appear in the northern reaches of New England, and the gradient would move upward with fair regularity all the way west to the Pacific Coast. The same gradient would appear, but much more sharply tilted still, as one moved southward to the Gulf of Mexico.[36]

The Survey Research Center did not discuss the long-term implications of the short-term impact of the "Southern strategy," but the trend in the South away from the Democratic party at the presidential level, evident before 1964, persisted and deepened through 1972 (the Democratic percentage of the presidential vote in the South dropped from 75 in 1944 to 50 in 1948, ranged between 48 and 53 from 1952 through 1964, and plunged to 33 in 1968 and even further in 1972[37]), and Southern Republican representation in Congress, which had consisted of no Senators and six members of the House in the 1950s, rose to ten Senators and thirty-seven members of the House in the Ninety-Third Congress, elected in 1972, with nearly all of them being former Democrats. By 1970 some political scientists, moreover, saw definite indications of a realignment of the electorate, which, as we shall see in chapter 6, they traced back to 1964. Meanwhile, the discussion of whether the development of ideologically distinct parties was desirable remained very much alive.

Between 1968 and 1972 A.E. Keir Nash, Allan C. Brownfield, Theodore J. Lowi, and David Broder, in *The Party's Over*, judged the present two-party system incapable of coping with current problems.[38] Reviewing Broder's book, among others, in mid-1972, Elizabeth Drew wrote, "The value of ideological parties is questionable. We are too nearly at each other's throats as it is; we are already too vulnerable to breaking apart. Ideological parties, moreover, might enhance, not diminish stalemate." Nor did Drew "think we can have anything like the British system of politics," in which the executive and the legislature are controlled by the same party.[39] One may add that reference to the British system as a preferred alternative to our ideologically indistinct parties rests on an unexamined assumption. In an article appearing in 1967, Jorgen S. Rasmussen refuted the view that American political parties would be more responsible and effective if they became more like British parties. He found that in many ways "British parties fail to meet the requisites of the responsible party model. Not only is applying the model to American politics questionable . . . the model is an inaccurate description of the British party system."[40]

In the early part of 1973 the decision of Representative Donald W. Riegle, Jr., a four-term Republican, to join the Democrats and the wide-spread expectation that former Governor John B. Connally, a Texas Democrat, would move into the Republican party caused a Washington correspondent to recall such switches in the past by Senators Wayne L. Morse of Oregon and J. Strom Thurmond of South Carolina and Representative Ogden R. Reid of New York. Such shifting, he concluded, "does not seem to carry any implications of the impending death of the two-party system. But it does seem to be an indication of a growing elasticity in party lines and a weakening of the old party organization discipline."[41] The *New York Times* noted that these changes were, on the other hand, applauded by those who believed in strict party responsibility and accountability. But the *Times* itself expressed misgivings:

> But for the nation as a whole there is still much to be said for having two national parties both of which span a broad ideological spectrum and make overlapping appeals. Such overlapping tends to soften the harshness of partisan combat. . . .
>
> Heterogeneous national parties are confusing and untidy but they lend stability to a diverse society which always needs a stabilizing influence. If political realignment brings gains in clarity of choice and enhanced party responsibility, it also brings its accompanying losses.[42]

Diverging views on the similarity of the major parties show that the political scientists, the journalists, and the historians of the consensus "school," or any other, are not required to endorse what they find.

Chapter Two
Causes of Consensus

Social Scientists on Causation

Why did ideological conformity, or the absence of ideology, emerge in American politics by 1840, or earlier? Posing this question provides an opportunity to point out that as the walls between disciplines have come tumbling down after the Second World War, history has not been the only discipline in which scholars in significant numbers have expounded the consensus view. Social scientists, too, have responded to external and internal pressures and much of their work is relevant to historians' causal explanations of consensus.

Sociologist Alvin W. Gouldner has traced the development of a concern with consensus among his colleagues. He contends that after 1815 Comte's Positivist movement made peace with the ruling industrial class in France, yielding leadership to the new industrial entrepreneurs and redefining the sociologist's role as a technical one in behalf of the interests of industrial society. But the new leadership's failure to take sufficient interest in social welfare produced a split in Positivist thought: a radical strand inclined toward Marxism and a conservative strand leaned toward Functionalism. Another sociologist, Bennett M. Berger, commenting on Gouldner's study, characterizes Functionalism as

> a theory which conceives of society as a "system" of interdependent parts having a natural propensity to equilibrium, and held together by the common values of its population which motivate each person to conform to the expectations of others. It

is a benign view of social order in which conflict is likely to be
regarded as pathology, and in which the sociologist's role is to
look for ways in which social systems adjust to internal tensions
and to external threats to their integration and stability. . . .
The work of Talcott Parsons, the single most influential and
comprehensive Functionalist of the past generation (to whom
Gouldner devotes more than 200 pages of consummately
detailed analysis and criticism) is interpreted as "American
Hegelianism," significant primarily for its attempts to rationalize
the crisis of laissez-faire capitalism in the 1930's and to cope with
the problems of Welfare State capitalism in the 1950's and
1960's.[1]

Parsons' assessment of the relationship between government
and business[2] is the sociological analogue of the consensus view
in economics, which we shall consider in chapter 7. Another
sociologist, Daniel Bell, in *The End of Ideology: On the Exhaustion of
Political Ideas in the Fifties* (1960), announced the emergence of
consensus on the mixed economy and the halfway welfare state
with the demise of the capitalism-versus-socialism conflict in the
United States.

More directly pertinent to our present concern than Parsons' numerous studies is the work of certain political
sociologists, particularly Seymour Martin Lipset, and a number
of political scientists, especially Dahl. Students of voter behavior
in American history posit, explicitly or implicitly, that changes
in objective conditions produce socioeconomic-cultural conflict
which, in turn, produces realignment of the electorate within
the American two-party system.[3] Lipset and Stein Rokkan,
using a comparative historical approach, pursue, as it were, the
prior question of why a consensual or competitive two-party
system arose in the United States. I cite their inquiry to underline
the interdisciplinary scope of concern with consensus. In their
analysis, changes in conditions result in conflict which, in turn,
results in the development of a particular kind of party system—
depending on "the genesis of the system of contrasts and cleavages within the national community . . . [and] the conditions for expression of protest and representation of interests
in each society."[4]

Inquiry into the translation of sociocultural conflict into party systems, Lipset and Rokkan conclude, suggests "a sequence of thresholds in the path of any movement pressing forward new sets of demands within a political system":

> *Legitimation*: Are all protests rejected as conspiratorial, or is there some recognition of the right of petition, criticism, and opposition?
>
> *Incorporation*: Are all or most of the supporters of the movement denied status as participants in the choice of representatives or are they given political citizen rights on a par with their opponents?
>
> *Representation*: Must the new movement join larger and older movements to ensure access to representative organs or can it gain representation on its own?
>
> *Majority Power*: Are there built-in checks and counterforces against numerical majority rule in the system or will victory at the polls give a party or an alliance power to bring about major structural changes in the national system?

Lipset and Rokkan show, in tabular form, that various nations at different times in history exemplify various combinations of high, medium, and low threshold levels. The United States, for example, represents an LLHH amalgam (Legitimation-Low, Incorporation-Low, Representation-High, Majority Power-High): "high-threshold majoritarian representation and separation of powers [in a] competitive party system under universal manhood suffrage but with high payoffs for alliances. . . ." The United States would be the best example in this category "if it were not for the restrictions on Communist Party activities and the low de facto enfranchisement of Negroes in the South."[5]

Although certain threshold-level combinations result in certain kinds of party systems, this four-variable typology of conditions for the development of party systems raises questions about the infinitely complex process whereby a nation changes from one combination to another. Lipset and Rokkan do not claim to explain the variations in sequences of change and in terminal stages of development. They call their essay a contribution to "an area of great fascination crying out for detailed comparative research."[6] Nevertheless, comparative studies of national party systems and attempts to construct a containing framework of developmental theory already constitute an imposing body of literature. Having considered one example of interdisciplinary concern with consensus, we may now turn to two statements on causation by political scientists that largely parallel the causal explanations of the generalizers among consensus historians.

Dan Nimmo and Thomas D. Ungs in *American Political Patterns: Conflict and Consensus* are brief and eclectic on causation. With respect to the "historical setting which has conditioned prevailing political values," they present Boorstin's and Hartz's views without comment.[7] They mention Turner's emphasis on "the democratizing and nationalizing influences of the frontier" while noting, "How much is explained by such an interpretation is open to question."[8] They list "several influences operating in conjunction with inherited Lockean ideals": geographical isolation from Europe; the vast area and enormous natural resources of an unsettled continent; the struggle of the agrarian tradition, as traced by Parrington, against wealth and concentrated authority; religious beliefs, especially the Protestant ethic—with its emphasis on the values of work, free choice, and private property—and the Social Gospel; and immigration, which has created diversity calling for accommodating democratic values such as "freedom of participation, dissent, uniqueness, and nonconformity."[9] Nimmo and Ungs are contradictory when they uncritically lump together Hartz's and Parrington's ideas since Hartz categorically rejects the Progressive approach to American history which Parrington's writings exemplify.[10] They also mention, in addition to the consensual effect of immigration, the conformity that often prevails within ethnic groups —an aspect of the nonconsensual "Beyond the Melting Pot" phenomenon which we shall discuss in chapter 3.

In *Pluralist Democracy in the United States: Conflict and Consent*, Dahl is brief and systematic on causation. Accounting for the development of a political consensus among Americans in the first half of the nineteenth century, he emphasizes the substantial degree of *equality* that prevailed in property, incomes, wealth, control over economic enterprise, education, and social relations, the principal reason for this equality of condition, at a level of general prosperity, being the availability of land. Homogeneity, ethnic and linguistic as well as economic and social, produced *unity*—the tacit "consent" of a large minority to the laws passed by the representatives of a majority. This unity was characterized by the unusually rapid development of a sense of nationhood and a remarkable similarity in attitudes and beliefs with respect to the virtues of equality, democracy, the constitutional system, and political compromise. This similarity, Dahl adds, was probably fostered also by physical isolation from Europe, relatively firm boundaries to the east, north, and south, and the "existence of a unique political system that united Americans in a bold new experiment in self-government." "Related to all these factors, there may be another, less flattering reason. . . . To use the modern jargon, Americans often appeared to Europeans as strongly 'conformist' and 'other-directed.' "[11]

Dahl, who views the Civil War as a singular, tragic illustration of the inability of American institutions to manage conflict,[12] carries his consideration of the sources of consensus into the post-Civil War period. Just as the origin of consensus calls for causal analysis, so does its persistence amid changing conditions. How, Dahl asks, did a political consensus continue to exist when the United States ceased to be a nation of small farmers? He attributes this persistence to (1) "the sheer inertia of an already venerable tradition"; (2) the survival of this tradition, which Dahl defines in Hartz's terms, through crises: each defeat of a rival ideology—aristocracy, slavocracy, socialism, plutocracy—has enhanced the traditional quality of the victorious older ideology; (3) the survival of "enough of the old 'equality of condition' [without which] these challenges might not have been overcome"; (4) the educational system: it espouses the dominant liberal-democratic ideology; (5) the influence of the mass media: their direct, manipulative influence on American attitudes is hard to assess and easy to overestimate, but it is essentially correct that "the amount of time and space devoted by the mass media to views openly hostile to the prevailing ideology is negligible."[13] At the same time, as we shall see in chapter 3, Dahl, like Nimmo and Ungs, imposes significant qualifications on the prevalence of consensus.

Hofstadter, Boorstin, and Hartz on Causation

Although Hofstadter deftly delineates and dissects the American culture as a capitalist-democratic one, he does not probe the ultimate origins of this phenomenon. In a brief reference to causation in *The Progressive Historians*, he associates the presence or absence of "comity" with the presence or absence of consensus. Comity "exists in a society to the degree that those enlisted in its contending interests have a basic minimal regard for each other."[1] In *The Genius of American Politics*, Boorstin presents a lengthy, subtle causal thesis which one can explicate only with considerable effort. In *The Liberal Tradition in America*, Hartz is brief and clear on causation.

Boorstin's treatment of causation has evoked this critical comment:

> Boorstin feels that because Americans did not use theory to construct their society, theory is thereby useless to explain it. I might argue with equal justice that because the water in a kettle does not take cognizance of the laws of thermodynamics, those laws cannot be used to explain why the water boils if put over a flame.[2]

One can understand why this criticism has been made, and one can also defend Boorstin against it. These two possibilities result from the confusing way Boorstin refers to "theory." The title of the first chapter of *The Genius of American Politics*, "How Belief in the Existence of an American Theory Has Made a Theory Superfluous," does not tell us precisely what the chapter is about. It does become evident that Boorstin is primarily concerned with Americans' making, more or less unwittingly, certain fundamental assumptions which serve the function of a theory and render us a people who eschew political theorizing. But he also raises the question: "Is there perhaps a theory behind our theory, or behind our lack of theory, which might itself have some validity as a conscious principle of political thought?"[3]

At the outset, Boorstin seems to dismiss this question with a negative answer: "To understand the uniqueness of American history is to begin to understand why no adequate theory of our political life can be written."⁴ But the question reappears. Boorstin, as noted in chapter 1, refers to the belief that "the earliest settlers or Founding Fathers equipped our nation at its birth with a perfect and complete political theory adequate to all our future needs"—a belief which accounts for "the poverty of our later theorizing." At various points he asks, "What circumstances of American history have made such a view possible?"; what are "the factors which have induced us to presuppose such an orthodoxy?"; and "How can we explain the origin, growth and vitality of this idea of 'givenness' in America?"⁵ Although occasional statements by Boorstin appear to preclude such an undertaking, he does theorize about the sources of Americans' nontheoretical approach to politics.

In *The Genius of American Politics* Boorstin discusses the belief in a perfect original doctrine under the heading "Values Given by the Past: The Preformation Ideal." He borrows the concept of "preformation" from out-of-date biology. It is "the idea that all parts of an organism pre-exist in perfect miniature in the seed. . . . It assumes that the values and theory of the nation were given once and for all in the very beginning." In response to the question, why did Americans come to hold "the belief that an explicit political theory is somehow superfluous precisely because we already somehow possess a satisfactory equivalent?," Boorstin cites: (1) the beginning of American civilization at a definite period in recent history, which has relieved us of the need to invent a mythology of original settlement; (2) the brevity of our history, which makes it easy for us to assume that our national life has had a clear purpose from the start; (3) the heterogeneous character of our population: "outcast Europeans have been eager to believe that they can find here a simplicity of theory lacking in the countries from which they came"; (4) "the fact that we have a written constitution and even our special way of interpreting it": we combine flexibility in applying the Constitution to specific practical problems while our framework, our political theory, remains rigid and unexperimental; (5) the practicality that is one of the main qualities of the doctrine in whose original perfection we believe: this may help us to grasp that "unique combination of empiricism and idealism which has characterized American political life."[6]

Boorstin discusses a second type of "givenness" under the heading "Values Given by the Landscape: The Land of the Free." He refers to these values as "the gift of the present" and "the golden land idea." Belief in them rests on: (1) abundance of resources; (2) a healthful climate; (3) the freedom to benefit from resources and climate, this freedom being "breathed in with our very air" and feeding "our belief in the mystical power of the land"; (4) our immigrant character: "We have been too well aware of our diversity to try to seek our values in our original cultures"; (5) our skipping the feudal phase of history; (6) geographical isolation; (7) special opportunities for expansion and exploitation within our own borders; (8) our remoteness from Europe; and other unnamed factors.[7]

The idea of "givenness" contains three elements. The first two are the "preformation ideal" or "the notion that we have received our values as a gift from the *past*," from the explicit ideals of the Founding Fathers, and the notion that American values are a gift from the *present*, "that our theory is always implicit in our institutions." They are given as axioms.[8] The third element, which links the other two, Pole writes, paraphrasing Boorstin, is "the homogeneity, the continuity of American history in a steady stream, free from violent oscillations of regime and void of violent ideological challenges."[9]

Pole emphasizes Boorstin's "controlling sense of distinction between theory and practice," his supposition of "the almost schematic opposition between theory and practical experience."[10] This distinction or opposition is apparently blurred by Boorstin's argument that ideas are the product of experience. Pole refers to Boorstin's "lasting preoccupation with the influence of the specifically American experience of life on the making of a specifically American mind" and to his thesis that "the concrete experience of [American] development, in all its ramifications, and not fixed ideology or preconceived political theory, has given America both its values and its characteristic methods of political action."[11] If one raises the question whether ideas can be divorced from experience if they are a product of it, one can still concede to Boorstin a meaningful separation on the basis of his consistent contention that experience is the ultimate causal factor. If one raises the question whether ideas, having come into existence from whatever source, can be denied any causal impact on subsequent experience and thought, one must recognize that Boorstin treats the role of ideas in American history at two levels. Although he denigrates the role of ideas in specific historical epochs or events, especially major conflicts,[12] he does ascribe causal significance to Americans' agreement on fundamentals—*but* this agreement is on fundamentals of a nontheoretical kind; it goes back to the beginning, when it arose from experience; and the United States owes its subsequent success to Americans' rejection of the teachings of theory and their eager embracing of experience.[13]

If the American experience "has given America its values and its characteristic methods of political action," what has determined the essential nature of that experience? Boorstin's reply, in effect, is "geography." It is worthwhile to compare this answer with Americans' beliefs, as described by Boorstin, concerning the determinants of their experience. Pole refers to "the feeling Boorstin discerns that American ideals and institutions all derive from an experience that was 'given' rather than being historically accumulated," and he quotes Boorstin directly: " 'Giveness' is the belief that values in America are in some way automatically defined: *given* by certain facts of geography or history peculiar to us."[14] The question arises whether "the feeling Boorstin discerns" among the American people and his own feeling are similar. They are. As pointed out in chapter 1, Boorstin's judgment of the people's belief that they possessed the equivalent of a political theory is that the people were mistaken. In the present case, Boorstin agrees with the people. At least to the extent that the people relate "givenness" to geography, Boorstin's view of causation is in accord with theirs, for, as Pole states, Boorstin "sees American society as a product of American geography"; his view that American values are a gift from the present "depends heavily on geography" in a way reminiscent of Turner; and the continuity which he sees as linking the gifts of the present to those of the past also depends heavily on geography—"our climate, our soil, and our mineral wealth."[15] Pole concludes: "Although movement and change are implicit as the subject of Boorstin's themes, his interests seldom call for intense analysis of specific processes; a vague determinism, mainly geographic in bias, underlies both events and social forms."[16]

Concerning causation, Hartz emphasizes the absence of a feudal past. Without an *ancien regime* and an opposing revolutionary tradition, America did not experience the ideological conflicts of Europe: "It is not accidental," Hartz maintains in *The Liberal Tradition in America*, "that America which has uniquely lacked a feudal tradition has uniquely lacked also a socialist tradition."[17] Hartz takes as his point of departure a quotation from Tocqueville: "The great advantage of Americans is, that they have arrived at a state of democracy without having to endure a democratic revolution; and that they are born equal, instead of becoming so."[18] Hartz, to be sure, was not the first scholar to stress the significance for American development of the fact that European feudalism was not brought to the seventeenth century English colonies,[19] but he "deserves credit for trying to convert an old insight into a tool of analysis."[20] What was brought to the seventeenth century English colonies was Lockean liberalism. In *The Liberal Tradition in America* (1955) Hartz more or less assumes this transference, a process which he later expounded as a "fragmentation theory" in *The Founding of New Societies* (1964). Nearly all the criticism of his causal analysis, including most of that which has appeared since 1964, focuses on the absence-of-feudalism emphasis of *The Liberal Tradition in America*. In the next section of this chapter we shall discuss the criticism bearing solely on *The Liberal Tradition in America*; in the following section we shall consider the criticism addressed to Hartz's fragmentation theory as well. This separation is called for because the earlier volume has had far greater influence on historians. At the same time, examination of the second volume sheds light on the basic concept of American development underlying the argument which Hartz presented in 1955.

Criticism of Hofstadter, Boorstin, and Hartz

Criticism of the ideas of the generalizers of consensus on causation—we shall consider criticism of their views in general in chapter 3—contains very little comment on Hofstadter's work, a substantial body of literature—especially essays by Pole and Diggins—on Boorstin's writings, and a number of relatively brief remarks on Hartz's causal explanation. The criticism of Hofstadter can be dealt with summarily. His emphasis on "comity," in David M. Potter's opinion, is not a causal explanation. Potter holds, as it were, that if comity causes consensus, Hofstadter does not tell us what causes comity. Comity, in fact, is synonymous with consensus—"more of a measure of the degree of toleration which prevails at a given time than the device for attaining toleration that he [Hofstadter] seems to think it is."[1] It is not possible, as the reader will probably suspect by now, to treat the criticism of Boorstin's ideas on causation with such dispatch.

In his analysis of Boorstin's interpretation of American history, Pole identifies two main logical difficulties or ambiguities: one is the endowing of facts with normative as well as descriptive qualities or making the "is" the "ought" (which we shall consider in chapter 3 in connection with Pole's criticism of Boorstin's selectivity); the other is the failure to separate illusion from reality. When Boorstin describes a belief in a fact—the Founding Fathers' legacy of a satisfactory substitute for a theory—rather than a fact per se, he seems, Pole writes, "to have prepared himself for the task of separating illusion from reality"[2] Having concluded that the belief is incorrect, Boorstin by implication assigns himself the task of distinguishing between what Americans thought they possessed in the way of a theory and what they actually possessed, but "he continues to speak of a 'belief' in 'givenness' rather than in the fact, and he never comes to the point of saying how much was valid, how much was illusory, what might have been valuable, what might have been pernicious, in either the illusion or the fact." Pole, who holds that the Founding Fathers *did* possess a theory and therefore sees no illusion on the part of the people in this regard, says, "In the end it turns out that Boorstin is himself encircled, that the illusion was the fact."[3]

This failure to expose the differences between the images and ideals that Americans derived from vague sources and the substance of history leads Pole to comment on the geographic bias in Boorstin's ideas on causation:

When Boorstin comes to the qualities given by the land itself, the argument is . . . elusive. Does Boorstin really believe that the encounter with the land gave Americans concrete values to live by, and does he himself proclaim these values, or is he only telling us that Americans were hallucinated into a kind of rapture, not unlike the mystique about the desert entertained by British contemporaries of T.E. Lawrence, and that this rapture acted as a substitute for systematic or connected thought? Such an explanation could in itself be valid; the sources of our beliefs, or ideals, are not necessarily rational; the trouble is that Boorstin fails, in his own analysis, to make the relevant distinctions.[4]

Near the end of his essay Pole asserts that the missing dimension in Boorstin's geographic determinism is historical explanation:

Why, we may ask, did political parties come into being? Why did community precede forms of government, and still more significant, why did Americans adopt these rather than other forms? The encounter with the land obviously presented hard necessities, but the land itself did not put into American heads the ideas of government and social organization on which they chose to act. Why did they choose as they did rather than otherwise? By ignoring the realm of preconceived ideas, the substratum of institutional thought, he has weakened his power of explanation.[5]

One of the primary targets of Pole's criticism, as we shall see again in chapter 3, is Boorstin's downgrading of the role of ideas in American history.

In his critique of Boorstin's interpretation of American history, Diggins asserts that Boorstin does theorize about the sources of Americans' nontheoretical approach to politics. Diggins addresses his essay to "the philosopher who has purged American history of theory only by theorizing about American history, and to the historian who has depreciated the role of ideas in it by imposing his ideas upon it." Not only does Boorstin "liberate the American past from ideology [by developing] a theory that is itself an ideology," but, according to Diggins, "his rejection of the role of theory and ideas in American history itself rests on a scaffolding of ideas that is as much European as American."[6]

Diggins points out that Boorstin's concept of the "preforma-tion ideal" clearly embodies "the Hegelian metaphysics of his-

tory, which infused nineteenth-century European thought."
Boorstin's presupposition of a self-contained, "embryonic" idea
at work in history from the very beginning is similar to one of
Hegel's basic assumptions. Boorstin's frequent use of mor-
phological metaphors—"his worship of 'the unity of our history'
and . . . his assertion that American institutions were not conceived but somehow sprouted as 'organisms which grew out of
the soil in which they are rooted and out of the tradition from
which they have sprung' "—echoes Hegel's description of the
organic unity of the "bud" and the "blossom," of the continuity
behind all change. Boorstin's endowing of facts with normative
as well as descriptive qualities—his making the empirical and the
ideal "one and the same . . . and his failure to draw the crucial
distinction between fact and value"—is similar to Hegel's implicitly fatalistic assertion that "the rational is actual; and the
actual is rational" and to Hegel's assumption that in historical
study "thought must be subordinated to what is given, to the
realities of fact." Boorstin, like Hegel, maintains that philosophy
and history are contradictory. He "banishes philosophy by incorporating it into the realm of history," and he is "convinced
that the study of history will better enable man to reconcile
himself to reality once human thought begins to correspond to
the actual world of fact."[7]

Diggins also identifies parallels between Boorstin's views
and those of Marx and interpreters of Marx such as E.H. Carr,
Plekhanov, and Engels. With respect to epistemology, Diggins
notes, the parallels between Boorstin's and Marx's phraseology
are "more than coincidental. They derive from the common
premise that action is a realm of knowledge and value higher
than thought itself." Thus the descriptive is the normative, the
empirical is the ideal, the "is" is the "ought." Boorstin completely
accepts Jefferson's conviction that the ideal, the moral, could not
be rooted in theory but only in the "life of action," and he has
faith in what he defines as the American tendency to "leave ideas
embodied in experience and a belief that truth somehow arises
out of experience." This acceptance and this faith, Diggins says,
are "curiously close to the Marxist theory of cognition, which
insists that truth is realized only in practical effort." Diggins also
finds it curious that

it is precisely this activist theory of knowledge and life . . . that is
the channeling ethos of communism as well as of capitalism. That
the meaning and value of life must be found in action is the faith
of the Stakhanovite as well as of the rugged individualist.
Whether the search is for socialism or salvation, both the Marxist
and the Protestant work ethic evoke an attitude of ceaseless
striving. . . .

Indeed, E.H. Carr has spent his scholarly career justifying Soviet
Russia with arguments resting on the same philosophical
assumptions Boorstin draws upon to explain the American past.
Carr still shares the pre-1914 faith in technological progress that
has enchanted America, and he is convinced that Soviet history
demonstrates [the Marxist law] that quantity can be transformed
into quality through revolutionary social change and that "values
can be derived from facts." Both Carr and Boorstin believe that
history is nothing more than process; both regard progress as
mastery of the environment. . . .

Literally, Carr states, "We are assured on all hands, and with the
utmost emphasis, that the dichotomy between "is" and "ought" is
absolute and cannot be derived from "facts." This is, I think, a
false trail.[8]

Since "action is a realm of knowledge and value higher than
thought itself," and since thought therefore must be "subordinated to . . . the realities of fact," philosophy can have an
antiphilosophic function. As Diggins comments,

Boorstin's Jeffersonian conviction that the major function of
philosophy is "prophylactic"—to dispel "the perils of
metaphysics"—is strikingly similar to Marx's conviction that true
philosophy is *praxis*—to reorient the mind from abstract
reflection to concrete activity.[9]

This attribution to philosophy of a "prophylactic" function is in
accord with Boorstin's appeal in *The Genius of American Politics* to
anti–status quo American intellectuals to exercise their only
freedom, which was to conserve God's gift, discoverable not in
abstract reason but in the details of life.

At the same time, according to both Boorstin and Marx,
philosophy can have a harmful impact:

from the common premise that action is a realm of knowledge
and value higher than thought itself . . . emerges the strangest
consensus in American historiography: for Marx the abstract
concepts of mind served mainly to delude man and thereby to
preserve the social order; for Boorstin such concepts serve mainly
to erode "a sense for the 'seamlessness' of experience" and
thereby radically undermine the continuity of institutions.
Assuming that theoretical man is the enemy, it is thus imperative
that Marx as revolutionary and Boorstin as conservative reject the
demands of ethical thought and the claims of autonomous ideas
in history.[10]

But this denial that abstract concepts have a causal role apparently amounts to repudiation by decree since Marx concedes
that they can help preserve the social order while Boorstin holds
that they can undermine the continuity of institutions. In the
end, however, Marx is consistent regarding the causal impact of
ideas. Abstract concepts can delay the demise of the social order,
but in the long run collapse is inevitable. Boorstin, for his part,
ultimately in *The Image* found the sources of America's departure from the Jeffersonian covenant not in ideology espoused by
the artificial elite of intellectuals but in corruption within "the
people."

Other parallels cited by Diggins between Boorstin's views
and those of Marxists are the similarity between Boorstin's declaration that America "would long profit from having been
born without ever having been conceived" and Plekhanov's assertion that "*Being* determines *thinking*"; and between Boorstin's
faith in "the moral plenitude of the American environment" and
Engels' faith in "the moral sufficiency of empirical facts." If
these and the other parallels Diggins cites are curious because
Boorstin is an anti-Marxist historian, they are not surprising,
Diggins holds, in view of the compatibility between Boorstin's
pragmatic naturalism and European Marxism: "Each assumes
the naturalistic supremacy of doing over being; each assumes
that the knowledge process is a practical, transforming activity;
and each is opposed to traditional philosophic dualism." Each,
moreover, has an attitude toward human nature that harmonizes with their common view on epistemology:

> When Antonio Gramsci asks, "What is man?" and tells us "we really mean 'What can man become?' " and then answers that "man is a process, and precisely the process of his actions," is this not Boorstin's definition of the American character? In his desire to liberate the American past from ideology Boorstin has developed a theory of history that is itself an ideology. . . .
>
> Boorstin is a philosopher of history in spite of himself, and the ideas with which he demonstrates the absence of ideas in American history are as rich and abstract as the European philosophies he finds so repugnant and un-American.[11]

Besides maintaining that Boorstin not only theorizes about the sources of Americans' nontheoretical approach to politics but theorizes in European-like terms, Diggins mounts a direct attack on Boorstin's ideas on causation. Just as Pole comments that Boorstin's "interests seldom call for intense analysis of specific processes," so Diggins asserts that Boorstin "consistently avoids the problems of causation."[12] Like Pole, Diggins stresses the downgrading of the role of ideas in American history as the basic flaw in Boorstin's views on causation. Diggins' attack on Boorstin's causal scheme, however, differs in detail from Pole's. Perhaps this distinction can be illuminated diagramatically.

Boorstin's Analysis According to Pole

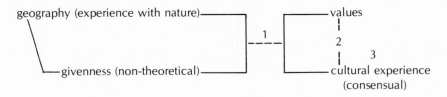

Geography is the ultimate causal factor, the source even of givenness since Americans' agreement on fundamentals goes back to the beginning, when it arose from experience. Pole specifies missing links in this causal chain at three points representing three levels of causation: Boorstin does not tell us (1) how the land gave Americans concrete values and a certain kind of cultural or total experience (for present purposes we do not follow the anthropologists' distinction between culture and society); (2) how values determined the general, consensual nature of the cultural or total experience; or (3) how, and what, specific choices were involved in the specific processes encompassed by the cultural or total experience. In Boorstin's view, to be sure, analysis of causation at levels (2) and (3) is unnecessary or, at most, of secondary importance since all developments, constituting one nonideological package, initially emerge from causation at level (1).

Pole's Own Analysis

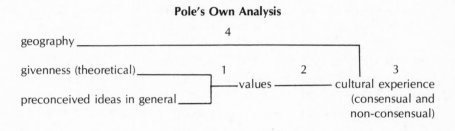

Pole's alternative scheme, derived from his analysis of Boorstin's writings, stresses (1) the intellectual sources of values, which, in turn, (2)determined the general, consensual and nonconsensual nature of the total or cultural experience as well as (3) entering into the specific choices involved in the specific processes encompassed by the total or cultural experience. Pole assigns a causal role to geography (4) of a general limiting kind—the "encounter with the land obviously presented hard necessities" so that, one may add, a cotton-based culture could not develop in Maine—but he denies that the land itself gave Americans the qualities or values which account for the particular cultural experience that occurred within the general outer limits imposed by geography.

Diggins' Own Analysis

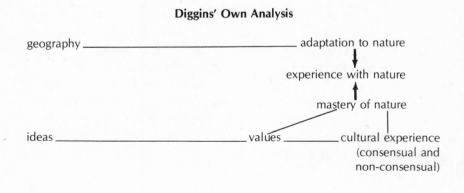

Like Pole, Diggins identifies ideas as the source of values and implicitly—in view of his comments on Boorstin's neglect of detailed causal analysis and in view of his basic agreement with Pole—he identifies values as the source of the specific choices involved in the specific processes encompassed by the total or cultural experience. Diggins sees the cultural experience and ideas as inseparable:

> Are the victors [in Boorstin's interpretation], then, responding to abstractions or experience, to doctrine or to fact, to principles or to precedent, to the demands of philosophy or to the pressures of history? In reality, such a dichotomous formulation poses a false problem, for . . . modern intellectual history [has seen] the erosion of these traditional epistemological dualisms.[13]

In addition to taking exception to Boorstin's neglect of the erosion of epistemological dualisms (his separating experience and ideas), Diggins objects to Boorstin's blurring of metaphysical dualisms (his uniting man's nature and physical nature). In this regard, Diggins holds that "nature was not a source of values but merely a dreary obstacle to be overcome,"[14] assigning geography, as it were, a causal role similar to that which Pole imputes to the "hard necessities" presented by the land. Yet, if geography had causal weight in that it called for adaptation (we may assume that Diggins would concede the impossibility of the development of a cotton-based culture in Maine), adaptation was only a part of Americans' experience with nature and, as we shall see momentarily, a factor decidedly subordinate to the other part—mastery of nature. In short, Diggins rejects the kind of relationship between man and the environment implied in the primary causal role Boorstin ascribes, especially in his chapter on the Puritans in *The Genius of American Politics*, to geography or experience with nature.

Boorstin, Diggins notes, interprets "the failure of Puritanism as the fulfillment of Puritanism":

> Although the Puritans became what they set out not to be, they achieved their historical purpose, as Boorstin would have it, in the obliteration of their spiritual purpose. "Puritanism in New England," Boorstin contends, "was to decline, not because it was defeated, but, in a sense, because it had succeeded." What

Puritanism succeeded in was the negation of its theology and the realization of the theory beyond theory, the idea of "givenness" that Boorstin assumes to have been inherent in both Puritanism and in the nature of America.[15]

Boorstin's contention, in Diggins' view, has an existentialist quality:

In truth, Boorstin is terribly anxious to de-Europeanize his Puritans, and in so doing he necessarily denies them their intrinsic spiritual nature, their heroic quest for "Being." He assumes that the Puritans were all along not what they conceived themselves to be but what they made of themselves. For Boorstin man has no essence; he is what he becomes. In his approach to history, meaning is therefore to be found in becoming, and in the context of his writings this means nothing less than the endless process of becoming American.[16]

The early Puritans themselves, Diggins writes, believed they embodied essence since they "doubted that man could change his nature by changing the natural world." Regardless of what they conceived themselves to be, however, "Boorstin seems certain that the first Americans were primarily doers and makers, men of self-actualizing activity." This certainty amounts to an "unspoken metaphysical premise about man's nature." This premise rejects the distinction between "the Puritans' self-conscious spiritual quest and the American environment which deflected that quest as they worked upon its materials"; it has the effect of "blurring the dualism between essence and becoming"; and it ignores the "teleological essence of Puritanism in order to make the New England Puritans a direct part of the American experience." "Givenness" has its own teleology: "all is process and continuity toward an end that is only a beginning."[17]

In merging man with the environment while subordinating him to it, Boorstin, Diggins insists, blends the immiscible:

With Hegel, Boorstin asks us to accept the "normative" significance of the past, to accept the empirically real as the American ideal. Once we see that what was actual had to determine what was possible, and once we become aware that no human theory was at work in American history, then we shall realize that the full meaning of that history can be grasped only by *understanding* its development. With Marx, on the other hand, Boorstin has asked us to accept the ontological supremacy of doing over being and the epistemological primacy of action over thought. He asks us to accept, that is, a pragmatic theory of knowledge, which leads to the conclusion that history is to be grasped not merely by comprehending it but by *changing* it.

Since "understanding" history is one thing and "changing" history is another, Boorstin's ideas, Diggins asserts, rest precariously on two incompatible premises, and this theoretical synthesis collapses under careful examination.[18]

Diggins further develops this line of criticism in commenting on Boorstin's concept of the "nirvana of success" or self-realization, which is "achieved in 'absorption,' 'oblivion,' and 'self-annihilation': it is consummated in the 'loss of identity.' " As Boorstin puts it, "the individual transcends his own personality to become part of what surrounds him," and Americanization is the attainment of a sense of oneness by "complete adaptation to the environment which involves seizing the opportunities it offers, by 'fitting in.' " When Boorstin writes that the "nirvana of success" in America has been "self-annihilation through mastery and adaptation," he suggests what Diggins calls "an almost romantic union of man and nature." Diggins objects to this fusion: "Adaptation and mastery are mutually exclusive. Forced to choose between the two, Americans chose not to adapt to but to master their environment. . . . Rather than be satisfied with 'a complete adaptation to the environment,' Americans strove to change it radically." The values expressed in this mastery, this subduing and appropriating, moreover, did not derive from nature. "It would seem truer to say," according to Diggins, "that in American history there has been a profound discontinuity between man and his environment, a perpetual divorce of humankind from the unity of nature." This alienation, for better or worse, involves the causal impact of man's essence, including his ideas. Thus, in his own terms, Boorstin introduces into his interpretation of American history a causal factor which he must denigrate to portray a geographically determined consensual development.[19]

Turning to Hartz's views on causation, we find that his critics often focus on the analysis signified in his dictum: "It is not accidental that America which has uniquely lacked a feudal tradition has uniquely lacked also a socialist tradition." Kenneth McNaught, for example, accepts the consensus thesis concerning politics, referring to "the extinction of party based dissent," but he judges untenable Hartz's assertion that socialism was bound to fail in America because there was no aristocracy for it to oppose. Socialism, McNaught claims, was both "in and of American society." He deplores the failure of historians to distinguish between opinionative and intrinsic irrelevance: "the fact that most Americans were persuaded that socialism was alien is taken as proof that socialism was alien."[20] Marvin Meyers comments that Hartz does not deal with the question of intrinsic irrelevance or relevance since he considers public opinion the historically determinative factor: "Hartz explains the failure of American Socialism as a political and intellectual movement not so much by exceptional 'objective' conditions or faulty theory as by the iron grip of liberal ideology on American minds."[21] McNaught, nevertheless, sees in Hartz's argument a deterministic quality which he attacks vigorously, stressing instead the importance of individuals' conscious decisions to abandon socialism and denying the *inevitability* of socialism's demise in America.[22]

Richard B. Morris considers Hartz's contention that the absence of a feudal tradition accounted for the absence of a socialist tradition a useful hypothesis but nevertheless an over-simplification which "minimizes the substantial evidence of vestigial feudalism in pre-Revolutionary America." It also fails to recognize that "the feudalism of the *ancien regime* by the time of the French Revolution bears little resemblance to the textbook stereotype."[23] Leonard Krieger maintains that the presence or absence of feudalism has played only a contributory role in the development of American and European liberalism. He finds Hartz's representation of the historical process behind the emergence of a more homogeneous, pervasive, and stable American liberalism "overly mechanical," *a* but not *the* explanation of the differences between American and European liberalism.[24]

Meyers draws a distinction between Hartz's and Tocqueville's versions of Americans being "born equal" in a society whose development was devoid of a feudal phase. Hartz "argues primarily from the single, special fact of equal birth; Tocqueville from the complex and as he thinks universal fact of equal social condition." Needless to say, equality in democratic civil and political terms is one thing; this kind of equality accompanied by equality of condition in general, and material condition in particular, is another. Tocqueville, Meyers states, emphasizes "equality of condition . . . as 'the fundamental fact from which all others seem to be derived.' " This leads him to consider a wider range of causal factors than Hartz does, "among them: religion, the specific legacy of English liberty, the decentralized pattern of settlement, and a wise constitution."[25] The key phrase here is "as he thinks." We shall deal with its implications in the concluding section of this chapter, where we consider Tocqueville's emphasis on equality of condition in the light of recent criticism of his work.

Perhaps the harshest critic of Hartz's causal analysis is Hartshorne, who, like Krieger, judges the absence-of-feudalism thesis inadequate. In Hartshorne's estimate it is even less than too narrow to begin with:

> To say, as Hartz did, that democracy was "inherent" in the American situation is to explain nothing at all. It may be correct, but by itself it is insufficient, for it begs an obvious question: Why was democracy inherent in the American situation? Hartz did not answer this question beyond stating that democracy grew up in the power vacuum created by the lack of feudal institutions in America. Again, this is insufficient. Why did *democracy* of all possible forms of government grow up in the United States? Granting the absence of feudal institutions, why was it not possible for them to grow as democracy did? It is not sufficient to assert that democracy grew because it was the only available alternative. It is necessary to determine *why* it was the only available alternative, and in order to do so it still seems necessary to resort to the Frontier Thesis or some other comparable historical generalization.[26]

If one argues in Hartz's behalf that he omits an analysis of the causes of the absence of feudalism and concentrates on its results, Hartshorne would reply that Hartz fails to eliminate the rise of feudalism as a possible outcome of the absence of feudalism.

Hartz's Fragmentation Theory

All of the criticism of Hartz's ideas just cited is addressed to *The Liberal Tradition in America*. The fact is that in *The Founding of New Societies* (1964) he advanced a general theory in which the same causes account for both the absence of feudalism and the presence of liberalism or democracy. Actually, in *The Liberal Tradition in America* Hartz had briefly presented the essence of his fragmentation theory—perhaps all too briefly for it to attract the attention it warrants as an integral part of his interpretation of American history. He frankly admitted that in dealing with the "absence of feudalism and the presence of the liberal idea," he was engaging in "single-factor" analysis by focusing on "the natural development of liberalism." He noted that the "escape from the old European order could be accompanied by other ideas," and he called for studies which would compare the positive cultural concepts of new societies with the European institutions they had left behind.[1] Having taken the presence of the liberal idea as his point of departure in *The Liberal Tradition in America*, Hartz returned to the antecedents of this presence in *The Founding of New Societies*, to which he contributed a lengthy exposition (pages 3–122) of his fragmentation theory of the development of new societies. Edward Handler, a political scientist, abstracts the essence of this theory:

> In *The Founding of New Societies* (1964), Louis Hartz builds on his
> earlier analysis of America as an archetypal nonfeudal
> society—*The Liberal Tradition in America* (1955)—to present a
> more general theory concerning five societies (Australia, Canada,
> Latin America, South Africa, and the United States) created by
> European migration. In each of these societies, Hartz explains, an
> ideological and social fragment detached itself from the larger
> whole of Europe to become the whole of the new nation. In these
> terms three centuries of American political experience can be
> traced to the original extraction of a bourgeois-liberal fragment
> from the turmoil of seventeenth-century England.[2]

When a part of English society became the whole of American society, the presence of liberalism was not the result of the absence of feudalism—both resulted from the process of fragmentation.

In 1963 Hartz published a briefer essay on his fragmentation theory,[3] and a summary of this version will serve present purposes. Hartz contrasts democracy's defeat in Europe with its triumph in America. Accounting for the failure of democracy to win out in the Old World, he identifies four main elements operative in the political arena of early nineteenth-century Europe: (1) the feudal, aristocratic right; (2) Whiggery, representing the ambition of the wealthier bourgeoisie, who had an enduring fear of the people; (3) the petit-bourgeoisie; and (4) labor. The democratic opposition to Whiggery was deeply divided: the peasant population was not quite an enemy of the right since it still had a strong affinity for the old feudal, conservative, aristocratic order; and the lower middle class was split off from both the peasantry and the workers. The lower middle class and labor lacked the political education required to lead the campaign against the right, and in the end they followed Whiggery in that campaign. Whiggery made limited reforms, while democratic elements demanded further reforms. They were unable to achieve them because Whiggery did an about-face and joined the *ancien regime*, depriving the democratic movement of its leadership as well as reducing its stregnth, and because democratic movement then split up as the leftward movement advanced, with the lower middle class becoming terrified of labor. "Battles break out, and democracy is defeated. This is the old European story."[4]

Why did the democrats triumph so easily in America? There were three major reasons for their victory: (1) a wider and more unified democratic majority; (2) an enlightened electorate; and (3) a simplification of political alignment. These three factors were analogues of each other:

> A wider and more cohesive democratic combination implies a larger degree of mass enlightenment, for it means that the predemocratic and antidemocratic dross on the European mind has been eliminated: the feudal spirit is gone from the land, the

proletarian outlook from the towns. And this necessarily means a simpler political alignment, for the right is gone and democracy has greatly grown.[5]

Arguing for the vastly greater unification of the democratic forces in America, Hartz tells us not to be misled by their hodgepodge quality into thinking that they were a "hopelessly disparate mass." American democratic politicians, to be sure, displayed political genius, but "the unity was already there":

> Indeed, the apparent looseness of the democratic combination is itself a clue to the point involved. For what the European scene presents us with is a series of sharp class breaks, involving deep mutual suspicions, and the bridging of these so effectively not even a master American politician could have accomplished.[6]

Nor was the triumph of the democrats simply a matter of sheer numbers and the acquisition of the franchise. "It is a matter of political consciousness as well," of the capacity of the mass of the people for a "very high degree of independent political activity":

> the shell of passivity and alienation cracked with comparative ease in the United States, bringing into existence the unified democratic alignment of American politics. . . .
>
> Once the democratic organization began, a degree of mass political enlightenment was manifested which had no parallel in the world.[7]

Although the third factor underlying democracy's triumph in America—a simplification of political alignment—is implied "automatically" by the first two, a summary of Hartz's discussion of this factor will shed some direct light on what was involved in the process of fragmentation. The right was "never transported to America in the first place." There was an American analogue of European Whiggery, and there was the democratic alliance. The democracy did not need Whiggery as an ally, "or at least not for very long." Whiggery stood alone. The democracy in Jacksonian America consisted almost wholly of the lower middle class. The small trader supported Jackson. In agriculture the dominant mood from the beginning was that of the independent entrepreneur, and the farmer was Jackson's ally, "not his sullen enemy." The workers in the towns never displayed the "sense of political alienation and depression" found among the urban proletariat in Europe. Their role in Jacksonian democracy is still debated by historians, but they were "not likely to strike out on terrifying revolutionary paths." In sum, in the American political arena the feudal aristocracy was missing from the right; an unenlightened peasantry and a threatened proletariat were missing from the left. Instead of four contenders there were two, and the triumph of democracy over Whiggery was inevitable: "The very wideness of the democratic alliance is proof that the political situation has been simplified, and the very enlightenment of the American electorate is proof that in this simplified picture it cannot be defeated."[8]

The forces which stood out in Europe in the nineteenth century were the forces which Americans had left behind in the seventeenth century: "The decisive moment in American history is the time of the great migration of the seventeenth century." Subsequent developments were an aftermath of this migration, "manifestations of the logic of New World settlement." With this assertion, Hartz turns from what Americans left behind to what they brought with them. If a wider and more unified democratic majority, an enlightened electorate, and a simplification of political alignment were analogues of each other, "there must surely be some deeper factor behind them all." This factor, extricated from the complex historic feudal culture of Europe, was the liberal-bourgeois element, common to American Whigs and democrats: "A liberal tradition arose in the New World, and this is the factor which, like some ultimate Hegelian force, keeps showing its face in the various aspects of American politics." Concerning this liberal tradition, Hartz writes, *"Now this was an idea, nothing more,"*[9] This assertion calls for special emphasis since it implies Hartz's basic views on ultimate causation and on the relationship between ideas and behavior or experience.

Hartz points out that in *The Liberal Tradition in America* he referred to Locke only as the symbol of the liberal idea "since there is much in his life and work which contradicts the American scheme of thought" (true, the concepts Hartz has in mind may be found in Locke's *Second Treatise*, but they also appear in the writings of various seventeenth- and eighteenth-century classical liberal thinkers). The common sharing of Lockean concepts or liberal values eliminated barriers to the unity of the democrats, and the experience of democratic liberalism, essentially the experience of the Jacobin or small entrepreneur in Europe, became the experience of nearly everyone in America. The liberal idea also stimulated political activism as the slogans of democratic liberalism became irrational in their appeal —became, that is, symbols which, as symbols, commanded widespread allegiance and generated continuous public participation in politics. Finally, the role of the liberal idea in the simplification of political alignment is clear: "When that idea is universal the politics of four dimensions becomes the politics of two dimensions, and the latter is contained within the bourgeois framework."[10]

When Hartz refers to the "experience" of democratic liberalism, to the "behavioral consequences" of an allegiance to different kinds of symbols, and to the simplification of political alignment as entailing a simplification of "cultural experience," it appears that there is something involved beyond "an idea, nothing more." There is, but Hartz does not separate thought and behavior, ideas and experience. On the contrary, the liberal concept, he holds, "transformed into operating modes of behavior, yielded the swift victories of American democracy." But it is extremely difficult, Hartz concedes, to track down democratic theory in America because the unchallenged liberal idea was elevated to an absolute, both as a faith and operationally. The democratic faith, indeed, lies far beneath the operational level of democracy. Scholars do not know this when, confusing a social with a philosophic process, they search for "democratic theory" instead of studying American political thought in order to shed light on the process of democracy. Nor do American politicians, as "victims of the universal mind," know this when they call each other names such as "Tory" or "leveler," failing to see the process which is at work.

> But is not this the final proof of the process itself? When a unifying idea has sunk so far beneath the surface of a culture that it can support a raging hyperbole which contradicts it, then surely

it has attained no mean victory. In such a world the search for "democratic theory," or even "political theory," is a beguiling quest. For it is the talent of such a world to take a single idea out of the conscious intellectual struggles of Europe and plunge it deep into unconscious behavior where it reigns, without philosophy, without criticism, as an operational absolute.[11]

Although Hartz accords causal weight in American development to experience or behavior, his view of the nature and role of experience cannot be equated with Boorstin's geographical or environmental determinism. In Hartz's analysis, experience, whatever self-perpetuating force it embodies, ultimately derives from the "power of the idea that was extracted from Europe and carried to the New World in the seventeenth century." He admits that an abundance of land and industrial working conditions less severe than those in Europe facilitated the triumph of democracy—although, he notes, they did not do so in certain other countries—but "fundamentally we are dealing with a psychic matter, the transforming impact of an idea . . . traceable in the end to a bourgeois trip that was taken in the seventeenth century which everyone has forgotten." Hartz concedes that his thesis is deterministic. He also points out that "abstraction itself is a process, yielding many of the crucial aspects of the American story, and it is not uniquely related to the liberal principle or for that matter to America itself."[12] In *The Founding of New Societies* he elaborates on the process of abstraction, dividing it into phases and describing different fragmentation patterns in different nations: "feudal" in French Canada and Latin America, "liberal" in English Canada, Boer South Africa, and the United States, "radical" in Australia.[13]

Just as the criticism of Hartz's causal explanation is addressed to *The Liberal Tradition in America* rather than to both this volume and *The Founding of New Societies*, so criticism of other aspects of Hartz's writings neglects the latter work. We shall have occasion to point this out again in our consideration of democracy in the next chapter and in some concluding comments about Hartz's views in the last chapter, but, to repeat, *The Liberal Tradition in America* has had far greater impact on historians than *The Founding of New Societies*. This becomes evident when one finds that in the literature on consensus historiography the most explicit recognition of Hartz's fragmentation theory is accorded in two commentaries by political scientists, Edward Handler and Neal Reimer.

In the introduction to his anthology on *The American Political Experience* (1968), Handler mentions Hartz's concept of the transplantation of a single European ideology, liberalism, to America, and in his bibliographical essay, as quoted above, he presents the essence of the fragmentation theory. In his introduction Handler also discusses interpretations of American political development under the heading "Environment or Inheritance," associating Boorstin's views with the former and Hartz's with the latter causal factor. Such categorizations, Handler's comments suggest, depend on relative emphases. Environmentalists like Ray Allen Billington, a neo-Turnerian, and David M. Potter, who stresses economic abundance, qualify their theses by assigning some weight to Old World historical and cultural inheritance (Potter calls cultural traits and dispositions the secondary—that is, nonphysical—environment). At the same time, nonenvironmentalists like Tocqueville and Hartz attribute some significance to physical circumstances, although in *The Liberal Tradition in America* notice of the material setting is fleeting. Handler quotes a single statement by Hartz: the liberal idea in America was "peculiarly fortified by the riches of a rich land" (in the same paragraph, on page 18, Hartz refers to a "Lockean idea fortified by material resources" and asserts that "the 'petit-bourgeois' giant of America, though ultimately a triumph of the liberal idea, could hardly have chosen a better material setting in which to flourish"). Boorstin, Handler's judgment implies, concedes even less to inheritance than Hartz does to environment: "Boorstin maintains that the baggage of 'idea' that the settlers brought with them often proved irrelevant, that their cultural inheritance had constantly to be unlearned."[14]

In his bibliographical essay Handler briefly summarizes the argument of his fellow political scientist, Reimer, who considers *The Founding of New Societies* as well as *The Liberal Tradition in America* and *The Genius of American Politics* and finds the key to American political development in the interaction of inheritance, environment, *and* his own version of the genius of American politics.[15] Although it is Reimer's exceptional performance among critics of consensus historiography—his consideration of Hartz's fragmentation theory—which has led us to an examination of his work, it seems appropriate to treat his commentaries on Boorstin and Hartz together. This will preserve the unity of his thought, which rests on his rejection both of Boorstin's discovery of the genius of American politics in its lack of ideology and Hartz's characterization of the genius of American politicians as their ability to exploit a unity that was already there.

Reimer expressed his disagreement with Boorstin in "Two Conceptions of the Genius of American Politics" (1958) and with both Boorstin and Hartz in *The Democratic Experiment* (1967).[16] In his article of 1958 Reimer interpreted political theorizing differently from Boorstin, arguing that it "need not involve one in 'extravagant and presumptuous speculations' [or] imply the construction of blueprints for remaking society." He argued further that

> there is both more and less in "givenness" than Boorstin emphasizes: that America has been *more* indebted to *past* theory and less a product of the American "landscape" than Boorstin appreciates; that we have had an explicit political theory and that there has been greater continuity in our *explicit* political theory than Boorstin may be willing to concede; and, finally, that our political theory has shaped in the past, as it must help shape in the future, new institutions if our democratic goals (our "large ends and unspoken values" to use Boorstin's phrase) are to be preserved.

Reimer used James Madison's political theory

> to *suggest* that, at least since 1787, America has had a theory which was, in part, the inevitable product of unique historical circumstances, and in part, the inevitable product of an incisive, creative, and synthesizing mind.[17]

The ability of the interpreters of our explicit democratic theory constantly to adjust it to new facts, with due regard to "both the limitations and the possibilities of past and present empirical reality, in order to advance the largely prescriptive values en-

shrined in the hearts of Western men"—"This," Reimer concluded, "is the true genius of American politics."[18]

In his book appearing in 1967, Reimer presented his tri-
causal thesis with confidence rather than suggestiveness. He
explicitly dissented not only from Boorstin's version of "givenness" and his unalloyed environmentalism but also from Hartz's
deterministic fragmentation theory, and he devoted 150 pages
to illustrating American political creativity based on conscious
choice. He asserted that the

> Old World Inheritance and the New World Environment were
> necessary but not sufficient conditions for The Democratic
> Experiment. American Democracy has not involved an automatic
> unfolding of a liberal English fragment from the 17th Century or
> an automatic response to a favorable American environment in
> the 17th, 18th, and 19th centuries! I hope the reader now sees
> that The Democratic Experiment required creative men to select
> and reject ingredients from the Old World Inheritance, and to
> adapt to and take advantage of the New World Environment.[19]

American creativity—creative acceptance and rejection of the
Old World Inheritance and creative use of New World
resources—was one of the three interacting ingredients of the
American experiment. It involved the "ethical, empirical, and
prudential components of political theory:that is,desirable ideals,
the realities of the struggle for power, and feasible policies."
In formulating public policies which would "maximize consciously conceived values in the light of the realities," Americans
made a creative contribution which rendered their ideas and
institutions something different from direct carryovers from the
Old World.[20] Reimer underlined the antideterministic quality of
this creativity, which involved both willing captivity by and conscious emancipation from inherited ideas, acknowledging in the
process that he, like Hartz, was indebted to Tocqueville:

> As Tocqueville perceived, creative leaders, and those who follow
> them, are not completely free of inheritance or environment. But
> as Tocqueville also saw, they are not completely enslaved. Their
> "captivity" may be a deliberate one. Moreover, within the "fatal
> circle" they are free to devise a new science of politics for a new
> world. In America, men of judgment did indeed devise a new
> science of politics for a new world. Not completely new—but new

in important respects! These men . . . devised and successfully
tested an experimental Federal Republic in a great revolutionary
epoch of the modern world.[21]

Elaborating his threefold causal thesis, Reimer acclaimed
the creativity of Roger Williams in choosing English con-
stitutionalism while rejecting religious or political authoritarianism. Williams' experiment drew on a radical Protestant Old World view and benefited from an open American
environment, but these factors "did not automatically produce
it, or—indeed—sustain it permanently in the 17th Century."
Reimer recognized the orthodox Puritans' encouragement
—admittedly initially unintended as such—of local autonomy
and self-government. Choosing the congregational principle of
church organization had been a "mistake" in that it weakened
theocracy, but it was a mistake the Puritans persisted in. Again,
Old World Inheritance—Protestant Reformation theory—and
New World Environment—the absence on the American Atlantic frontier of central control—played causal roles, but equally
important was a "conscious determination to persist in these
New World experiments in the interest of religious and political
freedom." Conscious choice rather than automatic response also
characterized Independence and Revolution. The British Whig
tradition, from which the Rebels chose heavily but selectively,
and the American landscape, which reinforced the choices they
made, did not account for the "creative mind at work, borrowing
from, and advancing, the Old World Inheritance in the receptive New World Environment."[22]

Reimer's assessment of Jefferson's accomplishment in 1776
illustrates his high regard for American intellectual creativity:

> Jefferson borrowed freely from Locke for the *Declaration of
> Independence*, and environmental circumstances strongly
> encouraged separatism and autonomy. But Jefferson pushed
> Locke's argument to democratic conclusions not found in the
> *Second Treatise on Civil Government* and not "given" miraculously
> by the American landscape.

Reimer lauds Jefferson's formulation of the American doctrine
of the continuing majority—his assertion, as Reimer puts it, that
"a majority of the people, in their own generation, should con-

trol their own fate; that they should be free to continue the Democratic Experiment afresh each generation." But Reimer bestows his highest praise on Madison, who "developed and defended the theory of the 'extensive republic' which guided the formation of the Constitution of 1787." Madison was "the great theorist of . . . this bold and immensely creative experiment in a Federal Republic." Nor did Madison's creative contributions to the Democratic Experiment, practical as well as theoretical, end with the masterful achievement of 1787. In the battle between the Federalists and Republicans in the 1790s he was "instrumental in developing a theory of republican constitutional opposition and, with Jefferson, a republican party which took over the nation peacefully in 1800." In the nullification controversy of the late 1820s and 1830s Madison condemned Calhoun's doctrines for their anarchistic implications while elaborating his significant, although sometimes ambiguous, theory of republican opposition.[23]

To sum up, in Reimer's view neither the emigration of Locke to America nor the unfolding of his ideas there necessarily in a certain way, nor the landscape on which this unfolding took place or which, alternatively, embodied "givenness" and thus precluded such a process of unfolding, adequately explains American political development. Reimer's disagreement with Hartz and Boorstin and his endowing of the role of creative men with causal weight equal to that of inheritance and environment is perhaps best exemplified in this passage:

> America's handling of the slavery question raises again the shortcomings of the view which holds that American Democracy is an automatic unfolding of a liberal British fragment or an automatic response to a favorable American environment. In the world of the 18th and 19th centuries, slavery was largely a unique American problem and called for a unique and creative solution. Such a solution was not to be found in the Old World Inheritance or in the New World Environment. It did not emerge out of what was "given" to Americans. . . . Their failure here, as their success elsewhere, is evidence of the shortcoming of that interpretation which ignores or minimizes the creative, if limited, role of men in shaping the American Democracy.[24]

Criticism of Tocqueville

Reimer attributes to Tocqueville recognition of the causal roles played by inheritance, environment, and Americans' creative thinking. Earlier we have noted that Handler classifies Tocqueville and Hartz as nonenvironmentalists, while Meyers takes exception to Hartz's nonenvironmentalist, Lockean reading of Tocqueville on equality of condition. Earlier still we have cited Dahl's emphasis on equality of condition in an inclusive sense as a source of consensus. Apparently it is possible to extract from *Democracy in America*, depending on which passages one selects, either a material or psychological version of equality of condition. Tocqueville, that is, at times refers to the fact of equality of material or economic condition and at other times to Americans' belief that such equality was a fact. Beliefs, of course, are themselves historical forces, but whether the facts are what the believers assume they are is, or should be, of vital importance to the historian. Actually, most historians, pro- and anti-Jacksonians alike, have, as Edward Pessen states, accepted a material version of Tocqueville's views on equality of condition.[1] Pessen extracts this version from *Democracy in America* and tests it. His findings suggest that Hartz—no doubt fortuitously since his interest in political thought accounts for his approach—avoided a snare when he presented a nonmaterial concept of equality of condition.

In an essay published in 1971, Benson, so to speak, anticipated Pessen's recent work on the subject of equality of condition. Benson hypothesized that developments in ideology, tremendous economic expansion, settlement over a greatly increased area, a high rate of physical mobility, and resultant changes in the "opportunity structure" produced a more democratic society by 1860. He asserted that neither Douglas T. Miller's contention that democracy advanced substantially in a political but not in a social or economic sense, nor Pessen's conclusion—in *Jacksonian America* (1969)—that democracy did not advance in any of these areas, nor his own claim that American political ideology and the American value system became significantly more democratic and egalitarian in the years

1825–60 or 1816–60 could be responsibly or confidently either accepted or rejected, either confirmed or disconfirmed, on the basis of the methodology and data available. Benson held that Miller's generalizations about social stratification rested on "proof by haphazard quotation [from] a haphazard sample of contemporary observers" and that Pessen's generalizations about social fluidity rested on data dealing only with movements from lower classes into the most favored class (movements, say, from classes ten through five into class one), a rare type of social mobility which tells us nothing of mobility of lesser degree (movements, say, from class seven to class five and so on) which is encompassed by the sociological concept of social mobility. Benson noted that his own views on the democratization of the central ideological tendency of the "Age of Egalitarianism" (his term) rested on the theoretical assumption of reciprocal relationships between a society's value system and behavior patterns, but he conceded that empirical studies of egalitarianism in its various ramifications were needed to test the validity of his hypothesis.[2]

In *Jacksonian America*, which Benson criticized in his essay of 1971, Pessen synthesized existing Jacksonian scholarship. Meanwhile he was engaged in research which, as it were, represented a response to Benson's call for empirical studies of egalitarianism. In the summer and fall of 1971 Pessen published three articles on wealth, mobility, and equality in the Jacksonian era. He abstracted from *Democracy in America* Tocqueville's egalitarian thesis concerning Jacksonian society and reduced it to a long paragraph. Distillation of Pessen's synthesis of Tocqueville's social theorem discloses a circular causal relationship: equality of condition fostered political democracy, which promoted social and economic democracy, which furthered equality of condition:

> The great mass of Americans consisted of the middling orders since there were very few rich—and they were rich only by American standards—and very few poor. Moreover, the rich were self-made men, for the poor did not stay poor very long and the rich did not stay rich very long.
>
> The limited and precarious nature of wealth reduced the influence of its possessors, resulting in the dominance of the great

mass of Americans or the middling orders. As restrictions on voting were eliminated, the politics of deference gave way to the strident rule of the masses. Class barriers loosened as social and economic democracy followed political democracy.

Abundant natural resources, technological advance, and human energy, present since colonial times, now combined with equality of opportunity to produce a near equality of condition.[3]

Pessen cited a number of studies, nearly all of them published in the period 1959–69, which emphasized Tocqueville's unreliability as a reporter and his weaknesses as a social analyst.[4] "That Tocqueville was ready to spin his marvelous theorems by reference more to logic than to pedestrian data," Pessen wrote, "is well known."[5] Tocqueville was "disinterested in mere facts, preferring to erect his model of American civilization on the basis of deduction and his great powers of imagination and generalization."[6] In his articles on *ante bellum* Boston, New York, Brooklyn, and Philadelphia Pessen provided data which did not square with Tocqueville's egalitarian thesis. In these studies, moreover, within their designated scope as to the meaning of "mobility," he met Benson's objections to his previous treatment of this phenomenon.[7] To his knowledge of the relevant literature Pessen added his own findings based on painstaking examination of tax records as well as other materials.

The data Pessen discovered and analyzed did not support the belief that there were very few rich men in "The Era of the Common Man": in the mid-1840s, according to assessed valuations of wealth (which nearly always undervalued holdings, particularly in regard to personal as distinguished from real property), there were 302 persons in New York, 361 in Philadelphia, 151 in Boston, and 26 in Brooklyn who were worth $100,000 or more.[8] Although fewer than one percent of wealthholders fell in the $100,000-plus category,[9] Pessen could have his cake and eat it too with respect to absolute and relative measurements: these wealthholders, although they were the "richest of the rich" or the "super rich,"[10] were more than a very few; at the same time the possession of wealth by them and by the lesser rich, both disproportionately *and* continuously, supported Pessen's conclusions concerning equality and mobility. Nor did the data substantiate the belief that the rich were rich only by American standards. Men assessed at $100,000 were usually worth many times that sum, but even that figure made them functional millionaires, worth about $4,000,000 in today's costs and prices.[11] In contemporary terms, the fortunes and life styles of the wealthiest Americans approximated those of the richest Europeans. Great American fortunes were newer than European landed wealth, and the American rich, unlike their European counterparts, were a working class—although out of choice rather than necessity—but their resources "would have been regarded as substantial wealth anywhere in the world."[12]

The beliefs that there were very few poor and that the rich were self-made men appear invalid as descriptions of Jacksonian society in view of Pessen's findings in the two areas to which he devotes the bulk of his inquiries: distribution of wealth and mobility (or opportunity). In regard to the distribution of wealth in Boston in 1833, Pessen places the richest taxpayers in five categories according to level of wealth:

Level	Number	Description
I. $100,000 +	83	"super rich"
II. $70,000–$100,000	54	"truly rich"
III. $40,000–$70,000	166	"truly rich"
IV. $20,000–$40,000	317	"not quite rich"
V. $6,000–$20,000	1195	"upper middle"

Persons in groups I–III were among the wealthiest one-half of one percent; all five groups comprised the wealthiest 2.5 percent of the population of Boston.[13] In a table showing the distribution of wealth in Boston in 1833 Pessen presents these data:

Level	Pct. of Population	Total Wealth	Pct. Noncorporate Wealth
$75,000 +	1	$19,439,000	33
$30,000–$75,000	3	$15,000,000	26
$5,000–$30,000	10	$16,047,000	27
Under $5,000	86	$ 8,331,000	14

A similar table for 1848 shows that the percentage of noncorporate wealth held by the upper 4 percent of wealthholders rose from 59 percent to 64 percent ($82,560,300) while the percen-

tage held by the lower 81 percent in 1848 was 4 percent
($6,000,000) compared to the 14 percent ($8,331,000) held by
the lower 86 percent in 1833.[14] Data for Brooklyn reveal that in
1810 seven of eight families paid taxes, in 1841 one of five.[15]
Tables on the distribution of wealth in Brooklyn show that 8
percent of the population held 55 percent of total wealth and
14 percent held 66 percent in 1810; that 3 percent of the population held 59 percent of total wealth and 12 percent held 83
percent in 1841.[16] Figures for New York City in 1828 and 1845
show a similar pattern: the top one percent held 41 percent of
total wealth in 1828 and 50 percent in 1845; the top 4 percent
held 53 percent in 1828 and 81 percent in 1845.[17] In brief, in
all three cities—despite the views of Tocqueville, many American contemporaries, and later historians—not only did the rich
hold a disproportionately large share of wealth but their share
increased during the age of equality.[18]

One might reconcile concentration in the distribution of
wealth with equality, at least in a certain sense, if mobility were
pervasive—if, as Pessen notes, "wealth and poverty were
ephemeral states" in a dynamic society marked by constant flux
comprising upward and downward mobility and creating a
"kaleidoscopic milieu."[19] Putting it another way, Pessen refers
to the argument that "equality of opportunity if not of condition prevailed in antebellum America."[20] The upshot of
Pessen's detailed analysis of tax records for Boston, New York,
and Brooklyn, and of other data for Philadelphia, is that in all
four cities very few of the rich were self-made men because,
with few exceptions, the poor did not rise; nor, with few exceptions, did the rich fall (and those who did fall, as the Boston
data for five-year intervals show, fell gradually rather than
suddenly[21]). Pessen concludes, "Only about two per cent of the
Jacksonian era's urban economic elite appear to have actually
been born poor, with no more than about six percent of middling social and economic status."[22] One's relative worth at the
beginning of the era was the most significant determinant of
one's chances of being among the rich at the end of the era[23];
the greater one's initial wealth, the greater were the chances
that it would increase[24]; and the greater one's original wealth,
the greater the increase was likely to be.[25] In sum, "During the
'age of the common man' opportunity was hardly more equal

than was material condition."[26] Toqueville's conclusions about
social or vertical mobility—his assertions that "most of the rich
were formerly poor," that fortunes were made and lost over-
night as wealth circulated with "inconceivable rapidity"[27]—do
not stand up in the face of "pervasive evidence of stability if not
rigidity in the possession of wealth."[28]

If in Brooklyn—as well as in the "strikingly similar" situations in Boston, New York, and Philadelphia—"there was little
of that 'constant movement up and down the ladder of wealth'
discerned by scholars since Tocqueville's day,"[29] does this conclusion apply to other areas of the nation? Conceding that the
four large Northeastern cities from which he has drawn his
evidence were "hardly typical of the nation as a whole," Pessen
cites studies of antebellum Baltimore, New Orleans, St. Louis,
Galveston, Natchez, Detroit, and Cincinnati, of cotton counties,
and of a county on the Northeastern frontier (in Michigan)
which show that inequality in the Southern and Western cities
was similar to the maldistribution in the four Northeastern
cities. Although the maldistribution in rural communities and
small towns was less than that in the cities, even in these areas
inequality was "dramatic and worsening."[30]

If Pessen's findings for four Northeastern cities apply in
varying degrees to other areas, how does the age of Jackson, as
he characterizes it in regard to inequality, compare with other
eras? Citing studies of seventeenth-century Salem; pre-
Revolutionary Boston, New York, and Philadelphia; and
post-Revolutionary New York, Pessen concludes, "When it is
compared with earlier periods in American history, the age of
egalitarianism appears to have been an age of increasing social
rigidity. . . . The evidence on the earlier period, scattered and
partial though it may be, suggests that a substantial upward
economic mobility that had characterized Northeastern urban
life came to a halt during the so-called age of the common
man."[31] It is true, Pessen notes, that during the colonial era
inequality increased as time went on, but during the Jacksonian
era the inegalitarian trend accelerated, the rate by which the
rich got proportionately richer becoming far more rapid than it
had been in the seventeenth and eighteenth centuries.[32] Comparing the age of Jackson to a later era, Pessen says, "Far from

being an age of equality, the *ante bellum* decades were featured by an inequality that surpasses anything experienced by the United States in the twentieth century."[33] This time factor, Pessen holds, has important implications for causation in American history. The popular view that industrialization pauperized the masses does not stand up when one notes that vast inequalities between the rich and the poor in the cities antedated industrialism.[34]

Another question that arises concerning Pessen's analysis is whether he meets Benson's objection to studies which focus on mobility only as it involves ascent into the highest socioeconomic category. The fact is that since few "new men" entered the top category while, as in Boston in 1848, 81 percent of the population shared 4 percent of noncorporate wealth, there could not have been great mobility below the top category. Pessen, moreover, can usually specify from what level a "new man" rose since the records he examines identify tax payers at the lowest levels (the Boston records include all persons who paid taxes on wealth worth twenty-five dollars or more[35]). True, the tax records do not list the nomadic poor, but their temporary presence in the city enhanced the inequality Pessen stresses: "A massive internal migration, above all of younger, marginal persons of little standing, into and out of the nation's cities increased both the power and the share of wealth commanded by more substantial and therefore more stable elements."[36] Internal migration is estimated by Peter R. Knights to have involved an annual population turnover in Boston of about 30 percent from 1830 to 1840 and about 40 percent from 1850 to 1860.[37] We shall have occasion in chapter 5 to refer to Stephan Thernstrom's comments on the geographically mobile but occupationally immobile, among others, in Newburyport in the latter part of the nineteenth century. At this point it is appropriate to note that in a recent study two economists conclude that geographical movement involved improvement of the migrants' economic status less in 1850 than at any time after that date.[38] This conclusion accords with Pessen's portrayal of a Jacksonian city with few rich and many, drifting poor.

Pessen's figures would be more useful if he showed the

wealth possessed by portions of the population in quintiles or deciles so that comparisons between his findings for the cities he studies and other scholars' findings for other locales could be made with more precision. A more important methodological matter is that the distribution of wealth has always been more inequitable than the distribution of income.[39] For example, recent studies of distribution, published in 1972, show that the top one percent of the population owns about eight times as much wealth as the bottom 50 percent, while the top 20 percent garners about eight times as much before-tax earnings as the lowest 20 percent.[40] Concentration or maldistribution of income, while less than that of wealth, still involves gross inequality. Yet, reference to income distribution raises questions that lead to nonquantitative considerations.

A breadwinner may have no income-producing wealth such as stocks, bonds, and real estate and yet have sufficient income to possess enough "inert" wealth such as a home and personal property to enjoy a comfortable life style; to expect, possibly, to advance further economically; and, in any case, to accept, with greater or lesser enthusiasm, the existing order of things. Comparatively, it is conceivable that two societies could exhibit the same pattern of distribution of wealth or income, with a member of one society at a given level—say in a given decile—enjoying a higher standard of living than a member of the other society at the same level. Pessen tells us that "American farmers and workingmen were better off than their European counterparts."[41] Was this relative overall well-being sufficient, despite inequality, to produce a consensual society, or was a combination of this factor and the egalitarian myth required to yield such a result? Certainly Pessen is aware of the importance of nonmaterial forces, for he discusses the complexity of the concept of mobility and the "immaterial or metaphysical" component of the egalitarian myth, pointing out that his studies attempt only the "measurement of the measurable."[42] Nevertheless, his findings are important for their implications as well as intrinsically.

Pessen claims that his investigation "undermines two of the main supports of the long-popular belief in antebellum mobility": the assumptions that the poor rose to wealth in significant numbers and that the rich remained wealthy for only a short time.[43] Can we hypothesize that the less the basis in fact for the Alger myth, the greater its force; that the invalidity of Tocqueville's thesis concerning material equality actually rein-. forces his conclusions concerning psychological equality? Did the Alger myth account for the consensual nature of American society? If not, what did? In the light of Pessen's work our answer cannot be "equality of material condition." Possible alternative answers seem innumerable, but it is not Pessen's purpose to pursue this line of inquiry. He does synthesize the political aspect of the Tocquevillean thesis—the limited and precarious nature of wealth reduced the influence of its possessors, with the politics of deference giving way to the strident rule of the masses—and he rejects it, concluding from his examination of the backgrounds of 210 winners of election to high office in Brooklyn in the years 1834–1844 that "deference by ordinary folk to their social and economic betters was evidently not passe even in the age of 'Tom, Dick and Harry.' "[44] (Meanwhile, the well-to-do exploited their position by reducing valuations of property and tax rates.[45])

A different conclusion concerning deference may be found in David Grimsted's article on "Rioting in Its Jacksonian Setting," where episodes of violence are treated as conflict within consensus—nondeferential in that they expressed the individualistic or anarchistic "higher code" component of democracy, as opposed to the legalistic component; deferential in that they did not involve attacks on the social system itself.[46] In any event, in subjecting Tocqueville's egalitarian thesis to empirical testing, Pessen—whose work on the age of Jackson has been characterized as neoentrepreneurial and an expression of the nonideological consensus view of Jacksonian politics[47]—has taken an important step beyond and beneath the area of party politics into the realm of the fundamental features of antebellum American society.[48]

Chapter Three
Confinement of
the Consensus View

The Critical Response to Consensus History

In an article published in 1956, Schlesinger wrote, "As historians of the '30's saw the American past too much in terms of conflict, so there is a danger that historians and political scientists today may see the past too much in terms of agreement."[1] This observation, however, was not an introduction to a full-blown attack on consensus history. It was prefatory to a brief description for a European audience of American liberalism, which, Schlesinger noted, clashed with conservatism within the liberal tradition as Hartz delineated it.[2] It was an article by John Higham, appearing in 1959, that really launched a wholesale critical response to the consensus view, a reaction which has had the effect of confinement—of reducing the portion of American history to which the consensus view applies. Higham deplored the emphasizing of consensus so as to exclude discontent and conflict from the nation's past, calling this process "Homogenizing Our History."[3] Since 1959 consensus historiography has been under continual attack. Some criticism maintains, in effect, that the consensus view may be informative as far as it goes, but it does not go far enough in accounting for the various ramifications of life and thought in America. In Mann's opinion, Hartz tells us that we have not had conflicts like Europe's but does not tell us about the conflicts we have had.[4] "For the participants of these struggles," writes J. Rogers Hollingsworth, "the battles were no less real than conflicts in any other society."[5]

Concerning the consensus concept of American political thought, Irving H. Bartlett concludes that the idea of an American liberal consensus is "most useful in helping us to distinguish American thinkers from Europeans; it does not help us a great deal in distinguishing American thinkers from each other."[6] According to Meyers, Hartz

> tells us broadly what we have not been—feudal or revolutionary—and therefore what we have not had—successful revolutionaries or socialists. That, I think, is a valuable beginning. "Locke" fills the whole space within these negative limits. In stretching the term over the full length and breadth of American politics, however, Professor Hartz makes it too indefinite and thin for the concrete uses of American history.[7]

Gatell accepts Hartz's contention that the absence of feudalism fundamentally affected American development, but "a problem remains":

> What is meant by "Whig"? In many places Hartz uses the term "Federalist-Whig," and he quotes amply from Hamilton and such backward-looking worthies as Fisher Ames. Hartz's Whiggery is essentially of the post-revolutionary variety; he is talking about the Federalist party of the 1790's. It is not useful to extend their concepts far into the nineteenth century.[8]

Other criticism cites particular aspects of American history which, it is held, cannot be understood adequately through the consensus approach. Dwight W. Hoover refers to the problems of the poverty-stricken, the urban masses, the blacks, and the South.[9] Burl Noggle makes the same point with respect to the South.[10] Hays asserts: "the increasing emphasis on the political and cultural homogeneity of American society has involved almost complete neglect of the examination of the structure of political groups."[11]

Among the writings which hold that consensus historiography does not go far enough, perhaps the most telling comment, if only because it flows from the pen of one of the prophets of consensus history, is Hofstadter's critique, "Conflict and Consensus in American History," the final chapter of *The Progressive Historians*, published twenty years after the appearance of *The American Political Tradition* in 1948. Pointing out, "I am discussing a tendency with which my own work has often been associated," Hofstadter expresses his determination "not to discuss my own work in these pages. . . . I trust it will be clear that while I still find use for insights derived from consensus history, it no longer seems as satisfactory to me as it did ten or twenty years ago."[12]

Before specifying the shortcomings of consensus history, Hofstadter asserts, "I see little point in denying that, for all its limitations, consensus as a general view of American history had certain distinct, if transitional merits [as] an indispensable corrective force as well as an insight of positive value." He lauds the consensus school for confronting the problem that "Turner glimpsed but did not really cope with, the task of getting this theme [of American uniqueness] into its necessary comparative frame"; for returning to an understanding of the pragmatic and pluralistic character of our history; and for forcing us to "think about the importance of those things Americans did not have to argue about." Finally, he commends consensus historiography as a necessary response to the Progressive historians' oversimplification and overemphasis of conflict and discontinuity,

> their sometimes too exclusive reliance on geographical or
> economic forces, their disposition to polarize, to simplify, to see
> history as the work of abstract universals, to see past conflicts as
> direct analogues of present conflicts, their reductionist stress on
> motives, their tendency toward Manicheanism, their occasional
> drift toward conspiratorial interpretations of events.[13]

"If there is a single way of characterizing what has happened in our historical writing since the 1950's," Hofstadter remarks, "it must be, I believe, the rediscovery of complexity in American history . . . the Progressive scheme of polarized conflict has been replaced by a pluralistic vision in which more factors are taken seriously into account."[14] At first glance this comment seems to imply a simplicity—complexity dialectic that does not accord with Hofstadter's assertion, which we shall consider momentarily, that the consensus historians' generalization is, like the one he says it supplants, oversimplifying. This apparent discrepancy dissolves in the light of the distinction Hofstadter makes between the "efforts, particularly by Louis Hartz and Daniel Boorstin, to generalize the consensus idea, to give it the positive status of a theory of American history," and "a whole series of concurrent special studies that broke sharply with the Progressives' pattern of interpretation." Hartz's and Boorstin's work were not the sources of these studies, which "may be regarded as a related and convergent but quite independent development."[15] These special studies simultaneously contributed to the rediscovery of "non-Progressive" complexity in American history and reinforced the consensus idea. They provided support for the concept of diversity amid concord.

The reaction of historians to the generalizing of consensus as a principle of historical interpretation, needless to say, has also contributed to the rediscovery of complexity in American history, to the disclosure of diversity beyond concord. Hofstadter himself, having commended the corrective, transitional merits of the idea of consensus in historiography, accords it, as an interpretive principle, "the status of an essentially negative proposition." As a positive principle "it does not go very far. . . . It has been developed as a counter-assertion more than as an empirical tool."[16] He concedes that Hartz is "right again and again in his learned comparative observations about the elements that are missing from the American scene [but] he cannot, with his device, get around to telling us quite enough about what is there . . . or give an adequate account of those conflicts that did take place."[17]

Hofstadter underlines the oversimplifying quality of the consensus approach by specifying those aspects of American history which it fails adequately to explain:

> There are three major areas in which a history of the United States organized around the guiding idea of consensus breaks down: first, I believe it cannot do justice to the genuinely revolutionary aspects of the American Revolution; second, it is quite helpless and irrelevant on the Civil War and the issues related to it; and finally, it disposes us to turn away from one of the most significant facts of American social life—the racial, ethnic, and religious conflict with which our history is saturated.[18]

More generally, Hofstadter observes that after 1789 the American people "about once in each generation . . . endured a crisis of real and troubling severity."[19] In referring to historians' treatment, or avoidance, of racial, ethnic, and religious conflict, Hofstadter finds the consensus theorists as neglectful as the Progressive historians had been.[20] "With the instructive effects of the debate over consensus history behind us," he concludes, "we can return to the assessment of conflict in American life without going straight back to the arms of the Progressives."[21]

Among those who hold that consensus historiography may be informative as far as it goes but does not go far enough in accounting for the various aspects of life and thought in America, Higham offers criticism of a different order in his article "Beyond Consensus: The Historian as Moral Critic." He asserts that some of the younger conservative historians of today, "while reacting against a reformist bias . . . continue to measure the past by pragmatic standards." They thus carry on the Progressive historians'

> tendency to dwell on means rather than ends—on the attainable results of an ideal rather than its intrinsic nature . . . a moral appraisal of the situation need not depend upon its outcome. A truly sensitive critic will go beyond the practical consequences of the process he describes . . . a working distinction between causal history and moral history . . . guards against pragmatic confusion between means and ends.

Here Higham attacks the tendency of some consensus historians to accept whatever "works" as desirable without considering its essential nature in moral terms, "its intrinsic value as a gesture of the human spirit."[22]

The Great Exception: The Civil War

Historians and political scientists, including most of those who emphasize consensus in American history, agree with Hofstadter on the Civil War. They usually refer to it with such labels as the Great Exception. In *The Genius of American Politics*, however, Boorstin confines this conflict to a consensus context by judging it the result of a nontheoretical clash between two descrip-

tive sociologies and two constitutional orthodoxies,[1] ⌐
as noted in chapter 1, in *The Americans: The National E*
he attributes to Southerners a "metaphysical politic
later view is similar to that of Hartz. In *The Liberal Tra*
America Hartz credits *ante bellum* Southern political t̶ ̶ ̶ ̶ ̶ ̶s
with an impressive effort as they concocted a feudal facade for
slavery—the equivalent of Boorstin's "metaphysical politics."
The Southerners were unable, however, finally to break the
grip of Locke, and their assault on the liberal tradition faded
rapidly after Appomattox as a significant element in American
political thought. Therefore, the Civil War, Hartz declares,
"symbolizes not the weakness of the American liberal idea but
its strength, its vitality, its utter dominion over the American
mind."[2] In other words, Hartz, who concedes the unique crisis
quality of the Civil War when he identifies slavery as "the only
problem in American history that has shattered completely the
framework of our legal institutions,"[3] relates this conflict to
consensus by stressing the outcome.

Commenting on Hartz's analysis, Harry V. Jaffa sees the
Civil War as the result of a conflict within the liberal tradition
between two views of the principle of equality. To the North,
slavery was inequality. To the South, basing its stand on the
Kentucky and Virginia Resolutions, the loss to a tyrannical majority of "the right to security of life and liberty, and the right to
judge of the means indispensable to that security, rights truly
sanctioned by the idea of equality," was inequality.[4] This interpretation differs from Hartz's portrayal of a conflict between the liberal tradition and a body of thought representing
an attempt to escape from that tradition. Jaffa also disagrees
with Boorstin. Since he maintains that the Southerners' argument went beyond states' rights as such to more fundamental
rights based on the principle of equality, his view is not like that
advanced in *The Genius of American Politics*, where Boorstin asserts, under the heading "Federalism Limits the Debate," that
the legal debate "never rose to the realm of natural law."[5]

In *The Genius of American Politics* Boorstin mentions the
heavy loss of life in the Civil War while indicating that his
concern is the significance of the debate preceding the conflict
for the American way of political thought. Hartz's concern is

the significance of the intellectual outcome of the conflict for
the history of American political thought. Hofstadter, on the
other hand, with his mastery of epigram, asserts that "consensus, to be effective, must be a matter of behavior as well as
thought, of institutions as well as theories."[6] Diggins, with his
talent for facile philosophical-historical analysis, elaborates and
modifies Hofstadter's aphorism, as it were, with respect to
Boorstin's treatment of the Civil War. He finds the argument in
the chapter of *The Genius of American Politics* entitled "The Civil
War and the Spirit of Compromise" to be "disarmingly simple."
Each section of the country claimed that it was not conceiving a
new society but was defending its fundamental institutions and
culture. Philosophizing about the issues, therefore, would have
been needless. Instead, to quote Boorstin, the Civil War is "an
admirable illustration of our tendency to make sociology do for
political theory, to merge the descriptive and the normative, to
draw the 'ought' out of the 'is.' Or, in a word, to confirm our
belief in 'givenness.' " Or, as Diggins summarizes Boorstin's
argument: both sides shunned ideology, and their belief in givenness was apparent in their assumption that social facts and
experience indicated *both* how life was and how it ought to be.[7]

Diggins holds that since geographical determinism failed
to produce consensus, Boorstin turned to intellectual history to
discover it: "although the natural environment may have determined the different behavioral attitudes of Northerners and
Southerners," Diggins paraphrases Boorstin, "a true continuity
of values still prevailed in the area of theoretical discourse."[8]
Diggins' response to this proposition is twofold. First, he restates, so to speak, Hofstadter's objection to the establishment
of consensus by subordinating behavior to thought: "similar
thought habits do not necessarily lead to similar modes of conduct. What impresses Boorstin is that Northerners and Southerners supposedly reasoned alike; but what depresses other
historians is that they behaved differently."[9] Secondly, Diggins
extends his analysis beyond Hofstadter's dictum, asserting not
only that consensus in the realm of thought unaccompanied by
consensus in the sphere of behavior poses a problem, but also
that there was no unity of mind to begin with. Diggins alleges,
as it were, that Boorstin mistakenly equates methodological
with substantive similarity.

Now Diggins is well aware that Boorstin knows that similar empirical thought-habits did not yield similar factual arguments—opposing sectional spokesmen, for example, affirmed or denied, as Boorstin points out, Southern or Northern progress and prosperity. Boorstin nevertheless stresses the consensus embodied in the elevation by both sides of sociology over ideology because, Diggins charges, he fails to recognize that the sources of substantive differences arising from the empirical reasoning which both sides employed lay beneath the domain of sociological discourse. Boorstin claims that both sides displayed an empirical mentality, but, Diggins writes, he

> seems scarcely troubled by this common attitude of the North and South. That both sides could appeal to the solidity of facts and arrive at hopelessly different conclusions is simply not a problem. Yet surely this fetish for facticity betrays something more than a gift for empirical discourse. Had Boorstin probed further, he might have discovered that both sides were using facts not as objective data but as subjective symbols (Becker), or nonlogical "sentiments" (Pareto) or class-conditioned "thought-processes" (Mannheim). To push historical analysis this far, however, is to open up a new dimension of reality. Now it is not my purpose to criticize Boorstin for failing to pursue this line of research. But it does seem proper to ask how he can see the Civil War as the "Spirit of Compromise" when the roots of the conflict obviously lie deeper than the empirical arguments reverberating across the Mason-Dixon.[10]

The key to Boorstin's failure to recognize the ultimate sources of sectional differences lies in the merging of the "is" and the "ought" entailed in his concepts of experience and "givenness." It is very unlikely, in Diggins' judgment, that

> empirical cognition itself could have resolved the crisis, and no amount of fact-gathering could have led Northerners and Southerners to an understanding of what *ought* to have been done. The "ought"—moral vision, ethical consciousness, human awareness, value judgment—this is the lost dimension in Boorstin's philosophy of history.[11]

Boorstin himself restored this lost dimension when he shifted, regarding the intellectual background of the Civil War, from the exclusion of ideology in *The Genius of American Politics* to the introduction of ideology in *The National Experience*. As Diggins comments:

> What is significant is not merely that a new South appears in the later work but that Boorstin implicitly concedes the shortcomings of his own philosophy. He now admits that in the South "this seeming identity of things as they were with things as they ought to be, came from a vision of society without conflict," while in "New England the sharp awareness of conflicting interests produced a reforming effervescence." What was formerly the American genius, then, became the fatal nemesis of a homogeneous South where the arts of compromise had gone unappreciated. The South suffered from too much consensus and not enough conflict.[12]

It seems to be a reasonable application of Hofstadter's comment on the behavioral as well as the intellectual requirements for effective consensus to note that Elijah Lovejoy would derive little comfort from reading that the debate preceding the Civil War took place within a nonideological, consensual framework. Similarly, to be informed that the conflict in which they engaged followed a nonideological debate (Boorstin in *The Genius of American Politics*) or a debate within the uni-ideological liberal Lockean tradition (Jaffa), or that it arose from a departure from the nonideological tradition that was unrealistic (Boorstin, *The National Experience*) or from an attack on the uni-ideological liberal tradition which could not escape Locke and which had only a limited and temporary impact on American thought (Hartz, *The Liberal Tradition in America*)—these alternatives would be of little comfort to the more than 400,000 combatants, Blue and Gray, who were wounded or the more than 600,000 who were killed. Finally, one may argue from Hofstadter's dictum that to learn that the Civil War's outcome in political thought was the triumph of Lockean liberalism would have done little to allay the disappointment of millions of blacks on plantations and in ghettos, for a hundred years after Appomattox, at the outcome for them. It seems naive, asserts John Rosenberg, a white man sympathetic to militant black thought, "to justify the slaughter of six hundred thousand men [one for every six slaves who were freed] for the slim reward of a formalistic and incomplete emancipation."[13]

We ought not to end this discussion of the Civil War, however, without mentioning Phillip S. Paludan's reconciliation of
violent behavior and consensus in his article, "The American
Civil War Considered as a Crisis in Law and Order." Although
a great deal has been written about secession, there is a need,
Paludan asserts, to look more closely at the Northern response
to secession—a response in which the concept of law and order
played an important role. This concept

> is a complex one, contemporary political rhetoric to the contrary
> notwithstanding. The order of a society depends on more than
> the rigid enforcement of all its laws. It depends on maintaining
> an enduring consensus about a people's fundamental goals and
> beliefs, and hence on the success of the institutions created to
> secure this consensus.

The defense of these institutions, Paludan holds, was the essential feature of the Northern response to secession. Americans'
daily experience with self-government, especially local self-
government, as lawmakers—as maintainers of law and order
through their own behavior—as close observers of legal contests, as jurors, as witnesses, as candidates, as officeholders, and
as highly active and partisan voters gave them "compelling personal reasons to be devoted to the preservation of law and
order." They associated their local personal experience with
the preservation of national institutions which enabled them to
rule themselves wherever they went—their attachment was to
self-government, not to place. Thus their loyalty to the nation
and their desire to save the union were personal concerns
rather than abstract issues. They were "loyal to nation as a
by-product of satisfaction achieved within non-national groups,
because the nation is believed to symbolize and sustain those
groups." In this context, "Northerners equated an attack on the
national government with a threat to the self-government they
had experienced." This attack threatened ordered liberty. Secession achieved by guns "was likely to produce disorder, anarchy, and a general disrespect for government." Accordingly,
the Northern response to secession indicates that "violence is
not necessarily the opposite of law and order." It may result
from "efforts to preserve, not to destroy, the existing order."[14]

The Abstract Quality of the Consensus Formula: "Capitalism"

Harvey Wish underlines the allegation that the exponents of the consensus view do not go far enough in interpreting the details of American life and thought when he calls consensus history a "new formalism." Its emphasis on abstractions, Wish holds, renders it inadequate as a means of understanding American history.[1] Certainly the consensus formula for universally held beliefs in America—capitalism and democracy—has an abstract quality that detracts from its value as an analytical tool. Consensus historians underscore Americans' repudiation of socialism and totalitarianism in favor of capitalism and democracy. This emphasis implies a marriage made in heaven of these economic and political systems, but other combinations are possible. Capitalistic Nazi Germany, for example, spurned democracy, while democratic Sweden largely rejects capitalism.[2] Now it is true that from the standpoint of consensus history the union of capitalism and democracy is an aspect of a unique, consensual America. Still, it is incumbent on the historian who stresses this marriage to delineate in some detail the development and traits of these partners in wedlock.

"Capitalism" as a general historical label connotes a static condition. It fails to indicate the transformation of America from a rural, agricultural to an urban, industrial nation. Nor does it disclose that Americans view capitalism in different ways. A discussion among economists of various nations reveals imposing conceptual problems involved in defining "capitalism,"[3] and—more relevant here—R. Joseph Monsen, Jr., shows that Americans look at capitalism according to five different "ideologies": classical, managerial, countervailing power, people's capitalism, and enterprise democracy.[4] These ideologies signify different interests which often clash. Differences, for example, between the "managerial" ideas of big business and the "classical" notions of small business, especially in regard to fiscal policy, are quite apparent. Under the New Deal, as Robert L. Heilbroner writes, "government investment was *meant* as a helping hand to business. It was *interpreted* by business as a threatening gesture."[5] By the 1960s big business had changed its views on public spending, but small business still clung to the older fiscal orthodoxy.[6]

The lexicon of "capitalism" contains corollaries, often used to denote consensus, which also manifest a misleading imprecision. The central point of a considerable body of "neo-Veblenian" literature is that with the separation of ownership and management and the rise of concentration in the corporate sector of the economy, nineteenth-century concepts of "private" property and "free" enterprise, as well as "capitalism," have become anachronistic.[7] To declare that we agree on "private property" tells us nothing of the disputes and changes involving the distribution of property and the concept of property itself. A new orthodoxy among social scientists and historians is the "mixed economy." This convention is employed to signify consensus—widespread support and widespread benefit—but it is being challenged by economists who contend that Keynesianism is not enough: it can stimulate overall growth but is ineffective as an alleviator of poverty because it does not affect the distribution of income; and it neglects the public sector because it does not influence the allocation of resources (the kinds of products composing an increasing Gross National Product). In this connection one often hears the phrase "military Keynesianism." The historian Basil Rauch asserts, "Defense and space exploration contracts and the enlarged armed forces serve—and overserve—the functions of New Deal agencies which were intended to be temporary, such as PWA and WPA."[8]

A corollary of "capitalism" that consensus literature often emphasizes is the "broker state," which stands for balance among economic interest groups competing for assistance from a mediating government—an equilibrium which, like the "mixed economy," enjoys widespread support and bestows widespread benefits. Oscar Handlin stresses the role, early in American history, of voluntary associations which fostered liberty and stability by enabling men to "make choices rather then face the brute alternatives of inaction or compulsion by the state." Handlin also insists that "it was never possible to define two distinct spheres: the public, reserved for the state, and the private, for the voluntary association."[9] With this division re-

maining ill-defined, the relationship between the public and
private spheres has produced not government regimentation
of private interests but government response to private pressures, and a consensus on capitalism is evident both in government intervention in the economy—stimulative and
regulatory—and in the demands the various economic interest
groups make of government. These requests generate the
competition that imposes on government the role of broker
and produces a rough intergroup equilibrium.

Robert A. Lively emphasizes the early origins and capitalist
aims of government intervention in the economy. He asserts
that the neomercantilist movement, "virtually unlimited as to
time and place, from Missouri to Maine, from the beginning to
the end of the nineteenth century," was the stimulation of
capitalist enterprise.[10] He also maintains that a "sturdy tradition of public responsibility for economic growth . . . seems
expanded in no theoretical respect by its uses in RFC, TVA,
and AEC."[11] (In 1959 Mario Einaudi observed that in the years
since 1933 the rate of growth of private industry had been
greater in the Tennessee Valley than in the rest of the
nation.[12]) Even the New Deal fiscal policies that business interpreted as a threat to its well-being were, as noted above, meant
to aid business, and by the 1960s big business came to favor
fiscal policies which were designed to spur economic growth
but which did not entail direct government intervention in business decision-making.[13]

The economic interest groups, for their part, often speak
the language of laissez faire or, to use Samuel Gompers' term,
"voluntarism," but each—while assuming a capitalist
economy—has in fact accepted or proposed government intervention which it has judged beneficial to itself or restrictive of
others while opposing intervention which it has deemed beneficial to others or restrictive of its own activities. Accordingly,
attitudes toward government intervention in the economy usually depend on whether stimulation or regulation is involved
and on whose ox is being gored.[14] "However adamant the business world might be in its opposition to the regulation of private enterprise by government," John D. Hicks writes in his
survey of the 1920s, "it had no slightest scruple against accept-

ing, or even soliciting, government aid of any sort or kind."[15] The agrarian reformers of 1900, John Morton Blum states, "would bring industrial units down to size. They would legislate their view of America."[16] In 1949 Rexford Tugwell, the farmers' spokesman in Roosevelt's Brains Trust, discerned in them "a feeling that agriculture ought to have everything else regulated in its interest."[17] As for labor, the violent episodes arising from labor's protest and the resistance to it suggest the possibility of an economic interest group's striving to achieve its aims outside the American consensus on capitalism. Certainly many Americans besides employers have labeled expressions of worker discontent "radical," and some labor organizations, it is true, have challenged the wage system—but they have failed. The successful unions have accepted the implications of the wage system and have sought, eventually with the help of government, to elevate labor's status within it.[18] Nevertheless, the violence marking organized labor's quest for a bigger slice of the capitalist pie has resulted from conflict that has been real enough for the combatants.

Criticism of the "broker state" involves enough dissenters to preclude labeling it unqualifiedly as consensual. Only the more articulate detractors publish their views, while other Americans—nostalgic or future-oriented—express their disapproval by voting for candidates for public office who disparage big, impersonal government and big business. Substantively, the critics of the "broker state" deny that it promotes the general interest. On the contrary, they insist that it serves special interests: the clients have their own way with the broker, and this undue influence, in turn, has obvious economic effects. Critics also deplore the neglect of the interests of those Americans who are not citizens of the "broker state."

The clients literally laying down the law to the broker is what Kolko, as noted in chapter 1, calls "political capitalism." More commonly one hears phrases such as "the regulated regulate the regulators" or, in academic circles, "co-optation." Tugwell took exception to this practice more than thirty years ago—a significant development in view of his basic ideas in political economy. Influenced in his college days by the pre–World War I views of Thorstein Veblen, Herbert Croly,

Charles R. Van Hise, Walter Weyl, Walter Lippmann, and
Theodore Roosevelt, Tugwell was an advocate of "concentration and control." Exponents of this doctrine claim that with
the emergence of bigness in industry in response to invincible
technological advance—the economies of mass production-
—only strong government can protect the public interest amid
the industrial giants. Tugwell in effect made a concession to the
critics of concentration-and-control when he wrote, in 1939,
"The ideological concomitant of the machine process can now
be seen to center in operational wholeness; and that was the
central, the *original* meaning of NRA."[19] In his view, the National Recovery Administration, in its actual workings,
amounted to concentration-without-control, a perversion, in
favor of special interests, of the potential in such an agency for
promoting the general interest.[20] In 1950, in a review of Philip
Selznick's study of TVA, Tugwell agreed with Selznick that the
promotion of the national interest by TVA, AAA, and the Soil
Conservation Service was hampered by "co-optation," the process whereby these agencies, in order to avert threats to their
stability or existence, share policy determination with "grass
tops" local interests which stand for the status quo.[21]

Nor was adverse criticism of concentration-and-control
heard only with the advent of the New Deal. Nearly sixty years
ago Louis D. Brandeis maintained that efficiency was not
necessarily either the cause of economic bigness ("no monopoly
in private industry in America has yet been attained by efficiency alone") or the result of economic bigness ("the unit in
business may be too large to be efficient, and this is no uncom-
mon incident of monopoly").[22] In 1955 Walter Adams and
Horace Gray concluded in *Monopoly in America: Government as
Promoter*, that "the current concentration level cannot be explained simply in terms of economic imperatives."[23] As the title
of their study implies, they contended that governmental
measures had enhanced concentration—horizontal, vertical,
and conglomerate—and reduced competition. If neither public
regulation, which the left prescribed, nor superintending of the
public interest by a private elite, which the right recommended,
could make concentration tolerable, we had to be willing,
Adams and Gray insisted, to "face up to the central problem
(both economic and political) of how to control power."[24]

As the economic effects of the corporations' use of political power became increasingly apparent after the Second World War, historians and students of other social sciences joined economists in the assault on the "broker state." Arthur A. Ekirch, Jr., in a book published in 1955, traced the historical trend away from traditional liberties and individual freedom toward privileges and freedoms that organized group pressures persuaded government to grant.[25] In the 1960s writers on the left such as Henry Kariel, Theodore Lowi, and Grant McConnell indicted modern liberalism, as Otis L. Graham, Jr., puts it, "for its assumption that the public interest would automatically be forwarded by the interplay of organized groups in the struggle for federal favors. New Deal efforts to build up the 'countervailing power' (Galbraith's phrase) of unorganized or underorganized groups were of insignificant effect."[26] Meanwhile, writers on the right, scornful of all leftist remedial prescriptions, made the same indictment of the "broker state." Yale Brozen, an economist of the laissez-faire "Chicago school," inquired, "Is Government the Source of Monopoly?" He concluded that because of featherbedding, overpayment of employees, overpricing of services, uneconomic locations, uneconomic scheduling in transportation, Department of Agriculture cartels, and monopolies by license and franchise, the cost to the country of regulation, of "governmentally fostered and supported monopolies," was fifty billion dollars per year.[27] Non-laissez-faire economists and historians do not share Bozen's views on ultimate causation. Big government, they argue, could not have destroyed the free-price, free-enterprise, free-market economy when it had already gone out of style by 1900 as the result of encroachments by big free enterprise.[28]

As this is written, Ralph Nader's charge that the regulated regulate the regulators, that regulatory agencies therefore promote special interests rather than the general interest, has struck a responsive chord. Meanwhile, enactment of government loan guarantees of $250 million for Lockheed Aircraft Corporation and up to two billion dollars for failing businesses (including Lockheed) has provoked considerable controversy. In connection with such legislation, an Associated Press writer reports that American private enterprise receives at least $28 billion and possibly as much as $38 billion a year in government subsidies and subsidy-like aid.[29] One of my neighbors has expressed dismay at the government's taking over Lockheed. In the light of Adams and Gray's analysis, one might put it the other way around. Richard J. Barber, in *The American Corporation* (1970), declares, "If 'government'—meaning those people denominated as politicians who are elected by and claim to serve the public—is to 'gain mastery over events,' a thorough reexamination of our whole range of public policies is necessary."[30]

The contention that the "broker state" is nonconsensual in regard to the forwarding of the general interest does not focus only on the organized interests which advance with impunity under its auspices. This protest also points to those Americans who do not belong to organized, articulate, politically influential interest groups, who have a minimal stake in the capitalist economy, who are not citizens of the "broker state," who, to use Higham's phrase in another sense, are "beyond consensus." The New Deal, as suggested above, dealt them few cards, but the benefits of organization and the price which those who fail to organize pay were evident before the 1930s. David J. Rothman concludes that the politicians of the late nineteenth century responded more to the demands of business than to those of agriculture and labor not because they were the tools of "robber barons" but because business interests were more effectively organized.[31] Michael Reagan asserts that our "governmental system is one that gives a vastly exaggerated weight to organized economic interests."[32] In the early 1970s previously unorganized groups such as migrant farm workers and sharecroppers were beginning to recognize and act on Reagan's maxim. If the capitalist "broker state" becomes more inclusive and thus more consensual, this development will result from continuing conflict.

The Abstract Quality of the Consensus Formula: "Democracy"

The affirmation that we agree on "democracy" does not inform us of changes in the definition of personal freedom or of the limitations and complexities that become evident in any detailed inquiry into Americans' beliefs and behavior regarding democracy. Kristol asserts that historians have given "very little

thought to the various meanings that democracy might have."
They both subscribe to and foster public acceptance of "an
ideology so powerful as to represent a religious faith. Indeed,
we can call this ideology 'the democratic faith.' " Kristol distinguishes between a *democratic faith*—which "may be attentive to
the problems of democracy [but] has great difficulty perceiving
or thinking about the *problematics* of democracy . . . those
kinds of problems that are inherent in, that are generated by
democracy itself"—and a *democratic political philosophy*, which is
concerned with the problematics of democracy. The Founding
Fathers, Kristol writes, were not political philosophers, but they
gave "serious thought to the traditional problems of political
philosophy. One of these . . . was the problematic character of
democracies." Their democratic political philosophy was
"gradually and inexorably transformed into a democratic faith
[and] in this transformation American historians have played a
significant role."[1]

Bancroft initiated this shift, taking a "giant step toward the
redefinition of the democratic idea." He proclaimed popular
infallibility while representing this notion as a "natural extension" of the Founding Fathers' thought. The gentlemen historians of the nineteenth century were not easy converts to the
transcendental faith in the common man, but, with the exception of Henry Adams, they dodged direct confrontation with
the replacement of an original political philosophy of democracy with a religious faith in democracy. Then Turner and
Beard redefined the democratic idea for the historical profession, explicitly repudiating the political philosophy of the
Founding Fathers. Turner's views on the frontier and Beard's
views on the Founding Fathers' motives were insignificant
compared with their ideological redefinition of the democratic
idea. The Progressive historians perpetuated a *simpliste*
conception of democracy, "one that cares much more about
ascertaining the sources and origin of political power than it
does about analyzing the existential consequences of this
power." For example, most historians consider the enactment
of the popular referendum as a victory for liberalism and
democracy, while, in fact, many American historians "in their
respective localities have seen some of their most cherished and

most liberal ideas . . . buried in a referendum [which is] the
most effective conservative piece of legislation passed by state
legislatures in this century." Meanwhile, the anti-Progressive
historians have not made it clear what they would put in place
of the Progressive concept. They, too, "shy away from raising
the basic issues of political philosophy that are involved," even
though

> the areas of American life that are becoming unstable and
> problematic are increasing in numbers and size every day. Yet,
> our initial response—and it usually remains our final
> response—is to echo Al Smith: "All the ills of democracy can be
> cured by more democracy." But is this really true? . . . Is it not
> possible that many of the ills of our democracy can be traced to
> this democracy itself—or, more explicitly, to this democracy's
> conception of itself? And how are we even to contemplate this
> possibility if historians seem so unaware of it?[2]

Kristol excepts Boorstin and Hartz from his complaint that
anti-Progressive historians have offered no alternative to the
Progressive view, but he is unhappy with their treatment of the
role of ideas in the American democracy. Boorstin, he notes,
concurs in this statement by Edmund Burke: "The bulk of
mankind on their part are not excessively curious concerning
any theories, whilst they are really happy; and one sure symp-
tom of an ill-conducted state is the propensity of the people to
resort to them." Although Kristol agrees with both Burke and
Boorstin on the validity of this thesis, he argues that Burke
"does not mean what Boorstin seems to think he does." Burke is

> talking about "the bulk of mankind" and "the people." He was
> *not* talking about political philosophers or historians or
> scholars—he was, after all, one himself. Burke thought it was a
> disaster when political philosophies became popular ideologies.
> But he never meant to suggest that truly thoughtful men should
> not engage in political philosophy. . . . Burke could not have
> had a high regard for a society where *no one* was engaging in the
> serious study of politics. . . . I do not think Burke, were he
> alive today, would regard the history of American democracy
> with the same satisfaction that Boorstin does. He might even be
> somewhat appalled at the enduring *mindlessness* of this
> democracy.[3]

Kristol is also "taken aback" at Hartz's conclusion that ideology is of no importance: "The system of democracy," Hartz writes, "works by virtue of certain processes which its theory never describes, to which, indeed, its theory is actually hostile." These processes involve "group coercion, crowd psychology, and economic power" and a conflict of interests from which an equilibrium roughly representing the public interest emerges. Interpreting Hartz, Kristol affirms, "If and when we examine the ideology of this democratic process and find it faulty or deficient, this is a crisis of democracy's image, not of its reality—[to quote Hartz] a mere 'agony of the mind rather than the real world.' " Kristol is surprised that a talented, perceptive historian of ideas whose "major work reveals the very great influence that a particular version of the democratic idea has had upon our history [could] end up with the assertion that the political mind has no dominion over political matter."[4] Kristol here refers to an essay Hartz wrote in 1960, a work which, in the light of Hartz's writings on his fragmentation theory published in 1963 and 1964, complements rather than conflicts with the main thesis of *The Liberal Tradition in America*. We shall return to this point after considering various criticisms of this thesis.

Hofstadter suggests that historians would do well to consider the findings of scholars in other disciplines concerning democratic theory and practice.[5] He cites several studies of this kind in his notes, but he does not summarize them. He refers to a "policy consensus" and a "constitutional consensus"[6]—what his Columbia colleague Charles Frankel, a philosopher, calls consensus on policy and consensus on framework. The former, Frankel writes, is arrived at within the context of the latter, through debate in which the members of the opposing sides hold a "shared allegiance to the rules of the democratic game."[7] However, political scientists' discoveries concerning consensus on framework, Nimmo and Ungs conclude, are not

> easily reconcilable with the classical theory of democracy or the long-held assumption that stability in American political processes has been the product of universal acceptance of fundamental values . . . there must be explanations for this stability, it would seem, other than mere assumptions about universal consensus.[8]

Nimmo and Ungs cite studies which show ambivalent and contradictory American attitudes toward democratic ideology, the operation of our political institutions, and specific policy issues. These investigations reveal "substantial consensus on abstract postulates about democratic precepts but little agreement on concrete application of these same principles." They also disclose definite differences in attitudes toward democratic values between the political leadership group (and better educated, higher income groups) and the general electorate. Nimmo and Ungs consider the higher degree of consensus on the specific application of the maxims of liberal democratic ideology among political "influentials" or activists than among the general electorate "decisive in shaping the context of limitations and taboos within which leaders accept the responsibility to govern." The attitudes of the leadership group are doubly decisive for sustaining democracy because Americans generally accept the making of political decisions on a day-to-day basis by this relatively small group. The assumption of universal "conscious and articulate acceptance of the creed" not only fails to allow for the crucial role of the leadership group, but, according to Nimmo and Ungs, it also overlooks another principal factor that makes for a stable democracy—habitual behavior patterns:

> despite individual ambivalence the collective polity operates as if a general consensus did exist . . . the absence of commitment to specific application does not mean hostility to the values themselves; absence of consensus may indicate indifference . . . lip-service consensus is supportive of political community, liberal democratic ideals, and constitutional procedures so long as people behave as if they *accept* the principles of each even though they may not actively *believe* in them.

Nimmo and Ungs list other "non-Hartzian"—or, as we shall see, allegedly "non-Hartzian"—factors as bases of stability: acquiescence in the values of liberal democracy "through its symbols, not necessarily through its content"; politico-constitutional "checks and balances"; and social "checks and balances" in pluralist America.[9] This assertion of the preponderance of behavior over belief as a support for democracy merits further scrutiny.

In 1955, when *The Liberal Tradition in America* appeared, Samuel A. Stouffer published *Communism, Conformity, and Civil Liberties*. He devoted a chapter to the question, "Are Civic Leaders More Tolerant Than Other People?" Stouffer compared the responses of a sample of fourteen types of community leaders with those of a cross-section of the population in the cities of 10,000 to 150,000 from which these leaders were selected, and with those of a cross-section of the entire nation, to questions concerning the civil rights of Socialists, atheists, alleged Communists who denied the charge, and admitted Communists. Although there was variation in the responses of the community leaders in the five categories to which Stouffer assigned the fourteen types (1, public officials; 2, political party chairmen; 3, industrial leaders; 4, heads of special patriotic groups; 5, others, in bar associations, women's clubs, parent-teachers' associations, and the press), every type of leader, without exception, was more willing to respect the civil rights —including the right to speak and the right to hold a job—of the four kinds of radicals or nonconformists specified than either the rank and file in the same cities as the leaders or the national cross-section. This mixed picture, Stouffer concluded, revealed the vital role which the leadership group played in the maintenance of democracy:

> the fact that responsible community leaders are more likely than the rank and file to give sober second thought to the civil rights of the nonconformists here studied can be of much significance to America's future. If the reverse had been found, the future might look dark indeed to those who view with anxiety current threats to historic liberties.[10]

In 1960 James W. Prothro and Charles M. Grigg published the results of their empirical examination of the proposition, recurrent in political theory, that consensus on fundamental principles is essential to democracy. For their purposes they interpreted this proposition as asserting that "a necessary condition for the existence of a democratic government is widespread agreement (approaching 100 percent) among the adult members of society on at least the basic questions about how political power is won."[11] Basing their research design on the major proposition that the United States is a democracy,

Prothro and Grigg prepared a questionnaire which asked for agreement or disagreement on statements about democracy at the abstract level:

Principle of Democracy Itself
  1. Democracy is the best form of government.

Principle of Majority Rule
  2. Public officials should be chosen by majority vote.
  3. Every citizen should have an equal chance to influence government policy.

Principle of Minority Rights
  4. The minority should be free to criticize majority decisions.
  5. People in the minority should be free to try to win majority support for their opinions.[12]

The responses of Prothro's and Grigg's sampling population —the registered voters of Ann Arbor, Michigan, and Tallahassee, Florida—showed agreement in support of these statements ranging from 94.7 to 98.0 percent: "consensus can be said to exist among the voters on the basic principles of democracy when they are put in abstract terms."[13]

The second part of the questionnaire consisted of ten specific embodiments, derived from the general statements in the first part, of the principles of democracy:

Principle of Majority Rule in Specific Terms	*Abstract Principle Referred to*	*Democratic Response*
1. In a city referendum only people who are well informed about the problem being voted on should be allowed to vote.	3	Disagree
2. In a city referendum deciding on tax-supported undertakings, only taxpayers should be allowed to vote.	3	Disagree
3. If a Negro were legally elected mayor of this city, the white people should not allow him to take office.	2	Disagree
4. If a Communist were legally elected mayor of this city, the people should not allow him to take office.	2	Disagree

	Abstract *Principle Re- ferred to*	Democratic *Response*
Principle of Majority Rule in Specific Terms		
5. A professional organization like the AMA (the American Medical Association) has a right to try to increase the influence of doctors by getting them to vote as a bloc in elections.	3	Agree
Principle of Minority Rights in Specific Terms		
6. If a person wanted to make a speech in this city against churches and religion, he should be allowed to speak.	4	Agree
7. If a person wanted to make a speech in this city favoring government ownership of all railroads and big industries, he should be allowed to speak.	4	Agree
8. If an admitted Communist wanted to make a speech in this city favoring Communism, he should be allowed to speak.	4	Agree
9. A Negro should not be allowed to run for mayor of this city.	5	Disagree
10. A Communist should not be allowed to run for mayor of this city.[14]	5	Disagree

The percentages of "democratic" responses to these statements are given below.

	Ann Arbor	Tallahassee
Majority Rule		
1.	*56.3*	*38.4*
2.	*20.8*	*21.2*
3.	*88.5*	*66.7*
4.	*46.9*	*45.5*
5.	*44.8*	*45.5*
Minority Rights		
6.	*67.4*	*56.6*
7.	*81.3*	*76.8*
8.	*51.4*	*33.3*
9.	*85.6*	*58.0*
10.	*44.1*	*38.2*[15]

A majority of the voters in Ann Arbor expressed "undemocratic" opinions on four statements (2, 4, 5, and 10), and a majority of the voters in Tallahassee expressed "undemocratic" opinions on six statements (1, 2, 4, 5, and 10). Prothro and Grigg concluded that "consensus does not exist on more concrete questions involving the application of democratic principles."[16]

Since a greater number of "correct" responses came from the Michigan than from the Florida community, regional subcultures, Prothro and Grigg noted, were one basis of differences in opinions on democratic principles. They also found that high, as opposed to low, education and high, as opposed to low, income were relatively pro-democratic in their effect on opinions. Those with high education gave the most democratic responses to all ten concrete propositions. "Partialling out" or controlling for the community, education, and income, Prothro and Grigg found that education was the "most consequential basis of opinions on basic democratic principles." Even among those with high education, however, there was no consensus in a meaningful sense—that is, 90 percent "correct" answers. Those in Ann Arbor with high education attained this percentage on only three of the ten specific statements, those in Tallahassee on none. "Even when the necessity of consensus is reformulated in terms of the group most in accord with democratic principles, then, consensus cannot be said to exist." Unlike Nimmo and Ungs and unlike Stouffer, Prothro and Grigg derived no assurance as to the vitality of democracy from the attitudes of the leadership or enlightened group of citizens:

> Assuming that the United States is a democracy, we cannot say without qualification that consensus on fundamental principles is a necessary condition for the existence of democracy. Nor does it appear valid to say that, although consensus need not pervade the entire voting population, it must exist at least among the highly educated, who are the carriers of the creed. Our data are not inconsistent, of course, with the qualified proposition that consensus on fundamental principles in a highly abstract form is a necessary condition for the existence of democracy. But the implication of political theory that consensus includes more specific principles is empirically invalid.[17]

Prothro and Grigg did derive some assurance about democracy's prospects from the function of apathy in our system: "many people express undemocratic principles in response to questioning but are too apathetic to act on their undemocratic opinions in concrete situations." Deeds differ from words, and, "fortunately for the democratic system, those with the most undemocratic principles are also those least likely to act." In fact, behavior of the citizenry in general, not just the apathetic, is crucial, Prothro and Grigg concluded, to the persistence of democracy: "Carl J. Friedrich appears to have been correct in asserting, eighteen years ago, that democracy depends on habitual patterns of behavior rather than on conscious agreement on democratic 'principles.' "[18]

This emphasis on habitual behavior, somewhat disconcerting to democratic ideologues and students of thought, was confirmed, in an indirect way, in an article by Herbert McClosky, published in 1964. McClosky did not stress habitual behavior as such, but he began his inquiry by referring to the dependence of democracy on acceptance of rather than belief in democratic norms and procedures, and he concluded by downgrading the role of ideas and intellectual processes in general as sources of stable democracy. This seemed to leave habitual behavior as the most likely candidate for causal primacy.

In 1957–58 McClosky carried out national surveys on two samples: 3,000 political "actives" or "leaders" drawn from the delegates and alternates who attended the conventions of the two major parties in 1956, and a representative national sample of 1,484 adults in the general population. In his tabulations he referred to the first group as the "Political Influentials" and to the second group as the "General Electorate." His first questionnaire called for responses to items involving "rules of the game"—for example, "Politicians have to cut a few corners if they are going to get anywhere." A majority of the general electorate supported the "rules of the game," but approval of these values, although not unanimous, was "significantly greater and more uniform among the influentials." Still, a "large proportion of the electorate has failed to grasp certain underlying ideas and principles on which the American political system rests."[19]

McClosky's second and third questionnaires correspond to
Prothro's and Grigg's. One called for responses to items expressing support for general statements of free speech and opinion,
the other for responses to items expressing support for specific
applications of free speech and procedural rights. Support for
items which expressed belief in freedom of speech and opinion
in a broad, general way was "remarkably high" for both samples,
but when converted into specific or applied forms, these principles were less widely and enthusiastically favored.[20] On both
questionnaires the political influentials displayed stronger support for democratic values than the general electorate.[21]
McClosky's findings were thus similar to Prothro's and Grigg's,
although there is one simple but significant difference between
the two analyses. McClosky calls the responses to items expressing support for general statements about free speech and opinion "remarkably high" for both samples. Of a total of sixteen
responses—answers by the two sample groups to eight
questions—the pro-democratic response is 90 percent or more
in only five instances: three for the political influentials (79.1,
81.4, 86.9, 87.8, 89.4, *90.6, 94.9, 96.4*) and two for the general
electorate (64.6, 77.0, 80.7, 81.8, 85.2, 88.9, *90.8, 94.3*). If we
apply the criterion for meaningful consensus of 90 percent
which Prothro and Grigg applied to those with high education,
what McClosky considers "remarkably high" support for basic
democratic values falls far short of meaningful consensus.

McClosky also presented findings which showed that the
political influentials registered higher scores than the general
electorate on pro-democratic attitude scales and lower scores on
anti-democratic attitude scales, although their repudiation of
anti-democratic attitudes was by no means unanimous.
McClosky then moved beyond aspects of democracy essentially
subsumed under "liberty" to a consideration of equality. While
Americans concurred substantially about liberty in the abstract,
both the political influentials and the general electorate divided
sharply on equalitarian values, whether political, social and ethnic, or economic. In the area of politics, both samples fell far
short of consensus on such questions as the capacity of the people for self-rule, although the influentials showed greater support for the equalitarian features of "popular" democracy. In

regard to economics, support for equality was slightly greater among the general electorate. Both samples split deeply on questions of social and ethnic equality. Both the public and its leaders, McClosky concluded, were "uncertain and ambivalent" about equality. He attributed this partly to complications associated with the concept of equality: the historical connection of democracy with capitalism; the diffuse, variegated nature of the concept resulting from its application to political, legal, economic, and moral domains; and the "common failure to distinguish equality as *fact* from equality as a *norm*." In addition, inevitable differences in rewards and opportunities in a complex society, and differences in the initial endowment individuals bring into the world, serve to "frustrate the realization of consensus around egalitarian values."[22]

In response to items expressing cynicism toward government and politics ("Most politicians are looking out for themselves above all else," for example) and items expressing a sense of political futility ("It seems to me that whoever you vote for, things go on pretty much the same," for example), the influentials proved substantially less cynical and less subject to a sense of futility than the general electorate. Meanwhile, the data revealed a "curious inconsistency." To the statement, "I usually have confidence that the government will do what is right," 89.6 percent of the otherwise relatively cynical general electorate (compared to 81.6 percent of the political influentials) responded in the affirmative. Americans are thus distrustful about the men and procedures involved in policy formation, but apparently they are not very dissatisfied with political outcomes. "They may be cynical about the operation of the political system," McClosky concluded, "but they do not question its legitimacy." This ambivalence in our tradition complicates the assessment of the various responses.[23]

McClosky carried his inquiry further than Prothro's and Grigg's, moving beyond attitudes toward democratic ideology and the rules of the game into the area of policy issues in order to ascertain whether an ideological consensus—some coherence and consistency of attitudes—existed beneath the level of basic values. He found that the political influentials were better informed than the general electorate on public questions and

more partisan and more consistent with their party preferences
in their issue orientations. Thus, "the political class is more
united than the electorate on fundamental political values but
divides more sharply by party affiliation on the issues which
separate the two parties." This was not a contradiction but,
rather, testified in each instance to the superior ideological
sophistication of the influentials. If it appears that selection of
political influentials for study amounts to stacking the deck,
McClosky noted that "similar (though less pronounced) differences emerge when we distinguish articulates from inarticulates
by criteria other than actual political activity." College education,
high-status occupation, and strong intellectual interests correlated by a significant margin with more positive attitudes toward
politics and government, and with greater coherence and consistency of attitudes on policy issues.[24]

Scholars who consider the possibility that the sources of
consensus lie in the realm of ideology do not, as noted above,
posit that consensus on policy issues is necessary so long as there
is consensus on basic democratic ideology or values and on
framework or rules of the game. McClosky seems to have taken a
different view:

> So far we have considered the question of ideology and consensus
> from the point of view of agreement on particular values. This,
> however, is a minimum criterion. Before one can say that a class
> or group or nation has achieved consensus around an ideology,
> one should be satisfied that they understand its values in a correct
> and coherent way.[25]

Then he presented his findings which showed that the political
influentials were more coherent, more partisan, and more consistent in their attitudes toward policy issues. Next he offered the
first of his six main conclusions: "American politics is widely
thought to be innocent of ideology but this opinion more ap-
propriately describes the electorate than the active political
minority."[26] Thus sharp, partisan division and intellectual
commitment—nonconsensus and adherence to ideology—went
together at the level of policy issues among the political influentials. All of which is somewhat confusing because McClosky
blended ideology and consensus, categories of manifestations of

democracy, and groups and the nation. To illustrate, he referred to "the question of ideology and consensus" and then presented data on activists' attitudes toward policy issues which showed ideological content but did not show consensus—which, indeed, showed its opposite. He specified understanding of an ideology's values in a coherent and correct way as a requirement of consensus of a class, group, or nation around an ideology, but his inquiry as to whether such an understanding existed focused not on values (by which he meant the democratic values he had examined up to this point) but on policy issues. This inquiry revealed consensus of two groups, Democratic and Republican activists, around two ideologies, which, at this level of analysis, precluded consensus of a nation around one ideology.

This confusion can be dispelled if we cling consistently to these categories:

1. Basic democratic ideology and values.
   The principle of democracy itself.
   The principle of majority rule.
   The principle of minority rights.
2. Framework or rules of the game.
   Basic democratic principles in specific terms.
3. Policy issues.

If, as McClosky asserted, consensus on levels 1 and 2 was a "minimum criterion" of consensus around an ideology, consensus on policy issues was presumably a maximum criterion—but, to repeat, activists' positions on policy issues involved consensus around two ideologies, and these two ideologies were in conflict. Indeed, whatever consensus was evident at level 3 existed among the general electorate: "not only do Democratic and Republican voters hold fairly similar opinions on issues," McClosky wrote, "but the latter's opinions are closer to the opinions of Democratic leaders than to those of their own leaders."[27] One can argue that this consensus, even though it may arise in part from lack of information on issues, prevents the clashing leadership groups from producing debilitating conflict by keeping them from moving very far off center—all of which relates to the matter, considered in chapter 1, of the similarity of the parties. In sum, if we depended on the general electorate for consensus on democratic ideology and the rules of the game, our faith would be unrealistic. If we relied on the leadership groups for consensus on policy issues, our trust would be misplaced. Could the society remain stable amid the kind of conflict which could conceivably arise over policy issues if there were no ideological consensus encompassing all or most Americans, as distinct from ideological consensuses embracing different groups? Which criteria are minimum and which maximum?

This comment is not meant to be caviling but to indicate the fundamental nature of the question we are ultimately concerned with: What accounts for the American consensus—inheritance or environment, ideas or experience, thought or behavior? Our concern at the moment is McClosky's response to this question. The first three of his six main conclusions pertained to the influentials. His first conclusion was that the influentials displayed a greater measure of unity than the general electorate on both abstract democratic principles and the rules of the game, especially the latter; that the coherency and consistency of the influentials' stands on policy issues were superior; that the evidence suggested that "it is the articulate classes rather than the public who serve as the major repository of the public conscience and as the carriers of the Creed. Responsibility for keeping the system going, hence, falls most heavily on them." McClosky's second conclusion was that the influentials were probably "better equipped for the role they are called upon to play in a democracy than the citizens are for *their* role." This finding, he maintained, refuted the widely held, intuitive expectation that a passion for democratic values arises spontaneously from the lowly, simple, "natural" folk of democratic ideology, Christian thought, and the works of Rousseau, Tolstoy, Marx, and other writers and social reformers. Did these conclusions mean that McClosky agreed with Nimmo and Ungs and with Stouffer that the influentials play a decisive role in sustaining democracy? Not quite. His third conclusion pointed in another direction: "While the active political minority affirms the underlying values of democracy more enthusiastically than the people do, consensus among them is far from perfect."[28]

McClosky thus set the stage for his fourth conclusion, which dealt with the "most crucial question suggested by the research findings, namely, what significance must be assigned to the fact that democratic ideology and consensus are poorly developed among the electorate and only imperfectly realized among the political influentials?" and his fifth and sixth conclusions, which related to the role played by intellectual factors in the attainment of democratic stability. His "first and most obvious" conclusion was that "contrary to the familiar claim, a democratic society can survive despite widespread popular misunderstanding and disagreement about basic democratic and constitutional values." Speculating as to why this was possible, McClosky, like Prothro and Grigg, mentioned the apathetic: a category most likely to include those who were most confused about democratic ideas. Although they did not contribute to the vitality of the system, they were not apt to do much harm. As for the influentials or the democratic elite, whether a consensus among them was "either a necessary or a sufficient condition for democratic stability is not really known." From this expression of uncertainty McClosky moved to further speculation about the relationship between consensus and stability:

> The opinion has long prevailed that consensus is needed to achieve stability, but the converse may be the more correct formulation, i.e., that so long as conditions remain stable, consensus is not required; it becomes essential only when social conditions are disorganized. Consensus may strengthen democratic viability, but its absence in an otherwise stable society need not be fatal or even particularly damaging.[29]

Finally, in addition to the apathy of the undemocratic and the stability of conditions, McClosky, like Nimmo and Ungs, referred to the democracy-sustaining role of politico-constitutional "checks and balances—federalism, separation of powers, bicameralism, the congressional committee system, the judicial practice of reconciling discrepant laws, a system of elections more often fought over local issues and personalities than over national questions, and the two-party system which blurs deep disagreements and accords with the reluctance of influentials to push intellectual disagreements all the way to the realm of action. McClosky, like Nimmo and Ungs, also mentioned social "checks and balances" in a pluralist society.[30]

In his final two conclusions McClosky asserted the limitations of the role played by intellectual factors in the attainment of democratic stability, then qualified this assertion by saying that the more strongly developed ideologically is a democratic nation's electorate, the sounder is the basis of democracy in that nation. Although the textbook model of democracy "can easily mislead us into placing more weight than the facts warrant upon cognitive elements—upon ideas, values, rational choice, consensus, etc.—as the cementing forces of a democratic society," it was not McClosky's intention to "imply that they are of no importance." Nor was the survival of democracy amid the limitations of consensus real grounds for complacency. The happy state of American democracy

> is not permanently guaranteed. Fundamental differences could *become* activated by political and economic crises; party differences could *develop* around fundamental constitutional questions, as they have in France and other democracies; and powerful extremist movements are too familiar a phenomenon of modern political life to take for granted their eternal absence from the American scene.

McClosky concluded on the hopeful note that since democratic ideology was associated with the articulate classes, its strength was likely to grow because the articulate class was growing.[31]

Implicit in McClosky's analysis was that students of politics would find it difficult to accept his central conclusion—that scholars had assigned an exaggerated role to ideas and intellectual processes in general, and that intellectual factors could not adequately explain many political phenomena which scholars, on *a priori* grounds, expected them to explain. It was natural, after all, McClosky noted, for scholars to take political ideas seriously and to endow them with crucial significance in the functioning of the state,[32] an occupational trait that accounted for both their error and their reluctance to recognize it. But it appears possible to deny McClosky the last word on this matter on other than *ad hominem* grounds.

McClosky's suggestion that the absence of consensus need not be fatal or even damaging in an otherwise stable society leaves us with some questions. If stability sustains democracy, it does not necessarily produce democracy. Stability for an extended time can, and has, marked nondemocratic societies. McClosky himself notes that "data from the observation of dictatorial and other nations further corroborates the conclusion that men may become attached to a party, a community, or a nation by forces that have nothing to do with ideology or consensus."[33] Such attachment, whether or not it is based on ideology of a particular kind, can be supportive of the stability of a dictatorship. If the stability of the United States has been that of a democracy, where did American democracy come from in the first place? If one holds that its origins lost their significance as the persistence of democracy eventually became primarily a behavioral phenomenon, how does one account for Americans' behavior during the Great Depression? Now it is conceivable that attachment to democracy as a behavioral phenomenon could sustain democracy in such a crisis, but McClosky himself states that consensus "becomes essential only when social conditions are disorganized." Since the Great Depression involved considerable social disorganization, consensus, rather than an "otherwise stable society," must have been essential in 1932 when 97.1 percent of the American voters cast their ballots for either Franklin D. Roosevelt (57.4 percent) or Herbert Hoover (39.7 percent), with the Socialist candidate Norman Thomas receiving 2.2 percent and the Communist candidate less than one percent—while 52 percent of the German voters cast their ballots for either a Nazi (37.4 percent) or Communist (14.6 percent) dictatorship. This reference to Germany is relevant because McClosky notes that some democratic governments such as Weimar Germany crumbled while others such as post–World War II France and Italy did not when faced with ideological conflicts among their political classes.[34] Postwar France and Italy, to be sure, were relatively "otherwise stable," whereas the Great Depression struck a devastating blow at Weimar Germany. But that is the point. No one will quarrel with the proposition that democracy has a better chance of surviving in an otherwise stable situation than in an otherwise unstable situation, but when it survives despite instability, this proposition does not explain its persistence.

It is not necessary to leap from the failure of the assumption of universal adherence to democratic ideology to pass empirical tests to the elimination of ideology as a significant causal factor. I had assumed that Hartz's thesis applied to about 95 percent of adult Americans—a figure I had used in the classroom—and McClosky's reduction of this figure, so to speak, is well taken. But how much of a change in degree is required to effect a change in kind? Prothro and Grigg tell us that 90 percent a- greement is the requirement for consensus. Do not scores on McClosky's questionnarie of 79.1, 81.4, 86.9, 87.8, 89.4, 90.6, 94.9, and 96.4 on general statements about free speech and opinion indicate enough consensus to sustain democracy? McClosky's answer is no, because these figures were attained only by the influentials and only on general principles as op- posed to their specific applications. Thus, consensus on the level of a 79.1–to–96.4 range is not enough as such, it is not enough when it is confined to the influentials—on whom, McClosky states, responsibility for keeping the system going falls most heavily—and it is not enough when it is confined to the level of broad democratic principles to account for the persistence of democracy. And "not enough" becomes, in effect, "grossly in- adequate." Fred H. Willhoite takes up these matters of numbers and levels of analysis, as well as other points, in his critique of Prothro's and Grigg's study.

Willhoite defines consensus as "agreement among citizens who are in any way politically minded . . . on the ends and means of political organization and activity." He then specifies types of consensus in terms of political ends and means, adding, as it were, another dimension to framework while also citing rules of the game and policy issues (although not in that order). In Willhoite's view, framework goes beyond the basic principles of democracy and democratic ideology as such; it encompasses "broad normative principles or long-term goals; for example, in a constitutional democracy, justice, fairness, integrity, impartial- ity, equality before the law." Government policies are another kind of end, "the very stuff of political controversy [but] the narrowest and least significant kind of consensus as regards the long-range prospect of creating and maintaining an ordered political community." The rules of the game are political means; they include the "formal and informal institutions and processes employed in gaining governmental power and exercising it." They are largely dependent for their successful operation, Will- hoite maintains, "upon a prior basis of generally agreed-upon broad-gauge political values and long-range goals. This means simply that a constitutional mechanism cannot of itself bring order out of political chaos."[35]

Willhoite offers a two-fold criticism of Prothro's and Grigg's treatment of consensus on framework: it assumes a perfect American democracy, and it neglects broad-gauge values and long-range goals. Prothro and Griggs assume that the United States is a democracy; they claim to show that the "highly abstract and rigid" set of principles which they consider the essence of democratic doctrine mean very little when applied in specific situations; and they thus claim to have demonstrated that meaningful consensus on principles is unnecessary to support the operation of a functioning democracy. Willhoite proposes starting with a more modest assumption: The United States is a political entity; each of the two cities—Ann Arbor and Tallahassee—is part of that larger entity; and each can be distinguished to some extent by differing political cultures. The question then arises, "exactly what kind of political order does exist in these two communities?" To what degree do the governments of Ann Arbor and Tallahassee conform to or diverge from Prothro's and Grigg's implicit model of democracy? "If it were discovered that in either or both instances there existed a 'democracy' conforming in practice to the authors' four rigid principles, despite an apparent lack of consensus on some hypothetical applications of these principles, then and only then might their general conclusion be verified." Willhoite's second criticism, with respect to framework, is that Prothro and Grigg do not mention broad-gauge values or goals. They concede, in their words, that their "data are not inconsistent, of course, with the qualified proposition that consensus on fundamental principles in a highly abstract form is a necessary condition for the existence of democracy"—that democracy can survive a lack of consensus on rules of the game so long as there is substantial consensus on framework—but this concession has to do with the framework of abstract principles of majority rule and minority rights rather than broad-gauge values and goals.[36]

Willhoite criticizes Prothro's and Grigg's treatment of the rules of the game—of issues about how political power should be won—on four counts: phraseology, the definition of consensus as 90 percent agreement, the divisiveness of the issues chosen, and the unreality of the situations presented. Willhoite considers one of Prothro's and Grigg's abstract principles—"Every citizen should have an equal chance to influence government policy"—and their finding that only a minority responded "democratically" to the application of this principle in questions concerning the restriction of voting in a city referendum to the well informed (49 percent), and the restriction of voting on tax-supported municipal undertakings to taxpayers (21 percent). Willhoite maintains that an "undemocratic" answer to these questions is not logically incompatible with agreement on the general proposition as it is stated. The establishment of such a logical gap would require presenting the general principle in such a manner as this: "Every citizen should have an equal right *through every means available to any citizen* to influence *every* government policy." In regard to the question about the right of the American Medical Association to try to get doctors to vote as a bloc, Willhoite holds that many laymen who deny this right—"undemocratically" according to Prothro and Grigg —may well consider bloc voting a "hindrance to the implementation of this abstract principle which expressly includes *every* citizen."[37]

Willhoite calls the requirement of 90 percent agreement an "arbitrary and overly rigid quantitative standard for determining the presence or absence of consensus." Prothro and Grigg, he writes, do not make a "serious attempt to justify their conclusion that there is a notable lack of consensus on these hypothetical examples to which three-fourths or four-fifths of their sample respond 'democratically.' " Although a principle is agreed to by less than 90 percent of the politically involved citizens, it could, Willhoite holds, create a "climate of expectation" in the community as to standards of public behavior and thereby exert a profound influence on conduct, including that of the undemocratic" apathetic citizens who refrain from acting on their views. Willhoite also notes that the highest degree of discord which Prothro and Grigg discovered related to propositions concerning "issues which in fact are extremely divisive on the American political scene—namely, civil rights of Negroes and the treatment of internal communism" (six of the ten propositions on the rules of the game refer to one or the other of these two factors, if one associates anti–anti-religion with anti-Communism as Willhoite does.) When Willhoite rejects Prothro's and Grigg's position—that the response of their sample to divisive issues indicates the nonexistence of significant consensus on the rules of the game—he is in accord with Lipset's and Rokkan's conclusion, noted in chapter 2, that the United States is a relatively highly consensual democratic society despite its nonconsensual or undemocratic restrictions of Communist activities and Negro voting. Finally, in regard to the rules of the game, Willhoite cites the "air of unreality" about Prothro's and Grigg's propositions: "These situations embodied in these propositions lie almost wholly outside the experience or normal expectations of most of the respondents." Therefore the responses to the hypothetical examples "merely indicate that at certain points communal consensus on means may well break down, but they do *not* indicate that no significant consensus whatsoever exists in this area of political life."[38]

Willhoite concludes by emphasizing his main methodological criticism of Prothro and Grigg: they neglect "the dependence of the means-principles (abstract as well as particular) upon prior value-assumptions." To illustrate this point he cites white supremacy as a potent broad-gauge value in the South and asserts that "the conflict between this principle and that of political equality, which is basic to the ideas of majority rule and minority rights, accounts for the breakdown of consensus on political means when applied hypothetically to questions concerning the rights of Negroes." If political order in a democratic state "is not and cannot be dependent primarily upon consensus on specific policies," it is dependent to some extent, Prothro's and Grigg's study notwithstanding, on consensus on political means. But consensus on the rules of the game is "not the most basic kind of agreement within a stable democratic order." Political means "serve the purposes of the broad-gauge values and goals that make up the fundamental consensus on ends which is of greatest significance for the communal order." These values and goals are, to be sure, very general, but they represent a "bedrock consensus," in the absence of which differences over political means could conceivably lead to the demise of democracy. To

put it another way, despite the deficiencies of consensus which
Prothro and Grigg specify, the United States has not become a
dictatorship or some other kind of non-democratic state. General agreement on broad-gauge purposes and values of the
organized community, Willhoite asserts, "makes a functioning
democratic system very different from what it might become
should, for example, the premises of social Darwinism or of a
Nietzschian power philosophy be accepted by the bulk of the
politically minded populace. . . . Those who would deny or
minimize the significance of consensus, of 'agreement on fundamentals,' in the construction and maintenance of political
order have yet to justify their claim."[39]

A matter which Prothro and Grigg, McClosky, and Willhoite discuss briefly—the apathy of the undemocratic
—warrants further consideration. While Willhoite goes beyond
the other authors, hypothesizing that this apathetic behavior
results from as well as contributes to consensus, Gerald Garvey
goes into more detail, distinguishing between two basic types of
political inactivity. He concludes that traditional political theory
concerning nonvoting overestimates apathy and underesti-
mates alienation or disaffection. The assumption that "apathy
tends to increase when citizens are satisfied that their interests
will not be seriously harmed, regardless of which party wins,"
neglects the possibility that a citizen who is "more concerned
over the fact that both parties have platforms which radically
differ from his preferences than over the fact that the two
parties are close together . . . would be likely not to vote as a
means of registering his protest rather than his passive consent
[to the election's outcome]." Garvey further concludes that
nonvoting—which, whether the result of apathy or alienation, is
a self-feeding phenomenon—creates forces that prevent elections from reflecting true social consensus. Political scientists
who focus on the behavior of the active electorate overlook
forces which, moreover, could destroy the consent, already subject to limitations, that is now obtained through two-party
elections.[40]

A Gallup Poll on voter turnout in the 1972 elections identified a group (10 percent), among the 46.5 percent of the
voting-age population who did not vote, who might well fit into

Garvey's category of voters who found both parties unacceptable. Citizens were nonvoters for these reasons:

10%	Lack of a good choice of presidential candidates.
28%	Lack of interest in politics.
24%	Health, job demands, travel.
38%	Failure to register, out of choice or because of residency requirements.[41]

One would also like to know how many among the 28 percent who indicated their lack of interest in politics were inactive because of apathy and how many because of alienation, how many among those who failed to register out of choice fell into each of these two categories, and how those who were stymied by residency requirements would have behaved in the absence of this obstacle. Voter turnout in the United States has fallen off sharply from the nineteenth to the twentieth centuries, as these percentages for presidential elections show:

1840	80.2%
1860	81.2%
1880	79.4%
1900	73.2%
1920	49.2%
1940	62.9%
1960	64.0%
1972	55.5%

Recent percentages of voter turnout in certain other democracies have been considerably higher than recent turnout in the United States: Australia, 97; Canada, 74; France, 82; Great Britain, 71; Ireland, 75; Italy, 93; Netherlands, 83; New Zealand, 90; West Germany, 91.[42] Burnham stresses the nonconsensual quality of political inactivity in the United States. Calling for the admission by the polity of non—middle-class values to political legitimacy in order fully to mobilize apolitical elements, he indicates the narrowness of the universe of active politics:

> The concentration of socially deprived characteristics among the more than forty million adult Americans who today are altogether outside the voting universe suggests active alienation—or its passive equivalent, political apathy—on a scale quite unknown anywhere else in the Western world.[43]

Nonvoting is, of course, an important feature of our politics, one reminder of the departure of real conditions from the textbook model of democracy. Kristol offers another such reminder when he refers to the actual effects of referenda, and Willhoite still another when he asks "exactly what kind of political order does exist in these two communities?" If Prothro and Grigg do not answer this question for Ann Arbor and Tallahassee, neither is it answered for the nation as a whole in a discussion of the relative importance of ideology and behavior as sources of democracy.

Having noted this limitation, let us conclude with a comment on ideology and behavior with respect to democracy, a comment prompted by Kristol's remarks, cited above, on Hartz's ideas. Kristol, the reader will recall, is surprised that a perceptive historian of ideas could "end up with the assertion that the political mind has no dominion over political matter." The occasion for wonder was his reading of Hartz: "If and when we examine the ideology of the democratic process and find it faulty or deficient, this is a crisis of democracy's image, not of its reality—[to quote Hartz] a mere 'agony of the mind rather than the real world.' "

In his article on "American Historians and the Democratic Idea," published in the winter 1969–70 issue of *American Scholar*, Kristol quotes an essay by Hartz on "Democracy: Image and Reality," published in 1960.[44] He might have been less shocked if he had also read Hartz's essay on "The Rise of the Democratic Idea," published in 1963, and *The Founding of New Societies*, which appeared in 1964, since the theory of fragmentation expounded in these writings enhances understanding of the essay of 1960. Even so, in "Democracy: Image and Reality," Hartz does not make a dichotomy between ideology and behavior and assign predominance to one. The deficiency of the textbook model of democratic theory is its failure to account for certain institutions and practices of democracy. The problems which result from this shortcoming, Hartz states, "expose our theory, which has room for none of them, but they do not expose [that is, "expose"] the real processes by which democracy has always worked."[45] In other words, we should not be amazed to learn that democracy in real life departs in many ways from the ideal political order portrayed in democratic theory. Hartz, it is true, can conceive of "problems of 'excess,' of the necessary machinery of the democratic world somehow getting out of hand."[46] But he maintains, as it were, that the divergence of democratic practice from democratic theory does not represent a deep, or in any event a new, crisis because this discrepancy has always been there. Nor does this deviation rule out democratic ideology as a causal factor in American political life. Hartz achieves his reconciliation of ideology and behavior through a historical explanation which anticipates, without explicitly mentioning, the theory of fragmentation which he spelled out a few years later.

Insisting that "no modern political system as it has risen to power has ever developed an image which corresponds to the real procedures by which it works,"[47] Hartz maintains that democratic theory arose as a negative reaction to the previous system. As such, it specified what should be destroyed, but it did not indicate what should be created. Just as Marxism is a negative picture of capitalism rather than a picture of a socialist society,

> the doctrine of liberal democracy, instead of being a description of democratic life, is a negative description of life in the old European world that democracy destroyed. Locke, Rousseau, and Bentham are in this sense not "theorists of democracy" at all: they are the inverted theorists of the "corporate society" of the Seventeenth and Eighteenth centuries.
>
> Once we go back to that society, it is clear enough why the democratic image these men gave us should be hostile to half the machinery that was later invented to make democracy work. The points at which they assailed the old corporate system were precisely the points at which that machinery was destined to appear.[48]

In this regard the democratic theorists are like active revolutionaries who focus on how to overthrow the evil regime but do not devote much attention to what they will do after they seize power. What happened in the case of democracy, Hartz writes, is that an ascendant social system struck "some middle ground between the blazing negative ideals of its origins and the operational necessities of actual life."[49] This middle ground thus incorporated both ideology and behavior. If Kristol reads an emphasis on behavior into Hartz's essay, "Democracy: Image and Reality," he will find, as I noted in chapter 2, that Hartz in his theory of fragmentation confines behavior to a broad ideological context. His treatment of ideology, it is true, makes it almost invisible, but he saves it from visual obscurity and causal impotence by demonstrating that its presence is what accounts for the broad-gauge differences between America, with all of its behavioral departures from ideal democracy, and other fragmented societies.

Yet it is not my intention to retreat from the main point made at the outset of this section. On the contrary, I hope that this consideration of relevant literature in political science will reinforce the argument that simply to speak of a consensus on democracy, although it tells us something important at a high level of generalization, leaves many significant things unsaid. At the same time, to use any failure of Hartz's Lockean consensus to encompass 90 percent of the population to deny ideology any role in the maintenance of democracy in America is to engage in overcorrection. But in agreeing with Hartz's generalization, one must also recognize that inquiry at lower levels of analysis reveals Americans' frequent ambivalence about democracy—a point Robert G. McCloskey makes in commenting on the findings of Stouffer, Prothro, and Grigg, and others[50]—the antidemocratic attitudes of some Americans,[51] and the undemocratic or violent behavior, which we shall consider in chapter 5, of one group or another of Americans at almost any given time.

Selectivity: "Givenness," Winners, and Ideology

The contention that the consensus view, informative as far as it goes, does not go far enough in accounting for the various ramifications of American life and thought, and the assertion that the consensus formula of capitalism and democracy is a broad abstraction from American reality amount to charges that the theory rests upon a selectivity which distorts historical reality. Hofstadter indicts Boorstin on this count:

> Where he is most successful in the two volumes of *The Americans* which we thus far have, is chiefly as a social historian writing about selected aspects of our social life in which conflict is not

uppermost. . . . As his work has progressed, he has turned his back on the basic problems of political conflict in our history, and often of social conflict as well. . . . Boorstin has not resolved the problem of conflict, he has simply abandoned it.[1]

Pole, too, emphasizes the selectivity he finds in Boorstin's writings:

> He adds the hope that the book [*The Genius of American Politics*] will "remind us how to keep our traditions alive," a hope that perhaps reveals more confidence than American traditions can be relied upon to bear. It depends which tradition one chooses. Racial discrimination is an American tradition; so also are equality, morality, and the rule of law.[2]

Boorstin, as noted in chapter 2, ties together his interpretation of the American experience with "the continuity of American history in a steady stream" in which conflict and ideas play relatively minor roles. To discern such continuity, Pole maintains, is to be selective with the evidence, and he devotes considerable attention to identifying such selectivity in Boorstin's writing. In his criticism of Boorstin's causal theory, as we have seen in chapter 2, Pole stresses the logical difficulty or ambiguity involved in Boorstin's failure to separate Americans' illusion from reality. A vague geographic determinism that does not separate myth from fact ignores the realm of preconceived ideas. The assertion of "givenness" without intensively assessing what Americans thought they had been given against what they had actually been given also entails, besides ambiguity, selectivity— "the extrusion of ideology from the substance of history."

Pole contends that the Founding Fathers did indeed subscribe to a theory, a fact Boorstin blurs. Pole cites Boorstin's widely quoted statement that the American Revolution was a "prudential decision taken by men of principle rather than the affirmation of a theory." Noting that the decision was prudential insofar as it was vindicated by events, Pole observes that the word *prudential* conceals the "frantic activity, passionate agitation, and background of military operations that brought the leadership up to, and past, the point of independence." He continues:

> And assuredly they were men of principle. But what principle? The answer, which Boorstin does not give, is that these men were

Whigs; their unifying principle was Whiggery; and despite their many and serious differences, it was enough to enable them to speak a common political language and to declare a common purpose. Why then, is it important, or even significant, that they do not affirm a theory? What theory other than that of their Whig principles could anyone have expected them to affirm?

If, as Boorstin says, the American leaders were men of principle (in a political sense; it would be trivial to say merely that they were "upright" or "men of honor"), then in fundamental matters they did possess a theory."[3]

One may argue that Americans' acting in accordance with their belief that they had inherited a theory renders unimportant the question of the theoretical or nontheoretical quality of this legacy. The nature of this legacy, however, involves the question of the role or nonrole, whether known or unknown to the actors themselves, of ideas in human behavior. It thus seems appropriate momentarily to interrupt Pole's critique of Boorstin to consider the content of the theory which he assigns to the Founding Fathers.

In an essay of 1962 Pole specified what he means by "Whiggery" or, as he put it then, "Whiggism," a concept of government "worked out in England and, both by extension and by original experience, in the American colonies." Whiggism, "like so many other things, derivable from Locke," was a theory of balanced or mixed government expressed in the form of a mixed constitution embracing different "orders" and giving security to each, with the commons being represented in the "democratical" arm, the assembly or commons house. The basic principle of the Whig view of government—of government-in-society—that preceded representative institutions was the compact, which people were supposed to have entered voluntarily to secure protection of both their property and their persons. In accordance with the component of Whig ideology which made a "stake in society" the basis of participation in government, the first requirement was the protection of property through some form of representation. The protection of persons was provided through the creation of a second house—a main feature of the Whig implementation of the compact. In practice, the postrevolutionary constitutions adapted Whig theory to a situation in which "all the 'orders' now drew their position in government from some form of popular representation." In fact, the "democratical" arm became preponderant in political power, but this did not produce democracy because there was an oligarchy, nontyrannical but powerful, which exercised its power "in, and through, the assembly itself." That the great mass of the common people gave their consent to "concepts of government that limited their own participation in ways completely at variance with the principle of modern democracy" can be attributed, Pole writes, to the irresistible sway of deference. The deferential American society finally dissolved with the emergence of Jacksonian democracy.[4]

The deference interpretation which Pole espouses has not, to be sure, gone unquestioned. In a comprehensive historiographical analysis and critique of the deference concept, John B. Kirby concludes that "democracy either in theory or practice was not widely subscribed to by colonists on the eve of the American Revolution," but the question of deference, Kirby believes, remains open. The elitist leadership appears to have accepted the deference concept. They probably believed that others also accepted it, since holders of power may "automatically assume, or at least might like to think that they owe their positions to the general accord of the rest of the population." We must know more about the attitudes of the nonelite, however, before we can consider deference a "sufficient explanation" of eighteenth-century American society. In any event, Kirby concludes, by the end of the Jacksonian period the status of the elite and its political power had declined considerably as America became a more open society. This evolution from Whiggery to democracy is germane here because it is a process that Hartz emphasizes in *The Founding of New Societies* (1964)—an emphasis which Kirby does not take into account. Referring only to *The Liberal Tradition in America* (1955), he says:

> Deference rests to a large extent on the assumption, long argued
> by the neo-Whigs, that American society in the seventeenth and
> eighteenth centuries was homogeneous, that there existed
> common values that colonials agreed upon, and that these values
> formed the basis of a stable social and political order. Writers like

Hartz and Boorstin have extended this "consensus" view of
colonial life to encompass the whole of American political
history.[5]

Now this comment, to be sure, is valid as far as it goes since
Hartz's (and Pole's) Whigs subscribe to basic Lockean principles; but Whiggery and democracy are different ways of
implementing these principles—representation of the general
interest through a disinterested, enlightened elite as opposed to
direct representation. In Hartz's account Whiggery and democracy clashed, and in the American situation, Hartz maintains,
democracy was bound to win. The virtual inevitability of this
outcome is an aspect of Hartz's fragmentation theory.

The significance which Pole and Hartz assign to Whig
ideology distinguishes their views of American development
from Boorstin's. It also suggests why Pole considers nonideological "givenness" a selective concept. The presentation of the
Founding Fathers' legacy as "principles" or a substitute for a
theory but *not* a theory, Pole implies, reflects Boorstin's finding
what he wanted to find. Since one of Boorstin's basic aims is to
contrast the pragmatic American historical experiment, which
he applauds, with a Europe whose institutions represent the
deliberate enactment of preconceived theories, a kind of development which he deplores, Boorstin tends to underestimate
the role of theory in American history and to overestimate its
significance in European history. Pole objects vigorously to the
way Boorstin uses the comparative approach:

> Here Boorstin's didactic purpose seems to have led him astray
> from his history. The kind of total theories of society, the desire to
> use revolutionary means to impose a schematic new order, that
> have caused such indescribable pain and suffering in our own
> twentieth century were almost unknown in the eighteenth. . . .
> Boorstin's carefully posed antithesis therefore becomes
> historically irrelevant and gives rise to the suspicion that he is
> using the weapons that belong to the eighteenth century to fight
> the battle of his own generation. . . . The contrast involves a
> good deal of oversimplification—and rather too often
> disparaging oversimplification—of European culture and
> institutions. Even when discussing modern European political
> parties, which, as he knows, often define themselves by

adherence to theoretical principles, he fails to observe how much European government is in fact coalition government.

In sum, the idea of "givenness" rests on selectivity—"the extrusion of ideology from history"; it is therefore ambiguous, and it leads to further selectivity since the "concept of 'givenness' controls the historian's selections and weakens his critical apparatus."[6]

Another ambiguity or logical difficulty that Pole identifies in Boorstin's interpretation of American history, one which also relates to selectivity, is his endowing facts with normative as well as descriptive qualities. Ironically, this ambiguity follows from one of Boorstin's own "deepest shafts of insight." In explaining the "apotheosis of nature" in Jeffersonian thought, Boorstin states:

> All facts were endowed with an ambiguous quality: they became normative as well as descriptive. . . . By describing a work of art as successful, we mean that it is hard to separate description from judgment, the "is" from the "ought," the facts about the work from the standards against which those facts are to be judged.

The key word here is *successful*, for, as Pole asserts,

> Men and women in America have achieved so much of what they have aspired to . . . that the historian relying largely on material that is in fact evidence of these successes, has difficulty in writing as though the history of facts were not also and necessarily the history of norms.

In short, Boorstin's history is about winners, not losers. One can appreciate the attraction of this approach when one considers how difficult it is, regardless of one's sympathies, to construct an alternative. As Pole states, "the history of failure or defeat can hardly become that of a *continuing* norm, even though it may recognize the existence of a conflict of values at some time in the past." Success as the continuing norm accords with Boorstin's belief in a mainstream of American history: "We view our history," he remarks, "—and the facts support us—as a single broad stream, the unbroken living current of the American Way of Life, not as a miscellaneous series of great epochs." But, Pole asks, asserting the epoch-making significance of the Revolution, the Civil War, and the closing of the frontier, "Which facts support us?" According to Pole, Boorstin's answer, as it were, is "Only those facts which are part of the mainstream."[7]

As Pole sees it, the outcome of Boorstin's selectivity is historiography which (1) accords inadequate recognition to "the passionate intensity of the major conflicts in American history"; (2) fails fully to take into account "the intellectual depth and seriousness of the opposed positions"; and (3) minimizes, through a "preoccupation with the conditions of success," the significance of conflict, especially because (4) conflict is viewed as irrelevant to the mainstream. Boorstin rejects any attempt to formulate a democratic philosophy, to define what Americans already agree on, and, Pole comments, "the presumption of real agreement . . . in fact controls much of the argument by defining outlines of relevance beyond which disagreements are merely factious or trivial." Boorstin ascribes irrelevance particularly to the intellectual content of conflicts, for, as Pole observes, "major issues of principle are treated rather as though, within the total context of 'givenness,' they ought to have been seen to be irrelevant." In this connection, Pole takes exception to Boorstin's treatment of the abolitionists' ideas, of war aims and concepts of national government expressed during the Civil War, of the thought underlying the achievements of the Radical Reconstructionists, and of the ideas of the Revolutionary leaders.[8]

Pole shows how the concept of a "mainstream" determines the selectivity that is evident in Boorstin's *The Americans: The Colonial Experience* and *The Americans: The National Experience*. Boorstin writes "neither social history without politics nor political history without society nor economic history without either; it is the history of a society in the widest sense." His objective is "not to establish sequences of events but rather to establish their context," the social texture from which they arose. He conceives the history of society as

> that of certain broad types of experience, some of which are shared by the vast majority but some of which are the result of special circumstances. It is essential to appreciate this implicit theme in Boorstin's work, that of the experience of the community, which continues whatever defeats some sections may suffer, whatever changes the rest may undergo. What is retained

through change, what has been absorbed into the bones of
American life, is constantly implied as he moves over the varied
ground both of the society and of the geography on which it
stands.

The method resulting from this concept involves a principle of
selection that, to repeat, minimizes the seriousness of the intellectual component of conflicts—"the major conflicts of interest
and opinion were due to prejudice, ignorance, or intellectual
error rather than to genuine convictions about fundamental
principles." This method also tends to dismiss "as incidental or
even irrelevant to the 'mainstream' of American history . . .
whatever past conflicts either obstruct the passage of his argument or more simply do not interest him." Many events which
ought not to have happened according to the American norm
did happen, "but they need not have done, and so can be treated
as of secondary importance."[9]
    Pole concludes his criticism of the first two volumes of *The
Americans* with a catalog of conflicts of opinion to which Boorstin
gives slight attention and which Pole feels were of such vital
importance—sometimes involving conflicts of ideals about the
future of the nation—that their resolution in a different way
would have resulted in a significant difference in the "development of the society that primarily interests Boorstin." To illustrate such slighting of important matters, Pole notes that the
Second Bank of the United States appears in Boorstin's account
"only incidentally in a passing reference to Nicholas Biddle,"
and Alexander Hamilton appears in the index only three times.
Pole's list of neglected conflicts includes those associated with
Independence, the Constitution, and the Confederation, and
the clashes of Robert Morris–Hamiltor *v.* John Taylor–
Jefferson, pro- *v.* anti-slavery, and the populists *v.* the industrial order. Yet, one might object in Boorstin's behalf, not
every book can be about everything, and Boorstin is entitled to
choose the history of social texture as the area of his concern. To
this objection Pole would reply that Boorstin's work is freighted
with a general interpretation of American history with primary
emphasis on geographically rooted experience, that although
Boorstin's argument, as Pole declares in an article on United
States historiography in general, "explains the sort of

phenomena that primarily interest Professor Boorstin . . . [they] are presented not merely as one aspect of what he calls the 'national experience': they *are* the national experience."[10]

Pole thinks highly of Boorstin's descriptive ability: "there is probably no living historian of America who is quite Boorstin's equal in the essential historian's power of bringing the past to life." Pole, moreover, attributes considerable explanatory force to Boorstin's consensus interpretation, subject to his own (Pole's) qualifications: the " 'preformation' theory describes a fact, after all, not simply a belief . . . and it provides later generations with a common political language and does much to explain the modern strength of the theory of consensus." In the end, however, Pole concludes that the consensus view may be informative as far as it goes, but it does not go far enough. To Hartz's negative concept—the absence of feudalism in American history—Boorstin adds another negative—the absence of dogma, of preconceived theory, even of too much formal knowledge—but this "theme is made to bear a greater burden of explanation than is usually required of absences, of spaces reserved but not filled." One may dissent from Pole's comment on Hartz since, as noted in chapter 2, the absence of feudalism is only part of Hartz's theory of causation, but Boorstin's writings, not Hartz's, are the subject of Pole's essay, and his comment on what can emerge from unfilled spaces will serve as a summary of his views on Boorstin's consensus history:

> The doctrine of "preformation" contains an obvious bedrock of truth: we know that the principles of the Founders, including the principle of compromise, had been handed down and resorted to by generation after generation of Americans, though often pursuing opposed ends with devious arguments; yet it was precisely in the interstices between the agreements of the Founders that the infection grew that would later burst into national conflict. Thus although "preformation" provides a valuable concept and a useful clue, it does not close the argument about what kind of country was being built.[11]

Diggins, like Pole, objects to the way Boorstin uses the comparative approach, to his "incessant contrasting of American practicality with European ideology." Insisting that "historical understanding consists in perceiving similarities as well as differences," Diggins asserts that Boorstin's assumptions about American uniqueness—the key to which is an anti-ideological mentality—rest on a misconception of European ideology. This error, Diggins maintains, derives from a selective interpretation of ideology—the image held by "the generation of the thirties —the generation in which Boorstin received his political baptism."[12]

Diggins points out that the Americans who praised Mussolini saw fascism as a "marvelous, pragmatic experiment," and those who were enchanted by Lenin and Stalin saw Bolshevism as an "exciting scientific adventure." Nor was such captivation by European ideologies confined, as Boorstin contends, to intellectuals. Henry Ford, for example, in explaining his dealings with the Soviet Union, stated, "Russia is beginning to build. It makes little difference what theory is back of the real work, for in the long run facts will control." In 1929, in *The Modern Temper*, Joseph Wood Krutch described the Russian people as being immersed in the conquest of a backward environment. Unconcerned with philosophical problems, not inclined to ask ultimate questions, and wholly absorbed in technique and process, they had transcended self and fully adjusted to the natural universe. "Ironically," Diggins comments, "the deified naturalism that Krutch found so disturbing in Russian Communism becomes in Boorstin's eyes the health of the American character."[13]

If Krutch found the Russians totally nontheoretical, "When," Diggins asks, "did Americans begin to assume that in Russia the urge to theorize had stifled the instinct for practicality?" When did the exciting scientific adventure become a "political nightmare"? For most Americans this change occurred during the cold war, but for many intellectuals ideology took on a "petrified cast" and became a "bugbear" and a "synonym for static doctrine" as a result of the incredible debates, the "woolly arguments," among the factions of the American Marxist Old Left. Thus, "when Boorstin assails European ideology, he may have in mind the intellectual foibles of American fellow travelers." The Old Left image of ideology, however, "has little to do," Diggins asserts, "with the real function of ideology in European politics."[14]

Although Boorstin contrasts American pragmatism, as the product of the absence of political theory, with European ideol-

ogy, as the fruit of philosophy, he fails, Diggins holds, to see that
modern European ideology was less the outgrowth of philosophy
than it was a revolt against formalism and a freeing of thought
from abstract theory and deductive treatises and systems. Conceding that the polemical connotations surrounding the concept
of ideology have produced imposing semantic problems, Diggins nevertheless asserts that the erosion in modern intellectual
history of epistemological dualisms such as abstractions-and-
experience or doctrine-and-fact has "rendered the ideologist
almost indistinguishable from the pragmatist":

> Once the debate over ideology arose in the nineteenth century
> there could no longer be a sharp distinction between the
> ideologist and the pragmatist, for pragmatism was implicit in the
> very label "ideological" since it compelled the man of ideas to
> prove that his thoughts could be realized in practice. . . .
> Attacked as being doctrinaire, the ideologist was perforce driven
> to accept the premise that, in Mannheim's words, "the only access
> to reality is to be sought in practical activity." The man of ideas
> therefore became the man of action, making "pragmatism" the
> "inevitable and appropriate outlook" for "modern man."
> Ideology thus produced . . . "a decisive turn in the formulation
> of the problem of the nature of reality." Writing in the twenties,
> Mannheim observed that . . . "The history of the concept of
> ideology from Napoleon to Marxism, despite changes in content,
> has retained the same political criterion of reality."

Examination of the function of European ideology shows that it
is marked by emotional intensity and that its appeal has to do
with power, as distinguished from Boorstin's claim that it is
characterized by intellectual consistency and that its appeal is
esthetic. Indeed, Boorstin's claim notwithstanding, Diggins concludes that "ideology is hardly alien to Boorstin's own philosophical premises . . . ironically, the functional nature of ideology corresponds to Boorstin's own philosophy of history
and partakes of what he calls America's 'naturalistic approach to
values.' "[15]

    While maintaining, as it were, that the contrast between an
ideological Europe and a pragmatic America exists only in the
minds of American Marxists (or ex-Marxists) with their highly
selective view of ideology, Diggins also shares Pole's objections to

Boorstin's selectivity in focusing on winners and making the "is" the "ought" so as to drain history of moral content. Diggins finds in Boorstin's work "no wise and courageous losers, no agonizing thoughts about might-have-beens. . . . What happened, happened. Those who survived, survived." Boorstin's regarding the triumphant facts as normative virtually amounts to "bestowing upon every victor the blessings of history." This view, moreover, "historicizes morality." The reduction of history to nature and experience "has confined ethics to precisely that natural world from which philosophers have sought to rescue it" and, in denying human causation, has created a "history without moral dimension." Boorstin's theory of history "takes ethics as a given, for it is based solely on the will and power to transform reality with no regard for the moral demands of the 'ought.' " Accordingly, "givenness"

> ignores the role of the active mind and thus rules out the possibility of ultimate value—the quest for transcendence. In rendering to "the mystical power of our land" the creative magic and higher awareness that properly pertain to the human mind . . . [Boorstin] denies Americans their highest freedom—their ability to distinguish the realm of morality from the realm of nature and to create values through conscious human choice.[16]

David Hackett Fischer also condemns the historicizing of morality. He refers, as Diggins does in his comments on the European-like qualities of Boorstin's ideas, to nineteenth-century European thought and to the writings of E.H. Carr as well as Boorstin. He defines the genetic fallacy as one which "mistakes the becoming of a thing for the thing which it has become." It involves the erroneous assumption that one can substitute the actual history of past developments for a nontemporal logical analysis of them and for the logical presentation of the interpretation resulting from that analysis. "The most hateful forms of the genetic fallacy," Fischer states, "are those which convert a temporal sequence into an ethical system—history into morality." The movement of historicism in Germany in the years 1790–1930 organized its ethics "around the nasty idea that whatever is becoming, is right." In the works of E.H. Carr "morality marches triumphant through history, always on the side of the big battalions." As for Boorstin's views, "Something of the fallacy of ethical historicism appears in the absurd and dangerous idea that America's rise to power and prosperity is a measure of its moral excellence—that the history of the Republic can be seen, in short, as a system of morality."[17]

An obvious corollary of the condemnation of treating the "is" and winners so as to historicize morality—triumph makes right—is the contention that losers are part of history, that historiography which omits them presents a distorted picture of the past. This argument, to be sure, was heard before the emergence of consensus history. It is the main theme of Herbert Butterfield's *The Whig Interpretation of History* which appeared in 1931. American historians who now echo Butterfield's protest in a different context do so with a sense of urgency: "The success fetish," Thomas A. Kreuger claims, "has almost completely blocked the downwardly mobile out of American history."[18] Objection to the enshrinement of winners has been accompanied, moreover, by an enormous increase in the publication of works about losers. Since the publication of Nathan Glazer's and Daniel P. Moynihan's *Beyond the Melting Pot* in 1963, scores of new historical studies of immigrant ethnic groups and blacks, as well as reprints, have appeared and this surge has reached the classroom.[19] The titles of three anthologies compiled for college students connote sympathetic concern for losers and resentment at the conduct of those who have defeated them: Melvin Steinfeld, *Cracks in the Melting Pot: Racism and Discrimination in American History* (1970); Thomas R. Frazier, *The Underside of American History: Other Readings* (1971), which considers Indians, immigrants, poor whites, blacks, and women; and Paul Jacobs, Saul Landau, and Eve Pell, *To Serve the Devil* (1971), which underlines the plight of Indians, blacks, Chicanos, Hawaiians, Japanese, Chinese, and Puerto Ricans.

Martin T. Katzman, writing in a scholarly journal, seems to point to losers when he concludes that ethnic concentration in the United States has been more static than generally believed, reflecting persistent economic inequalities.[20] In order to maintain a balanced perspective on winners and losers, however, one ought to bear in mind that many immigrants or their sons or grandsons, daughters or granddaughters, have become winners. This does not mean that they have necessarily been totally "melted," as the title of Michael Novak's recent book, *The Rise of the Unmeltable Ethnics*, suggests.[21] To the extent that ethnics maintain cultural enclaves, they are beyond the melting pot. At the same time, to the extent that they are active in politics, they are active winners—often engaged in conflict. Sociologist Milton M. Gordon provides a basis for understanding this difference, distinguishing between "behavioral assimilation" and "structural assimilation." The former refers to acculturation, the latter to "the entrance of the immigrants and their descendants into the social cliques, organizations, institutional activities, and general civic life of the receiving society." Gordon finds that acculturation or behavioral assimilation has taken place to a considerable degree but that structural assimilation, with some exceptions, has not been extensive. In this context, many ethnics might be culturally assimilated and politically inactive. Novak refers to the ethnic who is only to some extent culturally assimilated and is politically active. This activity does not necessarily make the ethnic fully assimilated in a structural way, however, because, as Gordon states, a "further distinction must be made between, on the one hand, those activities of the general civic life which involve earning a living, carrying out political responsibilities, and engaging in the instrumental affairs of the larger community, and, on the other hand, activities which create personal friendship patterns, frequent home intervisiting, communal worship, and communal recreation."[22]

Sociologists indicate the complexity of the question of variation in kinds and degrees of winning and losing in their studies of status inconsistency—discrepancies between an individual's relative ranks in achieved status systems (educational or occupational attainment) and ascribed status systems (race, religion, and ethnicity).[23] This question, as we shall see in chapter 7, is in a certain sense irrelevant to the historian who views American history from a New Left perspective and insists that even a winner—let us say an ethnic immigrant's grandson, an accountant and suburbanite who is assimilated in every way—is a loser. Meanwhile, the increased attention to Americans whose identification as losers is widely agreed upon pertains to a need felt by many historians of various persuasions—not just critics of consensus history. I.A. Newby quotes Hartz: "The distinctive element in American civilization [is] its social freedom, its social equality." Newby asserts that "this statement needs more modification than Hartz gives it to be applicable to the history of Negro Americans." Commenting on Boorstin's *The Americans: The Colonial Experience*, Newby makes an observation that until a short time ago applied to most writing on nearly all aspects of American history: "The colonial experience, to judge by his account, was a white man's experience."[24] Still, if history without losers is distorted history, so is history without winners. Sound history must pay due attention to both.

PART TWO

Consensus and

Public Policy

Chapter Four
Conflict within Consensus:
Party Politics

Abundance, Uniqueness, and Turning Outward

David M. Potter's important study, *People of Plenty: Economic Abundance and the American Character*, published in 1954, is essentially a consensus work. As we have seen in chapter 2, the various inquiries into the causes of the emergence of consensus contain frequent references to the abundance of land or resources or both. Dahl, for example, assigns a crucial role to this factor in both the pre-Civil War years when consensus developed and in the post-Civil War era when consensus persisted. Regarding the latter period, Howard Quint, a leading historian of socialism in America, also stresses the significance of abundance. He concedes that folk beliefs "have an amazing persistency and an undeniable importance in the shaping of the national character," but, noting that "most Americans could enjoy consumption goods beyond the reach of foreign workers," he observes:

> This latter factor bears attention in the light of repeated claims by cultural nationalists that the vista of the "American Dream" classless society, a fervently embraced idea of "uniqueness" and "givenness," and a frontier individualism were together responsible for counteracting socialism's appeal to the country's wage earners.[1]

Quint qualifies his assertion of the importance of abundance by expressing it relatively—Americans had greater access to consumption goods than foreign workers. Nor does Quint advance a monocausational thesis. Even a cursory inquiry into the relationship of abundance to national development indicates that such caution is appropriate. Citing the case of Venezuela, Thomas C. Cochran points out that the presence of the material requirements for abundance does not, in the absence of certain noneconomic factors, necessarily result in abundance—the conversion of ample natural resources into capital and consumer goods—while William N. Chambers, referring to today's new nations, says that workable solutions for noneconomic (political) problems do not automatically follow economic (and social) advance.[2] Samuel P. Huntington attributes violence and instability in the emerging nations to the lag of the development of political institutions behind social and economic change.[3] Cochran describes a situation in which noneconomic retardation is accompanied by economic retardation; Chambers and Huntington point to the persistence of noneconomic retardation despite economic advance. Such instances—and the constrasting combination in America of plentiful resources, prodigious exploitation of them, relatively wide distribution of the product, and a liberal-democratic political consensus, subject to confinement as we have seen in chapter 3—suggest that the American Way of Life is unique or, as Benson puts it, "relatively unique" in a "*combination* of characteristics."[4]

If the American Way of Life is unique, then we cannot induce other nations to emulate it. Boorstin subscribes to both parts of this proposition. The genius of American democracy, he claims, comes in part from a "peculiar and unrepeatable combination of historical circumstances."[5] He warns:

> if we rely on the "philosophy of American democracy" as a weapon in the world-wide struggle, we are relying on a weapon which may prove a dud. It may prove so because, as I shall try to show in this book, the peculiar strengths of American life have saved us from the European preoccupation with political dogmas and have left us inept and uninterested in political theory.[6]

Nontheoretical salesmen from a nation which "has had a unity and coherence unknown in Europe,"[7] cannot find customers for their product among ideologically divided Europeans. Boorstin thus labels the American Way of Life "Not for Export."[8] Similarly, Carl N. Degler, discussing the consequences of our lack of ideology for our present relations with the new nations, declares, "The fact is that we have no ideology, for by definition an

ideology is capable of being made universal."⁹ Accordingly, he
believes that democracy, in the Western sense, and capitalism
will make little, if any, headway in the underdeveloped areas in
the foreseeable future.¹⁰ Hartz observes, "Since the American
liberal creed is a submerged faith, even in its Alger form, it is
obviously not a theory which other people can easily appreciate
or understand."¹¹

We seem to be confronted with a paradox—to use one of
Hartz's favorite words. Once comparative analysis has established that American history is a singular phenomenon, with
what do we compare the unique? Meyers, so to speak, offers
one sort of answer. He writes that Hartz's cosmopolitan scholarship actually encourages a historiographical turning inward:
"once the ground has been cleared of spurious correlations,
new work should be built of native materials."¹² "Yet," Higham
comments, "the interest of the consensus historians focused so
exclusively on the differences between the United States and
Europe that they only prepared the way for a more explicit,
fully developed kind of comparative study."¹³ Taken together,
Meyers' and Higham's observations recommend that historians
simultaneously turn inward and outward.

In turning inward, as we shall do shortly, we do not deny
the great value of comparative analysis. Intelligent comparisons
will provide fresh insights and suggest questions which will,
in turn, produce more precise definitions of the nature of
similarities, if they are discovered, or of differences, if they
become evident.¹⁴ Nor does comparative history have to be
consensus history since it can, indeed, address itself to
similarities and differences between the conflicts in two or
more nations.¹⁵ Finally, we should not accept assertions of
America's uniqueness without taking cognizance of a number
of studies that call attention to the comparability of the American experience with that of other nations. "Certainly it is desirable," Hollingsworth writes, "for the historian to stress the distinctive quality of whatever subject he is studying. . . . But it is
also important for a society to understand the degree of similarity between itself and other societies."¹⁶ To cite only one striking example, Kenneth Barkin intensively compares American
and German Populism and concludes that "it is difficult to view
the two populisms . . . as anything but distinctive variations on a

common theme."[17] Reading Barkin's study, one can almost hear Mrs. Mary Elizabeth Lease exclaim to a German populist convention, "Deutscher Bauer, sie sollten nicht so viel Korn saen aber viel mehr Hölle erzeugen" (Raise less corn and more hell).

Socioeconomic Conditions, Politics, and Policies, 1914–1962

The frequent linking of abundance to consensus suggests, as just noted, noncomparative as well as comparative inquiry into American development. Summarizing recent studies of the implications of affluence in the 1960s for Americans' feelings of trust in others, optimism, social alienation, political partisanship, class awareness, religiosity and religious bias, and racial prejudice, Robert E. Lane cautions:

> The relationships between individual affluence and political attitudes are comparatively well known, but the relationships between communal affluence and political behavior are somewhat obscure. Even more obscure are the relationships between *change* in affluence and *change* in politics.

Implying a challenge to historians, Lane states, "We cannot explore (for want of time and survey data) these changes in the earlier period, so we will focus upon some recent changes."[1]

Since the early 1960s some political scientists have engaged in a type of research akin to that suggested by Lane's remark. They have examined relationships between (a) *socioeconomic conditions* (which comprise the degree of affluence—per capita and median income—as well as such factors as urbanization, industrialization, and percentage of foreign-born residents), (b) *political variables* (such as interparty competition and voter turnout), and (c) *public policies* (such as per pupil expenditure, old-age assistance, unemployment compensation, aid to the blind, and aid to dependent children). Their investigations to date show that a great deal remains to be done in order to delineate with some precision the relationships that Lane finds obscure. If affluence is related to consensus, the relationship between affluence and politics is, in view of disagreement among students of this subject, by no means clear.

Some of the investigators in this area assert that changes

in the degree of urbanization—a concomitant of *affluence*—produce changes in the degree of interparty competition—an aspect of *politics*.[2] Others do not find evidence supporting this proposition.[3] Much less attention has been devoted to this relationship, however, than to another question. In an a−b−c sequence—conditions, politics (competition), and policies—there is significant correlation between a and c, conditions and policies. The question arises, is b an intervening variable between a and c? What is the causal role of politics? Some scholars conclude that the states which are more highly developed socioeconomically—wealthier, more urbanized, more ethnically diversified—"tend to be more liberal in their public policies regardless of the level of party competition," that "the level of interparty competition is not the crucial factor intervening between socioeconomic factors and policy outputs."[4] In this view, changes in affluence are more significant as determinants of policy outputs than are changes in politics, whatever the sources of the latter. Other students, however, conclude that "even if there are direct effects from the environment, party competition still serves as an intervening variable [although] it is not possible to estimate the exact magnitude of the impact of party competition," and this impact varies depending on the policy in question (being greater with respect to aid to dependent children and unemployment compensation than with respect to per pupil expenditure, which "seems to be virtually a pure case of . . . function of the wealth of the state," and old-age assistance).[5]

Still other political scientists are very reluctant on the basis of any such correlations to assign special causal weight to any single factor in the a−b−c sequence—a restraint which is well founded since correlations, by themselves, do not definitively establish the cause of anything. These prudent researchers find greater correlation between the Welfare−Education dimension of state policy on the one hand and interparty competition *and* affluence on the other hand than between the Highway—Natural Resources dimension of public policy and these political and economic factors, but they underline *and* because they find that neither interparty competition nor affluence is "significantly more important than the other" an as independent variable affecting policy. They are wary of a "single determinant structure of causality" and stress "multidimensionality in state economics, politics, and public policy."[6]

It is neither possible nor necessary to offer a judgment here about causal relationships. As the authors of a review-essay on the relevant literature caution, "students of state politics must be extremely cautious and selective when building upon the foundations established by these studies, for they run the risk of erecting impressive structures upon shifting sands."[7] In any event, political scientists' concern with the causal role of interparty competition does suggest a question relevant to present concerns. Conclusions which emphasize the role of interparty competition as an independent variable are "consistent with the theory that given the advantages possessed by the haves, the organization, continuity, and visibility of alternatives provided through interparty competition is important for the capacity of the have-nots to attain policies in their own interests."[8] In other words, when the relative strength of the parties is 51–49, the haves will pay greater heed to the demands of the have-nots than when the ratio of party strength is, say, 58–42. The pertinent question here is: Who has the 51 (or 58) and who has the 49 (or 42)? Consideration of the identity of the majority (or winning) and minority parties is quite relevant to an assessment of consensus historians' main thesis regarding politics—the similarity of the major parties.

Thomas R. Dye concludes that Democratic or Republican control of a state government affects the extent to which revenue is obtained from the state and federal as opposed to local governments. "On the whole, however," he writes, "Democratic or Republican control of a state government is not a good predictor of state policy outcomes."[9] Ira Sharkansky, another leading student of state economics, politics, and policies, makes the same point, using as examples the cases of two one-party states, one Democratic and one Republican, appearing among the high-spending states and one Democratic-tending and two Republican-tending states found among the low-spending states as of 1962.[10] Sharkansky shows not only that Democratic or Republican control is inadequate as a predictor of state policy outcomes but also that (1) state expenditures tend to remain stable and minimal because of incremental budgeting

procedures—confinement of deliberations to consideration of
the increment of change that is proposed in existing tax and
spending policies—and (2) the pattern of historically conservative state budget decisions is modified significantly—that
is, new bases from which incrementalists begin subsequent
calculations are set—in response to nationwide influences:
the nationwide crises or trauma of depression, war, and postwar reconversion; increases in population; economic development (the automobile, for example); and federal spending
(which, needless to say, also changes in response to nationwide
stimuli).[11]

Yet the states' responses to nationwide inducements to
change are far from uniform. Sharkansky is able to demonstrate "Deviant Records of Government Expenditure" on the
part of individual states with considerable precision. Unlike
many other studies in the field which focus on total state expenditures (state plus local expenditures), his distinguishes between federal expenditures, state expenditures (which include
federal grants), and local expenditures. In tracing out patterns
of expenditures for the three levels of government from 1902
to 1966, Sharkansky reveals a "complicated shifting up and
down" of federal, state, and local shares of spending on "common domestic functions"—functions which involve expenditures by all three levels of government. He also finds "odd
collections" of states that deviate high and low from prevailing
nationwide trends in state expenditures in the successive
periods of depression, war, and postwar reconversion: "Both
the upward and downward deviants include states with relatively high and low levels of personal income per capita, urbanization, and industrialization; and each deviant includes
states that tend to be one-party Republican, one-party Democratic, and two-party competitive." Sharkansky concludes that
the impact of external pressures is conditioned by each state's
complex, peculiar political and economic environment, embracing particular values, alliances, and commitments. Nationwide forces do not "operate on a clean slate . . . personalities,
political opportunities, special economic and social conditions
may have a bearing on government expenditures." Regional
traditions, too, should appear in any list of "non-crisis
stimuli."[12]

Sharkansky presents additional complexities when he analyzes the relationship between state and local expenditures. On the one hand, state expenditures tend to increase in states where per capita state expenditures are relatively low or where per capita personal income is high. On the other hand, state expenditures sometimes show an inverse relationship with economic development: "In a number of poor states . . . the state government has assumed an abnormal proportion of financial responsibilities in order to compensate for the inadequacies of local tax bases." It is local government spending that is most consistent with the level of economic resources since it derives from tax revenues which depend on those resources. Additional indications of the complexity of spending policies are unnecessary here, and those that have been cited should not be permitted to obscure Sharkansky's conclusion which is most germane to our inquiry: "The political characteristics of voter turnout, the strength of the Democratic and Republican parties, the intensity of interparty competition, and the equity of legislative apportionment show little correspondence with state spending."[13] This conclusion accords with the consensus theme of similarity in policy amid political diversity. There are, it is true, states with particular characteristics in regard to the relative strength of the parties which deviate from trends in spending that prevail among other states with similar political traits—in this sense there is diversity in policy amid similarity in politics—but, as Sharkansky points out, within the various categories of deviant states the theme of similarity in policy amid political diversity applies.

When Dye, Sharkansky, and other political scientists illustrate with a few examples—that is, references to particular states—the point that Democratic or Republican control is not a reliable predictor of state policy outcomes, they arouse the historian's curiosity as to what would be shown by a comprehensive examination of the states on a state-by-state basis over an extended time span, in earlier eras as well as in the recent period. In a chapter, "Party Systems and Public Policy," Dye does treat the states in a comprehensive way in the process of examining the relationship in the years 1954–1962 between partisanship (party strength in seats in upper and lower houses and votes for governors) and state policy outcomes, while controlling for the effect of economic development, but in his correlational analysis he uses aggregate figures without referring to any particular state.[14] In his chapter, "Economic Development and State Political Systems," Dye provides data on the distribution of states by Democratic and Republican control of state governments in the decade 1954–1964 on a state-by-state basis,[15] but there he is not concerned with the relationship between party strength and policy outputs. He is concerned, rather, with the relationship between socioeconomic development and party strength—a matter we shall consider after we have looked at the relationship between partisanship and policy outcomes. (Incidentally, from his analyses of party strength and policy outcomes, controlling for economic development; of economic development and policy outcomes, controlling for party strength; and of interparty competition and policy outcomes, controlling for economic development, Dye concludes that economic development is a better predictor of policy outcome than party strength[16] and that "party competition itself appears to have little independent effect on policy outcomes."[17])

Richard E. Dawson specifies particular states when he examines the relationships between socioeconomic conditions (per capita income, median family income, urbanization, industrialization, ethnic diversity), interparty competition, and policy outputs over extended time periods—1914–1929, 1930–1945, 1946–1962—rather than focusing on these relationships, as other studies do, at a given point in time or for a period of a few years or a decade (although he measures socioeconomic development as of 1929, 1945, and 1963). However, he deals only incidentally with party strength—which party received what percentage of the vote—since his basic concern is with "the impact of interparty competition as an intervening variable between socioeconomic conditions and state policy outputs."[18] (His conclusion on this point, like Dye's, is that "the level of interparty competition is not the crucial factor, intervening between socioeconomic factors and policy outputs."[19]) We can present data appropriate to our concern here by combining data from various tables in Dawson's study and adding the factor of partisanship by indicating the number of gubernatorial victories for both major parties in each of the three periods which Dawson examines.[20] Victories in gubernatorial contests are useful in examining the relationship between partisanship and policy, but, of course, they do not constitute a precise measurement of time in office or of party strength at the polls. (In regard to time of incumbency, seventeen states of the thirty-six we shall con- sider first had four-year gubernatorial terms and twelve states had two-year terms during the entire period 1914–1962; five states switched during the period from two- to four-year terms, one from three- to four-year terms, and one from one- to two-year terms.[21] Calculations which reflect these differences yield percentages for lengths of party incumbency only slightly dif- ferent from the percentages based only on numbers of victories, as one might expect from a glance, given the nearly equal divi- sion of the seventeen states having four-year terms among Dawson's three categories of socioeconomic development—five High, seven Medium, five Low—and the numbers of Democrats and Republicans elected in these states: California, Delaware, Illinois, Pennsylvania, Washington—High; Florida, Indiana, Missouri, Montana, Oregon, Utah, Wyoming—Medium; Ala- bama, Kentucky, Mississippi, North Carolina, West Virginia —Low.)

We shall provide a precise measurement of party strength when we turn our attention to the relationship between socioeconomic conditions and partisanship. In fact, anticipating discussion of this matter, we shall group the states according to the levels of socioeconomic development which Dawson assigns to them, first presenting in this manner data for the thirty-six states which exhibited the same level of socioeconomic develop- ment for all three periods, 1914–1929, 1930–1945, 1946–1962. Then we shall discuss the impact on party strength of the Great Depression and Lane's question about the relationships between change in affluence and change in communal politics. In re- sponding to Lane's question we shall present data for the ten states which experienced a shift in level of socioeconomic devel- opment from one period to another (Minnesota and Nebraska are not analyzed in Dawson's study, presumably because their legislatures are elected on a nonpartisan ballot). Data on inter- party competition are provided not as part of a discussion of causal relationships but as the basis for some simple calcula- tions which will enable us to compare the politics of the period 1914–1962 with the politics of the era of the second party system, 1824–1854, which we shall consider in the last two sections of this chapter. In table 1, levels of socioeconomic development and policy outputs are designated H for High, M for Medium, and L for Low. The major parties are designated D for Democratic and R for Republican. Dawson's measurements of policy outputs are Per Capita Expenditures for Education, 1914–1929, and Per Pupil Expenditures for Education, 1930–1945 and 1946–1962. With respect to interparty competition, Dawson categorizes states according to composite percentage of the total vote received by the majority party gubernatorial candidate and the average proportions of seats held by the majority party in the upper and lower houses of state legislatures. 59.9 percent or less is highly competitive; 60.0–74.9 percent is medium, 75.0 percent and over is low.[22]

Table 1.

States High in Socioeconomic Development	1914–1929				1930–1945				1946–1962			
	Wins D	R	Policy Output	Compe- tition	Wins D	R	Policy Output	Compe- tition	Wins D	R	Policy Output	Compe- tition
California	0	3	H*	H*	1	3	H*	M	2	3	H*	H*
Connecticut	0	8	H*	M	6	2	H*	H*	4	2	H*	H*
Delaware	0	4	M	H*	1	3	H*	H*	2	2	H*	H*
Illinois	0	4	M	M	2	2	M	H*	2	2	H*	H*
Massachusetts	1	7	M	M	5	3	H*	H*	5	4	H*	H*
Michigan	1	7	H*	L	3	5	H*	M	7	2	M	M
New Jersey	4	2	H*	M	3	2	H*	M	3	2	H*	H*
New York	5	3	H*	H*	5	1	H*	H*	1	4	H*	H*
Ohio	5	3	M	M	5	3	M	H*	5	3	M	M
Pennsylvania	0	4	M	L	1	3	L	H*	2	3	H*	H*
Rhode Island	1	7	M	H*	6	2	H*	H*	7	2	H*	H*
Washington	1	3	M	L	3	1	H*	H*	2	2	H*	H*
	18	55			41	30			42	31		

States Medium in Socioeconomic Development

	Wins D	R	Policy Output	Compe- tition	Wins D	R	Policy Output	Compe- tition	Wins D	R	Policy Output	Compe- tition
Arizona	4	4	H	M*	8	0	H	L	4	5	H	L
Colorado	4	4	H	H	4	4	M*	H	5	3	M*	H
Florida	4	0	L	L	4	0	M*	L	5	0	M*	L
Indiana	0	4	M*	M*	3	1	M*	H	2	2	M*	H
Iowa	0	8	M*	L	3	5	M*	M*	3	6	M*	M*
Kansas	1	7	H	M*	2	5	M*	M*	2	7	M*	M*
Maine	1	7	L	M*	2	6	L	L	3	6	L	M*
Missouri	1	3	H	M*	3	1	H	H	4	0	H	H

Table 1 continued

States Medium in Socioeconomic Development	1914–1929				1930–1945				1946–1962			
	Wins D	R	Policy Output	Compe-tition	Wins D	R	Policy Output	Compe-tition	Wins D	R	Policy Output	Compe-tition
Montana	3	1	M*	H	2	2	L	M*	1	3	M*	H
Oregon	1	3	M*	L	1	2	H	M*	1	6	H	M*
Texas	8	0	L	L	8	0	L	L	9	0	M*	L
Utah	3	1	H	H	4	0	M*	M*	0	4	L	H
Wyoming	3	2	H	M*	3	2	H	H	2	3	H	H
	33	44			47	28			41	45		

States Low in Socioeconomic Development												
Alabama	4	0	L*	L*	4	0	L*	L*	5	0	L*	L*
Arkansas	8	0	L*	L*	8	0	L*	L*	9	0	L*	L*
Georgia	8	0	L*	L*	7	0	L*	L*	6	0	L*	L*
Kentucky	2	2	L*	M	3	1	M	M	4	0	L*	M
Mississippi	4	0	L*	L*	4	0	L*	L*	4	0	L*	L*
North Carolina	4	0	L*	L*	4	0	L*	L*	4	0	L*	L*
North Dakota	0	7	H	M	4	3	M	L*	2	8	M	L*
South Carolina	7	0	L*	L*	4	0	L*	L*	5	0	L*	L*
South Dakota	2	6	H	M	2	6	M	M	1	8	M	M
Tennessee	7	1	L*	M	8	0	L*	L*	7	0	L*	L*
West Virginia	1	3	M	M	4	0	L*	M	3	1	L*	M
	47	19			52	10			50	17		

*Same level as level of socioeconomic development

We shall not draw from these data any conclusions about the causal role of interparty competition—concerning which political scientists, using sophisticated quantitative analytical techniques, have failed as noted to arrive at any agreement. We can, however, indicate the complexity of this matter in a simple way by presenting these tabulations:

Socio-economic Develop-ment	Number of States	Number of States with Same Levels of Socio-economic Development and Party Competition			Number of States with Same Levels of Socio-economic Development and Policy Output		
		1914–29	1930–45	1946–62	1914–29	1930–45	1946–62
High	12	4	9	10	5	9	10
Medium	13	6	5	4	4	6	7
Low	11	6	8	8	8	8	9
	36	16	22	22	17	23	26

Overall totals show no significant differential between similarity of levels in regard to socioeconomic development and interparty competition (60 of 108 instances or 55.5 percent) and similarity of levels in regard to socioeconomic development and policy output (66 of 108 instances or 61.1 percent). Yet Dye concludes from correlational analysis of 54 policy outcomes, 1960–1964, divided into five categories (education, welfare, highways, regulation of public morality, taxation and revenue) that although 49 are "significantly associated with at least one of the measures of economic development . . . party competition has *no apparent independent effect* on 52 of the 54 policy outcomes investigated."[23]

Considering the time factor, one notes that the change from the first to the second and third periods in the number of states showing identity of levels was substantial in the high category of socioeconomic development in both the development-competition area (from 4 to 9 and 10) and the development-policy area (from 5 to 9 and 10), but not in the medium and low categories. This suggests differences in responses to the Great Depression—a matter to which we shall return below. A comment on the states in the low category of socioeconomic development is also appropriate. Political scientists who study nationwide political trends, especially those who utilize macroanalysis, invariably mention the special behavior of the eleven Southern (ex-Confederate) states, whose traits sociologist John Shelton Reed, using sophisticated analysis of opinion, identifies in *The Enduring South: Subcultural Persistence in Mass Society.*[24] Nine of the eleven states in the low category of socioeconomic development form a continuous geographical bloc, and seven of these nine (Kentucky and West Virginia are the exceptions) are in the Solid South. The appearance of the heavily Republican Dakotas in the low category raises the question whether states in this category tend to swing decisively one way or the other in partisanship. As we shall see, there is good reason to answer this question affirmatively.

Returning to our main concern, the relationship between partisanship and policy, we can readily see without engaging in sophisticated correlational analysis evidence of the consensus theme of the similarity of the major parties. If we look at the data for the twelve states in the high category of socioeconomic development in the latter two periods, we may note that these states display *limited variation in policy* (9 High, 2 Medium, 1 Low, 1930–1945, and 10 High, 2 Medium, 1946–1962) *amid political diversity* (limited variation in interparty competition—9 High, 3 Medium, 1930–1945, and 10 High, 2 Medium, 1946–1962 —but considerable variation between states and within states in results at the polls: within states both parties enjoyed at least one victory in every state in the second and third periods, whereas the Democrats had been winless in five states in the first period). Thus differences in the identity of the winning party from state to state at a given time or for the entire period 1930–1962 or within a given state from time to time did not, with the exception of Pennsylvania's low per pupil expenditure from 1930–1945, result in significant differences in policies between or within states.

As for the five states in the high socioeconomic-development category in which one party was all-victorious in the period 1914–1929 there was, to be sure, no variation between states at a given time or for the entire period or within states in the identity of the winning party, but the data for these states illustrate the consensus theme of the similarity of the parties in another way. If the data for the period 1930–1962 show similarity in policy amid diversity in politics, the five states in which the Republicans were all victorious in the period 1914–1929 display diversity in policy (2 High and 3 Medium) amid similarity in politics. True, to say that the same party adopted different policies in different states is not the same as saying different parties in different states adopted the same policies. Both of these findings, however, are in accord with Dye's and Sharkansky's conclusion that partisanship is not a good predictor of policy outputs, and this conclusion amounts to a negative expression of the consensus theme of the similarity of the parties. The first section of the following table (1914–1929) shows the same party following different policies (five predominantly Republican states are High in policy and four are Medium) and different parties following the same policy (three predominantly Democratic states and four predominantly Republican states are Medium in policy). The other sections provide similar examples. In table 2, the special regional quality of the states in the low category of socioeconomic development is also apparent: the one-party Democratic states are bunched in the low-policy-output column.

Table 2

Socio-economic Development	High Policy Output			Medium Policy Output			Low Policy Output		
	Dem.	Even	Rep.	Dem.	Even	Rep.	Dem.	Even	Rep.
				1914–1929					
High	0	0	8-0 3-0 7-1(2) 3-1	4-2 5-3(2)	0	4-0(3) 7-1	0	0	0
Medium	3-1 3-2	4-4(2)	7-1 3-1	3-1	0	8-0 4-0 3-1	8-0 4-0	0	7-1
Low	0	0	6-2 4-3	0	0	3-1	8-0(2) 7-0 4-0(3) 7-1	2-2	0
				1930–1945					
High	5-1 6-2(2) 3-1 5-3 3-2	0	3-1(2) 5-3	5-3	2-2	0	0	0	3-1
Medium	8-0 3-1 3-2	0	2-1	4-0(2) 3-1	4-4	5-2 5-3	8-0	2-2	6-2
Low	0	0	0	3-1	0	8-2 6-2	8-0(2) 7-0 4-0(5)	0	0
				1946–1962					
High	7-2 4-2 3-2 5-4	2-2(3)	4-1 3-2(2)	7-2 5-3	0	0	0		0
Medium	4-0	0	6-1 3-2 5-4	9-0 5-0 5-3	2-2	7-2 3-1 6-3	0	0	4-0 6-3

Key: 7–1(2) under Rep.: there were two states in which the Republicans won seven gubernatorial elections and the Democrats one in the period 1914-1929.

Table 2 continued

Socio-economic Develop-ment	High Policy Output			Medium Policy Output			Low Policy Output		
	Dem.	Even	Rep.	Dem.	Even	Rep.	Dem.	Even	Rep.
Low	0	0	0	0	0	8−1 8−2	9−0 7−0 6−0 5−0(2) 4−0(3) 3−1	0	0

Key: 7−1(2) under Rep.: there were two states in which the Republicans won seven gubernatorial elections and the Democrats one in the period 1914-1929.

Although one who has a penchant for gambling would not bet a month's pay on the predictive power of the party affiliation of the occupant of the state house with respect to level of policy output for the states in the high and medium categories of socioeconomic development, one cannot claim to have constructed an explanatory universe from policy outputs in the single area of expenditures for education, which Dawson utilizes for the period 1914−1962, or even from policy outputs in the several areas which Dye analyzes for the period 1960−1964. At the same time, one is impressed by the importance which James T. Patterson, the author of the most comprehensive study of depression-born social policies in the various states, attaches to the kinds of inquiries we have been discussing. Concluding that the variety in state policy in the 1930s is perplexing, Patterson notes that the findings of Dawson, Dye, Sharkansky, and other political scientists are suggestive regarding the question as to why some states were "little New Deal" states and others were not. Commenting on the possible causal roles of urbanization, voter participation, interparty competition, and socioeconomic development, Patterson says, "But the *sine qua non* of state progressivism seems to have been per capita wealth. Those states which had broad tax bases were able to provide more generous services than those which did not." He also concedes that the political scientists' studies in question do not account for variations in the politics and policies among states of similar socioeconomic character. He sees clues to an answer to this "riddle" in tradition—a reform tradition in some "little New Deal" states and, ironically, a tradition of reaction in others. Finally, "Perhaps the indispensable ingredient was the governor himself."[25]

If socioeconomic development was the *sine qua non* of generous policy outputs, further consideration of this factor may be in order. We have noted that the substitution of party strength for party competition in the development–politics –policy sequence with which so many political scientists are concerned yields, as it were, a consensus conclusion since partisanship does not explain policy outcomes. Is more detailed examination of the relationship between socioeconomic development and party strength justifiable? It would seem so because the assertion and denial of class conflict in American politics are components of the conflict–consensus controversy. If well-to-do folk tend to be more favorably disposed toward one party and poorer people toward the other, these tendencies should be reflected in significant differences in the relative strength of the two parties as between wealthier and poorer states. For purposes of examining this hypothesis we need a precise measurement of party strength and have thus utilized the composite which Paul T. David designates "the best general measure of party strength": a combination of data on voting for governor, senator, and representative in Congress—data from "two offices that are always voted on statewide and from a third that can be cumulated on a statewide basis."[26] David converts these data into percentages of the total popular vote for the Democratic, Republican, and "other" parties and manipulates them to present percentages for every even year from 1872 to 1970. By using Dawson's levels of socioeconomic development and David's figures for party strength, we can tabulate development and partisanship on a state-by-state basis for the periods 1914–1929, 1930–1945, and 1946–1962. Before we consider these tabulations, however, we might consider Dye's relevant findings for the period 1954–1964.

While Dye's examination of the relationships between socioeconomic development, party competition, and policy outputs utilizes macro-analysis, as noted above, he does cite the fifty states individually and places them into several ranked groups, according to precise criteria as of 1959 or 1960, under each of four headings in the area of economic development: industrialization, urbanization, income, and education.[27] He also names the states individually in classifying them into five groups according to party strength—Strong Republican, Moderate Republican, Divided, Moderate Democratic, Strong Democratic —in three tables indicating percentages of seats held by Democrats in lower and upper houses and Democratic percentages in votes for governor, 1954–1964. His measurements of party strength, unlike David's, are based only in part on voting statistics, and he employs a scale of 0–20, 20–40, etc.[28] Still, when Dye combines his three measurements of party strength and cross-tabulates these composite data with medians for four aspects of economic development (while indicating in a note which states are in each category of party strength), he provides a table (given here as table 3) which is relevant to our concern.

Table 3
Economic Development and Party Affiliation in State Government

	Strong Republican	Moderate Republican	Divided	Strong Democratic	Moderate Democratic
Urbanization	47.8	64.0	72.9	64.8	54.5
Industrialization	83.0	90.2	93.8	93.2	89.0
Income	$4989	$5620	$6063	$5897	$4069
Education	11.0	11.1	11.0	11.0	9.2

Urbanization: Percentage of the population living in urban areas, 1960
Industrialization: Percentage of the work force not in agriculture,
    fisheries, and forestry, 1960
Income: Median family income in dollars, 1959
Education: Median school year completed by population, age 25
    and over, 1960[29]

Dye offers two comments on these data. The first pertains to a matter mentioned above: "Strong Democratic and Strong Republican states tend to resemble each other in socioeconomic composition more than they resemble the divided states."[30] The figures for the divided states suggest that "economic development may be more closely related to party *competition* than to Democratic or Republican party success."[31] In fact, Dye points out that significant relationships between economic development and party success virtually disappear if one drops the eleven Southern states from the calculations: "there is really no relationship in the 39 non-Southern states between Democratic or Republican party success and urbanization, income, or education. There is, however, a significant relationship between

Democratic success and industrialization in the non-Southern states.[32]

Dye does not separate the Southern states in the analysis which he presents in his book, and we have pursued this point further by combining his groupings of states in the four areas of economic development with median figures for 1954–1964 derived from David's measurement of party strength; this is given in table 4.

Table 4

50 States

Group	Industrialization No. of States	Median D	R	Urbanization No. of States	Median D	R	Income No. of States	Median D	R	Education No. of States	Median D	R
1	11	52.7	47.1	6	50.5	48.6	1	57.4	42.3	7	50.1	49.4
2	18	52.6	46.8	12	53.3	45.8	14	52.0	47.6	13	50.8	49.0
3	11	58.0	41.2	11	53.4	46.1	17	50.1	49.4	17	50.8	48.4
4	5	53.4	46.2	10	51.7	48.2	13	56.3	43.7	5	65.1	27.0
5	3	48.0	52.0	6	59.6	40.3	4	84.5	15.1	8	75.9	23.8
6	2	45.6	53.3	5	45.8	52.2	1	97.5	2.4			

39 States

Group	Industrialization No. of States	Median D	R	Urbanization No. of States	Median D	R	Income No. of States	Median D	R	Education No. of States	Median D	R
1	11	52.7	47.1	6	50.5	48.6	1	57.4	42.3	7	50.1	49.4
2	14	50.8	48.9	10	51.4	48.4	14	52.0	47.6	13	50.8	49.0
3	6	49.5	48.4	10	52.3	47.2	16	50.1	49.6	15	50.6	49.2
4	4	52.9	46.8	6	47.9	51.9	8	48.1	50.6	2	51.0	48.9
5	2	46.1	53.7	3	53.7	46.2				2	55.0	44.9
6	2	45.6	53.3	4	45.6	53.3						

Industrialization: percentage of the work force not in agriculture, fisheries, or forestry, 1960.
Group 1: 96–100; Group 2: 91–95; Group 3: 86–90; Group 4: 81–85; Group 5: 76–80; Group 6: 61–75.
Urbanization: percentage of population living in urban areas, 1960.
Group 1: 80–89; Group 2: 70–79; Group 3: 60–69; Group 4: 50–59; Group 5: 40–49; Group 6: 30–39.
Income: median family income in dollars, 1959.
Group 1: 7,000; Group 2: 6,000–6,999; Group 3: 5,000–5,999; Group 4: 4,000–4,999; Group 5: 3,000–3,999; Group 6: 2,000–2,999.
Education: median school year completed by population, age 25 and over, 1960.
Group 1: 12–12.9; Group 2: 11–11.9; Group 3: 10–10.9; Group 4: 9–9.9; Group 5: 8–8.9.[33]

The data for 39 states might be refined through rank-order correlation of the states' figures for economic development and party strength, but their essential accord with Dye's observations is evident, even though the relationship between increasing industrialization and increasing Democratic strength does not show an unbroken progression, and there is a relationship be-

tween increasing income and increasing Democratic strength
even if one omits Alaska, the only state in Group 1. These data
afford no basis for generalizations about differences in levels of
economic development as a source of social conflict which, in
turn, affects the alignment of the electorate.

Dye's work is impressive, but in table 5 we have elected to
use Dawson's categories of socioeconomic development (combined with David's measure of party strength) because, as noted
above, Dawson covers a considerable time span. This will also
enable us to see whether Dye's observations hold for earlier
periods.

Table 5

States High in Socioeconomic Development	1914–1929 Dem.	Rep.	1930–1945 Dem.	Rep.	1946–1962 Dem.	Rep.
California	24.7	60.4	39.2	57.1	46.7	52.8
Connecticut	43.3	53.1	48.9	47.2	48.0	50.1
Delaware	45.2	52.9	47.4	51.0	49.3	50.7
Illinois	40.1	55.5	52.7	46.0	50.3	49.4
Massachusetts	43.1	52.7	48.0	48.5	51.6	47.9
Michigan	36.6	61.3	46.8	51.6	51.1	48.7
New Jersey	44.4	52.9	47.6	51.4	47.9	51.2
New York	44.2	47.7	52.4	44.1	45.9	51.5
Ohio	46.6	51.8	49.2	50.5	48.3	51.0
Pennsylvania	30.9	60.5	47.5	50.5	48.9	50.8
Rhode Island	44.6	52.5	55.0	43.5	59.0	40.9
Washington	34.0	54.6	56.4	42.2	50.9	49.7
	43.2	53.0	48.4	49.5	49.1	50.4
States Medium in Socioeconomic Development						
Arizona	56.9	40.5	71.3	28.4	54.0	46.0
Colorado	46.2	49.2	53.8	45.0	50.4	49.3
Florida	90.9	15.3	86.8	13.2	80.2	19.8
Indiana	45.9	52.0	51.0	48.3	46.9	52.3
Iowa	35.6	64.3	46.2	53.1	47.3	52.7
Kansas	36.4	59.7	43.2	53.0	43.3	55.8
Maine	41.5	58.5	42.2	56.8	43.1	56.9
Missouri	47.3	50.9	54.5	45.2	54.9	45.0
Montana	49.8	45.0	55.1	41.7	50.8	49.2
Oregon	34.4	50.5	37.6	51.7	46.3	53.7

Table 5 continued

States Medium in Socioeconomic Development	1914–1929 Dem.	Rep.	1930–1945 Dem.	Rep.	1946–1962 Dem.	Rep.
Texas	82.4	15.0	94.1	5.7	82.6	16.1
Utah	46.6	48.8	56.4	42.3	47.0	51.0
Wyoming	46.5	51.4	49.1	50.1	47.4	51.9
	46.5	50.5	53.8	45.2	47.4	51.0
States Low in Socioeconomic Development						
Alabama	80.1	14.2	88.3	10.2	89.0	10.8
Arkansas	77.7	18.0	89.8	6.7	89.3	9.6
Georgia	96.9	0.7	97.5	1.1	99.1	0.5
Kentucky	51.1	47.7	57.1	42.3	54.0	46.0
Mississippi	96.9	0.0	100.0	0.0	98.5	0.5
North Carolina	59.5	40.1	69.4	30.6	67.8	32.1
North Dakota	29.4	58.2	35.1	50.6	32.8	65.4
South Carolina	99.5	0.2	99.1	0.8	97.2	1.4
South Dakota	36.2	52.7	44.2	54.8	42.2	57.8
Tennessee	60.9	37.9	67.9	27.1	68.6	24.0
West Virginia	47.1	51.1	55.5	43.8	55.4	44.6
	60.9	37.9	69.4	27.1	68.6	24.0

At least two facts are readily apparent from a glance at the figures in table 5: the impact of the Great Depression and the inconclusiveness of the figures for the states in the high and medium categories of socioeconomic development in regard to the relationship between development and partisanship. From 1914–1929 to 1930–1945 the Democrats gained *and* the Republicans lost strength in thirty-three of the thirty-six states —the exceptions being Oregon, South Carolina, and South Dakota—but the shift was from Republican dominance to a competitive situation rather than to Democratic dominance as one would conclude from "party systems" analyses based on voting in presidential elections. Democratic strength, in median medians, rose 5.2 percentage points (from 43.2 to 48.4) in the high group and 7.3 percentage points (from 46.5 to 53.8) in the medium group, but in the third period, 1946–1962, although Democratic strength continued to rise (to 49.1) in the high group, it fell (to 47.4) in the medium group. This suggests the possibility that "the bigger they are the harder they fall," that the impact of the depression on the political behavior of the most industrialized states was more lasting. If one looks beneath the median median for the high group in the period 1946–1962, however, one finds that in the seven states which accounted for about half the nation's unemployment during the depression, Illinois and Massachusetts were only slightly Democratic while California, New Jersey, New York, Ohio, and Pennsylvania were slightly Republican. The assumption that "the bigger they are the harder they fall" conflicts, of course, with the assumption that Democratic strength rises as socioeconomic development declines. This latter assumption also collapses when one drops from consideration the states in the low category of socioeconomic development, with their special attributes.

One may call the Great Depression a downward change in affluence, a euphemism which its victims would not relish, but the data presented above do not provide an answer to Lane's question about the relationships between change in affluence and change in communal politics. In order to respond to his question in some fashion, we must turn our attention to the states which experienced a change in level of socioeconomic development from one period to another, as indicated in table 6:

Table 6

	Development		Competition		Policy		Gubernatorial Victories				Party Strength			
Level of Socioeconomic Development							D	R	D	k	D	R	D	R
Rises I to II	I	II	I	II	I	II	I		II		I		II	
Maryland	M	H	M	M*	M	M*	4	0	3	1‡	50.3	47.3	57.5	41.3
Nevada	M	H	H	H*	H	H*	3	1	3	1*	46.5	44.0	59.7	38.9
New Mexico	L	M	H	M	M	M*	3	4	8	0	48.4	49.9	56.6	43.1
Oklahoma	L	M	M	L	L	L*	4	0	4	0	50.4	45.3	62.3	36.4
Level of Socioeconomic Development Falls I to II														
Louisiana	M	L	L	L*	L	M	3	0	3	0*	93.4	0.5	99.9	0.1
New Hampshire	H	M	M	H	L	M	1	7	0	8†	42.7	55.4	46.8	52.9
Vermont	M	L	L	L*	M	M*	0	8	0	8*	25.9	71.5	35.5	64.9
Wisconsin	H	M	L	H	M	M*	0	8	1	4+	23.4	61.3	24.2	42.8

Table 6 continued

	Devel- opment	Compe- tition	Policy	Gubernatorial Victories		Party Strength			
Level of Socioeconomic Development				D	R	D	R		
Rises II to III	II III	II III	II III	II	III	II		III	
Virginia	L M	L L*	L L*	4 0	5 0†	77.5 13.7		67.6 22.5	
Level of Socioeconomic Development Falls II to III									
Idaho	M L	H H*	L L*	6 2	0 5	51.0 48.9		48.5 50.5	

I=1914−1929   II=1930−1945   III=1946−1962
*=No change   †=Insignificant or temporary change

‡Maryland had a Republican governor, 1935−1939; from 1900 to 1935 there was only one Republican governor, 1912−1916; the governors were Democrats, 1939−1951. From 1899 to 1959 New Hampshire had two Democratic governors, 1913−1915 and 1923−1925. Wisconsin had two non-Republican governors from 1901 to 1959: a Democrat, 1933−1935, and a Progressive, 1935−1939.

The median medians for Democratic strength indicate that change in party strength was greater in the eight states which experienced a change (four up and four down) in the level of socioeconomic development from period I to period II than in the twenty-five states (twelve high and thirteen medium) which did not experience such a change:

	Democratic Strength		
	I	II	Plus
Change in Level of Socioeconomic Development (8)	47.4	57.0	9.6
No Change in Level of Socioeconomic Development (25)	44.6	49.2	4.6

A somewhat different picture emerges when one considers the states in question in four categories:

Change in Level of Socioeconomic Dev't., Up	49.3	58.6	9.3
Change in Level of Socioeconomic Dev't., Down	34.3	41.1	6.8
No change in Level of Socioeconomic Dev't., High	43.2	48.4	5.2
No Change in Level of Socioeconomic Dev't., Medium	46.5	53.8	7.3

If one is concerned with macro-analysis and theory of causation, one could hypothesize that political units which experience an upward change in level of socioeconomic development from one period to another experience a greater change in the relative strength of the parties than units which experience a downward change or no change in level of socioeconomic development in the same time span. This hypothesis would have to be tested for many units and many periods. When one introduces the factor of partisanship by identifying the parties which enjoyed an increase or suffered a decline in strength, one must consider the historical developments in general and the political trends in particular of any period one examines. In the period we are concerned with, while the Democrats gained *and* the Republicans lost strength in all eight states which experienced a change in level of socioeconomic development from 1914–1929 to 1930–1945, the same kind of change in party strength occurred in twenty-four of the twenty-five states which were high or medium in socioeconomic development in both periods (and in thirty-three of the thirty-six states which were high, medium, or low in socioeconomic development in both periods).

Shifting our attention from theory of causation to practical politics, we can see that a change from a median percentage of 25.9 Democratic to 35.5 Democratic or from 23.4 to 24.2, from 1914–1929 to 1930–1945, did not afford much comfort for the Democrats of Vermont and Wisconsin. More comprehensively, among the twenty-five states whch were high or medium in level of socioeconomic development in both periods, nine states (Colorado, Connecticut, Illinois, Indiana, Missouri, New York, Rhode Island, Washington, and Utah) experienced a change in the identity of the party enjoying majority or superior strength, while among the eight states in which there was a shift in the level of socioeconomic development from one period to the next, only one (Nevada) experienced such a change. No matter what a well grounded theory of causation will show, moreover, a slightly higher change in party strength in four states out of forty-six —the four states in which the level of socioeconomic development rose from period I to period II—does not amount to a substantial alteration of the national political picture. It is possible that the percentage of units showing significant change of the kind we are concerned with would be greater if more units, say counties, were examined. If this possibility were to materialize, this outcome would differ from the findings of students of the Jacksonian era who, as we shall see, discover that certain counties which experienced a change in level of socioeconomic development continued to show the same alignment of the electorate. In sum, our response to Lane's question, tentative because it is based on limited data, suggests that neither change nor the absence of change in the level of socioeconomic development of a state produces significant social conflict having substantial impact on party strength.

Democrats and Republicans

If the relationships between partisanship and policy and between socioeconomic conditions and partisanship are nonrelationships, does this mean that our socioeconomic and political systems have been static, that what change has occurred happened smoothly and in accordance with a preordained plan? Hardly, for the investigations we have been considering, although valuable, take place at a relatively high or general level of analysis without examining political developments in detail. Their limitations become apparent when one considers the particulars of party legislative behavior at the national and state levels and voter behavior at the national, state, and local levels. To put it another way, let us turn to the second and third components of the tripartite theme of this chapter: (1) aggregate figures for socioeconomic development, voting, and policy outputs for large areal units suggest consensus, but (2) they tend to conceal the conflict which is evident at lesser levels of aggregation, but (3) this conflict occurs within the context of agreement on capitalism and democracy.

In considering legislative behavior in Congress, for present purposes we can select from a long shelf of literature a brief compilation by Clinton Rossiter, given here as table 7. These figures for the New Deal era are taken from his tabulation of voting records for the period 1933–1952. He does not claim scientific accuracy for them but seeks evidence of tendencies that distinguish the two parties:

> I have done my best to choose examples of votes in which the conflict between "liberalism" and "conservatism" . . . was a matter

of common knowledge, in which opposition to (or support of) the President was a relatively minor factor in sharpening the division, and in which the final vote . . . was the "crucial" vote on the particular issue.[1]

Table 7

Domestic Issues	Party	House Vote For	House Vote Against	Senate Vote For	Senate Vote Against
T.V.A., 1933	Dem.	284	2	48	3
	Rep.	17	89	14	17
	Other	5	—	1	—
N.R.A., 1933	Dem.	266	25	46	4
	Rep.	53	50	10	20
	Other	4	—	1	—
A.A.A., 1933	Dem.	272	24	48	5
	Rep.	39	73	14	15
	Other	4	1	1	—
Public Utilities, 1934	Dem.	203	59		
	Rep.	7	83	Voice Vote	
	Other	9	0		
Social Security, 1935	Dem.	287	13	60	1
	Rep.	77	18	14	5
	Other	7	2	2	—
Rider to Return Control of Re-lief to States, 1936	Dem.	Not		1	50
	Rep.	Before		13	4
	Other	House		—	3
Soil Conserva-tion, 1936	Dem.	246	25	49	9
	Rep.	20	64	5	11
	Other	1	8	2	—
Housing, 1937	Dem.	239	38	55	8
	Rep.	24	48	6	8
	Other	12	—	3	—
Wages and Hours, 1938	Dem.	247	41		
	Rep.	31	48	Voice Vote	
	Other	12	—		
A.A.A., 1938	Dem.	243	54	53	17
	Rep.	14	74	2	11
	Other	6	7	1	3[2]

"Did it make any difference in the 1930s and 1940s whether one voted Republican or Democrat?," Rossiter asks. "Surely it did," since Democrats provided the bulk of support for New Deal measures."[3] In view of the results of the elections of 1934 and 1936, we can assert that the electorate shared Congress' pro–New Deal sentiments. This assertion may seem superfluous, but the relationship in regard to policy between party leaders, officeholders, and activists on the one hand and rank-and-file on the other is not a simple matter, and it varies in complexity from one time to another. Comparing the positions on policy issues of party leaders and followers in the late 1950s—when the New Deal was relatively noncontroversial and "middle-of-the-roadism" marked American politics—political scientists Herbert McClosky, Paul J. Hoffman, and Rosemary O'Hara conclude: "Whereas the leaders of the two parties diverge strongly, their followers differ only moderately in their attitudes toward issues. . . . Republican followers, in fact, disagree far more with their own leaders than with leaders of the Democratic party."[4] This conclusion (stated in a 1960 article and cited by McClosky in his 1964 article summarized in chapter 3) suggests that leaders and activists are more ideological on policy issues than are followers. This does not necessarily mean, however, that the electorate was no more ideological in the 1930s than in the 1950s. It may indicate that leaders clung to ideological positions of the 1930s longer than followers did. In fact this appears to be what actually happened in many cases, for in the 1930s the electorate as well as the elected exhibited considerable partisanship and ideological commitment, both colored by a large measure of emotion.

Unusual partisanship, ideological commitment, and emotion were certainly evident in the campaign and election of 1936. The election of 1932, Burnham says, was "the last of the sequence beginning in 1896 rather than the first of the New Deal generation."[5] The depression vote of 1932, Lubell writes, "still mirrored the orbit of conflict of the old Republican order."[6] With the election of 1936, on the other hand, American politics became a new ball game, qualitatively as well as quantitatively. This change, Lubell concludes, was evident before the election: "Not only in Washington but throughout the country 1935 was the year of decision. To go back to the old order or to move forward to something different? That was the question posed for decision in 1935, in countless different ways, in every phase of life."[7] It was in "The Year of Decision" that the "shift in the basis of Roosevelt's appeal 'from acreage to population,' to use Raymond Moley's phrase, occurred . . . the key to the change was the rise of a common class consciousness among all workers."[8] Unlike previous realignments of the electorate, which had been largely sectional, the New Deal realignment drew "the same class-conscious line of economic interest across the entire country."[9] Nor was class consciousness confined to workers: "The balloting revealed as much class feeling among the higher-income Republicans. If Roosevelt solidified the lower class, he also welded the upper class."[10]

William E. Leuchtenburg also emphasizes class consciousness in the 1930s and the ideological division which accompanied it:

> Labor's support of FDR riveted attention on the most significant political development of the Roosevelt years, the nationalization of American politics. Class replaced section as the critical determinant of partisan disposition. . . .
>
> This sharp cleavage was the result of the impact not only of the Great Depression but also of the New Deal, which established the Democrats as the party of big government and the workingman, the Republicans as the party of limited government and business. . . .
>
> In the thirties, the parties became more polarized, and it became easier for voters to relate their decisions at the polls to policy preferences. Although the two parties remained loose confederations of local organizations, many of which had small interest in ideology, they could now be distinguished by their attitudes toward the welfare state.[11]

Leuchtenburg also makes an observation which historians who contrast the independence from class of American politics with the class orientation of European politics may ponder: "By 1948, nearly 80 percent of workers were voting Democratic, a percentage which, as Seymour Lipset had pointed out, is higher than that ever reported by left-wing parties in Europe."[12]

In 1936, Hofstadter notes, "the various reform and recovery measures instituted by Franklin D. Roosevelt were challenged almost in their totality by Republicans who saw in them the end of the American system."[13] The emotion which marked the clash between challengers and defenders of the New Deal in 1936 is difficult to recapture, but Leuchtenburg is helpful:

> As the 1936 campaign got underway, the note of class conflict sometimes reached a high pitch. At an excited night meeting at Forbes Field in Pittsburgh, a stern-faced Danton, State Senator Warren Roberts, spat out the names of the Republican oligarchs: Mellon, Grundy, Pew, Rockefeller. The crowd greeted each name with a resounding "boo." "You could almost hear the swish of the guillotine blade," wrote one reporter afterwards. Then came Governor George Earle, their handsome Mirabeau, and he too churned up the crowd against the enemies of their class. "There are the Mellons, who have grown fabulously wealthy from the toil of men of iron and steel . . . Grundy, whose sweatshop operators have been the shame and disgrace of Pennsylvania for a generation; Pew, who strives to build a political and economic empire with himself as dictator; the duPonts, whose dollars were earned with the blood of American soldiers; Morgan, financier of war." As he sounded each name, the crowd interrupted him with a chorus of jeers against the business leaders. Then the gates opened at a far corner of the park; a motor-cycle convoy put-putted its way into the field, followed by an open car in which rode Franklin Delano Roosevelt, grinning and waving his hat, and the crowd, whipped to a frenzy, roared its welcome to their champion.[14]

Today's youth may attribute the impact of Leuchtenburg's report to his facile pen, his selectivity, the exaggeration typical of political rhetoric, or unsophisticated politics, but Americans who remember the thirties will find this anecdote of a piece with the temper of the times—marked not just by emotion but by emotion arising from division along socioeconomic lines.

For anyone who has some knowledge of the 1930s, the partisanship, class-ideological commitment (or position on welfare statism), and emotion of the decade are, it is true, implicit in the voting record Rossiter presents, but aggregate figures on legislative roll calls do not tell us directly about the battles within and between parties and the clashes of interest groups that precede the legislation of policy. "These figures," Rossiter writes, "give no indication of the jockeying that went on for weeks

before each final vote, nor do they account for the range of
enthusiasm or the varieties of motivation that marked the votes
of the Fors and Againsts on each major issue."[15] Daniel Nelson's
account of the passage of the Social Security Act illustrates
Rossiter's point. The friends of unemployment insurance were
bitterly divided over a number of issues: a national system vs. a
state system, the latter involving questions of tax offsets and state
discretion vs. state differentials; inclusion vs. exclusion of em-
ployee contributions; and actuarially determined vs. dole-like
benefits, which were an aspect of the basic, long-standing prevention vs. compensation conflict. The politicians and adminis-
trators who formulated the measure necessarily took into account political and constitutional limitations, both of which mili-
tated against a national system. Labor, temporarily peeved at
Roosevelt, was passive, and the influence of the New Emphasis
men in the business community was swiftly declining. With opposition to the New Deal rapidly rising, it may have been, Nelson
implies, the last chance to enact an unemployment-insurance
law—at least for an indefinite period.[16] One cannot infer from
the overwhelmingly favorable vote, the most one-sided in
Rossiter's table, this story which, as Nelson tells it, is a cliff-
hanger.

Nor do aggregate voting figures for relatively large areas
tell us about individual voters—who, for example, the affluent
or nonaffluent were, how they stood on particular issues,
whether they voted, how they voted, and why they voted the way
they did. A case in point at the national level may be found in the
writings of political scientists who identify party systems by
alignments of the electorate. They maintain that we have had
only five party systems since the founding of the nation:
1789–1820, 1828–1854/60, 1860–1893, 1894–1932, 1932–?[17]
The over-all trends in voting in the periods 1914–1929 and
1930–1945 cited above indicate at the state level what students
of the alignment of the electorate at the national level designate as the shift from the fourth to the fifth party system, from
the "Industrialist System" to the "New Deal System." Under the
fourth system the Republican Party and under the fifth system
the Democratic Party enjoyed "normal majority status." According to the Survey Research Center at the University of Michi-

gan, the presidential candidate of the party enjoying normal
majority status, other things being equal ("if short-term forces
associated with the election favored neither party in particular"), can expect to receive 53–54 percent of the two-party
vote.[18] Normal majority status comprises quantitative and
qualitative elements. The quantitative component is entailed,
by definition, in the expectation of a majority of the vote. The
qualitative ingredient is party identification or party loyalty—
voters' tendency to vote according to party preference. Obviously, if a particular candidate, like Eisenhower, or a particular issue, like Kennedy's religion, overcomes this tendency
among a significant number of voters, everything else is not
equal.[19]

One must concede to the party-systems analysts that the
trend embodied in Roosevelt's receiving 57.3, 60.8, 54.7, and
52.8 percent of the popular vote in four successive elections is a
significant fact in American electoral history—and in American
history in general. At the same time, one must insist that the
probable representation by each of these four totals of combinations of individuals' votes different from the combinations represented by the other three totals is also a significant fact in
American electoral history. In other words, aggregate figures do
not indicate shifting on the part of individual voters, much less
their reasons for shifting. Data on such shifting is admittedly
much less adequate for the elections of the 1930s and 1940s than
for later ones, but it seems reasonable to assume that a significant
amount of shifting occurred in earlier as well as in later elections. The Survey Research Center emphasizes the crucial role
shifting played in the election of 1960,[20] and V. O. Key, Jr., cites
the shifting which accompanied Eisenhower's triumphs at the
polls:

> One may note that Eisenhower polled 55.4 per cent of the
> major-party vote in 1952 and 57.8 percent in 1956. Then one
> may easily slip into the belief that from 1952 to 1956 only 2.4 per
> cent of the 1952 voters changed their allegiance; in fact five or
> six times as large a proportion switched their preference.[21]

The error Key refers to, as Gerald Pomper explains it, is the
assumption that the net change between parties is the total

change.[22] Key also makes an observation on shifting which is
relevant to Roosevelt's victories. Political scientists classify the
elections of 1936, 1940, and 1944 as "maintaining" elections
—contests in which the normal majority party wins its expected
victory.[23] Key writes:

> A series of maintaining elections occurs only in consequence of a
> complex process of interaction between government and
> populace in which old friends are sustained, old enemies are
> converted into new friends, old friends become bitter
> opponents, and new voters are attracted to the cause—all in
> proper proportions to produce repeatedly for the dominant
> party its apparent stable and continuing majority.[24]

Aggregate voting figures, particularly at the national level, fail
to convey a sense of this turbulence in the electorate at large
and within individual voters.

The political scientists who analyze correlations between
conditions, politics, and policies, it is true, use aggregate figures
at the state rather than the national level. Even when these
figures are supplemented by the identity of the winning party
in gubernatorial elections, however, they are still subject to the
kinds of limitations which apply to aggregate data at the national level in regard to both party and voter behavior. Concerning party behavior at the state level, Sharkansky comments:

> By focusing on the dollars and cents of appropriations or
> expenditures, we ignore important qualitative decisions that are
> made during the budget process. Decisions that govern the
> allocation of money to specific projects or certain locations may
> be at the focus of intense political and economic disputes, but
> they will not reveal themselves in our analysis. Our data also fail
> to reveal important information about the motivations that
> affect expenditures. We cannot determine, for example, if
> spending levels reflect the interests of a legislature or governor
> with respect to a particular service; if they represent a reciprocal
> action taken in response to a federal grant; or if they reflect the
> effort of one party in a political struggle to reward (or provoke)
> another participant with whom he is engaged in important
> negotiations on other business.[25]

Regarding voter behavior, Pomper asserts,"We examine the voting patterns of states, not that of individuals, whose behavior must be inferred rather than directly examined . . . Apparent stability in the total state returns might disguise considerable but countervailing shifts by individual voters." At the same time, although we must avoid the "ecological fallacy," recognizing that "acres or political units are not people" and correlations between voters of certain demographic and psychological characteristics and particular parties do not definitively establish causal relationships, analysis of areal units has some intellectual validity, Pomper maintains, when "smaller geographical units are analyzed and social . . . characteristics are correlated with political material." The most desirable kind of data are derived from surveys—carefully conducted depth interviewing of individuals in a representative sample of voters. Yet even citation of survey data often involves total figures: "The evidence that party identification has been stable is largely based on aggregate figures from the surveys, not on analysis of individual behavior." [26]

Analysis of voting behavior in smaller areal units shows that the relationship between change in conditions and change in politics is extremely complicated and that we do not know enough about it. Key presents a line graph showing that the Democratic percentage of the two-party vote in Auglaize County, Ohio, from 1880 to 1956 involved deviations from a secular or long-term trend—two of them (in 1932 and 1936) running against and two of them (in 1920 and 1940) running ahead of this trend—but "all these deviations occur around a long-term decline in Democratic strength." In "Secular Realignment and the Party System"(1959) Key presents a number of other illustrative examples, and he hypothesizes that "some objective change in the status of a group of persons is the condition most frequently associated with such a long-term partisan shift" (a change in economic conditions would be only one kind of change in status or social change). Political change lags behind social change, which suggests that a "complex social process . . . mediates between social change and its political consequences." Nor does change in the status of a group by itself produce a realignment. It does, however, create "oppor-

tunities for exploitation by political leadership. Agitation to
that end may be aided by a sequence of events whose impact
reinforces the oratory of the agitator." For example, Bull
Moose progressivism, Wilsonianism, the secondary postwar
depression of 1921, Al Smith's candidacy, the primary postwar
or Great Depression, and the New Deal "all pushed in the same
direction." A secular trend, accordingly, "may, and probably
often does, reflect not a single factor operative continuously
through time but the impact of separated events that happen to
push in the same direction."[27]

In "Social Determinism and Electoral Decision: The Case
of Indiana," (1959) Key and Frank Munger examine short-
term as well as long-term disturbances of partisan patterns and
are impressed by the failure of social determinism to explain
some shifts in partisan strength over four-year periods:

> it is not uncommon for people of the most diverse social groups
> to shift their political sentiments in the same direction.
> Decisions, i.e., to change, may well be conditioned, at least in
> some elections, by factors more or less independent of social
> characteristics. It could be that persons of different
> characteristics shift in the same direction for different reasons,
> yet that seems inadequate to account for the drastic shifts
> affecting all types of persons in some elections.[28]

Considering the nation as a whole, one may assume that such a
shift in the electorate occurred from 1928, when Hoover received 58.2 percent of the popular vote, to 1932, when
Roosevelt received 57.3 percent, but studies of voting behavior
in the counties of Pennsylvania and in Chicago show that even
in 1932 noneconomic social characteristics affected some voters, that the durability of party attachment, which Key surmises
has something to do with the slowness of the process of secular
change,[29] was evident amid the shift from a Hoover landslide to
a Roosevelt landslide. Certainly the Great Depression benefited
the out party in the election of 1932. Yet a study of this election
in Pennsylvania, the largest of the six states Hoover carried,
shows that while thirteen of the twenty counties with an unemployment percentage of more than thirty in May 1932 went
Democratic in November, which is not surprising, only six of
the twenty-five counties having an unemployment percentage

between 25.0 and 29.9 went Democratic, which is more or less "unexpected." The author of this study concludes that "the real margin of Republican victory was the *margin of habit*."[30] Similarly, two students of the election of 1932 in Chicago, where Roosevelt received 59.2 percent of the vote, conclude that although "an increase in economic insecurity produces a reaction against the party in power . . . there is a distinct lag in the adjustment of political attitudes to changing material conditions." And John M. Allswang shows that the blacks lagged behind other ethnic groups in Chicago in shifting to the Democratic party in the 1930s.[31]

Another approach, besides the use of aggregate figures to indicate socioeconomic conditions, legislative and voter behavior, and policies—that is, expenditures— which can be misleading with respect to the partisan, ideological, and emotional content of American politics is the "me-tooism" argument. This line of reasoning often appears in accounts of the New Deal. Rossiter expresses it plainly: "The Republicans have been following the same road as the Democrats, but they are ten to fifteen years behind and have not enjoyed the trip half so much."[32] John Kenneth Galbraith agrees with Rossiter: "Debate is almost invariably confined to measures that have not yet been enacted. One of the most surprising features of social welfare legislation is its inability to sustain controversy once it has been enacted into law."[33] In this connection Galbraith mentions the Social Security Act of 1935, and public-opinion polls support his contention. In 1952 a survey of regular Republican sentiment on social security laws disclosed that 85 percent thought they were a "Good Thing," 6 percent judged them a "Mistake," 7 percent considered them "Neither Good Nor Bad," and 3 percent had "No Opinion."[34] Many other writers comment on the Republicans' eventual acceptance of the New Deal.[35] Yet, as many writers, including Rossiter, have shown, the lag of one of the major parties behind the other of "only" fifteen years has resulted in continual controversy as our political system has facilitated—adequately or inadequately—the transformation of America from a rural, agricultural nation to an urban, industrial, welfare state.

Yet the "me-tooism" argument, despite all that has been said here about how it contributes, along with the use of aggregate figures, to concealing turbulence in American politics, brings us back to a level of generalization at which consensus cannot be denied. In the first place, looking back from 1973, when party loyalty is declining and President Nixon has been re-elected with substantial support from blue-collar workers, one can see that the partisanship and the class composition of the alignment of the electorate in the 1930s were unusual. Walter Dean Burnham discusses in "The Onward March of Party Decomposition" a depoliticizing and antipartisan process of which split-ticket voting is a primary indicator. This trend toward disaggregation, Burnham writes, got underway about 1900, underwent a reversal in the period 1932–1948, resumed with "double force" in the early 1950s, and expanded geometrically in the mid-1960s with a steep rise in the number of independents. In the light of these developments, Burnham says,

> the post-1952 resumption of the march toward electoral
> disintegration leads one to suspect the possibility that, in terms
> of the history of American voting behavior at least, the New Deal
> might come to be regarded one day as a temporary if massive
> deviation from a secular trend toward the gradual
> disappearance of the political party in the United States.[36]

Not only was the partisanship of the New Deal era unusual, so was the movement of politics off center, as gauged by the enactment of policy measures, As Leuchtenburg points out, under the "4-Party System," which includes a conservative congressional coalition of Republicans and Southern Democrats, the politics of dead center has prevailed, except for an interruption in 1964 and 1965, since 1938.[37] There are book titles like *The Age of Reform: From Bryan to FDR*—and the reform tradition has continuity as an intellectual phenomenon—but with respect to legislation one may underline Leuchtenburg's point by noting that in the fifty-eight years from 1916 (when Wilson signed the Adamson Act and a Populist-like tax bill) to 1973 there have been eight years, 1933–1938 and 1964–1965, in which Congress has enacted significant innovative domestic measures. Leuchtenburg also notes that the emergence in the 1930s of the Democrats as the party of big government and the Republicans as the party of limited government represented a reversal of the pattern of the late nineteenth century when "the Republicans had been more closely identified with central government, the Democrats with states' rights."[38] This remark has implications for consensus, for concerning a similar reversal in the early nineteenth century, Charles M. Wiltse, as noted in chapter 1, declares that "the last ideological differences between the parties were gone."

The most important consensual quality of the policies of the 1930s, however, was that they were policies—that is, the controversy over them did not involve either the framework of democratic ideology or the "rules of the game" discussed in chapter 3—and these policies, including welfare statism, were capitalist policies. As McClosky, Hoffman, and O'Hara assert, "contests of the capitalism vs. socialism variety have never achieved an important role in American politics."[39] Thus our socioeconomic system has not been static—we are no longer a nation of small farmers—and the response to changing conditions through the political system has not been smooth or in accordance with a plan. Response has taken the form of delayed, spasmodic reactions to new realities, and the belatedness, fitfulness, and limitedness of these adjustments have reflected the sway of Lockean capitalism and democracy—a predominance not preordained but, it is true, prepackaged, according to Hartz, for export to America. The political controversy accompanying these adjustments amounts, then, to conflict within consensus.

The phrase "conflict within consensus" is not only descriptive; it also suggests a methodological point: it is unsound to employ inferences from data gathered at one level of analysis to answer questions posed at a different level. At the beginning of this section we noted that political scientists' inquiries into conditions, politics, and policies do not involve analysis of political developments in detail—party or legislative behavior and voter behavior. Presenting Rossiter's summary of voting records in Congress, we noted that his tabulation, although it does provide a quantitative indication of differences between the two major parties, does not, as Rossiter himself comments, provide any insight into individual legislators' motives and maneuvers and only implicitly evokes the partisanship, ideological commitment, and emotion of American politics in the New Deal era. Just as aggregate figures on voting records in Congress are one thing and the motives and conduct of the individual legislator are another, so aggregate voting figures for the general electorate—as a comparison of data on overall and net shifting shows—supply no information about the individual voter. We do get closer to him as we move down the continuum of electoral units—from the nation, to the state (Indiana), to counties (in Pennsylvania), to localities and their political subdivisions (Chicago). Ideally, we would have comprehensive data for the traits and behavior of all voters and units, say every precinct, through time.

None of which is meant to imply disapproval of generalization at any level. Such disparagement would be inconsistent since I have cited not only Sharkansky's strictures concerning the analytical limitations of policy-outcomes studies but also Patterson's urging that political historians consider the findings of policy-outcomes studies. Too, I have supported the concept of consensus, within which conflict occurs, by means of high level generalizations concerning widespread acceptance of capitalism and democracy—an acceptance which, it must be conceded, is subject to limitations in the light of Burnham's objections (noted in chapter 3) about the narrowness of the American political universe. By ordering generalizations on an intelligible scale for various times we can see top-down and bottom-up relationships between levels without mixing levels—in this case how and when Democrats and Republicans were different and how and when they were alike.

Party Strength and Internal Improvements, 1836–1852

A historian might ask whether our conclusions concerning socioeconomic conditions, partisanship, and public policies in recent times hold for earlier periods. In fact, in 1968 political scientist David R. Mayhew, commenting on Dawson's study which appeared in 1967, expressed his curiosity about correlations between socioeconomic indices and party competition in the Whig-Jacksonian era[1]—a period of special interest here since historians often associate the emergence of consensus with it. It should be noted, however, that Mayhew's question is not the one emphasized in our consideration of conditions, politics, and policies in the years 1914–1962. In view of political scientists' disagreement as to whether interparty competition is an intervening variable between conditions and policies, and for other reasons, we stressed the correlation, or its absence, between partisanship and policies and between socioeconomic conditions and partisanship. It is difficult to apply this approach to the Jacksonian era, as we shall see momentarily, but meanwhile we can reach some kind of answer to Mayhew's question.

We have calculated the percentages of the two-party vote which the Democratic and Whig candidates received in the twenty-five states voting in all presidential elections, 1836–1852.[2] These five elections were chosen for examination because in the years in question American politics exhibited characteristics that enable us to make inferences about state politics from the voting in national elections—something that we cannot do for the twentieth century. McCormick states that the second party system "assumed the character that it did because political leaders in every state related their actions closely to the presidential contests [and] the second party system was characterized by similar alignments of voters in both state and national elections in every state."[3] We have calculated for each state the average percentage of the two-party vote received in the five elections, 1836–1852, by the victorious presidential candidates and used Dawson's criteria to assign a level to the degree of interparty competition in each state. In addition, we have again introduced the factor of partisanship, indicating the number of victories both parties achieved in each state. In regard to socioeconomic development, we have drawn on a study by Charles Sellers, who divides the twenty-five states under consideration into three categories (which we shall call High, Medium, and Low) according to density of population, urbanization and economic and social diversity.[4] (Sellers also classifies these states by interparty competition, but we employ Dawson's criteria to attain comparability.)

In the area of policy outputs, we have chosen internal improvements policies for two reasons: whether involving public ownership of enterprise or public subsidization of private enterprise, they are cited by writers who emphasize consensus on the mixed but predominantly capitalist economy, and—like the policies considered for later periods but unlike policies flowing from other issues of the Jacksonian era such as banking, public lands, Indian removal, slavery, tariffs, political and social reforms, and regulation of corporations and currency—they involve expenditures which have been measured for all states and which persisted over several decades. Using George Rogers Taylor's figures, we shall designate internal improvements expenditures as "Rising" or R (which was the case in every state in the period 1830–1838, when state debts increased from 20.8 to 170.8 millions, 109.6 millions of this increase being contracted for the financing of internal improvements; in the period 1853–1860, when state debts increased from 193 to 257.5 millions; and in five states in the period 1841–1853, when state debts rose only from 190 to 193 millions), "Stable" or S (which was the case in seventeen states in the period 1841–1853), and "Falling" or F (which was the case in three states that notably reduced their debts in the period 1841–1853).[5] These data are presented in table 8.

Table 8

States	Socio-economic Develop-ment	Interparty Competition		Victories		Debt for Internal Improvements		
		Avg. Pct. 2-Party Vote for Winning Candidates	Level	Dem.	Whig	30–38	41–53	53–60
Connecticut	H	52.8	H	2	3	R	S	R
Delaware	H	52.4	H	1	4	R	S	R
Louisiana	H	53.9	H	3	2	R	F	R
Maryland	H	53.1	H	1	4	R	S	R
Massachusetts	H	57.4	H	0	5	R	S	R
New Jersey	H	51.7	H	1	4	R	S	R
New York	H	55.0	H	2	3	R	R	R
Ohio	H	52.6	H	2	3	R	S	R
Pennsylvania	H	51.4	H	3	2	R	S	R
Rhode Island	H	58.6	H	2	3	R	S	R

Table 8 continued

States	Socio-economic Develop-ment	Interparty Competition		Victories		Debt for Internal Improvements		
		Avg. Pct. 2-Party Vote for Winning Candidates	Level	Dem.	Whig	30—38	41—53	53—60
Illinois	M	53.7	H	5	0	R	F	R
Indiana	M	53.6	H	3	2	R	S	R
Kentucky	M	56.1	H	0	5	R	S	R
Maine	M	55.3	H	4	1	R	S	R
Michigan	M	54.3	H	4	1	R	S	R
No. Carolina	M	53.8	H	2	3	R	R	R
Tennessee	M	53.4	H	0	5	R	R	R
Virginia	M	53.7	H	5	0	R	R	R
Alabama	L	56.7	H	5	0	R	F	R
Arkansas	L	60.1	M	5	0	R	S	R
Georgia	L	55.6	H	2	3	R	S	R
Mississippi	L	54.5	H	4	1	R	S	R
Missouri	L	57.2	H	5	0	R	R	R
N. Hampshire	L	64.2	M	5	0	R	S	R
Vermont	L	63.0	M	0	5	R	S	R

In response to Mayhew's question, we may note that the levels of socioeconomic development and of interparty competition were the same in ten of twenty-five instances—the ten states in the High category of socioeconomic development—or 40 per cent. The corresponding figures for the periods 1914–1929, 1930–1945, and 1946–1962 are 16 of 36 instances or 44.4 percent, 22 of 36 instances or 61.1 percent, and 22 of 36 instances or 61.1 percent, respectively. These figures cannot be taken as the basis for a definitive comparison since Dawson's and Sellers' measurements of socioeconomic development differ, but they do reflect the unusually high degree of party competition across the nation in the Jacksonian era. In other words, levels of socioeconomic development and competition differed in more instances in the earlier period because competition tended to be high regardless of the level of socioeconomic development. McCormick points out that there were no "one-party" regions during the period 1824–1854,[6] and our own calculations indicate the presence of balanced parties in every section and nearly every state: in 125 elections (five in each of twenty-five states) the victorious party's percentage of the two-party vote in presidential contests was in the 50.1–60.9 range in all but sixteen instances.[7]

With respect to our immediate concern, comparison of election results with internal improvements policies reveals conformity in policy amid political diversity in the periods 1830–1838 and 1853–1860, when state debts increased substantially. In the years 1841–1853, when state debts rose only slightly, eight states significantly increased or reduced their debts, thereby increasing or reducing their expenditures for internal improvements:

	Victories	
	Dem.	*Whig*
States Which Increased Debts	.	
Missouri	5	0
New York	3	2
North Carolina	2	3
Tennessee	0	5
Virginia	5	0
States Which Reduced Debts		
Alabama	5	0
Illinois	5	0
Louisiana	3	2

Similar policies were adopted by states with different political situations—compare Whig-dominated Tennessee with Democratic-dominated Missouri and Virginia—and states with similar political situations adopted different policies—Missouri and Virginia on the one hand and Alabama and Illinois on the other. In any event, the situation of the 1840s was temporary and was caused not by a shift in attitudes toward internal improvements but by financial exigencies.[8] The indicated conclusion is that the states needed and wanted internal improvements and supported them, regardless of the relative strength of the parties, until they exhausted their financial resources; when their credit was restored, they resumed their support, regardless of the relative strength of the parties.

This conclusion suggests that internal improvements policies cannot be explained by generalizations about sections, classes, or parties. Nor is it in accord with the contention that the Whigs were closer than their Democratic rivals to the New Dealers—a contention which may be considered a response to the reverse proposition advanced by Schlesinger, whose criteria include "executive vigor" as well as policy.[9] Benson and William S. Hoffman, it should be pointed out, refer to similarities between Whigs and the New Dealers only in regard to New York and North Carolina, respectively.[10] Glyndon G. Van Deusen draws the comparison more broadly: "For the Whig attitude toward the function of government, at least at the national level, bears a closer resemblance to that of the New Deal than did the attitude toward government of Jackson and Van Buren."[11] Degler, on the other hand, states that "laissez faire" did not apply to the Jacksonians' attitude toward governmental stimulation, as distinguished from regulation, of economic activity either in theory or, the Maysville veto notwithstanding, in practice.[12] With respect to regulation, Gatell, as we shall see, emphasizes the non-laissez-faire policies of the Jacksonians at both the national and state levels. In any case, governmental support of internal improvements in the pre-Civil War era was far more important at the state than the national level,[13] and the Whigs-New Dealers analogy does not hold for Missouri and Virginia, where the all-triumphant Democratic party sponsored expansion of internal improvements in the 1840s despite the financial exigencies of that decade.

In his study of economic policy in Missouri from 1820 to 1860, James Neal Primm concludes that the government in undertaking an active, positive role was neither hampered by laissez-faire ideas nor motivated by a theory of state action: "Missourians . . . were essentially pragmatic."[14] Similarly, in his study of internal improvements in Virginia from 1816 to 1861, Carter Goodrich finds that discussions involved some clash of economic interests but "ran more in terms of specific proposals than of broad economic policy." There were government, private, and mixed enterprises. The latter were the most important, despite a predominant doctrinal preference for purely private enterprise, because for the building of a transportation system "unaided business enterprise in ante-bellum Virginia was manifestly inadequate." In 1828 Governor Giles declared: "These improvements are demanded by so many considerations of public and private interests, that they will be acceptable to the country through which they pass on any terms they can get them."[15]

Does this decisive weight of practical considerations not only account for uniformity in internal improvements policies amid political diversity—thereby negating Van Deusen's generalization—but also substantiate Boorstin's thesis which elevates experience and denigrates ideology as causal factors in American development? Although this phenomenon demands the historian's attention, it would be hazardous either to reject Van Deusen's conclusion on the basis of the exceptional behavior of two states among eight or to accept Boorstin's sweeping assertion about the nature of American history on the basis of the similar behavior of most states in one policy area. The fact is—and it has not been our intention to set up a straw man—that internal improvements expenditures, as we shall see in the next section of this chapter, were one of the less controversial policy issues of the Jacksonian era.

Before discussing politics in that era in some detail, we may briefly consider together, as we did for the period 1914–1962, the factors of socioeconomic development and partisanship, employing Sellers' classification for the former and median percentages of the two-party vote received by Democratic and Whig candidates in the twenty-five states voting in all presidential elections from 1836 to 1852:

High Socio-economic Development	Dem.	Whig	Medium Socio-economic Development	Dem.	Whig	Low Socio-economic Development	Dem.	Whig
Conn.	47.6	52.4	Ill.	54.8	45.2	Vt.	37.0	63.0
Mass.	43.6	56.4	Ind.	50.8	49.2	N.H.	64.9	35.1
R.I.	39.7	60.3	Me.	56.1	43.9	Mo.	56.8	43.2
N.J.	49.4	50.6	Mich.	54.5	45.5	Ga.	48.5	51.5
N.Y.	50.5	49.5	N.C.	47.3	52.7	Ala.	55.4	44.6
Pa.	51.1	48.9	Va.	53.0	47.0	Miss.	51.0	49.0
Ohio	49.0	51.0	Ky.	46.1	53.9	Ark.	62.1	37.9
Del.	48.0	52.0	Tenn.	47.5	52.5			
Md.	47.7	52.3						
La.	51.3	48.7						
	48.5	51.5		51.9	48.1		55.4	44.6

In certain respects these figures do not display the inconclusiveness of the figures for 1914–1962. The Southern states are
distributed among the three categories of socioeconomic development; they exhibit, with the exception of Arkansas, a high degree of competition—especially striking in the case of Mississippi; and they are not uniformly predominantly Democratic
since the Whig candidates attained a majority for the period in
Georgia, North Carolina, and Tennessee. The one-party regional factor is thus not present. The steady increase in Democratic strength with a decrease in the level of socioeconomic
development and the reverse in regard to Whig strength warrant attention despite the narrowness of the Democratic range
(48.5 to 51.9 to 55.4) and the Whig range (51.5 to 48.1 to 44.6),
understandable under conditions of high party competition across the nation, and despite the minority of states in each category which do not fit the pattern of the median medians.
Further inquiry, of course, will require more precise measurements of socioeconomic conditions and party strength than
those used here. Historians have only recently begun systematically to investigate socioeconomic conditions in the Jacksonian
era and their relationships to party strength, and, as we shall
see, some of them are more impressed than others by the
power of conditions to explain political behavior.

Democrats and Whigs

As in writing on the politics of the 1930s, recent literature on
the details of politics in the Jacksonian era reveals qualities
which aggregate figures for socioeconomic conditions and
party strength do not disclose. Any discussion of the studies
which have appeared since the publication in 1964 of Alfred A.
Cave's concise, comprehensive volume on Jacksonian historiography must begin with a reference to the main interpretations
Cave dealt with in his concluding chapter on recent trends.[1]
The publication of Schlesinger's *The Age of Jackson* in 1945
began a new era in Jacksonian historiography. Schlesinger's
thesis that militant, class-concious Eastern labor played a major
role in shaping the radical aspects of the Jacksonian program
and his broad assumption that Jacksonian democracy was a
movement "on the part of the other sections of society to re-

strain the business community" provoked a storm of controversy. Dorfman, Hofstadter, and Hammond, as noted in
chapter 1, maintained that the party battles of the Jacksonian
era were not conflicts between social classes but clashes arising
from the interests and aspirations of small entrepreneurs and
nascent-entrepreneur laborers who wanted to democratize business by creating wider opportunity through the elimination of
law-created privileges. Schlesinger was charged with undue
present-mindedness, with reading worker-capitalist relationships of the New Deal era back into the pre-Civil War period.
Students of voter behavior in Philadelphia and Boston and of the
workingmen's movement of the Jacksonian era rejected Schlesinger's "urban labor" thesis, concluding that the workers' mood
was not one of proletarian resentment but of capitalist aspira-
tion. Meanwhile, other scholars questioned attributing pro-cap-
italist sentiments to workers; also questioned were the analysts'
statistical techniques in studying workers' voting behavior.
There was thus no consensus on the question whether labor
voted for Jackson.[2]

In 1949 Schlesinger himself, in a somewhat uncharacteristic
reaction to criticism, wrote a short defensive letter to the editor
of the *American Historical Review*.[3] Finally, in 1969, he commented at length on Hofstadter's "intelligent and searching criticism of the viewpoint set forth by this writer in *The Age of
Jackson*." The entrepreneurial thesis of Jacksonian democracy,
he noted,

> soon swept the field. Indeed, it was eventually carried to the
> point where it almost obliterated the difference between the
> Jacksonians and the Whigs and made the bitter political conflict
> of the age of Jackson a mystery. This was doubtless further than
> Hofstadter intended to go. . . . Presumably the Whigs were
> expectant capitalists, too, just as eager to open up the
> competitive game; and if this were so, what was the political
> shouting all about? Hofstadter did not take up this question,
> except to imply that the quarrel may have been between old
> (Whig) and new (Democratic) money.[4]

Marvin Meyers, a Hofstadter protege, took up the question in
The Jacksonian Persuasion: Politics and Belief (1957). He distinguished between forward-looking Whigs and paradoxical Jack-

sonians torn between past and future, desiring to "preserve the virtues of a simple agrarian republic without sacrificing the rewards and conveniences of modern capitalism." In this view, Jacksonians appealed in their public pronouncements to Old Republican restorationism, and their supporters responded because, as they pursued the dollar in an age of rising capitalism, they yearned for the austere good old days. Meyers thus offered a consensus interpretation. "Both parties," he held, "must have reached broadly similar class constituencies." He found the difference between the Jacksonians and the Whigs in their attitudes toward change, the Jacksonians feeling threatened by it, the Whigs rejoicing in it: "The Whig party spoke to the explicit hopes of Americans as Jacksonians addressed their diffuse fears and resentments."[5]

Other students of Jacksonian America have followed Meyers' lead by analyzing attitudes toward change. Major L. Wilson asserts that "one possible method . . . for recovering the substance of dialogue among [Hartz's] liberals is to make fully explicit the concepts of time found in their pleadings." Arguing for conflict within consensus, Wilson describes the Whigs as contemplating qualitative improvement of an unfinished society through time and the Jacksonians as demanding quantitative expansion through space of a presently finished society.[6] Elliot R. Barkan takes a somewhat different view of Whigs: "The evidence in New York State leaves little doubt that the Whigs envisioned quantitative changes that would enhance the material wealth and opportunities for all Americans as well as qualitative changes that would improve the social, moral, and intellectual climate of the state and nation."[7]

Meyers improved on the entrepreneurial thesis in regard to partisanship, but he left some questions unanswered. If, as he held, Jacksonians feared change and Whigs welcomed it, in a certain sense both favored change. The Jacksonians were restorationists, and the Whigs, so to speak, were modernists. Undoubtedly both were both, but the Jacksonian was torn between restorationism and modernism in a ratio of, say, 50−50 (if it were possible to quantify such feelings), while the Whig was inclined toward modernism in a ratio of, say, 75−25. Up to this point, putting empirical considerations aside, there is nothing in Meyers' view to quarrel with. He has been criticized for "creat-

ing hybrid, Janus-like, confused, paradoxical Jacksonians,"[8] and
his use of the term *paradox* is perhaps unfortunate. I would
say rather, *lag*—ideas formed in an earlier age have a persisting grip on men's minds even though conditions have changed.

The idea on which the Jacksonian era restorationist impulse rested was the agrarian ideology as John Taylor of
Caroline had expressed it. Taylor's agrarian ideal, as summarized by Henry Bamford Parkes, depicted a society of many,
small, equal, independent units resulting from opportunity,
which, in turn, resulted from prevention of and abstinence
from the transfer of property from producers to nonproducers
through the use of political power to give away economic
privileges—through the use of financial devices such as high
interest rates on bonds, legal devices such as privileged corporate charters, and legislative devices such as the tariff. In such
a society economic freedom involved ownership of productive
property—men owned the land on which they lived and
worked—and the maintenance of such a society required austerity and restraint. In violation of this agrarian ideal, Hamilton sinned by transferring property to an elite of the wise, the
rich, and the well-born; Jefferson sinned by failing to undo the
Hamiltonian system; the badly managed War of 1812 saw the
rise of nationalism (with a desire for a strong, rich nation
guided and aided by a paternalistic government) and the abandonment of agrarianism; and the postwar period saw the democratization of Hamiltonian transfer—the transfer of property,
through federal subsidies and distribution of privileges, not just
to an elite but on a wider basis. Thus by 1822 Taylor concluded,
bitterly, that the agrarian ideal was dead.[9]

In Meyers' analysis, since "both parties must have reached
broadly similar class constituencies" and farmers were thus not
the only Jacksonians, the agrarian ideal, with its accompanying
restorationist impulse, was not confined to agrarians. Historians have in fact discerned an analogue of the Taylor ideal
among "urban agrarians,"[10] and, as noted above, they have
investigated and debated the impact of the Jacksonian appeal
among laborers—some of whom, in Meyers' analysis, would
have been nascent entrepreneurs. Presumably, too, the Jacksonian appeal struck a responsive chord among actual as well as

would-be entrepreneurs. This doctrinal-psychological reconstruction of the politics of the Jacksonian era must, of course, be
considered in the light of empirical evidence, and we shall cite
some of the relevant findings of recent studies and questions
raised by them in the areas of policy, party politics, and the
political behavior of entrepreneurs.

That the Jacksonians were torn between past and future
was evident, as noted above, in the gap between their laissez-
faire profession and their interventionist practice in the area of
internal improvements. To cite still another instance of this
discrepancy, Richard T. Farrell concludes from his study of
internal improvements in Southwestern Ohio from 1815 to
1834: "Committed as were most Americans to the principles of
laissez faire, they nevertheless were willing to seek government
assistance to solve problems which blocked economic
progress.[11] John A. Monroe's study,"Neo-Hamiltonian Jacksonianism: the Treasury Plan of 1831," analyzes a proposal—a vic-
tim of the Bank War—by Secretary of the Treasury Louis
McLane for a national fiscal program, encouraging, among
other things, state-supported internal improvements.[12] Gatell
carries this argument for the Jacksonians' inconsistency
further, passing from stimulation to regulation of economic
activity. He contrasts the laissez-faire demands (according to
the entrepreneurial interpretation) of the newly arrived, expectant Jacksonian capitalists in their battle against entrenched
capital with the non−laissez-faire regulatory banking policies
of the Jacksonians at both the national and state levels.[13] Again,
this contrast is consonant with the "lag" discerned by Meyers
in seeing the Jacksonians as subject to the conflicting attrac-
tions of past and future.

In regard to party politics, although the restorationist or
radical perspective of Taylor affords the basis for a tidy, consistent summary of ideology and politics from 1789 to 1822, it
encompasses only a part of the story. Richard E. Ellis points out
that when Jefferson became President, the Republican party
was heterogeneous in composition and viewpoint: "Indeed,
two of the most important groups in the coalition, commercial
farmers and agrarian democrats, had very little in common and
were even political enemies on many local issues." Ellis rejects

the charge that "the Republican Party, while victorious at the polls, nevertheless failed to implement its program after it came to power in 1800." Given the division in the party between the moderates and the radical agrarians, "it was by no means clear what Jefferson's victory in 1800 signified," and the major political battles of the next decade were between the moderate and radical Republicans. The moderates' victory was crucial to the development of the nation:

> The real meaning of Jeffersonian Democracy, it would seem, is to be found in the political triumph of the moderate Republicans and their eventual amalgamation with the moderate wing of the Federalist party. This represented a victory of moderation over the extremism of the ultra-nationalist, neo-mercantile wing of the Federalist party on the one hand, and the particularistic, Anti-Federalist–Old Republican wing of the Democratic-Republican party on the other.[14]

This did not mean, however, as many historians have argued, that "all the Republicans in power did was to out-federalize the Federalists." Unlike the Federalists, the Jeffersonians were "unqualifiedly committed to a republican form of government" and were "prepared for and capable of playing the game of democratic politics when circumstances required." Unlike the Federalists, the moderate Republicans emphasized agricultural rather than mercantile development, but they were concerned about the well-being of all sectors of the economy as they stressed self-sufficiency rather than dependence on England. Unlike the Federalists, too, the moderate Republicans favored the settlement of the West and the promotion of its economic development through internal improvements. "The moderate Republicans," Ellis concludes, "during the years of their ascendancy, created a new political and economic synthesis from the old dichotomies of the Revolution . . . what the moderate Jeffersonians did was to democratize business enterprise." Ellis' analysis, emphasizing a fusion of moderates and the rejection of extremes, is more probing than that of the historians who, as noted in chapter 1, describe the emergence of consensus as Republican acceptance or adoption of

Federalist ways. It is with this greater depth of inquiry in mind that we can fully appreciate Ellis' consensus conclusion: "the Jeffersonian triumph of 1800 probably secured the liberal tradition in America."[15]

Ellis' investigation of the pre-Jacksonian era is relevant here in two ways. First, while the entrepreneurial thesis did not specify who were Democrats and who were Whigs, Meyers saw an answer in the groups' attitudes toward change: the restorationists were Democrats and the forward-looking were Whigs. Ellis finds that in the pre-Jacksonian era the radical agrarian restorationists were Democrats, but so were the democratizers of business, some of whom presumably resembled Meyers' forward-looking Whigs. Secondly, studies of the bank question in various states, discussed below, find the Democratic party still split between moderates and radical agrarians, with a coalition of Democratic moderates and Whigs often determining the outcome, just as an alliance of Republican moderates and Federalists had, according to Ellis, secured the liberal tradition in the years 1800–1810. The question arises: did significant numbers of moderate Democrats defect to the Whigs during "the rise of liberal capitalism" (the phrase Hofstadter uses to characterize the Jacksonian era) or, more precisely, did entrepreneurs tend to be Democrats or Whigs?

In his analysis Meyers takes an additional step which is pertinent to this question. He notes that by 1846 the practical meaning of the differences in economic policy between the Jacksonians and the Whigs had faded, but

> they still could not let their differences go. If only by the shading of a constitutional clause, a Whig must press his special concern for endless progress under democratic capitalism stimulated by the state. A Jacksonian must insist that the changing world is full of terrors, and hint at least that once there was a better, even as he helps perfect the instruments of change.[16]

This comment suggests that entrepreneurs divided fairly evenly between laissez-faire Jacksonians and neomercantilist Whigs who called for state stimulation of economic development. This possibility, however, leaves us with a rephrased

question: Why did some rising entrepreneurs prefer a restorationist laissez-faire and anti-privilege position—in profession if not always in practice—and the Democracy while other
rising entrepreneurs preferred the "American System" and
Whiggery?

This discussion of Meyers' observation is, of course, a deductive exercise, and one must turn to empirical findings relevant to the questions raised here. In "Beyond Jacksonian Consensus," published in 1970, Gatell surveyed literature which
revealed an increasing wariness of the consensus-entrepreneurial interpretation of Jacksonian politics, "a growing
reluctance to abandon altogether traditional interpretive roads
to Jacksonianism." Undergoing re-examination were the emphases of the consensus historians, who in their treatment of
party politics minimized or neglected class conflict. They
stressed

> the absence of ideological differences between Democrat and
> Whig, and the presence of all sorts of viewpoints within the
> amorphous coalitions that then passed for national parties.
> Jacksonians might be ex-Federalists, Whigs might be
> ex-Jeffersonians; and whatever they had been or were, however
> boisterously or sincerely they fought party battles, they agreed
> on fundamentals.

Gatell conceded that some ex-Federalists, like Roger B. Taney
and James Buchanan, thrived in Jacksonian politics, but activist
Federalist Jacksonians did not take their beliefs with them, and
the exceptions do not vindicate the rule: available information
suggests many ex-Federalist defectors from the Democracy in
the 1830s and, with respect to the general electorate, a
Federalist-to-anti-Jackson voting pattern. Gatell also conceded
that the Jacksonian coalition of 1828 included many leading
entrepreneurs, but they, too, were exceptions, becoming more
exceptional—as the result of defections—by the late 1830s, and
they did not manage Jacksonian politics, which "failed to conform to the mold of the consensus historians."[17]

The literature Gatell reviewed, and to which he himself
had contributed, led him to conclude that the party battles of
the Jacksonian era were not "the clank of tin swords" but rang
with "the sound of clashing steel." "Men could and did argue

about national economic issues, if not altogether intelligently, then certainly passionately," and this clash affected political alignments:

> *Perhaps* many of the Jacksonians were nascent capitalists, as Hartz claims. *Perhaps* no basic ideological quarrels raged between the parties. But the Whig party had the aura of economic elitism around it, and the voters knew it. It was no secret, however many individual exceptions can be produced, that the leading entrepreneurs were Whigs, especially by the late 1830s. Men like Thurlow Weed knew that elections could not be won by defending banks. The Whig appeal had to be masked behind a strained camaraderie of supposedly complementary interests. American politics was much more than a simple tale of rich against poor, but with the rich men preferring one party, and with the poor going to the polls, it is no surprise that Whigs experienced so much trouble.

Gatell was more appreciative of *The Age of Jackson* than he had been a decade earlier, but, he wrote, "Jacksonian historiography cannot be the same as before the entrepreneurial-consensus critique." At the same time, he asserted, "we should be extremely cautious before we banish the conflict-with-capital factor from Jacksonian politics."[18]

In conceding that many Jacksonians were perhaps nascent capitalists while asserting that the leading entrepreneurs were Whigs, Gatell accepts the portrayal of Jacksonian era politics as a struggle of little capitalists against big capitalists, but he breaks out of the confines of the entrepreneurial interpretation when he assigns the combatants to opposing parties and when he refers, in a general way, to the poor. His distinction between Jacksonian "on the make" capitalists and Whig "made" capitalists is also different from the division of "on the make" capitalists between the two parties on the basis of attitudes toward change postulated by Meyers.

Gatell's observations in fact accord in some ways with Hartz's analysis of politics in the age of Jackson. Hartz pits the wealthy, upper-middle-class, capitalist Whigs against the lower middle class, which, at least with respect to attitudes, includes everybody else in America, "where the aristocracies, peasantries, and proletariats of Europe are missing, where virtually everyone, including the nascent industrial worker, has the mentality of the independent entrepreneur." In this situation the Whigs' crime was not villainy but stupidity: "the democracy was closer to them than anywhere else in the West, and yet instead of embracing it, they feared it and they fought it." Whiggery should have made "a big issue out of the unity of American life, the fact that all Americans were bitten with the capitalist ethos it was trying to foster." If the Whigs had adapted to the realities of American life, donning the garb of Alger and Carnegie before the Civil War (after first seeing the light only in 1840), "they would have confused the issue considerably." The price they paid for their stupidity was that they were simultaneously condemned as "parasitic 'aristocrats' and exploitative 'capitalists' " ("when in fact they are only capitalists") whose protective tariffs and "American System" symbolized "monopoly."[19]

Nor does Hartz characterize political conflict as the "clank of tin swords." The Whigs' unrealistic advocacy—at least until 1840—of representative government without universal (white) manhood suffrage was a matter of basic ideology, and the condemnation of the Whigs by Taylor and Leggett was "punishment" and "abuse." In Hartz's view, Taylor was, to be sure, a participant not in a struggle between agrarianism and capitalism or labor and capitalism but in one between agrarian capitalism and industrial capitalism.[20] If Hartz's account of Jacksonian era politics conveys the impression of conflict of limited intensity and significance, however, perhaps it is because he insists that the opponents were grossly mismatched —given the Whigs' stupidity, they could not win. The most important difference between Hartz and Gatell is Hartz's failure to mention the poor. Hartz, it is true, as a student of political thought, expounds the social aspect of Tocquevillean equality rather than equality of condition, and thus his thesis does not depend on denying the kind of evidence, cited in chapter 2, which undermines assumptions of equality of condition in Jacksonian America. His failure to allude to the poor in his interpretation of Jacksonian politics undoubtedly derives in part from the fact that the only book he wrote before he completed *The Liberal Tradition in America* focused on fiercely capitalistic entrepreneurs of the *ante bellum* era.[21]

If the entrepreneurs divided between the parties as Gatell and Hartz say they did, there may be no need to pursue Meyers' distinction between backward- and forward-looking "men on the make." We cannot forgo further inquiry into the entrepreneurs' politics, however, in the light of Ronald P. Formisano's tentative conclusions about entrepreneurs in his recent study of party formation in Michigan in the years 1827–1861. Formisano states, "It has frequently been assumed that most entrepreneurs and promoters in the old Northwest were largely Whigs. Yet even a cursory look at enterprise in Michigan during the 1830s reveals the heady involvement of Democrats in growth-related business enterprises."[22] He also concludes that "Democrats engaged heavily in entrepreneurial pursuits, but that Democrats were newer capitalists 'on the make' in Michigan is yet to be demonstrated." In identifying Democrats among the entrepreneurs, Formisano does not deny partisan tendencies—"The economic elite in Wayne County [the Detroit area] was predominantly Whig." But neither does he espouse an economic-class interpretation of partisanship—if the economic elite was mostly Whig, this was "not because that party simply reflected its economic interest."[23] Formisano's explanation of partisan preferences, as we shall see, stresses ethno-religious factors. When he refers to the uncertainty as to whether or not the Democratic entrepreneurs were newer capitalists "on the make," he touches on a crucial methodological and substantive matter. If entrepreneur A owned a certain amount of property and enjoyed a certain income as of, say, 1840, and his worth in both areas had been increasing for ten years, his situation was not the same as that of entrepreneur B who, in 1840, possessed property of the same value and had the same income but whose worth in both areas had been declining for ten years. Michael A. Lebowitz raises the question of who was rising and who was falling in a provocative discussion of the age of Jackson. He hypothesizes that declining men—and not just entrepreneurs—as well as rising men responded to the Jacksonian restorationist appeal and "unit[ed] under the same banner."[24]

By 1969 Schlesinger had good reason to write that "I think

I am not wrong in detecting a reaction today against exaggerated statements of the entrepreneurial view."[25] In fact, three major studies of the banking issue which have appeared since 1969—those by Roger Sharp (1970), William G. Shade (1972), and John M. McFaul (1972)—reject the entrepreneurial thesis, as Jean Alexander Wilburn had done in her 1967 study of the bank war. To reject Hammond, however, is not necessarily to accept Schlesinger, as McFaul indicates: "A basic fault of both the anti-business and pro-business approaches to Jacksonian Democracy has been to concentrate on economics and interest-group motives. The present analysis has argued that economic interests were subordinated to political interests."[26] It should also be noted that while studies of Jacksonian politics in Georgia, Florida (Doherty), Missouri, New Hampshire, and Pennsylvania—some of which Schlesinger cited in 1969—reveal class differences between the major parties, studies of Alabama, Florida (Thompson), Mississippi, New York, North Carolina, and Ohio do not.[27] Meanwhile, as we shall see, very recent studies have revised Edwin A. Miles's contention that Andrew Jackson's personal popularity outweighed all socioeconomic divisions in Mississippi and Harry R. Stevens' conclusion that at the beginning of the Jacksonian era there was very little difference between the two major parties in Ohio.

Thus the intensive inquiry into the age of Jackson triggered by Schlesinger's presentation of (1) the class conflict thesis has produced (2) the entrepreneurial interpretation, a consensus analysis which fails to grapple with the problem of explaining partisan affiliations, (3) a psychological elaboration of the entrepreneurial thesis which denies that there was partisanship along class lines while asserting that partisan preferences related to rising men's attitudes toward change (a construction which raises questions still to be answered and neglects the question whether declining men played a significant role in politics), and (4) an analysis which emphasizes ethnoreligious factors—"cultural politics" or "political subcultures." Whether this analysis, which rejects both the class-conflict and entrepreneurial interpretations, is a consensus or conflict view depends on how one looks at it. Donald J. Ratcliffe maintains that it supports the consensus (5) electoral-machine thesis, according to which American political parties are designed primarily for nominating candidates and electing them to office. This thesis, Ratcliffe writes, has been "strengthened by recent studies of Jacksonian voting behavior [which] emphasize that the electorate divides along ethnic and cultural lines and was largely uninfluenced by the political debates and power struggles of the politicians."[28] (There is, as we shall point out, another way of looking at cultural politics. A renewed emphasis on (6) agrarian radicalism is also expressed in some recent studies, and one of them, Sharp's, ascribes some significance to (7) socioeconomic factors. Finally, some writings refer to (8) regional or sectional subcultures.

As its label suggests, category (8) involves more than geographical factors like climate and crops. People living in a given location may hold similar views, but the reasons for this will differ from place to place. This variation becomes apparent in historians' writings on areal units—whether an ethnic neighborhood, a portion of a state (Shade describes political conflict in Illinois as involving regional subcultures, each with its own distinctive economic life-style[29]), a region embracing several states, or a section (which in general historical usage usually connotes an area somewhat larger than a region). In this regard, it is revisionist to emphasize agrarian radicalism since the class-conflict, entrepreneurial, and entrepreneurial-psychological interpretations focus on the East.[30] Ratcliffe describes an East-West division over internal improvements and a North-South division over slavery—*the* sectional issue which Ratcliffe judges to have had an important impact on the second party system from its beginning to its end.

Analyzing voting statistics and socioeconomic and demographic data for Michigan localities, Formisano concludes that ethno-religious factors were not only far more important than economic-class conflicts as determinants of party choice (his chapters on "Religious Groups and Parties: 1837–1852" and "Ethnocultural Groups and Parties: 1837–1852" treat almost precisely the period we are concerned with here[31]) but also the source of contrasting world views. Among social groups with certain religious and cultural values, revivalism fostered an evangelical perspective which called for the use of government to control social behavior. This perspective was antiorganizational and shunned compromise for political purposes. Thus the Whig party, which gave expression to the evangelical impulse, was handicapped by ineffective organization and its inflexibility on various issues. The more cosmopolitan Democrats exploited the Whigs' hindrances, voicing egalitarian appeals for social and personal freedom in opposition to the Whigs' exclusivist call for a restricted society, and they were successful until the second party system broke up in the 1850s when the Republican leaders combined evangelical anti-Democracy with egalitarian anti-Southernism. Formisano believes that his findings concerning the social causes of party attachment in Michigan have implications for the nation as a whole: "the kinds of value conflicts and social cleavages moving voters in the 1830s and 1850s in Michigan were characteristic phenomena of American society and politics. The kinds of social conflicts underlying Michigan politics cut across this highly mobile society and, in a sense, traveled with footloose Americans."[32]

Now one may argue that cultural politics involves conflict which is not over abstract principles but, rather, arises from feelings of familiarity or group identity which move citizens of certain ethnoreligious traits to vote for a candidate from their group or to exhibit reference-group behavior by supporting or rejecting a candidate on the basis of his standing with another ethnoreligious group toward which the first group is either favorably or unfavorably disposed. On the other hand, pluralism is itself a principle, for the "recognition" which a group attains is not only a matter of material benefit, power, and psychology but also of democracy—although this rendering of democracy clashes with the melting-pot myth. In any event, if "recognition" were the sole content of cultural politics, Ratcliffe's distinction between cultural politics and politics proper could be accepted with little qualification. The kind of cultural politics Formisano describes, however, transcends specific, immediate interests of groups as ethnoreligious bodies. It encompasses ideologies or world views which affect the partisan affiliation of their holders. Thus cultural politics is politics.

In his study of the banking question from 1832 to 1865, Shade, using quantitative techniques, shows how "a party system rooted in the conflict of [ethnoreligious] subcultures could polarize around an economic question, the bank issue." This issue had both "real" and symbolic dimensions: economically, its outcome affected the distribution of benefits; symbolically, its function was "to characterize, often in highly moralistic terms, group differences, not only over the evolving economic order but also over the cultural identity of the society."[33] Although McFaul in *The Politics of Jacksonian Finance* focuses on decision-makers—politics from the inside out—and not on analysis of demographic and electoral data, he concludes with a tribute to Formisano's work and delineates the central role of concepts of morality in Jacksonian politics.

McFaul rejects the entrepreneurial thesis with respect to the bank issue. He also rejects the class conflict view. The nature of the controversy, he concludes, was not economic but political. Initially, therefore, McFaul seems about to advocate the electoral machine thesis in a simplistic way, but, in fact, his argument is quite sophisticated. He does not share the determinism of the econometricians, who have recently dominated the economic analysis of the Jacksonian era, stressing the impact of the international economy on American development, or of the psychological historians "who search the rhetoric of the period for peculiar distortions of reality and their significance." "The significant event during the Jacksonian era," McFaul writes, "was not the triumph of laissez faire or a protoregulatory state but the emergence and establishment of a new party system." Within this political framework, however, he portrays a complex mixture of motives and considerations influencing the decisions of the inner circle of Jacksonian political decision makers "as rational, freewilled men" in regard to federal policy on state banking. The pet banking operation was not intended to sanction wild speculation and laissez-faire avarice; it was an attempt to protect society against the "Monster" Bank of the United States while meeting society's economic needs, and, like Van Buren's independent treasury proposal, it compelled the Jacksonians to reconcile the imposition of controls with their decentralization creed. Secretary of the Treasury Levi Woodbury illustrated the politician's simultaneous response to political self-interest, to special interests, to social forces, to a sense of responsibility for the public interest, and to ideology. Ideology, moreover, came after as well as before the fact—that is, the insiders often "made political decisions and then justified them on abstract ideological grounds." In turn, "political rhetoric became a vital force in itself," often compelling the Jacksonians "to act politically in ways which threatened the stability of the coalition which they had so artfully constructed." The Jacksonian "fetish for specie" illustrates the reconciliation of the agrarian ideology or economic primitivism and the need for regulation of a volatile economy. In this light, the attraction of specie was that, in the Jacksonians' view, it would serve as an impersonal regulator, a "financial *deus ex machina.*" In the end, however, hard-money rhetoric, while easing the Jacksonian conscience as an apparent expression of an antibank position, "served as a verbal camouflage for the regulations."[34]

McFaul does not confine his conclusions to commentary on politicians as responders to various forces. He identifies two basic themes in the American experience which influenced political action: a dichotomy consisting of belief in a homogeneous society and fear of alien, subversive forces; and the "dramatization of the money issue into a moral event." In the antibank crusade the Jacksonians very effectively politicized fears that liberty might be lost, but they often did not know what to do with their victory: "Jacksonians were more interested in denouncing banks than in regulating them." Referring to the writings of Walter T.K. Nugent and of Irwin Unger, McFaul emphasizes the firm hold on nineteenth-century Americans of moral values in general and the moral quality of the money issue in particular—an issue which "perpetrated a moral exchange between members of society about the meaning of life." The Jacksonians' moral positions derived from a sense that the "quickening tempo of economic change somehow violated Calvinist loyalties to hard work, thrift, and duty." The Whigs, too, stressed morality. While the Jacksonians made a moral issue of the money question, which the Whigs considered political, the Whigs—and in this connection McFaul cites

Formisano—made political issues of matters such as religion and prohibition, which the Jacksonians considered moral questions: "The Jacksonians preferred to moralize politics while the Whigs attempted to politicize morality."[35]

In a review of Formisano's book, Joel H. Silbey notes that "most of his efforts are directed toward structuring these ideologies out of manuscript materials, newspapers, and individual local histories."[36] In other words, Formisano moves from who the voters were (socioeconomically and demographically) to what they (or some of them) said; but he does not deal comprehensively with who the people they elected were or what they did (how they voted on bills) and what they said (although officeholders are among the people whom Formisano quotes). It is understandable that Silbey, as a leading student of legislative behavior, should make such a comment (while paying high tribute to Formisano's industry, sensitivity, precision, and persuasiveness). In light of Silbey's remark, it is pertinent to note that two recent studies of legislative behavior in the Jacksonian era, one of which presents the electoral machine thesis implicitly and the other explicitly, indicate what legislators did and said but largely discount what they said.

At the outset of his study of the development of party loyalty in Congress from 1830 to 1840, David J. Russo asserts that if one accepts Edward Pessen's portrait, as he, Russo, characterizes it, of "the Jacksonian politician as opportunist *par excellence*, one who cared more for winning office and wielding power than in applying principles or even being politically consistent, then politics becomes a game whose players are characteristically motivated by unattractive personal considerations and not by concern for the interests of a locality or the nation." Russo accepts the fact of party loyalty after 1836: "Concerned only with the *measurement* of party loyalty, Silbey and Alexander [in their analyses of Congressional voting behavior[37]] do not go on to *explain* the phenomenon." The question is, "*Why* did some issues become known as 'party' and others as distinctly 'non-party' matters?" Russo concludes that the issues which became "party" issues—banking, public lands, removal of Indians to reservations, and slavery—"all shared in common the strong advocacy of either a president or an opposition leader. All also had the characteristic of being national in the sense that politicians *could* allow general and not local considerations to determine their position." Other issues—especially internal improvements and protective tariffs—"turned on local considerations" and were by common consent nonpartisan. It is as if a hypothetical party leader said to a Congressman, "We expect you to follow the party line, but when local pressures are overriding you are on your own." As Russo puts it, "it was considerably easier for Congressmen to respond to pressures other than those from their own electors on some issues than on others."[38]

Concerning politicians' motivations, Russo denies that purely selfish opportunism is an important explanation and in that sense claims that he rejects the electoral machine thesis. Larger than self is party: it is "overly simplistic to argue that politicians were opportunistic and selfish. They were also, at certain times and in particular places, highly loyal to political organizations."[39] Russo, as noted above, also designates "concern for the interests of a locality" as a motive above self-interest. Is it not possible, however, that loyalty to party and concern for local considerations can be reasonably construed, in certain situations, as aspects of political self-preservation? Moreover, if Congressmen expressed loyalty to party when they could allow "general and not local considerations" to determine their positions, unless "general considerations" refers to broad principles, Russo is specifying loyalty to party as party. In fact, Russo's citations of politicians' expressions of broad principles are followed by disclaimers: Democratic Congressmen's analyses of the nature and history of parties were "for the most part . . . convenient oversimplifications, accepted without much thought, and designed to make the Democratic party and its predecessor appear as the people's party"[40]—but this lack of sophistication did not preclude belief in principles. At the same time, one may note that Russo judges the tariff and banking issues to have been of "great concern" to politicians and voters alike, and he is careful to point out that party loyalty was "only one of a number of influences" which affected Congressional voting behavior.[41] Still, Russo's explanation of why some issues became party issues and others did not is essentially institutional and thus falls within the scope of the electoral machine thesis.

Rodney O. Davis, in his presentation of the first thorough scalogram analysis by a historian of a state legislature—the Illinois General Assembly in the years 1834–1841—explicitly endorses Van Deusen's 1958 assertion, cited in chapter 1, of the electoral machine thesis: parties battled to control the government rather than to promote opposing political and social ideals. Davis finds that "little overt Jacksonian anti-state-bank sentiment was abroad in Illinois before the panic [of 1837]." After 1837 "Whig and Jacksonian rhetoric regarding business enterprise was reflected in legislative behavior, at least insofar as that enterprise was associated with banks." It was only when hard times set in that legislative attitudes toward banks became polarized. On corporation issues such as charter grants the Whigs were unified while the Democrats were fairly evenly split by 1836 between moderates and antis. When resolutions called for local endorsement of national policies, the Illinois legislators "could be quite emphatic in registering their collective sentiments . . . Illinois Democrats, and to a lesser extent Whigs, were willing to follow their national leaders." Davis, however, discounts this division: "yet we may not exaggerate by saying that . . . contests involving national partisan matters were over non-issues in Illinois."[42]

Davis is well aware of political rhetoric which emphasized differences between the parties: "The public (and sometimes private) images that Illinois Whigs and Democrats cast of themselves and of each other, especially after the Panic of 1837, were not much different from those that historians have derived from the traditional sources."[43] Like Russo, however, Davis tends to depreciate the significance of this rhetoric. In Russo's analysis Congressmen are freer to vote their partisanship on national issues. In Davis' view state legislators are freer to vote their sentiments. One may ask whether Congressmen and state legislators were freer on national issues to vote their deep beliefs which they related to party. This question, to be sure, is arrived at deductively, but Davis' conclusion becomes less convincing when one simply glances at Shade's maps showing Illinois counties' positions on the bank question in the Constitutional Convention of 1847 and in a referendum of 1851—not to mention Shade's quantitative analysis of demographic data which also reveals regional subcultures—and when

one notes Ershkowitz's conclusion from analysis of party voting
patterns in the New Jersey Assembly of 1835–1836 on banking
and corporation issues—patterns very similar to those Davis
finds in Illinois—that there was a definite doctrinal distinction
between Democrats and Whigs.[44]

Recent studies of the bank war and the bank question underline the differences between the parties. Erickson and
Sharp find the Whigs to have been overwhelmingly pro-bank
while they identify a division among Democrats between hard
and soft money groups. Farmers in particular have always been
torn between the John Taylor of Caroline view of soft money as
a means by which manipulators and speculators will fleece the
farmer of his hard-won gains and the agriculturalist's special
dependence on credit to carry him from planting to harvest
time—a conflict between ideology and exigency which Erickson
aptly describes:

> Hard-money Democrats worked for abolition of banks of issue
> because they believed sufficient gold and silver existed to serve
> as a circulating medium; in theory they opted for slow economic
> development and an inelastic currency supply. This was,
> however, a time of tremendous economic expansion in the state,
> and this policy was unacceptable to most Iowans in their conduct
> of everyday affairs, regardless of how they had voted on the
> issue. In practice the people kept up an incessant demand for
> credit after Iowa outlawed banks of issue, demonstrating that
> what they really wanted was rapid economic development with
> the aid of an elastic currency.[45]

Using Guttmann scale techniques to analyze voting in the ter-
ritorial House and Council and in the constitutional conventions of 1844 and 1846, Erickson characterizes the main party
groups:

> The Whigs favored an elastic currency created by banks of issue
> (under general incorporation laws) regulated by a federally
> chartered national bank. The Democratic party on the other
> hand was seriously split on the question. The hard-money
> radicals (self-styled Democrats of the "old school"), believing
> gold and silver the only true and constitutional currency,
> opposed all such banks. The conservative (or bank) Democrats

opposed the Whig-proposed national bank but favored a
flexible currency issued by stringently regulated, locally
controlled (state) banks of issue.[46]

A main theme in Erickson's discussion of the politics of banking
is the shifting balance between the two groups of Democrats,
with the conservative Democrats sometimes joining with moderate Whigs in support of strict regulation.[47]

Sharp surveys the politics of banking in other states while
presenting a detailed analysis of the issue in Mississippi, Ohio,
and Virginia. He, too, finds the Whigs to have been pro-bank
while the Democrats were divided between hard and soft
money factions. Sharp also identifies a group of Democrats
who were more concerned about party unity than the bank
issue. Sharp, however, rejects the electoral machine as well as
the entrepreneurial thesis. The antibank position, he argues,
rested on egalitarian sentiment and the attitudes of the nostalgic Democratic "heirs of John Taylor of Caroline and his cult of
agrarianism." Like Formisano, Sharp presents correlational
analysis of party (Democratic) strength and measures of
economic standing (taxable wealth, slaveholding, and aggregate real estate wealth). Unlike Formisano, Sharp is impressed
by the possibility of a causal relationship between socioeconomic conditions and partisanship—Democratic strength appears to have been greater in poorer areas—but in his analysis
of conditions and constituencies at the county level in Mississippi, Ohio, and Virginia he is cautious on the question of
causation since the apparent influence of wealth or lack of
wealth on political affiliation varied from area to area. Other
variables such as degree of economic maturity, stage of political
development, density of population, participation or nonpar-
ticipation in the market economy, rising or declining wealth,
power, and prestige and the accompanying attitude toward the
future, degree of urbanization, the presence or absence of
laissez-faire urban radicals, ethnic composition, and the presence or absence of antibank citizens of German descent appear
to have been related to differences from one area to another in
the correlations between wealth and the division of the electorate between the two major parties.[48]

It is obviously very difficult to answer Lane's question for the Jacksonian era about the relationship between conditions and communal politics and between change in one and change in the other. Pessen's comments on the latter relationship indicate its complexity. He cites studies of a number of counties which show that "certain counties in election after election reported the same distribution of votes between major parties despite changes in the socioeconomic situation within counties." Analyses of voting in Missouri and New Hampshire indicate that although "economics undoubtedly had much to do with it . . . the choice of party was not a simple function of a community's wealth or poverty." The characteristic traits of anti-Jackson towns in these two states were not "aristocratic" tendencies or wealth *per se* but "closeness to rivers, ties with other communities, the presence of a number of churches, particularly those of evangelical tendency, a sizable population, an educated citizenry, a general atmosphere of vitality."[49]

Finally, we may consider two recent studies which bring together several themes concerning Jacksonian politics while frontally attacking the electoral machine thesis. Ratcliffe's article, "The Role of Voters and Issues in Party Formation in Ohio, 1824," is important in this regard because exponents of the electoral machine thesis have based their argument in part on Harry R. Stevens' study of *The Early Jackson Party in Ohio*. Stevens analyzed in great detail the background and social position of twelve hundred known supporters of the three major presidential candidates in 1824 and found essential similarity with respect to economic interests, ethnic origins, and geographical sections: "The composition and structure of each party was essentially the same." On basic issues, moreover, "there was very little difference between one party and another." In 1824 the "more fundamental issue was the most simple and obvious one, that the contest involved the election of a president." Stevens discussed this "more fundamental issue" in institutional terms—the questions about party structure and activities arising from a nationwide political effort—but in fairness one ought to note that he allows for the possibility that the formation of the Jackson party involved factors transcending institutional considerations. He declines to generalize for all states from the case of Ohio, and he speculates that the emergence of professional politicians may have been greater among support- ers of Clay and Adams than of Jackson, that this change may have represented "the maturing of a frontier society," in which case the Ohio Jacksonians were a backward-looking group whose democracy and Democracy reflected an attachment to the old frontier.[50] Yet, Stevens' study, as far as it goes, stresses the basic similarity of the parties and thus expresses the elec- toral machine view.

Ratcliffe questions the validity of Stevens' sample: "It is always dangerous to base an analysis of a party's character on an investigation of its identifiable supporters." This skepticism have been justified by the fate of a line of inquiry into the Pro- gressive Party of 1912 begun in the 1950s when Stevens was studying the Jacksonians. Alfred D. Chandler and George Mowry assumed that the Progressive and Republican parties had different aims and proceeded to characterize the Progres- sive leaders. Subsequent studies for various localities added a comparative analytical dimension to the inquiry and showed that the leaders of the Regular Republicans and of the Demo- crats exhibited the same characteristics as the leaders of the Progressives. The result, as it were, was a single stratum model: leaders of the three parties came from the same social class. These comparative studies also demolished Hofstadter's psychological elaboration of Mowry's and Chandler's work since his status anxiety thesis regarding the Progressives ex- plained a reform impulse through personal traits which, it turns out, were not peculiar to the reformers.[51] That different par- ties in 1912 had similar leadership with respect to social stratum suggests, even though 1824 is not 1912, that it is risky to assume that similarity in leadership meant similar parties. It is also appropriate to note that Stevens suggested that psychology might hold the answer to voting behavior: "it would seem that . . . men with a given outlook on life might be inclined to favor one presidential candidate rather than another. The more energetic and overtly aggressive might prefer Jackson, the more judicious and reflective, Adams, the more skilled in 'wire-working,' Clay."[52] Ratcliffe does not explore this psy- chological area further—why was a man aggressive or judicious or manipulative?—but rather utilizes more conventional techniques for explaining voter behavior.

Ratcliffe begins with a statement of the electoral machine view of party formation. Ambitious politicians developed effective state organizations, and powerful state leaders cooperated to control the presidency. Political issues were largely irrelevant to this process since political conflict in the 1820s was a clash of personalities and because, in any case, American political parties' fundamental objective is to win elections. The electorate's attitudes and interests were also largely irrelevant since "the politicians had mastered the techniques of winning votes and could therefore lead their constituents." Ratcliffe emphatically rejects this view. He concludes that leaders were, so to speak, followers since they acted in accordance with their constituents' interests, prejudices, and, above all, their stands on issues: "Deference to political leaders and the manipulative skills of the politician were of negligible importance in this respect [the nature of the division of 1824] in Ohio." The party division which developed in 1824–1825 involved competing appeals and "real and explicable" differences. It persisted—even dictating to some extent the nature of the collapse of the second party system which first became evident in 1848—despite changing political circumstances, including an enormous increase in voter turnout in 1828; a decline in party differences over issues, especially internal improvements; and the emergence of new interests that had not been politically relevant during the formative period: "some constituents might continue to vote for a party whose policies were no longer appropriate to their interests and prejudices." Ratcliffe thus recognizes the force of loyalty to party as party—the kind of lag which, as noted above, accompanied the shift from the fourth to the fifth (or New Deal) party system. The division of 1824 developed "a thrust and momentum of its own." Under the second party system politicians compromised, obscuring their policies and principles, in order to form coalitions for electoral contests, but these later ambiguities "in no way contradict the argument that the initial organization of [the parties'] component elements was prompted by a concern over political issues and that for many of their supporters the parties continued to possess the identity and significance that they had acquired in the controversies which first brought them to life."[53]

Ratcliffe devotes the bulk of his article to an analysis of the Clay, Adams, and Jackson votes in 1824 and 1828, cross tabulating location, ethnocultural traits, attitudes on internal improvements, and the impact of the Panic of 1819, felt most in the southwestern counties around Cincinnati. Voters most keenly interested in internal improvements, regardless of location, favored a western candidate, "be it Jackson, or Clay, or even Calhoun." New Englanders or Yankees everywhere preferred the northern candidate, probably because of antislavery sentiments arising from the Missouri crises of 1819–1821. The Scotch-Irish and "Pennsylvania Dutch" in all parts of the state were attracted toward the general who had defeated the British at New Orleans. Those who suffered most from the Panic of 1819 also supported Jackson. Ratcliffe also mentions an anti-"ins" or antiestablishment impulse, "widespread, if half-muted mistrust of those in authority," which benefited Old Hickory: "the widespread resentment of privilege and governmental corruption, which local politicians had cultivated in the past, provided fertile soil in 1824 for the cause of the candidate who was seen as a strong-minded patriot hero risen from the people and unconnected with politics." Ratcliffe suggests that the reactions of the four main groups of voters to various issues in Ohio were "probably typical of the reactions of similar groups in other states."[54]

When Ratcliffe writes that internal improvements advocates preferred "even" Calhoun because he was a western candidate, he suggests the tension between pro-American System and antislavery interests which marked the northwestern quarter of the nation while the northeastern quarter was antislavery and anti-internal improvements, the southwestern quarter proslavery and pro-internal improvements, and the southeastern quarter proslavery and anti-internal improvements——dualisms which rendered the first party system irrelevant and underlay the coalition-through-compromise that marked the second party system.[55] In the end, the issue that arose in 1819 on the eve of the formation of the second party system was evident in the demise of that system. Formisano, in his

study of Ohio's neighbor, entitles one chapter, among five devoted to this demise, "Crusade for White Freedom"—a status
quo and anti-Southern rather than a humanitarian
movement.[56] Reference to Formisano's book also suggests
another comment about Ratcliffe's analysis. Ratcliffe, as noted
above, begins by designating studies, including Formisano's,[57]
which stress ethnocultural factors as supporting the electoral
machine thesis, yet he stresses the "ethnocultural homogeneity"
of the Scotch-Irish, the "Pennsylvania Dutch," and the "Universal Yankee Nation" as determining these groups' reactions to
various issues. This source of differences between the parties is
neglected by the electoral machine thesis, which in any case
renders issues largely irrelevant to the political process.[58] Cultural politics thus becomes part of politics proper.

While Russo and Davis espouse the electoral machine
thesis, the other authors we have cited maintain, in various
ways, that there were important differences between the
Democrats and the Whigs. None of these studies, understandably, treats in great detail all of the components of the continuum encountered by the analyst of political behavior: where
voters and legislators came from (the socioeconomic conditions
of their areas), who they were (cultural-demographic traits),
what they did (how they voted on candidates and bills), and
what they said. They also exhibit limitations regarding policy
issues and geography. Aside from Russo's assessment of Congressional voting behavior, which tends to minimize the significance of what politicians said, these studies deal with one policy
area in one state, one policy area in several states, or several
policy areas in one state. In an impressive analysis of the differences between Democrats and Whigs, Herbert Ershkowitz and
Shade examine what legislators did with respect to various issues in various states and then relate what the legislators did to
what they said. And they emphatically reject the electoral
machine thesis.

Pointing out that Silbey's and Alexander's studies of congressional voting behavior indicate definite differences between the parties at the national level, Ershkowitz and Shade
note that the electoral machine thesis rests mainly on differing
practices at the state and local levels. They judge this thesis

inadequate as the result of their examination of legislative behavior in the years 1833—1843 in six geographically dispersed
states—New Hampshire, Pennsylvania, Ohio, New Jersey, Virginia, and Missouri—in five policy areas: regulation of corporations, regulation of banking, currency, internal improvements,
and political and social reforms, the latter including
humanitarian reforms (militia reform, abolition of capital
punishment, temperance, prison and asylum reform, antislavery and pro-Negro measures), economic reforms (abolition of
imprisonment for debt and relief for debtors), and support for
public education.[59] The six states examined displayed "an
amazing consistency both in the problems their legislators discussed and in the positions the political parties maintained on
these issues."[60] Jacksonians opposed and Whigs supported corporations, banks, and paper currency; Jacksonians showed little enthusiasm for humanitarian reform while Whigs favored
it. Voting along party lines prevailed by 1836, and by 1840
four-fifths or more of the legislators adhered to dominant
party views. These "distinct and contrasting" positions indicate
that the Whig party was not just a coalition of anti-Jackson
politicians, that both parties were more than alliances of politicians whose main objectives were the election of a president
and the dispensing of patronage.[61]

Spelling out the contrasting ideological perspective of the
parties, Ershkowitz and Shade relate the Whigs' views on the
positive role of corporations and credit in economic expansion
to "their conception of republican society as a commonwealth
of interrelated interests and their belief that government
should encourage the development of society." Corporations,
especially under limited liability, banks, and credit and currency not only fostered economic expansion and prosperity but
also promoted opportunity and democratization of the
economy. The commonwealth concept of society was also evident in the Northern Whigs' position on humanitarian reform
and "their emphasis on the role of government in encouraging
socially beneficial behavior and individual opportunity." Encouragement of sobriety and education would make self-
government viable and enable the poor to rise in an expanding
economy. Southern Whigs shared the Yankee Whigs' views on

promoting economic growth, but they did not wish to legislate morality. Their "unwillingness to join the movements for humanitarian reform reveals a deep fissure in the Whig party which could be covered only so long as these issues remained local matters."[62]

The Democrats' preconceptions about government and society, evident in their legislative behavior, were marked by less optimism and more fear of concentration of power than the Whigs' world view. They stressed limited government "to insure individual liberty rather than to create opportunity," an emphasis in accord with the Taylor of Caroline idea that opportunity results from not using political power to give away economic privileges. This notion of liberty and opportunity also related to the Taylor concept of the economy. As Ershkowitz and Shade put it, "the Democrats pictured the economy as a "static 'zero-sum' game in which certain groups—usually with the aid of corrupt government—enriched themselves at the expense of others." This game entailed a particular view of politics: "In sharp contrast to the Whig emphasis on community, the Jacksonians described a 'politics of conflict.'" The Democrats' economic and political views also referred to moral considerations: "Corporations illustrated the evils of government interference by giving advantages to privileged individuals while removing the moral restraints of personal responsibility." Similarly, banks, credit, and paper money not only denied natural economic laws, which were the key to creating wealth while assuring its equitable distribution, but also undermined morality. In sum, the Whigs and the Democrats "represented contrasting belief systems and differed about more than the spoils of office."[63]

Ershkowitz and Shade tentatively assert that "the dissimilarities of the major parties on the national level, were, with only modest alterations, reflected in the behavior and thought of state party leaders." This assertion, in itself, does not necessarily clash with the conclusion of Russo (who did not compare legislative behavior at the national and state levels) and Davis (who did not compare legislative behavior in Illinois with that in other states) that partisanship was associated with national issues and nonpartisanship with local issues. Ershkowitz and

Shade, in fact, taking cognizance of issues on which Democrats and Whigs voted together, say that "most often such instances were the product of convergence of different ideological strains or local interests rather than an indication of the basic similarities of the parties."[64] The methodological distinctiveness of Ershkowitz's and Shade's study, which enables them to recognize such convergence while asserting fundamental differences between the parties, lies in their considerably more comprehensive treatment of policy issues voted on, their taking seriously what men said as well as what they did, and their juxtaposition of word and deed to construct "attitude structures" or "ideologies" or "belief systems" with which Democrats and Whigs rationalized their behavior.

Still, although the Democratic-Whig division was similar at the national and state levels, one cannot disregard recent studies of partisanship at the local level. Benson, Gatell, Pessen, and Robert Rich have investigated and debated the question of the partisanship of the well-to-do in Northeastern cities.[65] In his study of the wealthy men of Boston, Rich asserts that it is unsound to generalize about the party affiliations of a socioeconomic group from the backgrounds of political leaders—as Benson did when he offered a consensus hypothesis concerning the general partisanship of the well-to-do on the basis of his tentative conclusion that the leaders of both parties in New York were well-to-do. To supplement Gatell's analysis of the political attachments of the rich in New York City, thereby further testing Benson's hypothesis, Rich examines the political affiliations of Boston's wealthy men. He finds that in "this citadel of Whiggery, the wealthy men were even more staunchly Whig [89 percent] than the rest of the city's voters."[66] Rich, however, does not attribute this Whig preponderance among the well-to-do solely to wealth. Among Boston's elitists ethnicity, religion, family upbringing, and personal conviction blended with business interests and economic status to produce political conformity. To the aristocracy a wealthy, renegade Democrat was still a "common man."[67] Yet, if we put aside Benson's general hypothesis about the partisanship of the wealthy, we can see that the debate is really not a debate at all. When Benson writes that all leaders,

Whigs and Democrats, were wealthy, and Rich notes that most wealthy men were Whigs, they are dealing with two different problems: the relationship between socioeconomic status and political leadership on the one hand and the relationship between socioeconomic status and political affiliation on the other.

Pessen turns to another question in a recent article, "Who Governed the Nation's Cities in the 'Era of the Common Man'"?, when he considers the relationship between leaders and followers. In regard to officeholding in New York City, Brooklyn, Philadelphia, and Boston in the years 1825–1850, "Although their number diminished significantly during the 1840's, rich men at mid-century continued to be inordinately represented in city government," and throughout the period wealthy men were elected by relatively poor voters. In regard to policy, "Antebellum cities were governed largely by the propertied for the propertied." Expenditures for public relief, social services, sanitation, and police protection were limited, while in the area of street improvements "prosperous districts got the first, the most, and the best attention." City governments were also sensitive to the needs of the well-to-do in assessing wealth, granting access to valuable real estate through leases on easy terms or sales at low prices, and financing improvements in transportation which businessmen wanted. If these policies were the policies of the wealthy, who were predominantly Whig, the common man could not obtain rectification by electing Democrats, so long as rich men dominated officeholding: "There is little evidence that the national party preferences of wealthy Democrats in municipal office led them to support policies and expenditures that were either distinctly Democratic or inimical to the interests of large property owners." Among rich men, class meant more than party.[68]

Pessen's portrayal of common men without power or even influence differs markedly from Ratcliffe's description of the relationship between leaders and followers in Ohio politics, and Pessen's disclosure of the absence of conflict between the leaders of the two parties over policy issues is quite different from the findings regarding such conflict presented in the various studies considered above of politics at the national and state levels. Pessen does ascribe discernible partisan preferences at

the national level to local leaders, and this attribution, together
with Ershkowitz and Shade's discovery of similarity in partisan
voting behavior between congressmen and state legislators, indicates that local politics is one thing and state and national
politics another. Historians have only recently begun to follow
Samuel P. Hays's suggestion, which we shall consider in chapter
5, that they abandon a uniform perspective on local and national political history.

Since 1945 Jacksonian historiography, impressive in quantity and quality, has provided some answers and raised a
number of questions, as advances in historical studies will always do—unless one assumes that historians move inexorably
toward the time when one of them, perfectly objective and
having access to all relevant data, will produce a definitive answer to a given problem in historical understanding. One cannot say that Schlesinger was wholly wrong and Van Deusen was
wholly right about Schlesinger's Jacksonians—New Dealers
analogy, but the Workingmen's movement of the Jacksonian
era was not the C.I.O. and, given the restorationist, laissez faire
tendencies of the Jacksonians and the interventionist, modern-
ist inclinations of the Whigs in the area of political economy,
Van Deusen appears to have the better of the argument. At the
same time, the consensus-entrepreneurial thesis has been badly
battered, especially in studies of the banking issue, and
Schlesinger was right to insist that all the political shouting
meant conflict over something more than winning elections.
Beneath this high level of generalization, however, one has to
say that Schlesinger's explanation of conflict has been substantially modified, although, given the aura of elitism that sur-
rounded the Whigs and despite the very impressive work by
Formisano and Shade, one is not quite prepared to conclude
that socioeconomic factors were largely subsumed under ethnocultural factors. This is not meant to admit into American
history class conflict in its Marxist form, for which the American left has long searched in vain.

After nearly twenty years Meyers' psychological variant of
the entrepreneurial thesis, for all its shortcomings, is impressive in that, given his focus on intellectual history and the pau-
city of relevant behavioral studies at the time he was writing, his

inquiry, which is a detailed analysis of the thought of several men, led him to distinguish between rising, backward-looking Jacksonians and rising, forward-looking Whigs. Later studies have substantiated this distinction, although recent works treat with a specificity that Meyers' book lacked the question of who the Whigs and Democrats were while relating their partisan identity to their various traits, and their voting behavior on candidates and policies to their thought. These recent studies, moreover, taking cognizance of Formisano's work, endow the distinction which Meyers presented in a consensus context with a quality of deep, intense conflict between belief systems. Meyers, as noted above, also confined his inquiry to an entrepreneurial framework, raising questions about entrepreneurs' politics which have yet to be answered while neglecting the possible role in Jacksonian politics of men whose fortunes were declining. Meyers nevertheless anticipated, even if inadvertently, the picture of Jacksonian-era politics which is emerging in the early 1970s.

Finally, it ought to be noted that the telling assaults on the electoral-machine thesis do not amount to a total victory. Interests involving self, party, and principle are both interdependent and independent, with their relationships and relative motive force varying from individual to individual at a given time and within a given individual from time to time. In other words, to hold that Russo's distinction between interest in self and interest in party falls within the electoral-machine thesis is not to deny that interest in party as party, and thus parties themselves, has independent causal weight in American politics.

The question of declining men also arises in connection with the symbolism of Andrew Jackson, which emerges as a major element in studies of the bank war. Russo asserts, and no one denies, that the banking issue was "*the* political issue of the 1830's."[69] Taking "political" to mean politics as politics or politics as party loyalty, one can readily understand how concentration on the banking issue might lead one to concur in the electoral machine thesis. Such assent, however, is subject to at least two qualifications: positions on the banking issue, as we have seen, fitted into contrasting belief systems which can be constructed from positions on a number of other policies as well, and the banking issue involved one of the more striking figures in American political history, "Old Hickory." In *Biddle's Bank* Wilburn lists the twenty Senators who voted against the Bank before Jackson's veto, when Jackson's wishes had less impact on the legislators than they did later,[70] and she identifies nine of the twenty as men who actually favored the bank but voted contrary to their feelings on the issue (she finds "no indication that any senator known to be against the bank actually voted in favor of it").[71] Did these nine senators, and voters in general, vote for Jackson as Democrat—as an advocate of other desirable policies who must be conceded to on this particular policy—Jackson as a charismatic personality, or Jackson as symbol of a belief system? Did Jackson's appeal attract the support of declining as well as rising men?

In *Andrew Jackson: Symbol for an Age* (1955), John William Ward concluded: "The unchecked development of the individual was the chief implication of the ideas of nature, providence, and will. It is in this respect that the figure of Andrew Jackson most completely embodies the spirit of the age." Both the theme of nature and the theme of will demanded tremendous exertion of the isolated man, but

> For the weak who might take fright at such a limitless prospect, or for the tender who might recoil from the buccaneering overtones of the theme of self-help, there was always the idea of providence. Man in America could commit himself violently to a course of action because in the final analysis he was not responsible; God was in control.[72]

This conclusion accords with the entrepreneurial, rising men thesis, which, McFaul observes, portrays "the Old Hero . . . as the moralist who eased the guilt feelings of the public by defining its rapacious actions as a disinterested crusade against the aristocratic enemies of the virtuous Republic."[73]

A recent, provocative essay by Michael Fellman suggests the possibility that if Jackson as symbol was not all things to all men, he was at least capable of attracting the support of men whose nostalgia was heightened by their declining fortunes in the new order as well as of backward-looking but rising men. Fellman distinguishes between the earthbound, tainted Jackson and the depoliticized, pure quality of the three transcendant members of the American Pantheon: Washington, Jefferson, and Lincoln. Jackson serves the function in American mythology, perhaps a necessary one, of a go-between who relates "ageless truths to an equally pervasive practical American experience."[74] It is conceivable that various facets of Fellman's democrat as realist appealed to different men in different situations, to declining as well as rising men. Ward's pioneering inquiry into the symbolism of Andrew Jackson should be supplemented by studies which combine intellectual and behavioral history. Ward's work suggests that there are social bases for a political figure's attractiveness, and recent commentaries, both behavioral and impressionistic, on the appeal of Ike and FDR indicate that historians should be extremely hesitant to rely on the explanatory power of charisma.[75]

Thus, as in the case of the recent period, beneath aggregate figures on socioeconomic conditions, party competition, party strength, and general and legislative voting behavior lay conflict which the consensus view minimized but which is now being recognized and defined in new ways. Given the party decomposition since 1900 (with a temporary reversal in the New Deal era) which Burnham describes, Perry M. Goldman's conclusion that by 1840 "politics had become an all-pervasive phenomenon and 'party' had become the most significant form of organizational activity in an age of voluntary associations,"[76] and the contrasting Democratic and Whig world views described in recent literature, one is inclined to believe that party meant more then than it does now, that the differences between Democrats and Whigs were far from superficial. Yet we must hesitate to generalize about party affiliations for the American electorate as a whole. The need for many more local studies is underlined by Burton W. Folsom's analysis of the party allegiance of the prominent men in Davidson County (around Nashville) Tennessee. Referring to studies of New York, Boston, and Wayne county, Michigan, and Pessen's conclusion that "rich men were evidently Whig," Folsom presents data on education, occupation, religion, ethnicity, and slaveholding which show that "no clear socioeconomic differences existed between the prominent adherents of the two political parties." In view of the persuasiveness of recent ethnocultural interpretations, the ethnic factor in Davidson County is especially significant. Nashville, Folsom concludes, "may represent a specific type of community not yet sufficiently explored —the ethnically homogeneous southern town."[77]

Still, there is evidence of deep political conflict in some areas. If one ascends to the level of generalization which stresses agreement on capitalism and (white) democracy, however, one must recognize the validity of this emphasis as far as it goes. In a sense the Whigs, who finally embraced democracy,[78] lost the battle but won the war. We can now see that the Jacksonian economy was transitory, that a fragmented agricultural economy gave way to a corporate industrial economy, that partial laissez faire (if such a term can be used) succumbed to the interventionist, welfare state. Again we encounter conflict within consensus, which is what Schlesinger referred to in 1945 when he wrote in the preface to *The Age of Jackson* about a "time of bitter social tension," the kind of crisis in which "our democracy has, save for the tragic exception, thus far avoided the terror of violent revolution."[79] In 1973 Pessen restated this view in his article, "Why the United States Has Never Had a Revolution—Only 'Revolutions.'"[80]

PART THREE

Departure

from Consensus

Chapter Five
The Belated Recognition
of Violence in Our Past

Beyond Political Economy

In this chapter we shall consider departure from consensus in the past and some reasons why it has only belatedly been recognized. In chapter 6 we shall consider departure from consensus in the 1960s. This later departure contributed not only to recognition of nonconsensual developments in the past but also to the departure by many historians in the 1960s from the consensus view, the subject of chapters 7 and 8. Still, departure from the consensus *view* did not mean departure from the *fact* of consensus. It conprehended not a denial of the fact of consensus but a refusal to accept that fact as virtually the whole story of the American past

Clashes primarily over issues in political economy were the concern of chapter 4. Burnham imposes limitations on the significance of this conflict:

> Controversies over public involvement in the economy have essentially tended to be differences . . . over what "minimum intervention" ought to be at any given time . . . . But this hardly means that there have been no political conflicts—or even that there have been no significant elements of class conflict—in our history. Still less does it mean that the party system itself has played an insignificant role in that history.[1]

Moving from political economy, where politics and economics meet, to the economy itself—from legislatures to factories and

mines and fields, from lobbying and debates over labor-rela-
tions bills to nongovernmental resolution of differences—we
encounter not only bloody battles between capital and labor,
but also, as Michael Wallace reminds us, "food riots, bank riots,
tollgate riots, Luddite violence, antirent disturbances, agrarian
land riots, and antieviction riots."[2] The departure from the
consensus view in the late 1960s by many historians appears to
be attributable in part to belated recognition of the frequency
and intensity of economic violence in American history. This
trend among historians can also be ascribed in part to belated
recognition of the significance of struggles in two other areas,
distinguishable from although not necessarily unrelated to the
fields of political economy and economics: racial and ethnic or
religious violence.[3] (It can be argued, to be sure, that while
belated recognition of violence in our past contributed to the
departure from the consensus view, the reverse is also true.)

Perhaps both the belatedness and the eventual emergence
of recognition of the importance of violence in American history
resulted in part from the sway of consensus history, which, with
its depreciation of conflict, dominated for a season but in time
produced a critical response. This reaction is now evident, as
noted in chapter 3, in a recent development in publishing so
large that it has qualitative implications for the study of history—a trend, or explosion, which can be identified merely by
referring to the huge Arno Press historical reprint series on
black history and literature, religion, immigrant ethnic groups,
and "Mass Violence in America," not to mention new historical
studies in these fields. Taking cognizance of the most recent
development in the inner dialectic of ideas in the writing of
history leaves us with a question: how could the consensus historians so underplay conflict in American history? One could, if
one wished, refer to the inner dialectic of ideas to answer this
question as well by pointing to the consensus historians' reaction
to their Progressive predecessors' overworking of the theme of
conflict—but one would have to bear in mind that even the
Progressive historians neglected conflict outside the sphere of
political economy.

Although much of the political conflict of American
history—particularly since the Civil War—has centered on "the

proper role of government in relation to the economy," as James P. Young writes, "there is more to ideology than economics."[4] Young's remark suggests another maxim: "There is more to politics than politics." If this proposition appears to be redundant, Allan G. Bogue dispels this impression:

> To prove consensus in our political history, the historian must define politics, political ideas, and the American political system narrowly. In reality it is as much a political act to exclude a racial or an economic minority from participation in formal political institutions, or to keep a depressed sector of the population in bondage by failing to provide adequate educational and economic opportunities, as it is to share in the task of choosing a presidential candidate. With this understood, American political life becomes once more the scene of fundamental political conflict.[5]

Benson finds Hofstadter's thesis of the unchallenged, or insignificantly challenged, legitimacy of the capitalist system consonant with conflicts not only within but also beyond the realms of political economy. It can be reconciled with struggles arising from

> different conceptions of the proper balance of agriculture, commerce, and industry in a liberal capitalist society. Also consonant with it are clashes over the division of profits, or over the best way to develop and preserve a liberal capitalist society.... [R]ather than deduce that agreement on fundamentals will necessarily produce harmony, it seems logical to deduce that agreement on fundamentals will permit almost every other kind of social conflict, tension, and difference to find political expression.[6]

Agreement on capitalism does not preclude controversy in political economy, which can occur simultaneously with controversy in other areas. Relative quiescence in political economy in the 1920s did not preclude controversy in other fields. Referring to struggles "waged over prohibition, religion, immigration restriction, the rights of Catholics and Jews, struggles which symbolize the cultural schism between rural and urban America," Lawrence W. Levine writes: "To call an era marked by conflict of this nature one of apathy and complacence is incorrect. To millions of Americans in the Twenties these were the conflicts and issues which were of primary importance, and it was into these channels that they poured their idealism and fervor and energy."[7] Nor were any of these issues nonpolitical. Discussing Al Smith's victory in Massachusetts in 1928, J. Joseph Huthmacher writes:

> Attributing the Democrats' gains to the ethnic aspects of Smith's campaign, Republican leaders trusted that they were merely temporary. "Strike out all the nonpolitical factors, the prejudices and passions which have marked the campaign in this state," declared the *Boston Herald*, "and the net result is a state as fundamentally Republican as it has ever been."

> The *Herald's* notion, that ethnic politics and cultural liberalism were somehow "non-political factors," was wrong; for indeed those were the most significant issues of American politics in the 1920's.[8]

Burnham's conclusions about conflict accord with Bogue's condemnation of narrow definitions of politics and Benson's views on conflict over matters other than capitalism. Surveying our political history, Burnham designates three types of cleavage as being of "paramount importance": the conflict of sectional subcultures; the friction among ethnocultural groups, stressed by Benson; and the clash between "community" and "society," emphasized by Hays.[9] Hays acknowledges as a source of inspiration the work of the sociologist Robert D. Merton, who introduced the distinction between "locals" and "cosmopolitans" at a time when consensus historiography was beginning its ascent.[10] "Locals" participate in "networks of primary interpersonal relationships within a limited geographical context" and are preoccupied with affairs arising from daily personal life, which is the source of their knowledge and the means of their action. "Cosmopolitans" enjoy secondary contacts over wide geographical areas and considerable geographical and ideological mobility, "with much variety of choice and of what one can do, think, and be." They develop "human relationships on the basis of similar functions . . . organizational structures to coordinate activities beyond the confines of the community, and . . . techniques to influence affairs over broad geographic areas." Historians, Hays contends,

> have erroneously assumed a uniform perspective in local and

national political history, emphasizing that national history is
either local and state history writ large or that local and state
history is national history writ small. But political life at one level
is of an entirely different order from that at another. They are
linked not by logical similarity but by human interaction.

Hays maintains that a "community-society dimension" provides
a framework which will "account for the different levels of
political behavior and the interaction between them."[11] This
interaction, one may add, encompasses more than politics in the
narrow sense and political economy. It involves diverging world
views.

A search for conflict extending beyond controversy over
issues in political economy not only reveals friction arising from
other factors, it also discloses the main sources of the clashes
which have produced violence—the kind of conflict we are concerned with at this point. In his introduction to a collection of
documents illustrating political violence; economic violence; racial violence, religious and ethnic violence; antiradical and
police violence; assassination, terrorism, and political murders;
and violence in the name of law, order, and morality, Hofstadter
observes, "When these are examined, one is quickly driven to the
conclusion that ethnic, religious, and racial mixture—above all
the last of these—are the fundamental determinants of American violence."[12]

Some Reasons for Historians' Neglect of Violence

Political economy is neither politics as such nor economics as
such; it includes the area where the two meet. In everyday
usage this territory is designated as the relations between government and the economy or the relations between government and business or some other sector of the economy. That
historians have devoted much attention to controversy in this
area is understandable. Possibly concentration on this type
of friction has contributed to the neglect of economic
conflict—clashes within and between various sectors of the
economy—as well as racial, ethnic, and religious conflict. Still,
focusing on one kind of conflict does not necessarily preclude
consideration of other kinds. It would seem that the nature of
other types of conflict has had something to do with their neg-

lect. It would also seem that belated recognition of their significance in American history was related to the nature of the times in which this overdue awareness came.

Wallace's comments on the quality and dimensions of economic, racial, ethnic, and religious violence help us to account for the delay in the perception of this strife. "But *why*," he asks, "have we forgotten about our violence?"[1] He first cites a factor unconnected with the violence itself: the Horatio Alger myth, which assumed an open, fluid system, the melting pot, and the redress of grievances through the democratic political system.[2] Then, turning to the attributes of our violence, Wallace points out that

> with the exception of the Civil War and Reconstruction, only a
> tiny fraction of our violence has been directed against the state.
> Perhaps because we have been conditioned by the European
> experience to consider only antistate violence truly significant,
> we have been prone to dismiss the American varieties. But if
> we shift our focus on violence and look at its place in relations
> between groups rather than in relation to the state, violence
> assumes a much larger significance in our history.[3]

A third factor Wallace cites is the nature of ethnic violence:

> the wavelike character of the migrations and the multiplicity of
> groups prevented the formation of a rigid ethnic hierarchy; that
> is, there was never an overwhelmingly predominant group for
> very long. Ethnic conflicts were thus seldom as lopsided as
> economic or racial clashes.[4]

In addition, without conceding any contradiction of his previous assertion of the importance of violence in American history, Wallace observes that although there is a tradition in our history of violence by the oppressed, striking features of this violence, besides its failure to challenge the legitimacy of the state, are

> its relative scarcity (our bread riots and Luddite violence were
> faint echoes of vigorous European traditions, for example); its
> characteristically low level (subordinate groups have engaged
> far more often in acts of force than violence, and even their
> violence has been primarily directed against property rather
> than persons).[5]

Finally, Wallace points out that a "seemingly simple explanation for the relative nonviolence of the oppressed is that our subordinate groups have been *minorities*. They have been outnumbered. They have been outgunned."[6] If minority groups refrain from resorting to violence because they are outgunned, they are also likely, for the same reason, to suffer defeat if they do have recourse to violence—and losers have usually received little attention in historical works.

If the rare and low level violence was not directed against the state, against what or whom was it directed? In general, it has consisted of conflict between groups vying for places in the power structure. "In the main, violence has been used most frequently and effectively by dominant groups [whites, capital, established immigrants] seeking to preserve their power and less frequently and effectively by subordinate groups [blacks, labor, recent immigrants] seeking to protest or improve their situation. The great bulk of violence . . . has been *repressive* rather than expressive or insurrectionary."[7] In regard to economic violence, more precisely labor violence, most of it has pitted workers against workers in clashes that were frequently exacerbated by racial and ethnic animosities. Established or dominant workers violently repressed aspiring or subordinate workers. The other main type of labor violence, worker versus employer, Wallace writes, "might more aptly be named 'capitalist violence,' " although it should be pointed out that private forms of violence (such as the Pinkertons and the Coal and Iron Police) were often supplemented in attacks on unions and strikers by the assistance of the state. When, during depressions, the unemployed demanded bread and work, they, too, were quickly suppressed.[8]

If various groups have used violence mainly against each other, why has their action not been directed at the state, and what factors in addition to those just mentioned account for its relative scarcity and its characteristically low level? Wallace prefaces his answer with a reference to Hartz:

> To be subordinate is not automatically to be rebellious. I think
> that, on a gross level, Louis Hartz's notion of a Lockean
> consensus is largely correct: most groups at the bottom of the
> social and economic scale have not raised *fundamental* objections

to the nature of bourgeois, capitalist America. They have
attempted to become part of it, to get "more," in Samuel
Gompers' words. Violence, therefore, would have been a most
inappropriate tactic. Those who do not want to overthrow, but
to be admitted, generally avoid violence. Still, there has been no
lack of dissatisfied, angry groups who might readily have turned
to violence to better their lot, so this explanation is not
sufficient.[9]

An additional reason that violence has not been directed at
the state is that much of our repressive violence has been informal and nongovernmental: "Subordinate groups have often
suffered more violence from dominant groups than from the
state." But the state often aided the dominant groups. How
could it do so without turning the thwarted workers into lasting
enemies or potential revolutionaries? The numerous explanations include:

> the realities of power, the ethnic and racial divisions among
> the working class, and the vitiating effects of bourgeois ideology,
> but perhaps one explanation is that the state was considered to
> be a satellite, firmly within the orbit of some dominant group.
> This may partly account for why it was seldom held directly
> and primarily responsible.[10]

Exoneration of the state, Wallace maintains, is an American
characteristic with deep roots. It is the hallmark of the vigilante
tradition, which is

> a product of the weakness of the early American state,
> particularly on the frontier, but also in urban areas where police
> forces were slow to develop. Partly it is due to the fragmentation
> of the American state into nation, state, county, town, and city
> governments, many of them often at odds with one another.
> More directly the dismissal of the state is related to the way
> decisions have been made in this country. A large number of
> critical decisions about the allocation of power and privilege
> have been made in private arenas.[11]

Wallace also notes that very early in American history most
white males participated in the formal political process—"We
had a voting proletariat before we had an organized pro-

letariat"—and that men who were economically subordinate but belonged to a racially dominant group felt they were represented to some extent by the state.[12] Meanwhile, ethnic groups often clashed—sometimes violently—over control of the state, "a prize worth fighting for."[13]

Access to the polls and electoral victories not only fostered exoneration of the state, but, along with numerical disadvantage or minority status, they also accounted in part for the nonviolence of the discontented. Blacks, for example, "have consistently avoided *revolutionary* action, and with good reason. Even if they successfully overthrew the government they would have to rule the other eighty-five or ninety per cent."[14] Conversely, most of our dominant groups have been majorities, repressive of what they have viewed as challenges to their own position and subject to only slight restrictions when they have contemplated resort to violence and to few limitations when they have used violence. Industrialists, it is true, were even a smaller minority than workers, but the "crucial fact is that the values of the capitalists were accepted by a majority of the country." In this regard, Wallace mentions the "widespread diffusion of property and the Horatio Alger mythology." They promoted a "monolithic consensus" which enabled the industrialists to "transmute a defense of privilege into a defense of something more abstract, more acceptable to the majority: the defense of law, order, and property."[15] Like Hartz's *ante bellum* Southern political thinkers, Wallace, who deplores the consensus historians' neglect of violence, finds it difficult to break the grip of Locke—that is, in his case, to eliminate Locke as a significant explanatory factor. He also echoes John Taylor of Caroline's complaint in the early nineteenth century that the moneyed interests were able to convince the people that an attack on ill-gotten property was an attack on all property.

Violence and Consensus

Wallace's references to violence, nonviolence, Alger, and Hartz suggest at least a few brief comments. It is trite to say that the Alger legend was a myth as an all-encompassing characterization of the realities of American life but was not a myth as a historical force. Yet this stale remark raises some important questions. If mobility was usually somewhat less than "rags to riches" or involved less than a high percentage of the population, how much mobility did it take to sustain the myth? Certainly the labor unions which accepted the wage system and endured had abandoned the Alger myth, but, as Stephan Thernstrom concludes in his study of Newburyport, Massachusetts, although industrial workers seldom moved out of their class, they had the opportunity to make advances in skill and to accumulate some property: they had occupational and property mobility. What percentage of the working class did they comprise? In other words, were there not many other laborers who might have mounted a formidable protest? No, Thernstrom says, as it were, because the other workers were drifters. They had geographical mobility, which in their case was not an asset: "The bottom layer of the social order in the nineteenth-century American city was thus a group of families who appear to have been transients, buffeted about from place to place, never quite able to sink roots." They were poor material for a protest: "By no means everyone at the bottom was upwardly mobile; the point is rather that those who were not were largely invisible . . . alienated but invisible and impotent." Thus a permanent proletariat of the Marxist type did not develop because, in part, "Few Americans have stayed in one place, one workplace, or even one city long enough to discover a sense of common identity and common grievance."[1]

If the nomadic American laborers failed to follow the Marxist prognosis, would they have done so if they had stayed put? The assumption or implication that they would have is at least quasi-Marxist. True, one might argue that if they had remained in one place, in the nature of the case which Thernstrom presents they would not have been down-and-outers, but the experiences of massive cyclical unemployment in the Great Depression and substantial structural unemployment in generally affluent times indicate that large groups of down-and-outers can be both stationary (remaining in the same locality if not the same dwelling) and apathetic.[2] That the drifters were not only invisible but also, as Thernstrom notes, alienated means that we cannot equate the absence of violence with consensus. As Wiebe asserts in a brief, perceptive note on "The Confinements of Consensus," the absence of violence, "which has been used to prove a consensus may actually demonstrate its opposite," for blacks, immigrants, and the poor often failed to engage in "ideological debate, hard political battle, and armed conflict" with the comfortable and educated "not because they really agreed on the fundamentals" but because they lacked articulateness, organization, and power. Absence of strife "may indicate social distance and power differentials so great that they preclude any direct confrontation."[3] But Wiebe leaves us with a question. Can we say that subordinate groups failed to fight not because they did not want to but because they could not? Or is it possible that they did not even want to fight? In order to have been articulate, organized, and powerful, they would have had to be different—in a different stage of social development and in a different situation—from what they were. This very lack of the attributes needed to acquire weapons for combat could also have rendered them apathetic. This is not to argue that the subordinate groups had only themselves to blame for their plight. We need mention only one manifestation of the power confronting them: David Brody shows how the steel companies kept their workers unorganized through a combination of repression, welfare programs, and exploitation of ethnic and racial differences.[4]

All of which leads us to Hartz and paradox: the nonviolence of the alienated or nonconsensual and the violence of the nonalienated or consensual. If alienation represented a limitation of consensus among the inactive, resort to violence represented a limitation of consensus among the active. The behavior of the active, however, was merely paradoxical—that is, only seemingly contradictory—for beneath the gross level at which subordinate groups accepted the Lockean consensus, some of them sometimes turned to violence in order to get "more." It should be noted in this connection that Wallace thinks that the concept of relative deprivation—the discrepancy between what people believe they are entitled to and what they actually manage to obtain—does little to account for the behavior of those who resort to violence in order to obtain "more": "Crowds are not irrational herds, nor are they mechanistic bodies reacting reflexively to stimuli like 'relative deprivation'; they are acting politically—with passion perhaps but usually with a clear sense of what they are about."[5] Nevertheless, as I examined the literature on the motives and conduct of active protesters in the early years of the Great Depression, I was impressed with the explanatory power of the idea of relative deprivation, but with reservations.[6]

The active protesters in the Farmers' Holiday Association in 1932 came from the better off—or recently better off—farmers in western Iowa, eastern Nebraska, and southern Minnesota who presumably had a strong sense of relative deprivation. If a farmer's income dropped from $3,000 to $1,000 a year, there was, it is true, nothing mechanistic about his engaging passionately in political action (3,000 farmers marched through Lincoln, Nebraska, in February 1933) with a clear sense of what he was about (in Nebraska a mortgage moratorium bill became law three weeks after the march through the capital). At the same time, this behavior is not irreconcilable with relative deprivation as a perception and a feeling which moved a farmer to act rather than a stimulus which, together with a mechanistic response to it, is an abstraction apparent only to behavioral theorists. The concept of relative deprivation, however, leaves some questions about protest among Midwestern farmers unanswered. Only about one-fifth of the previously well-to-do farm families in the areas in question were represented among the Holiday activists. In other words, all of the activists suffered from relative deprivation, but by no means were all of the farmers who suffered from relative deprivation activists. We need to know much more about the comparative qualities of the active and inactive. Nor can we assert without misgivings that relative deprivation is a behavioral phenomenon not subject to intellectual forces. David Grimsted writes to this point:

> Ted Robert Gurr, who has constructed the most complex and
> satisfactory sociological model for violence, argues that
> ideological sanctions for violence are important, but in "a
> secondary, rationalizing" way. Because "relative deprivation" is
> his key concept, Gurr claims that social tensions develop first, and

from these grow intellectual sanctions for violence. One could argue equally well that deprivation relative to something or other is always with us, and violence depends more on ideological or cultural channeling.[7]

There is also the question whether relative deprivation produces or does not produce violence, depending on general conditions. To put it another way, during the Great Depression demands for "more" increased after it became apparent that the bottom was not going to fall out of the economy, after partial recovery made it clear that there was something to get more of, and after the protesters had enjoyed at least a little more of it or had become aware that such enjoyment was possible. The unemployed, for example, although they staged a number of demonstrations in the years 1930–1932, were poor material for a revolution, and the significant activism on the part of laborers was undertaken by employed workers after partial recovery and after the rise—with the help of society at large in the form of New Deal legislation—of the unions. A major riot in Harlem came in 1935, after it was apparent that the very worst of the depression was over, and the same theme marks the conduct of the most poverty-striken farmers: the Southern Tenant Farmers' Union was not formed until 1934, and important sharecroppers' demonstrations did not take place until well into the 1930s.

It is conceivable, to be sure, that those who later demanded more of the system could have voiced, during the hopeless early stages of the depression, demands for another kind of system. Since there was only half a pie to cut up, they could have called for the baking of a whole pie in a new way. Lest we lose perspective, however, it should be noted that active protesters, early and later, were neither socialists for the most part nor more than a small minority of the population. After the depression struck, most Americans simply sat around waiting for something to happen—a phenomenon for which I have suggested several reasons: historical, intellectual, nationalistic, psychological, and political.[8] These factors were consensual either in themselves or in their effect—the absence of violent protest against the system. The ideas and values of the masses were essentially consensual, part of the context for the kind of protest that did occur.

Aileen Kraditor, a serious, brilliant socialist historian, states that

> those radical historians who deal with the ideas and ideals of past radicals rarely discuss the ideas and ideals of the majority of the people and of the ruling elites. Although radicals by calling recognize the reality of class power, American radical historians have rarely recognized one necessary support of that power. The *sine qua non* is the masses' acceptance not of the legitimacy of the ruling class and its power but of a whole complex of ideas and attitudes that indirectly support that power and indirectly legitimize the position of its wielders.[9]

Kraditor emphasizes two illusions: the illusion, which persisted despite great differences in wealth and status, that there is no ruling class in America; and the illusion that the workers have power (as well as an interest). The first illusion, she writes, is maintained because the ruling class is able to remain invisible as a ruling class; it does not claim that it is a good ruling class: it fosters the widely held belief that there is no ruling class. Meanwhile, the illusion of workers' power, which leads them to consider threats to the ideological hegemony of the ruling class as threats to democracy and the power of all, is sustained by the partial reality of the workers' interest. The hegemonic group considers other groups' interests and, without giving up its decisive role in the economy, makes concessions to these interests. Illusion is thus not total illusion:

> If it were a total fraud, the fraud could not have lasted as long as it has. The majority of Americans are better educated, have more opportunities for career choice, are better fed, housed, and clothed, and are freer in many ways than the majority of most nations' populations. A radical, of course, attributes their advantages to other things, but it is easy to see why the average American worker is convinced the system works in his interest. Supporting this conviction is the logic described above: the equation of loyalty to the established order with loyalty to democracy itself.[10]

It is difficult to disagree with Kraditor about results—widespread consensus on capitalism and democracy. One may disagree with her about causes, however, and Gabriel Kolko does so when he emphasizes the prevalence of consensus on the basis not of the carrot of concessions by the ruling class but as the result of the stick of repression. Certainly when the New Left moved off the campus and onto the streets, it met with the kind of repression encountered by many earlier movements that dissented from consensus. In regard to the 1930s, for example, I have asserted the applicability of George Rude's conclusion, with respect to social unrest in France and England in the period 1730–1848, that the violence of authority exceeded the violence of the protesters.[11] Kolko notes that despite "an economic context of inequality, poverty, and many years of unemployment, there never has been a class opposition to constituted politics and power." He concedes that a "sufficiently monolithic consensus might voluntarily exist on the fundamental questions indispensable to the continuation of the existing political economic elites." But, in the end, it is irrelevant whether the masses' consent is "voluntaristic or otherwise." The views and values they accept are those of the dominant class: "The prevailing conception of interests, the critical values of society, did not have to be essentially classless as Louis Hartz and recent theorists of consensus have argued." In the absence of voluntary acceptance—"during those rare periods when consensus breaks down"—the dominant class will resort to discipline. In Kolko's structural-functional, deterministic analysis the ruling class does what it has to do in a capitalist society. In the nature of the situation, it has the need, the desire, and the capacity to compel conformity, using its agent, the state, if necessary, to enforce a consensus which protects and promotes its interests. Kolko is realistic in recognizing the absence of class consciousness among American proletarians, while he is Marxist in his determinism and his epistemology in regard to the bourgeoisie, insisting that capitalist class interests, not the personal interests of bureaucrats or the pattern of recruitment of decision makers, ultimately determines policy.[12] Kolko's argument must be taken seriously and calls for comment.

Consensus, of course, does not exist if one accepts as the criterion agreement on the part of 100 percent of the population. Kolko alludes only to a "sufficiently monolithic consensus." Similarly, the total absence of repression as a requirement for consensus precludes its existence. Toward the other extreme lies constant, nearly total repression—in the capitalist world, fascism or gangsterized capitalism. Kolko does not place the United States at this end of the spectrum since he refers to the "relatively rare exercise of ever latent authority and repression."[13] He might reply that this rarity means that violence need not be used overtly but that the threat of repression is always there and is adequate to the needs of the ruling class. We may inquire, however, as to whether anticonsensus protests have been rare and protesters few in number because of the ever-present threat of repression, or whether repression has been rare because anticonsensus protests have been rare and protesters few in number for other reasons. These questions bring us back to the basic problem of the roles of ideas and force in history. There are two main approaches to this problem. The Marxist-Hobbesian view is that men naturally clash, that, as James P. Young puts it, "it is ultimately force rather than a complex system of shared values which holds society together and preserves order." The Durkheim-Parsons view is that force by itself cannot hold a society together, that there is conflict but it "takes place within a genuine consensual framework of shared values," a framework whose demise will threaten a society with dissolution. In regard to the distribution of power, there are unicentrists or elitists like sociologist C. Wright Mills, who attribute consensus in America to manipulation by a single "power elite," and multicentrists or pluralists like political scientists David Truman and Dahl, who see competing interests—admittedly, often competing elites—resolving their conflicts over policies within a consensual framework.[14] Kraditor, as it were, subtly combines these approaches, recognizing both the socialist's reality of a ruling class and the ideas of the masses, the latter resulting partly from mass interests and partly from elite manipulation, while Kolko espouses a materialist interpretation of history and is in the end a coercion theorist.

Most repression, as Wallace points out, has been exerted by "in" groups against others seeking to participate in the American system, but even when the state is involved, we cannot summarily dismiss the ideas of those who actually carry out the repression. The crucial role of the defection of the army to the people in the French and Russian Revolutions is well known. These defections were, to quote Rude, "a social and political rather than a military question."[15] Likewise, in the United States the army, the national guard, and the police have not failed to defect to the protesters because they have been tools, lackeys, or dupes of vested interests or the government. They have believed in the system or the American Way of Life as they have seen it, and most of the people have shared their belief.

Neglect of the ideas of the masses is also evident in Kolko's explanation of racism in industry: "It is the commitments of those able to implement their beliefs and goals, rather than of the powerless, that creates racism in the employment practices of corporations; and it is elite authoritarianism, which remains constant in the historical process, rather than working-class biases—which vary with circumstances and interest and often disappear functionally—that leads to authoritarian, institutions."[16] Certainly the rise of industry has exacerbated problems in race relations. The decline of unskilled labor has put at a great disadvantage the blacks who have moved to the cities with the liquidation of the plantation economy. But racism antedates industrialism. It is the government—Kolko's agent of the capitalists—which has enacted fair employment practice measures, and it is the white unions which have often excluded blacks.[17] One can make a case that the capitalists' employment practices have followed working class biases, that those biases have disappeared functionally when black workers have entered the industrial labor force as the result of pressures originating outside the labor movement. One may even pose a Marxist dilemma for Kolko: if capitalists can extract more surplus value from black workers than from white workers, why did they not exercise their elite authoritarianism and dictate the admission of masses of blacks into the industrial labor force a long time ago? The fact is that racism has marked both management and labor—although there are managers and managers as well as unions and unions, and elite racism is unlike working-class racism which arises in part from the white worker's view of the black as a competitor for employment. In other words racism transcends capitalism.

When we refer to the beliefs of most of the people, which Kolko recognizes but to which he denies a causal role, we introduce the question of numbers that Wallace discusses. One may argue that when 85 per cent of the population imposes its views on the other 15 percent, the very ease of imposition shows consensus—the repressors triumph without difficulty because they are so preponderant in number. On the other hand, a ratio of, say, 60–40 between the opposing sides might make repression so difficult that we would speak of a civil war. This argument from numbers, however, involves a certain perversity since arithmetic is not a valid test of a democratic consensus. What Murray B. Levin calls *The Democratic Capacity for Repression*[18] is by definition contradictory and does not accord with Hofstadter's insistence that consensus must be a matter of behavior as well as thought. Yet undemocratic behavior is reconciled with democratic thought in the repressors' minds when, as in the special case, discussed in chapter 3, of the Civil War—special if only for its magnitude—or as in the more typical case of Kent State, they uphold "law and order" by repressing what they consider a threat to democracy.[19] As McClosky concludes, "Among Americans . . . the principal danger is not that they will reject democratic ideals in favor of some hostile ideology, but that they will fail to understand the very institutions they believe themselves to be defending and may end up undermining them rather than safeguarding them."[20] Writing a decade before Watergate, McClosky presumably had in mind various extremist groups across the nation, not the president and his aides in Washington, D.C.

The Time of Recognition

Kolko's comments on repression appear in a book on foreign policy, and in this area, too, as we shall maintain in chapter 7, his materialist interpretation of history can be criticized on conceptual, methodological, and empirical grounds. To assign a causal role to the ideas of the masses in the maintenance of consensus is not, however, to drain American history of violence and conflict, which have been there in abundance. Any reference to the belated recognition of their presence in our past should take cognizance of the times in which the discovery occurred. Wallace notes that the great bulk of our violence has been repressive "at least until the 1960's," and he feels that violence may be losing its non-antistate quality as "blacks and radicals now clearly perceive the national state as a source of both oppression and possible relief."[1] Harvey Wish states that the "tempestuous nature of the postwar decades revealed the obvious importance of conflict studies as a clue to the struggles of our times."[2] A concomitant of recognition of the extent of conflict has been the assertion of the limitations of consensus both as fact and as a principle of historical interpretation. Upon returning to the United States recently, Bernard Crick, an Englishman who spent four years at Harvard in the 1950s, discerned a breakdown of unity into an unconsensual polity, a development we shall discuss in chapter 6. "It was said of Herbert Spencer," Crick comments, "that his only idea of tragedy was a theory killed by fact: this could cruelly be said of the Hartz thesis nowadays—at least we await a reply."[3]

No, the American experience has not been characterized by stasis and conformity to a preordained plan, and this nation has had its conflicts—from Shays' Rebellion to the Homestead and Pullman strikes to Watts and Newark and Detroit. Dahl declares:

> From the very first years under the new Constitution American political life has undergone, about once every generation, a conflict over national politics of extreme severity . . . . Whoever supposes, then, that American politics has been nothing more than a moving consensus, a sort of Rotary Club luncheon, has not sufficiently reflected on the recurrence of intense conflict, crisis, and violence in American history.[4]

Violence may or may not be, as H. Rap Brown proclaims, "as American as cherry pie," but as *American Heritage Magazine* asserts in bold type in an appeal for subscribers, "It's Part of the American Heritage," and, as Wallace concludes, " it is not too early to suggest that the use of violence has been a fundamental and grim characteristic of the American past."[5] Yet historians have "dwelt rather nostalgically," C. Vann Woodward commented in his American Historical Association presidential address of 1969, "upon what was appealing and virtuous in the American past, and rarely on the darker, more violent, and tragic aspects of the national experience."[6] (Woodward himself, although he had, as Michael O'Brien notes, "kept up a running dialogue with the consensus perception" in stressing the absence of consensus evident in the differences between North and

South, had enjoyed "no advantage over Northern historians in seeing suffering north of the Potomac."[7]) Still, lest we lose perspective, we should bear in mind Kraditor's main methodological point (to which we shall return in chapter 8): the historian must consider together the contents of conflict and the contents of consensus, including the ideas and values of the majority of the people, if he is to gain an adequate understanding of both.[8]

Chapter Six
Consensus
and the Politics
of Affluence

The Decline of the Conventional Dichotomy

In chapter 4 we referred to how change in political behavior lags
behind change in conditions. Burnham identifies such lag as the
source of the critical realignments of the electorate such as those
of 1893–1896 and 1928–1936. The lag is evident, on the one
hand, in the emergence of "increasingly visible social maladjustments . . . the product of dynamic transformations in a quite
separately developing socioeconomic system," and, on the other
hand, in the inability of the American policy structure or the two
major party organizations to take a long-range, or even an
intermediate-range, view of socioeconomic transformations,
and in the protests of groups injured or threatened by injury as
the result of the uneven distribution of the social costs of such
transformations.[1] If the policy structure and the party organizations were able to overcome the arguments of "already-organ-
ized shared-interest groups," the constraints of their own "consensual liberal-pluralist ideology," and the lack of time, they
could react to social maladjustments before a flash point is
reached, before demands become "so intense that it no longer
seems safe to defer them any longer."[2] Instead of continual,
small, relatively smooth adjustments, we have had periodic,
major, critical realignments. The belated response of the policy
structure and the parties to change in conditions, moreover, is
followed, as we have seen, by lag on the part of a significant
portion of the electorate.

Burnham discerns socioeconomic transformations in the 1960s which are sources of protest and counterprotest and may produce a critical realignment of the electorate: the "massive but uneven spread of material affluence"; the impact on the social structure of spectacular postwar technological advance; and one of the greatest transfers of population in modern history—the movement of rural Southern proletarians, especially blacks, into the cities. The uneven distribution of affluence has undermined the Alger component of the dominant Lockean ideology, particularly among the "children of affluence" in the colleges. Post-industrial technology is changing the old industrial pattern of stratification—upper, middle, and working classes—into a pattern made up of the technologically competent (a professional-technical-managerial elite), the technologically obsolescent (older local elites, white-collar employees, and white production workers), and the technologically superfluous (whites and blacks in hardcore poverty areas). The massive migration of rural Southern blacks has "nationalized the racial polarity and hostility which has long been a hallmark of the South." Burnham ascribes politically relevant traits to the three technologically defined groups: a considerable portion of the "competent" elite approves of the federal government's domestic social activism, and this elite tends to be "more politically cosmopolitan and socially permissive than does the society as a whole"; the "obsolescent"—often called "the great middle" or "middle America"—are the "chief carriers and defenders of the old middle-class dream and its associated values"; the "superfluous" are clients and natural political allies of significant parts of the competent elite.[3]

The political implications of Burnham's analysis are clear: he identifies the sources of a possible, if not actual, confrontation between an upper-lower alliance, which mobilizes a protest against the existing political structure, and the middle, or middle-white, group, which countermobilizes resistance to "new demands for redefinitions of social allocations through political means."[4] Before Burnham discusses these implications, he writes, "Reorganizations of what might be called politically relevant patterns of social structure have almost always produced not only economic and status conflict, but—in greater or lesser degree—profound cultural polarization as well." To the extent that current divisions in American society are cultural struggles between intensely held "world views," Burnham asserts, they "cannot be satisfactorily settled in liberal-pluralist terms or through liberal-pluralist political institutions." This is because, unlike conflicts over tariffs, taxes, or minimum wages, they "inherently involve not questions of more or less, but of either-or." Struggles between culturally antagonistic groups

> may, if they are not too intense or if the groups are small enough, be "institutionalized" through strong identification by one group with the party which is seen to be the enemy of the other; they may gradually wither away; or they may escalate to the point of civil war, genocide, or an imposed dictatorship over the one "side" and its groups by the other "side."[5]

In short, a realignment of the electorate resulting from escalation of cultural conflict could have dire consequences for our political system. We shall consider Burnham's extended discussion of the political implications of his analysis below. For the present I wish to emphasize the cultural-conflict component of the process of electoral realignment which, in his view, appears to have been underway since 1964.

While Burnham merely mentions conflict over status, another political scientist, Everett Carll Ladd, Jr., who analyzes ideological shifts among Americans from the 1930s to the 1960s emphasizes the rise of status politics as opposed to the politics of clashing economic interest groups. Ladd characterizes the "Conventional Dichotomy" which emerged with the New Deal as a division between liberalism—"the ideological statement of the interests of the 'have not' class of industrial workers and their allies who found the good society not in some agrarian past but in a future of more humanized industrialism and who evoked government to get there"—and conservatism—"the ideological defense of those of an elitist inclination opposed to the use of government on behalf of a broader extension of values." Conservatism was espoused by two quite different groups: a rural and small-town backward-looking but parochial elite and an urban, industrial nationalizing elite, forward-looking but deeply dissatisfied with being displaced by government as supervisor of nationalizing developments. Ladd then describes post-

1930 changes in the structure of society that have produced
new patterns of ideological conflict to which the "Conventional
Dichotomy" no longer speaks. He mentions nationalization of
the economy, communications, and culture; mass-extended affluence; the emergence of a new "ruling class" or socioeconomic group which "the balance of political power has as its
fulcrum" ("a white-collar, corporate based, new middle class
. . . residing principally in the suburban fringe around the central cities"); the massive development of status politics in which
new groups see demands for change as threats; and the "rapid
growth, maturation, and extension" of a scientific culture or
orthodoxy representing "a new way of conceptualizing public
problems." These have created a society with patterns of ideological conflict best understood, he concludes, as a Cosmopoli-
tan-Parochial polarity[6] (terminology similar to that of Hays
and Merton cited in chapter 5).

In stressing the explosion in affluence from 1961 to
1968—when Gross National Product expanded by a third—and
the rise of status politics, Ladd does not neglect the limitations of
this affluence. Poverty is still with us, and he discerns two opposite reactions to it. The proportion of American families below
the poverty line having been reduced to 17 percent by 1965,
some "serious men can begin to talk about the elimination of
poverty"—if we can go this far, let us go all the way. On the other
hand, there is the strong possibility that when poverty-stricken
people comprise only a fifth of the population, the other four-
fifths will forget them. To make this point Ladd cites Michael
Harrington's well known distinction between the meaning of
poverty in the past, when it was "general in the unskilled and
semi-skilled work force [and] the poor were all mixed together"
and today, when the poor are "the first minority poor in
history—the first poor not to be seen."[7]

Yet it is doubtful that the poor are invisible, even if they are
seen by many only in the press and on television, or that most
Americans are capable of indifference toward the poor. Even
hostility is not indifference, and poverty is widely recognized as a
major problem. It appears that Young made an observation that
was premature when, in 1968, he wrote, "Where once economic

affairs were the primary divisive forces in American politics, the evidence . . . indicates that foreign relations and civil rights will in the future dominate our political struggles."[8] As soon after this remark was made as 1972 there were signs that foreign affairs would become less divisive in view of President Nixon's abandonment of the Cold War as Holy War and the general acceptance of this departure (in August 1972, respondents to a Gallup Poll specified the President's trips to China—59 percent—and Russia—54 percent—as his two most important achievements, while all other issues rated 38 percent or less[9]). Meanwhile, TRB of the *New Republic* commented in September 1972, "As we come to the end of the 20th century, the two great issues are Race and Poverty."[10]

While one almost daily encounters commentaries on American society which imply the absence of poverty, Burnham and Ladd do recognize its presence as they point to the rise of affluence. Their writings, however, ought not to cause the reader to overestimate affluence among the nonpoverty stricken. In *The Myth of the Middle Class: Notes on Affluence and Poverty* (1972), Richard Parker notes that according to the official definition, about 13 percent of the population is "poor," having annual incomes of less than $4,000. The lower middle class, however, having incomes between $4,000 and $10,000, also suffers, in Parker's opinion, from material and cultural deprivation. Only the upper middle class and the rich, who comprise about 50 percent of the population, enjoy the affluence that is often erroneously attributed to most of the nation. Many suburbanites whose incomes exceed $10,000, moreover, undoubtedly fall into the category that Ladd designates as "marginal haves." Ladd, in fact, emphasizing the importance of the white-collar suburbanites' "swing" role in politics, neglects the blue-collar suburbanites who are often marginal haves, who do not share the cosmopolitan suburbanites' concern with the cities, civil rights, and foreign policy, and whose antitaxes, antiblack, increasingly isolationist views have considerable importance in politics.

Nor ought one to overestimate affluence and stress cultural and status concerns so as to dismiss interest politics—voting one's economic concerns—as being of little or no consequence.

Just as cultural conflict flourished during the New Deal era, when, as Burnham notes, economic issues were of "exceptional salience,"[11] so interest politics are significant now. The precise weight of this significance is difficult to determine, whether one consults comments on the 1972 elections or more general observations. For all the emphasis on the counter culture as the source of the "generation gap," Lubell concludes that "Currently one of the strongest obstacles to a reconciliation of the younger and older generations is this lack of work for young people."[12] Stressing economic concerns and micro- as opposed to macropolitics, James Burnham asserts that most Americans "translate political issues into their practical and relatively short-run bearing on their own lives and affairs." He predicted that McGovern would be "lucky to carry the District of Columbia."[13] Thomas S. Berry, an economist, correlating Gross National Product with presidential election results—macroanalysis—classifies presidential years in six categories according to average change in Gross National Product in the two preceding years: boom, brisk, good, fair, poor, bust. The party in power has always won in boom and brisk years and lost in poor and bust years. Berry predicted President Nixon's reelection because 1972 was a brisk year.[14]

In 1968, in his study of political ideology since the Second World War, Young distinguished between economic and noneconomic liberalism, between a "liberalism concerned with the distribution of economic benefits and one concerned with such problems as civil liberties, race relations, and foreign affairs."[15] In 1970, in *The Real Majority*, a widely discussed, comprehensive study of voter attitudes, Richard M. Scammon and Ben J. Wattenberg distinguished between the economic issue, which gave the Democrats majority status after 1929 when poverty overtook many of the middle class, and the social issue, which emerged as a major voting issue sometime in the 1960s:

> For several decades Americans have voted basically along the lines of bread-and-butter economic issues. Now, in addition to the older, more potent economic concerns, Americans are apparently beginning to array themselves politically along the axes of certain social situations as well. These situations have been described variously as law and order, backlash, antiyouth, malaise, change, or alienation.

But it is clear that Scammon and Wattenburg do not cast aside interest politics:

> The ever-potent Economic Issue always hold a high priority, and in time of economic crisis—great inflation, depression, or deep and lengthy recession—the Economic Issue will likely be the crucial Voting Issue in a national election. This is as it has been, as it is, and as it will likely continue to be.[16]

When Scammon and Wattenberg refer to the potency of the economic issue in a time of economic crisis and to voters behaving along the lines of economic issues for several decades, they are really dealing with quite different matters—a distinction which is relevant to our consideration of change in the alignment of the electorate from the 1930s to the 1960s. Voter behavior in an economic crisis, when enough members of all economic groups move in the same direction to determine the outcome of an election, is quite different from voter behavior and partisan attachments in a longer run. To establish that pocketbook or economic or interest politics explains shifts in the electorate in economic crises is not to establish that economic factors determine party loyalties which persist for extended periods and are expressed at the polls when everything else is equal—to borrow a concept which, as noted in chapter 4, the Survey Research Center uses to define "normal majority status." Needless to say, in a severe economic crisis everything else is not equal.

If it is necessary to draw this distinction, with its crucial temporal component, one must also point out that distinctions between economic or interest politics on the one hand and status and cultural politics on the other hand can be overdrawn in at least two ways. First, occupational achievement, an aspect of status, as noted in chapter 3, often relates to income, an economic fact; while race, religion, and ethnicity, also aspects of status, pertain to cultural politics and, in many cases, to income. Secondly, and of immediate concern here, interest and cultural factors affect politics simultaneously. This can be obscured by the assertion that the impact on voter behavior of interest politics rises and of cultural politics falls in bad times, and the opposite occurs in good times. Walter Dean Burnham, as noted above, avoids this distinction when he notes that changes in the social structure which relate to critical realignments involve cultural clashes. Accordingly, the Roosevelt coalition which formed during the depression–New Deal era reflected cultural as well as economic concerns. As Leuchtenberg remarks:

> When Roosevelt took office, the country, to a very large degree, responded to the will of a single element: the white, Anglo-Saxon, Protestant property-holding class. Under the New Deal, new groups took their place in the sun. It was not merely that they received benefits they had not had before but that they were "recognized" as having a place in the commonwealth.[17]

Thus to demonstrate the impact of economic interest on voter behavior in the short run is not the same thing as showing the impact of economic factors on voter behavior in a longer run. Two sociologists, David R. Segal and David Knoke, using data gathered in 1965, conclude that (1) economic factors have limited explanatory power with respect to persisting patterns of partisanship, and (2) insofar as economic factors affect partisanship in a longer run, they exert this influence in a way quite unlike that assigned to them by the class-conflict, Marxist model of political behavior. Before turning to Segal's and Knoke's analysis of the sources of long-run partisanship, we may recall the study of the counties of Pennsylvania, cited in chapter 4, which minimized the impact of economic factors on voting even in the depression year of 1932. We may also note these findings for Lima, Ohio: in the presidential elections from 1924 through 1940 the most Republican of the six wards of the city was the wealthiest ward in assessed value of real property, and the second most Republican ward was the poorest ward.[18] And one must ponder the results of a post-election poll by the Columbia Broadcasting System in which 47 percent of the unemployed said they had voted for the incumbent president in 1972, and Robert Axelrod's finding that in presidential elections, 1952–1968, the vote of both the poor (annual family income under $3,000) and the nonpoor (annual family income over $3,000) generally divided between the two major parties within a few percentage points of the division of the entire nation's vote.[19]

Segal and Knoke conclude that social structural factors —region, religion, race, occupation, and education—are more important than economic factors as sources of partisanship, and that to the extent that economic factors are influential, consumption is more important than production. Segal and Knoke define consumption by position in the commodity market (ownership of major appliances and automobiles) and position in the credit market (home ownership, liquid assets, income, and automobile financing). Production refers to position in the labor market (employment status, whether or not self-employed, reasons for considering a job change, and desire to go into business for oneself). Since the decline in the political significance of the production factor, the monistic Marxist view of political behavior has lost explanatory power because the Marxist model assumes that social relations are built upon an economic substructure defined by productive relationships.[20]

Segal and Knoke point out that some theorists who accept the Marxist explanation conclude from its withering applicability and from decreasing conflict in the productive sector that "cleavages in American society have lost most of their impact for most people and have been transformed into a consensual political style." Their data, Segal and Knoke assert, do not support this inference. In the absence of traditional class conflict politics, they conclude, the new consumption modes of economic differentiation serve as the bases of political cleavage; residues of earlier real economic cleavages persist as part of subculture systems (an obvious example is the *gradual* nature of the drift of the South away from regional politics since its economic base changed with a sharp increase in industrialization in the 1920s); and "non-economic cleavages, particularly along racial lines, still await resolution." These noneconomic cleavages do not "lend themselves to simple solutions based on economic rationality."[21] One may ponder the precise meaning of Segal's and Knoke's findings for politics since the partisan Democratic preference expressed by 71 percent of their survey sample diverges widely from actual voting patterns not only in presidential elections but also in elections in nonpresidential years, which are less volatile and more reliable as indicators of partisan identification than presidential elections.[22] Our main concern at this point, however, is that Segal's and Knoke's refinement of economic factors as political motives, although it departs from the "Conventional Dichotomy," provides no support for the argument that conflict is vanishing from the American scene as consensus becomes pervasive.

Realignment or Partyless Politics?

Having considered analyses of changes since the 1930s which have undermined the power of the conventional or New Deal dichotomy to explain voter behavior, while citing comments and studies which in their variety commend caution to anyone who would formulate a new explanation, we may now turn to Burnham's analysis of the alignment of the electorate as well as the realignment he sees emerging and its implications for the consensus idea.

Burnham points out that critical realignments have occurred every thirty to thirty-eight years, a fact that probably owes more to coincidence than to any inevitable cycle in the events themselves. The major party bolt type of third-party activity—the Bull Moose defection of 1912, for example—has not borne any significant relationship to subsequent realignment, but the protest movement type of third-party activity which has attained 5 percent or more of the popular vote has been a proto-realignment phenomenon, a harbinger of realignment and the basic issues of the next electoral era. Burnham puts the American Independence Party of 1968 in the latter category while pointing to the "remarkable" showing made by George Wallace in the Democratic presidential primaries during the spring of 1964. Although the protest movement type of third-party activity has usually had a "leftist" orientation, the AIP had a "rightist" orientation. Its antielitist objective, however, is common to all such movements, which have entailed "expressions of acute center-periphery tension at the polls." The AIP seeks to produce a "popular uprising against the conspiracy of top political elites, intellectuals, blacks, and others against the 'common man.'"[1]

On the basis of his historical analysis of critical realignments, Burnham hypothesizes that

> a certain kind of realignment may be in the offing, one in which the Democratic Party may come to be increasingly the party of

the technologically competent and the technologically superfluous strata . . . while the Republican Party may become more and more explicity the partisan vehicle for the defense of white "middle-America," the interests of the periphery against the center, and the values of the disintegrating Lockian-Horatio Alger creed which has dominated the country's political culture until very recently.[2]

Such a development would place "enormous strains on consensus," for all critical realignments have had civil war potential, a potential which was actually realized in one instance. The kind of realignment which may have begun in the "profoundly transitional" 1960s could involve

either the speedy liquidation of those aspects of the traditional American political formula which have stood in the way of central planning for change or—and perhaps more probably—a last-ditch effort to reimpose that formula's dominant position in the political culture by force if necessary.

"More probably" relates to Burnham's belief that the short and intermediate range prospects of the Republican Party, which in his analysis would not represent "Republicanism" in its familiar "me-too" form, are better than those of the Democratic Party, whose long-run prospects are good—if the run lasts long enough. In any event, "it is probable that any force great enough to produce 'classical' critical realignment under present conditions would also be great enough to break the system altogether, with consequences of incalculable magnitude."[3]

There is a strong possibility, however, that the growing process of party decomposition, noted in chapter 4, will prevent a traditional critical realignment, since by definition such a realignment involves a shift in the identity of the party whose normal majority status is due to the loyalty of its partisans. It is also possible that the mobilization of "middle America" and party decomposition may develop simultaneously. Various analyses of the 1972 elections, indeed, accord with this possibility, although one must bear in mind that in receiving 60.9 percent of the total popular vote Richard Nixon undoubtedly benefited from upper and lower as well as middle support. In September 1972, Lubell called the predicted Nixon majority a "shape-up coalition" composed of those who fit the economy as it now stands, who use "welfare" as a code word for racial resentment and attack it in an "effort to compel both black and white workers to 'shape up' to 'work ethic' standards"—although their antigovernment views do not rule out the use of government to further their own economic interests.[4] This rallying to the Lockean-Alger creed, meanwhile, was accompanied by spectacular ticket splitting.

In the nation as a whole, one careful study shows, the percentage of voters who consider themselves independents rose from 22 percent in November 1962 (the same as the percentage for October 1952) to 31 percent in November 1970.[5] The liberal TRB of the *New Republic* notes that "ticket-splitting couldn't have gone further than it did in 1972 with Mr. Nixon's lonely landslide."[6] The liberal Republican Ripon Society asserts that the 1972 election results foreshadowed not a period of party realignment but a trend toward "nonalignment" of voters.[7] The conservative *National Review* remarks that the Republican performance in the congressional elections did not validate—"not yet, at any rate"—Kevin Phillips' prediction that the GOP would become the normal majority party for the next decades.[8] Examples of ticket splitting are numerous. To cite only a few, analysis of the voting in a heavily Republican ward of Toledo, Ohio, indicates that Republicans in that city did even more ticket splitting than Democrats.[9] In Illinois an upper-lower combination carried Chicago's Cook County for Republicans Bernard Carey, candidate for state's attorney, and Senator Charles Percy as well as for George McGovern. Nixon carried Wyoming by 100,000 to 44,000, Republican Senator Clifford Hansen won reelection by 101,000 to 40,000, and Represtative Teno Roncalio, a Democrat, was reelected by 75,000 to 70,000—"a model of ticket splitting."[10]

Should we feel relieved that nonalignment or "dissolution of party identification and voting behavior at the mass base" may already have gone far enough to prevent a critical realignment which could break the system altogether? Hardly. Burnham believes that the emergence of partyless politics would mark "one of the great turning points in the history of American politics" and could be as dangerous as a classical realignment. He declines to predict precisely what American

politics without a high degree of partisanship would be like, but
he supposes that "political decision-makers would have wider
discretion, particularly in foreign and military issue areas, than
they have even now, and that specific interest groups would
enjoy even more influence on policy-making than they do
now."[11] TRB makes a complementary comment: "For 50 years
presidential power has grown and two-party discipline has
shrunk. But you can't run our 18th-century system of checks
and balances without effective party structure, short of piling
up presidential power. And indeed that's what's happened."[12]
That is not to imply that President Nixon is the American coun-
terpart of the European "man on horseback," but Burnham is
uncertain whether partyless politics is preferable to the kind of
critical realignment, with its sinister overtones, that he sketches:

> To the extent that erosion of party at the mass base is joined with
> mobilization for self-defense within the American "great
> middle"—as may very well happen—we would probably find
> that the political system had attempted to take for its motto
> the last sentence of the preface to *1066 and All That*:
> "History is at an end; this History is therefore final."[13]

As one might expect, Burnham's pessimism about the capacity of the American political system to accommodate current
shifts in the electorate through the traditional realignment process is shared by some political scientists but not by others.
James W. Lindeen, in a study of state-level support for Republican presidential candidates from 1896 to 1968, offers an implicitly optimistic conclusion: "It is testimony to the adaptability
and flexibility of the American party system that a return to
'regular politics' has followed each critical election period."[14]
John Roos, on the other hand, is skeptical concerning Kevin
Phillips' traditional interpretation that, as Roos puts it, "once
again an accommodation has been found by the two parties,"
with a moderately conservative Republican party emerging
from a realignment as the vehicle for continued majoritarian
consensus. In view of the militancy of the blacks and the left
and the militancy and "strange diffuseness" of the Wallace and
McGovern vote, Roos believed, as of early or mid-1972, that
"discontent appears to be wider and deeper than any accom-
modations presently being offered by any of the candidates of

the two major parties," He saw the possibility of deceptive electoral developments in which "either of the two parties could weld together a seemingly majoritarian coalition in 1972, and yet the underlying malaise might remain just the same."[15]

Moods, Values and Attitudes toward Change

Are we witnessing, as David S. Broder claims in *The Party's Over*, a breakdown of the two-party system which is related to a breakdown of American society as a whole? Is our condition aptly characterized by titles such as "The Sixties: 'This Slum of a Decade,'" *Coming Apart: An Informal History of America in the 1960's, The Troubled Land, A Nation of Strangers*, and *The Neurotic Trillionaire: A Survey of Mr. Nixon's America*?[1] Have the war in Vietnam and race relations caused, as David Brudnoy believes, "unparalleled division of the United States in this century, divisive to young, to old, to all parties and philosophies"?[2] Or have we heard this song before, as in 1932, when Louis Adamic found the United States "more a jungle than a civilization—a land of deep economic, social, spiritual and intellectual chaos"? Is the mobility of our population which Vance Packard claims has made us strangers any greater than that of other eras when it did not shatter social order?[3] Did we move in about 1945, as Rowland Berthoff holds, from an age of imbalance, disintegration, or disorder into a period of balance, integration, or order?[4] How do Americans feel about the state of the union?

Certainly attempts to capture the national mood, an elusive but important phenomenon since it both reflects and contributes to the state of the nation, do not encourage complacency. In 1970 John R. Brooks characterized six successive post–World War II moods: the nest-building mood with its boom in marriages, births, and home construction and lack of protest; the mood of dismay as the Korean War shattered only five years of peace and of frustration in the face of a "limited war"; the McCarthy era mood of fear and distrust; the Eisenhower mood of long-deferred self-indulgence; the Kennedy mood of responsibility and optimism that we could overcome our problems (the latter rested more on JFK's style than on practical accomplishments—although the denouement of the missile crisis and the test-ban treaty did dispel the old fear of nuclear war); and the present mood—arising amid steady, beneficent material change—of paralysis and violence, reappraisal and gloom or doubt and disillusion verging on despair. Brooks was not certain when it was that the national mood shifted, but he posited that a dramatic reversal occurred sometime recently—probably in 1965. Nor was he certain what had initiated this change, although he referred to Lee Harvey Oswald (in which case developments in 1965 would have been the result of accumulated momentum), the escalation of the war in Vietnam beginning in early 1965, and the Watts riot of August 1965, which made many Americans aware for the first time of the rage and despair of urban blacks outside the South. Brooks also specified possible longer-run causal factors: the computer revolution, which has caused mechanical thinking to be mimicked in everyday life and has provoked a reaction in the cult of irrationality; and television and jet travel, which have made the world a village while fostering tribal village methods of instinctual communications as well as passive receptivity.[5]

Brooks illustrated the present mood in several ways. With respect to attitudes toward military affairs and especially toward our own military, he noted that popular reactions to a uniform were enthusiastic during the Second World War, neutral in the postwar period, and often negative after 1963. Broad expressions of patriotism were generally considered commendable in 1945, harmless in 1963, and subsequently, for about half the population, indicative of extremist political and social views. Among our leaders Brooks discerned a paralysis of will, a demoralization which has spread to many Americans. Finally, he underlined changes in attitudes and values among the young, evident in campus revolts, the cult of irrationality (astrology, Oriental occultism, and drugs), and the redefinition of sex roles. Brooks' reference to the young made his prognosis grim, for he pointed out that the latest shift in mood occurred precisely with the coming of age of the post–VJ Day generation—which truly belonged to the new TV, jet, space, computer, nuclear world.[6]

The title of Brooks' article, "A Clean Break with the Past," suggests that something snapped in 1965. It is difficult for a historian to accept unquestioningly an interpretation which hinges on such an abrupt disjuncture. Brooks, however, did not necessarily argue for a departure without roots in the past, since the post–VJ Day generation had had twenty years to acquire its views before coming of age and vocalizing them. Some of the views of the new generation, moreover, were expressed by the "Beat Generation" of the 1950s,[7] while the historian of culture and social thought can identify in the late 1930s and the 1940s direct antecedents of post–Second World War radicalism in these areas.[8] Nor should we accept the concept of a sudden severance without recognizing that it is unrealistic to treat the post–VJ Day generation as a monolith. There is also evidence that the current mood which Brooks described exists among the "over thirty" portion of the population as well.

In any case, national moods, which Brooks portrayed as following in staccato-like succession, seem more volatile than national values or basic attitudes toward change. The anthropologist Clyde Kluckhohn, in a survey of literature on shifts in American values published in 1958, concluded, "The most generally agreed upon, the best documented, and the most pervasive value shift is what Whyte (1956) has called 'the decline of the Protestant ethic,'" which embraces both Puritan morality (respectability, thrift, self-denial, sexual constraint) and the work-success ethic ("austerity, individualism, and devotion to occupations and callings").[9] Some students of this shift, Kluckhohn noted, traced its beginnings to the latter part of the nineteenth century.[10] In his presidential address to the American Historical Association in 1972, Thomas C. Cochran observed, "In the 1920's particularly, older American values were being eroded by new scientific ideas." He was especially concerned with business management, but he asserted, "The weakening of the belief that success was self-justifying had profound ramifications outside of business."[11] Still, Burnham believes that the persisting grip of Lockean values—the consensus historians' analogue of the Protestant ethic—on the minds of many Americans is, in view of the irrelevance of those values to new conditions, dangerously disruptive. Crick, on the other hand, feels that out of disunity—friction between adherents to

Lockean values and defectors from them—may emerge a new kind of stability. We shall take up these contrasting prognoses after a brief consideration of recent attempts to gauge the national mood in general and attitudes toward change in particular.

Opinion samplings of public qualms or contentment concerning self and society reveal both satisfaction and malaise. A national survey of January 1971 by Potomac Associates showed that 47 percent of the people (and a majority of those having an opinion) believed that unrest and ill-feeling were "likely to lead to a real breakdown in this country."[12] A Gallup Poll of mid-1971 presented a mixed picture. Large majorities of Americans were highly satisfied with the basic circumstances of their lives: jobs (81 percent), income (62 percent), housing (74 percent), education (63 percent). These figures, however, represented declines since a 1969 survey of 6, 3, 4, and 1 percent, respectively. The percentages for blacks, moreover, were lower—63, 41, 51, and 57—than the overall percentages, but they represented a rising trend since 1963. With respect to the "quality of life" in their communities, 78 percent of the whites but only 51 percent of the blacks said they were satisfied. These figures do not justify complacency, much less euphoria, and caution against such a response to these data is the burden of the interviewees' attitudes toward the future facing them: in this regard 56 percent of whites and 43 percent of blacks said they were satisfied. Finally, one American in eight said he would like to emigrate to some other nation if given the opportunity.[13]

In mid-1972 Potomac Associates found that fears of imminent breakdown, evident in their poll of January 1971, had abated. Although Americans no longer felt a sense of national deterioration, however, they showed little enthusiasm about where they stood, either personally or as a nation. They had a tempered sense of progress in some areas, but they rated the state of the nation as just fair to middling.[14] In fall 1972, the Harris Survey found Americans somewhat more pessimistic than they appeared to be in the second Potomac Associates poll. The Harris Survey asked people to state whether they had "a great deal of confidence, only some confidence, or hardly any confidence" in the leadership in various areas of public interest. In 1966 the Harris Survey had asked the same question. This is how some of the results of the two polls compare:

Area of Public Interest	Percentage Expressing Great Confidence in the Leadership	
	1966	1972
Press	29	18
Television	25	17
Advertising	21	12
Medicine	72	48
Banking and Finance	67	39
Scientific Community	56	37
Educational Institutions	61	33
Federal Executive Branch	41	27
Congress	42	21
Supreme Court	51	28

These figures, in James J. Kilpatrick's estimate, were "sobering, dismaying, frightening," indicative of a "disenchantment with old institutions, a kind of alienation between people and their government, a feeling of frustration that emerged as contempt. It was a malaise of the spirit, pervasive and contagious."[15]

In the fall of 1972 a seminar of eight writers, educators, and polltakers, discussing the mood of the nation, used such words as "lethargy," "resignation," "frustration," "impotence," "disillusionment," and "chaos." Betty Friedan, author of *The Feminine Mystique,* said, "There's a tuning out of the old politics and nothing is coming in that tunes in to the needs of the people." George Reedy, President Lyndon Johnson's press secretary, observed that apparent lethargy did not mean that people were "losing their moral sense, but only a sort of feeling that they cannot do anything about it." On a somewhat brighter note, the pollster Daniel Yankelovich said, "Most people are not pessimistic about their personal situation but about what is happening in the country at large." In the opinion of George Gallup, the mood of the nation was downbeat but far from one of helplessness. He suggested the impermanence of moods when he commented that "the mood has changed in the last six months from despair to watchful waiting; people are beginning to believe that things can change as a result of agreements with China and Russia and the improving economic situation." While Gallup referred to a short-run change in mood, Robert Semple, Jr., White House correspondent of the *New York Times,* argued that disillusionment had spread because "The speed of events has outrun man's ability to keep pace with them."[16]

Semple's proposition is one that historians have weighed, and will continue to ponder, since in their attempts to make sense out of the past they try to avoid becoming so fascinated with particular events or developments in a narrow time span that they neglect longer-term forces. Short-run shifts in national mood may tell us something about a society, but they do not afford an adequate explanation of the lag of changes in thought and institutions behind changes in conditions. Without contradicting this stricture, perhaps we may properly consider current opinion, focusing briefly not on national mood as such but on attitudes toward change. Then we shall consider the prospects for our accommodating changes in conditions amid changes in the state of the Lockean consensus.

Americans' attitudes toward change were the subject of many commentaries on the presidential election of 1972. In companion articles in the *New York Times Magazine* in the summer of 1972, Arthur M. Schlesinger, Jr., predicted that McGovern would win, and Kevin Phillips asserted that President Nixon's long lead in the polls would hold up on election day. Both writers, however, viewed the contest as one between a Democratic candidate who believed that Americans wanted change and a Republican candidate who saw Americans as feeling threatened by change.[17] Did the accuracy of Phillips' forecast mean that his estimate of Americans' attitudes toward change was also valid? Opinions varied. Mike Feinsilber of United Press International called the outcome of the election a "massive endorsement of the status quo."[18] The pollster Lou Harris, on the other hand, in an address to the National Press Club, declared that, far from voting for the status quo, the people gave the President a "powerful mandate" for change in foreign policy and a Democratic Congress a similar mandate for change in domestic affairs.[19]

Harris saw the nation divided almost evenly between pro-change and anti-change coalitions. His analysis of these groups accorded to some extent with Burnham's upper-lower versus the

middle assessment of the alignment of the electorate. The pro-
change coalition largely consisted of under-thirty suburban independents with some college education and incomes of
$15,000 or more. The anti-change coalition mostly comprised
"those over fifty, union members, those with an eighth-grade
education or less, small-town residents, and those with incomes
between $5,000 and $10,000 a year," but their numbers were
shrinking. President Nixon's majority, Harris concluded, drew
on both the pro- and anti-change coalitions. Many members of
the pro-change group voted for Nixon because they were
"committed to change—concrete and pragmatic, not ideological
but real," and McGovern, who began his campaign as the candidate of change, "proved incapable of communicating a message
of orderly as opposed to radical change."[20] One may add that
Nixon benefited from an anti-change feeling with respect to
foreign affairs, a reluctance to change horses in the middle of
the stream. In another sense, this feeling was pro-change since it
reflected approval of the President's new departures in relations
with the Soviet Union and China. Harris, in fact, contended that
if the election had turned on domestic issues alone, Nixon could
have lost, or won by a far more narrow margin than he did.[21]

Nor did attitudes of party activists and analysts toward
change present a clear picture. The election in December 1972
of Texas conservative Robert Strauss as Democratic national
chairman represented the emergence among Democrats of
"me-tooism"—a stance which Old Guard Republicans had long
ascribed deploringly to the liberal wing of their own party. At
about the same time Governor John J. Gilligan of Ohio stated
that under the leadership of liberals like himself, the Democratic
party had alienated middle America and that it should now
make a turn to the right to regain the loyalty of the working class.
Gilligan called for a "realistic" rather than a "conservative" shift
involving programs which, unlike those of the 1960s, would be
of "general benefit" rather than helpful "only to one group of
people." He insisted that governors and mayors should play an
important role in the design and administration of the new
programs.[22] Meanwhile, columnists Clayton Fritchey and
Stewart Alsop pointed to the possibility that me-tooism may be
out of date by 1976 as issues such as Vietnam, amnesty, busing,
and marijuana fade;[23] and Kevin Phillips declared that if

Nixon's majority were to become a normal majority, more than the dismantling of the ineffectual and unpopular programs of the sixties was needed:

> Conservatism must evolve its own positive approaches to housing, education, unemployment, productivity and the rest of the national challenges. This activism is the baton which the New Majority must accept from the exhausted New Deal coalition if conservatism is to win the next lap of American politics.[24]

Like columnists and pollsters, scholars offer various findings about Americans' attitudes toward change. Lloyd A. Free and Hadley Cantril to some extent account for the way that people accept in practice changes that they profess to condemn by pointing out that not only nine-tenths of ideological liberals but also one-fourth of ideological conservatives are "operational liberals."[25] On the crucial question of individualism and social control or collectivism, Americans show ambivalence—something that is widely known but brilliantly spelled out and documented in Ellis Hawley's *The New Deal and the Problem of Monopoly: A Study in Economic Ambivalence* (1966). Like Roosevelt and the New Dealers, who could not choose between antitrustism and collectivism, ordinary citizens daily express both individualist and collectivist values—sometimes in successive sentences. While ambivalence denotes absence of choice or resolution in the face of change, compromise, according to William G. McLoughlin, is pursued by Americans as a way of dealing with change and of resolving problems, but it becomes an end in itself or, at another level of analysis, a means to an end since Americans believe that an indefinite succession of compromises will lead to utopia.[26] The result is watered-down measures rather than effective attacks on social problems. We are, indeed, what Michael Kammen entitles a dazzling piece of scholarship, a *People of Paradox* or, as the title of an earlier work of Kammen's puts it, a *Contrapuntal Civilization* in which polarity or biformity is so pervasive that America is, to borrow Marcus Cunliffe's phrase, "a dialectic without a synthesis."[27] Can this kind of society mount a thrust sufficiently effective in coping with change to sustain stability? I will risk a response to this question in the concluding section of this chapter after presenting others' pessimistic and optimistic replies.

The Breakdown of Consensus: Pessimism and Optimism

It should come as no surprise to the reader that we have drawn on Burnham's writings to represent the pessimistic estimate of our present state and the prospects for democracy. His analysis of recent developments in the alignment of the electorate has been summarized above: government and parties lag behind changes in conditions, resulting in periodic critical realignments; the current emergence of an upper-lower versus the middle division with cultural dimensions may result in a critical realignment which could be dangerous, conceivably shattering the traditional political system; or a critical realignment may be prevented by the rise of partyless politics, a situation which could be equally perilous. What needs to be emphasized here is the vital role in Burnham's analysis of the acceptance by the overwhelming majority of Americans of "bourgeois individualism and its Lockean-liberal political variant as their consensual value system."[1]

This value system has produced both a relatively unchanging political system and the separation of this system from a dynamically developing socioeconomic system. The survival of the political system in such a disjunctive situation is attributable, again, to the "reception of Lockean individualism," which has prevented any large group within the society from developing the motivation to "organize for the capture of state power in order to inaugurate central control over and transformation of the socioeconomic system." The Civil War was the only case in which "antagonisms over social fundamentals burst through this elaborate Lockean defensive network." It is conceivable, Burnham writes, that given steady economic growth which is "not seriously undercut by depression" fundamental changes in the political system in a society such as ours might never occur. But the "Lockean cultural monolith . . . is based upon a social assumption which comes repeatedly into collision with reality." This assumption is that socioeconomic development, autonomous—as it should be—from political direction, will proceed with "enough smoothness, uniformity, and general benefits to individuals that it will be entirely compatible with the

usual functioning of Lockean political structures." Yet there
have been recurring social or economic maladjustments great
enough to produce political effects which the normal processes
of American politics cannot contain. This is where critical
realignment enters the picture as the chief tension management
device of the political system. It permits, for a generation or so, a
"restabilization of our politics and redefinition of the dominant
Lockean formula." Still, this kind of adjustment is symptomatic
of political nonevolution because it has taken place "thus far
always within a liberal-Lockean context."[2]

We are a people, Burnham states, which is "socially
heterogeneous but is overwhelmingly committed to an individualist, middle-class, achievement-oriented social value system." We have been able, moreover, to apply the "Lockean
individualist dogma" to larger social or economic units than the
classical atomic human being, but the "price which has been paid
in our public life for the survival of the Lockean political dispen-
sation into an era of big organization and high industrialism
has been very high." Only recently have scholars and political
activists begun to assess some of these costs. The task which the
American polity now faces is "no less than the construction of
instrumentalities of domestic sovereignty to limit individual
freedom in the name of collective necessity." Such construction
will not result from a critical realignment because of continuous
party decomposition. It could result from drastic changes in
party structure and mass behavior, but this would require a
revolution in social values. Such a revolution, however, would in
all probability be overwhelmed by a counterrevolution among
a majority of the population. In sum, the breakdown of consensus—the defection by a minority from individualist values
—could result in the imposition of consensus by the majority. Burnham is thus very pessimistic about the prospects for
democracy as we face the crisis of our time, "at bottom the crisis
of traditional Lockean ideology and institutions in an age
marked by their increasingly obvious irrelevance to the policy
choices at hand."[3]

While Burnham delineates the persistence of the Lockean
values among some Americans and the weakening of their hold
on others, Crick also sees the end of the monolithic hold of the

Lockean consensus. But in his prognosis Crick does not share
Burnham's pessimism. Like Burnham, he cites Hartz's work,
crediting *The Liberal Tradition in America* with a "profound effect"
on many American historians. He accepts Hartz's thesis of universal liberalism, which shows that by any possible European
comparisons the so-called American traditions of reaction and
progressivism appear virtually identical. In foreign affairs this
irrational liberalism resulted in an all-or-nothing stance, a "fear-
some sense of imperial mission" or isolationist escape, "either a
liberal conduct of foreign relations, or as few foreign relations as
possible—so as to preserve liberalism at home from contamina-
tion." In economic matters, "as well as the lack of any fundamental disagreements about how to organize the economy, there has
been an almost universal belief in its ever-expansive power and
affluence." In politics liberal unity resulted in the politics of
interests groups. American parties, from the English point of
view, did not lack ideas but simply did not differ in their ideas.
"A pragmatic politics could be assumed and practiced not because of the absence of values, but precisely because of their
presence and unity."[4]

As the decade of the 1970s began, Crick saw the breakdown
of liberal unity in America. In foreign affairs there was the
"abandonment of the idea of victory, even of forward containment, still less of ideological victory." In economic matters there
was some doubt concerning the myth of infinite expansion and
abundance. Even while deflationary policies were being pursued, the end of involvement in Vietnam seemed to require
inflationary policies. In politics there was the failure of the party
system and the federal government to deal effectively with great
social problems such as urban decay, race relations, residual
poverty, and law and order. As unity gave way to disunity, the
antiwar movement on the campuses revealed "empirical intensity in hitherto highly intellectual concepts like 'anomie' and
'alienation.'" An exotic literature of protest and exotic brands of
socialism, anarchism, and even rejection of all political action
flourished, although not among the society at large. Still, that the
protesters were taken seriously was impressive because they
questioned "some of the assumptions of an acquisitive society."
They were not the first to criticize the "puritan religion of work

and labour as the highest values." When Niebuhr, Arendt, and others had criticized "possessive individualism," however, no one paid any attention to them. Americans had moved from a consensual into an "unconsensual polity," which perhaps accounted for their present malaise, but despair was not in order:

> Americans are having to adjust, rather suddenly, to a condition long familiar to inhabitants of many other countries: living in a society that can no longer pretend to be a nation in the sense of a unified culture agreeing on basic values. The consensus has broken down. But did the consensus ever have to be that consensual? Perhaps once, in the new nation and the nation of mass immigration; but plenty of states have survived amid a plurality of values, have seen their consensus and sense of nationality narrowly but strongly in the political institutions themselves, neither in something that is compulsive and compulsory, as in the Communist States, nor perhaps as meaninglessly vague as the late General Eisenhower's frequent appeals to "our common Hebraic-Graeco-Roman civilization."[5]

In the remainder of his essay Crick specifies what is required if the United States is to survive amid a plurality of values, and he points to some signs that these requirements may be met. Crick's formula stresses stability, which rests on effective government, which, in turn, derives from a "hard" pluralism. He observes that "even political scientists come to believe that strong government has something to do with the cohesion of society." In order to be effective, government must assure opportunities for the young and show "intolerance towards discrimination and social and economic inequalities of the kind that permanently doom an individual to remain always a member of 'his community' whether he wishes to or not." Political institutions must be capable of "conciliating and compromising genuine differences of morality and policy, such as they now are," for a "plurality of values simply based upon hardship and oppression is the seed-ground of rebellion."[6] Crick's causal sequence of "hard" pluralism, effective government, and stability despite the absence of consensus suggests McClosky's conclusion, noted in chapter 3, that "so long as conditions remain stable, consensus is not required . . . its absence in an otherwise stable society need not be fatal or even particularly damaging."

Crick's concept of "compromise," different from McLoughlin's, is central to his diagnosis and prescription. Amid a unity of values Americans have been able to resolve conflicts of interest by bargaining, by counting votes or cash. Suddenly, amid a conflict of values, "the habitual processes of bargaining appear to have broken down." It is evident that bargaining "works within a culture, but not among cultures; among cultures a mixture of empathy and realism is called for." This mixture marks "hard" (as distinguished from "soft") pluralism, which makes compromise possible. Crick considers soft pluralism—the "acceptance of diversity for the sake of diversity"—as fatuous, a "failure to choose, to make qualitative decisions, and as a pseudo-social science and destructive politics in which, in fact, the organized interests always defeat the unorganized majorities." Hard pluralism, on the other hand, is "not an acceptance of a plurality of values and interests as such, but a toleration of necessary differences that are based on real diversities of the dimension of cultures, or at least of subcultures." This kind of toleration is the "limited acceptance that one extends, out of a mixture of policy and humanity, to those things of which one disapproves." It is based on recognition that the nation's safety does not depend on uni-ideological conformity, that in a mature, complex American society Hartzian liberal unity has long since served its purpose, that Americans "have to learn to disapprove openly of each other." It is, in fact, compromise: "when one knowingly allows a value that one holds, and will not give up holding, to be diluted in a given circumstance (usually because of some other value that one also holds, respect for law, peace, stability, sometimes even because of respect for the sincerity of another of whose values and objectives one disapproves)."[7]

Crick is not dismayed by the "end if ideology," which has really been the "end of a particular ideology, that of the necessary unity of American liberalism." In its place has arisen a plethora of political "doctrines," a term Crick chooses deliberately to denote "sets of concrete policy-objectives based upon theory—each group may have its own ideology." He bids good riddance to ideologies "either as single total solutions, or as the total complacency—as it now seems—of the belief in a unified liberalism." Indeed, Crick detects certain signs that at a time when "the majority is being asked to compromise with aroused and articulate minorities in a way that it feels affects its principles," America may acquire the capacity to compromise so as to achieve stability together with social justice. The disappearance of the illusion of American omnipotence in foreign relations, involving the demise of both the bi-polar and the convergence theses of international politics and Nixon's acceptance of coexistence, is a significant adjustment. The defeat of Goldwater, the drawing back of the student militants, and the emergence of a programmatic literature of reform which considers various policy alternatives and does not call for absolute commitment—all are encouraging indications of progress in that they represent avoidance of extremes. Crick believes that a "new consciousness of the need for coherent public policies is emerging." Americans are beginning to ask questions about how, given genuinely differing perceptions of interests, priorities should be determined. Such questions suggest that "the theory of consensus as a necessary social cement is beginning to be abandoned." Finally, fear itself of breakdown or of continuing trouble at an intolerable level may produce a general interest in conciliating differences. In sum, Crick believes Americans "are, indeed, beginning to discover a hard and sensible, not amorphous, sense of pluralism."[8]

Bad Times and Good Times: Change and Politics

Having examined analyses by Ladd, Burnham, and Crick of the politics of affluence, we may note that while during the Great Depression political partisanship increased and normal majority status passed from one major party to the other, during the rise of affluence since the Second World War political partisanship has decreased and "independence" and ticket splitting have risen substantially. These developments, together with a critical realignment of the electorate at the time of a severe depression in the 1890s, tempt me to offer a historical law or at least a rule of thumb—political partisanship increases in bad times and decreases in good times—but I hesitate to do so until we know much more about the secular trend in party decomposition which began around 1900.

One is also tempted to accept Hofstadter's proposition that, although both are always present, interest or economic or class politics tends to prevail in bad times and lead to a variety of

reforms, and status or cultural politics tends to prevail in good
times, resulting in various irrational pseudoreforms as expressions of status anxieties.[1] At least two additional considerations,
one historiographical and one empirical, caution against uncriti-
cal acceptance of this proposition. The historiographical consideration pertains to periodization and perspective. A generation
of historians viewed the 1920s as a conservative or reactionary
period falling between the Progressive era and the New Deal;
but if one recognizes that from 1920 to 1973, with respect to
significant innovative domestic legislation, politics has been off
center only eight years, 1933–1938 and 1964–1965, the New
Deal becomes the exceptional period when poverty, which is
always with us, threatened the middle class. From this standpoint, the earlier perception of a reform-reaction-reform sequence has resulted in an exaggeration of the relative weight of
interest politics and underestimation of the persistence and importance of cultural politics. True, both are always there, but to
say this while maintaining that one declines as the other rises is to
convey the wrong impression in regard to cultural politics, which
in fact is not only always there but is present at a high level of
intensity in bad times and good times alike. In any event, one
ought not to ignore cultural politics without taking into account
the work of Allswang and Mann on the 1930s and of Benson,
Formisano, and Shade on the antebellum era, cited in chapter 4;
studies by Richard Jensen, Paul Kleppner, Frederick C. Leubke,
and Samuel T. McSeveney of the late nineteenth century and by
Don S. Kirschner of the 1920s; and Thomas P. Jahnige's attempt
to develop a theory that economic factors have triggered electoral realignments while ethno-class-cultural groups have been
transmitters of this process.[2]

　　Kirschner subjects Hofstadter's proposition to empirical
testing in *City and Country: Rural Responses to Urbanization in the
1920's* (1970). Using legislative roll call analysis in this study of
Iowa and Illinois, Kirschner delineates a very complex situation
in which ruralities agreed on cultural matters and disagreed on
economics, reflecting the cultural homogeneity and economic
diversity of the country districts, while the cities united on
economic issues but, differing in ethnic composition, disagreed
on cultural matters. Kirschner concludes that Hofstadter's

model is flawed in relation to the 1920s because it assumes that farmers were "in fairly good shape economically. In fact, they were not . . . . There is simply no evidence to indicate that farmers had few economic problems, or that they were at all placid about the ones they had." At the same time, farmers "did feel status insecurities before the new kinds of people and new style of life centered in the cities, and there is no denying that they met the challenge by reasserting their own life style in a set of issues that were of supreme importance in the legislative affairs of the Midwest." Rejecting the explanation of this reassertion of rural values as a luxury the farmers could afford in good times, Kirschner avers that the "most reasonable explanation is the most obvious one: cultural issues lived a life of their own and flourished on their own terms. They did not ebb and flow with the erratic pulse of crop prices, and they did not vary greatly from the more affluent to the less affluent farm areas." Finally, on the question of irrational pseudoreforms resulting from cultural problems, Krischner refers to the difficulty of making judgments on this point because it involves questions of definition, difficult-to-measure subjective or psychological elements, and the historian's own values. Still, he reasons that "people who try to regain lost status are probably acting rationally as long as their actions are relevant to the situation." He personally considers the cultural reform efforts of the 1920s—such as rural resistance to the legalization of liquor, boxing, and horse racing—"narrow, bigoted, perhaps immoral, and certainly outrageous," but they were real enough to ruralities who considered them "absolutely necessary to preserve a nation that they had cherished and, equally important, a nation that had cherished them."[3]

Another dualism encountered in historical literature and elsewhere, at least implicitly, is that people are happy in bad times and unhappy in good times. A blurb on the cover of a 1972 paperback describes a "novel of the Thirties that celebrates life in a happy vanished time."[4] In an article on "The 1930's: America's Major Nostalgia," Robert Nisbet introduces the second part of the dualism: "Only in ages of affluence, it seems, does humor wane."[5] To be sure, humor or its absence is not necessarily the equivalent of widespread happiness or its absence, but one wonders whether the humor of the thirties was the whistling-in-the-graveyard type, an outlet for desperation or despair not very far below the surface, and whether present estimates of its amount and significance are affected by nostalgia. Warren Susman asserts that it is against a psychological background of fear and shame that we can begin to sense

> the importance of a certain type of comedy that played such a vital role whether in the writing of a Thurber, the leading radio comedy shows (perhaps like "Fibber McGee and Molly"), or the classic film comedies of Frank Capra. All, in some degree, depend initially on a kind of ritual humiliation of the hero, a humiliation that is often painful and even cruel but from which the hero ultimately emerges with some kind of triumph, even though it is a minor one. The theme, of course, is not new to comedy in this era; but this was to be a golden age of comedy in all media, and rather than simple escape it provided a special kind of identification for those whose self-image had become less than favorable. This was especially to be the case for enormously swollen radio and movie middle-class audiences.[6]

I have had students write histories of families from welfare files of the 1930s for Lima, Ohio, and while the welfare rolls comprised only a portion of the population, it is obvious that these cases provide very few laughs. Even if inquiries are confined to formal humor, generalization about bad times and good times is difficult. Eric Goldman calls the affluent 1950s "The Stuffy Decade" and deplores the era's humorlessness, but before one concludes therefore that humor declines when the business cycle rises, one must note that Goldman also emphasizes the importance of H.L. Mencken's humor in the 1920s.[7]

As for happiness, shortly before I write, I watched a television special on life in Birmingham, Michigan, an affluent suburb of Detroit, whose burden was that money does not buy happiness. Does that mean that lack of money makes for bliss? The philosopher Morris Cohen once said, "If ignorance were bliss, the world would be a much happier place than it is." The same may be said of poverty. In his presidential address to the American Historical Association in 1972, Cochran refers to the 1960s and 1970s as "a period in which it has become clear that greater affluence has failed to cure relative or 'psychic' poverty, or necessarily to increase happiness."[8] The implication of this remark is well taken. Unhappiness, like cultural politics in Kirschner's analysis, has a life of its own, flourishes on its own terms, and does not ebb and flow with the erratic pulse of the business cycle. Still, it must be specified what kind of unhappiness, arising from what sources, is meant when generalizations are offered. Certain kinds of unhappiness are obviously present in good times, but the impressionistic notion is unacceptable that in the 1930s everyone was laughing it up, inwardly as well as outwardly, when the business cycle was down.

Although the bad times–good times dualisms with respect to political partisanship, economic and cultural politics, and humor and happiness appear to me unconvincing, it seems apparent that unity in regard to Lockean-Alger values increases in bad times and decreases *to some extent* in good times. Amid the depths of the Great Depression there might have been widespread rejection of the American experience and American values, but most Americans, in a display of what John A. Garraty calls perverse patriotism,[9] affirmed the virtues of the American people and the American past which, as Alfred H. Jones shows, nonradical writers rediscovered.[10] And the movies, as Andrew Bergman demonstrates, subtly fostered the survival of traditional institutions and values.[11] The basic theme implicit in Charles G. Alexander's *Nationalism in American Thought 1930–1945* is "There is nothing wrong with the American Way and the American People, but they have been betrayed by a selfish, irresponsible elite." The majority of Americans called for change in the form of restoration of America to "the people."[12] Their assumptions, as well as those of the New Deal, were essentially Lockean. They desired democracy and did not call for a new kind of economic pie but rather for the creation of a bigger capitalist pie, with everyone being assured a minimum portion and having the opportunity to acquire a larger portion in the traditional Alger way. Thus, while blending the themes of security and opportunity, they also displayed a certain perversity or inconsistency in their causal analysis, condemning certain groups for betraying the American Way while nevertheless, as shown by considerable empirical data, often, in Alger fashion, blaming themselves for their plight.[13] With the passing of the nadir of the depression, it is true, stepped-up demands for "more" produced friction in labor-management relations and heated partisan controversy in politics, but this controversy, as we have seen in chapter 4, involved differences not over democratic framework or rules of the game but over policy issues.

While the society rallied around old values in bad times, portions of it, especially among the children of affluence, as Burnham points out, defected from the Lockean-Alger ethic in good times. This observation, however, calls for some attention to problems of definition and measurement. In *Changing Values on Campus*, Daniel Yankelovich, on the basis of polls of students over the period 1965–1971, reports these findings concerning attitudes toward the work ethic:

Believe That Hard Work Will Pay Off			
1968	*1969*	*1970*	*1971*
69%	56%	45%	39%[14]

When I presented these figures to undergraduates in a course in recent American history, a number of students objected that the work ethic was often confused with the middle-class success ethic, that many of their generation believed that hard work would pay off, although in psychic rather than in material rewards. They denied that they were loafers or shunned success. They were prepared to work hard and, hopefully, successfully at jobs which might pay relatively little. This definitional refinement is well taken, and more data based on inquiries that recognize such a distinction are needed.

Not only are there definitional problems in specifying the nature and degree of defection from the work ethic, but it is necessary to recognize that a number of obvious defectors cannot be considered active opponents of the system. Without passing any value judgments on the counter culture, sociologists Peter L. and Brigette Berger conclude that the "green" revolution—Charles A. Reich's *Greening of America*—like the red and black revolutions envisioned on the left, displays a "sovereign disregard for the realities of technological society in general, and for the realities of class and power in America." The cultural revolution, rooted in opposition to some of the basic values of bourgeois society, is disproportionately evident among the college-educated children of the nonfundamentalist Protestant and Jewish upper-middle class. This radicalism, however, is not "simply in opposition to the particular form of technological society embodied in bourgeois capitalism but to the very idea of technological society." The counter-culture youth "drop out," but the personnel requirements of the technological society —despite predictions that automation will make it possible to keep the technological society going with fewer people— continue and grow. The positions which upper-middle-class young people disdain, the Bergers write, will be filled by the newly educated children of the Fundamentalist Protestant and non-Wasp lower-middle and working classes, who will not remain unaffected by their exposure in their college years to the counter culture but will cling to the essence of the old, achievement-oriented Protestant ethic. The classes which are most untouched by the "green" revolution will enjoy new prospects of upward social mobility. The "system"—the class and occupational structure of the society—will not change as the result of the "greening" of America. It will simply draw its personnel from new sources in a Paretian "circulation of elites." "Far from 'greening' America," the Bergers conclude, "the alleged cultural revolution will serve to strengthen the vitality of the technological society against which it is directed." As the Bergers suggest in the title of their article, we may be witnessing "The Blueing of America."[15]

In assessing defection from traditional values, one must also recognize that the inertia or staying power of the system is evident not only in "The Blueing of America" but also in the phenomenon of the intellectual and emotional defectors who "go along." A number of students have told me that they fall into this category. Having rejected the commune as well as the system and being unable to secure employment in the areas of teaching or social service, they are resigned to working at in-system jobs as the only practical alternative. The troubling question of individual adjustment or inner turmoil aside, in societal terms those who "go along" do not constitute a threat, at least not immediately, to the system.

Finally, in appraising defection one has to consider the time
at which previous appraisals were made. Many of them appeared in the period 1968–1971 when campus unrest was at its
height. Even as early as 1973 it appears that some observers
overestimated both the quantitative and qualitative dimensions
of the student revolution or, in any case, the depth and durability of student militancy. The education editor of *Newsweek,*
touring colleges across the country, quotes a professor at San
Francisco State on the malaise which engulfs reformers on
most campuses: "If you like the '50s, you'll love the '70s."[16]
Newsweek's reporter, however, distinguishes between the qui-
etude of the 1950s, with its unquestioning acceptance of the
status quo, and the placidity of the 1970s, which is only on the
surface and conceals a difficult-to-define uneasiness devoid of
identification with the restless students of the late 1960s and
marked by decreasing social concern[17] (a finding which does not
apply to the students, cited above, who profess declining material but increasing social concern). The contrast between the
campuses of the late 1960s and the campuses of the early 1970s
is underlined when one reads *The Harvard Strike*, published in
1970,[18] and columnist Nick Thimmesch's account of his visit to
Harvard in early 1973, when he found that "the big worries are
over money and career. Students are jaded about activism, especially politics," although the "new life styles haven't changed
since they emerged."[19]

There is no intention here of implying that values do not
change. They do and they will. The question is how fast and,
with respect to their nature and the number of people or value-
holders involved, how far? Turning from the children of affluence in the colleges to the blue-collar workers, whose increasing
aversion to boring mass production jobs is the subject of a recent
flood of writings,[20] one perceives not only the special problems
of a particular group in regard to the work ethic but also a
technologically derived development with broad, long-term social implications. All of which brings us back to Burnham's deep
misgivings over our inability to close the gap between a dynamically developing socioeconomic system rooted in technological
advance and responses to it through a political system dominated by Lockean-Alger values—an inability which has produced defection by some from traditional values—and to Crick's

relatively optimistic estimate of our capacity to cope with the breakdown of consensus.

Burnham does not envision imminent violent conflict between adherents of old values and defectors from them. If defection now encompassed, say, half the population and if the defectors were prepared to engage in militant action, violent conflict would be more likely than in a situation involving, say, a 70–30 or 80–20 ratio between adherents or inactive defectors on the one hand and militant defectors on the other. Burnham contemplates the eventual development of a situation in which the defectors would be no longer outnumbered or outgunned—a dangerous situation in which one side might impose its values on the other through a dominant party or through a dictator in a partyless political system. In any event, one must not lose sight of the basic source of the pessimistic prognosis in Burnham's analysis—the lag of thought and values of the bulk of the population behind changing reality.

If Crick is right—if hard pluralism now prevails or is about to become the general attitude—ratios between adherents to and defectors from traditional values will, of course, have little bearing on the possibility of strife, since each group of value-holders will recognize the interests of the other groups. As a historian with a comparative perspective, Crick is telling us not to panic because the liberal consensus has broken down—other nations have survived without such a consensus, and this nation can survive in freedom without unity on Lockean values. Horace Kallen, who stressed cultural pluralism fifty years ago when it was not a popular concept, agreed with Crick, as it were, when he said in December 1972 at the age of ninety, "Since people have to live together, plurality is a basic condition of existence. The need is to bring differences together to make a union, not unity."[21] There is no pollyanna in Crick's prescription; he does not claim that adoption of a hard pluralism is easy. It requires, for one thing, rejection of the melting-pot myth. Hard pluralism, for another thing, is in a certain sense "softer" than broker-state pluralism since the beneficiaries of the latter are hard-nosed or hard-hearted in their denial or neglect of the interests of those who are not citizens of the broker state. This "softness" requires a hard-headed empathy that is difficult to attain.

Both Burnham's and Crick's views contain certain short-

comings as remedial prescriptions. Lockean doctrine, as Burnham knows, embraces both economic and political concepts or
values, both capitalism and democracy. Can we throw out the
bath without throwing out the baby? Can we discard individualistic, acquisitive capitalism while retaining democracy, in
view of Americans' close association of the two? Burnham's
pessimism reflects his awareness of this problem. As for Crick's
pluralism, it is, albeit hard, still pluralism. Can the energy crisis,
to mention one of many national problems, be "solved" by a
pluralistic approach, even a hard one, on the part of producers,
distributors, consumers, and environmentalists, or is a disinterested holistic approach required if the society is to surmount
this difficulty in a manageable, equitable way? Crick's prescription or prognosis, moreover, follows from a faulty diagnosis.
Presumably writing in 1971 (his essay appeared in early 1972),
he described as a breakdown in consensus what was in fact a
limited defection, and he tended to downplay the persistence of
cultural pluralism in its old, soft form—evident in politics not
only in voter behavior but also in the widespread adverse
reaction to the hard pluralism of the Democrats' quota system
for the selection of delegates to their 1972 convention.

In the end, as noted above, the crucial question is how
American society will accommodate change—how changing
conditions and changing values will affect attitudes toward
change, and how these attitudes will translate themselves into
politics and, through politics, into policy. Our bad times—good
times comparison affords no reason to feel that relative affluence will preclude either a willingness or a positive desire to see
changes in policy. With respect to bad times, one ought not to
underestimate the force of the hanging-on or restorative impulse during the Great Depression. Daniel Snowman, an English
historian, argues that the New Deal was "a holding action, an
attempt to salvage and perpetuate certain American values."
The depression, Snowman believes, "acted as a brake on the
reformist tendencies of the era and assured that those in positions of official responsibility would have to move heaven and
earth in their efforts merely to perpetuate an existing but
threatened social system."[22] Snowman is favorably impressed by
Arthur M. Schlesinger, Jr.'s contention that the discontent of the

1920s would have produced a new deal in the 1930s—different from and probably more progressive than FDR's New Deal—if good times had continued unabated.[23]

Schlesinger's hypothesis can be neither proved nor disproved, and one cannot easily generalize about present-day values, attitudes toward change, and politics since changes in values cannot be related either to shifts in attitudes toward change or to politics on a one-to-one basis. When Yankelovich asked the political views of college students who agreed with the statement, "Hard work will pay off," to the extent of 69 percent in 1968 and 39 percent in 1971, only 11 percent identified themselves as radicals.[24] A study by the American Council on Education of freshmen's attitudes, based on questionnaires returned by 188,900 freshmen in colleges of all types across the nation and published in 1973, reveals a definite trend away from liberal views toward conservative opinions. With respect to political orientation, the freshmen see themselves this way: Far Left—2.4 percent; Liberal—32.8 percent; Middle of the Road —48.2 percent; Conservative—15.6 percent; Far Right—1.0 percent. From 1971 to 1972 the Liberal—plus—Far Left sector declined 2.9 percent while the Middle of the Road category rose 1.5 percent and the Conservative—plus—Far Right group increased 1.4 percent.[25] These figures suggest that the changing age structure of the population and a rising level of education will not have the immediate, deep liberalizing impact on politics that some observers suppose. Of 200 million Americans alive in 1970, 38.7 million were born in the period 1946–1955 and 36 million were born in the years 1956–1965.[26] In the 1930s just over 10 percent of high school graduates went to college, in 1950 more than 20 percent, and in the 1970s more than 50 percent will go on for some college education.[27] Yet, although the presidential election of 1972 generally resembled the contest between Calvin and Socrates depicted by Frederick G. Dutton in a chapter, "The Generational Struggle in Politics,"[28] the "youth vote," college and noncollege, divided nearly evenly, with McGovern receiving just over 50 percent.[29]

We can be certain, in any case, that the 1970s will witness continuous change in conditions, and that Americans' response will be crucial to the nation's development. This response, to be

sure, could be a nonresponse or repressive resistance to a positive response. James Reston contrasts the 1930s, when the majority were at the bottom, with the present, when the majority is
in the well-to-do middle, and he sees certain politicians appealing to "The Selfish Majority." But he believes that this appeal will
not succeed in the end, that the comfortable voters, out of fear of
the alleged threat of anarchy, will not spurn the afflicted.[30]
Stewart Alsop shares this feeling; after the election of 1972, he
wrote, "A lot of voters who do not want to have their children
bused into the inner cities also . . . would like to see the black
children in the ghetto schools get a decent break."[31] One can
find support for these journalists' views in the striking case of
Mayor Roman S. Gribbs of Detroit. In late 1972 Mayor Gribbs
delivered a presidential address to the National League of
Cities which must be evaluated in the light of his earlier law-
and-order candidacy. He recognized, so to speak, that law-and-
order as an abstraction has limitations, that ultimately, if it is
not to be maintained by continuous repression, it must rest on
justice and widespread well-being:

> As a nation we are resting and recuperating from a decade of
> unprecedented social challenge. The major challenge we face in
> the '70s is to accommodate a people's caution to a nation's
> needs. It would be tragic if, in our desire to rest, we closed our
> eyes to critical needs that must be met if we are to achieve the
> stability we so fervently seek. The very old, the very young, the
> very poor have a claim on the American conscience that
> cannot be ignored. There are national problems—crime,
> unemployment, drug abuse, deteriorating housing, pollution,
> school finance—that we must solve collectively if we are to
> solve them at all.[32]

Agreeing with the findings of Lou Harris cited above, I do
not feel that the presidential election of 1972 represented a
massive endorsement of the status quo. In fact, as Harris suggests, it appears to have obscured a desire for change—orderly
change. As the Democrats, typified by Governor Gilligan of
Ohio, quoted above, move away from identification with radical
change and toward the middle, Middle American spokesman
Kevin Phillips, as noted above, urges conservatives to seize the
baton of activism from the exhausted New Deal coalition. Ap-

parently political activists and analysts recognize the need for change, as a response both to conditions and to voters' attitudes. If the desire for change continues to grow, especially as Americans shift their priorities from foreign to domestic concerns, as they appear to be doing, it is likely, as Gilligan's and Phillips' statements suggest, that both parties—regardless of which holds the allegiance of Middle America—will sponsor roughly parallel policy changes, thereby behaving in accordance with the consensus historians' thesis concerning the similarity of the major parties. If this likelihood materializes, party politics will not accord with Burnham's prognosis of the emergence of either an upper-lower versus the middle division or partyless politics, or with the multiparty politics which Dutton sees as a long-term possibility.[33] Optimists may assume that centrist party politics will enable us to "muddle through" or, as Dutton puts it, "middle through,"[34] but this kind of politics does not preclude the continuing and potentially "fatal" lag of thought and policy behind changes in reality which Burnham fears.

To be sure, when Burnham uses the phrase "politics without parties," he denotes not necessarily the literal disappearance of parties but the anomaly—at least to a political scientist—of parties without partisanship. There may be limitations on electoral disaggregation, however, which could prevent this process from proceeding to the point where partisanship literally disappears. John C. Pierce points out that the partisanship of some strong Republican and some strong Democratic identifiers —twice as many of the former as of the latter—rests on ideology, and that these ideologues, although they are minorities, can exert a profound influence on politics. Pierce's findings and comments suggest that amid continuing electoral decomposition these ideological partisans would have great discretion, determining the choices available to the electorate. If this were the case, these choices could both reflect and foster intense political conflict and radicalization or ideological polarization of politics—possible consequences, Pierce notes, of concentrations of ideologues within partisan organizations of a political system. On the other hand, if even ideologues concede to the quest for votes, polarization could be prevented by the movement of both parties toward roughly similar positions. Yet, competition between the two parties for the middle will not have the traditional

moderating effect which many historians assign to it if, as Burnham maintains, the middle is reactionary. Whether competition for the middle will make for moderation can be questioned,
moreover, in the light of Pierce's finding that there is a significant proportion of ideologues among "independents"—smaller
than among Republican loyalists but larger than among Democratic partisans. This brings us back to Burnham's concern, for
Pierce sees in the independent ideologues "the potential for
ideologically generated conflict which is not bounded or con-
strained by traditional party politics in America."[35]

To sum up, in the late 1960s some children of affluence
expressed alienation from Lockean-Alger values, but—unless
one insists on 100 percent agreement—this defection did not
amount to a breakdown of consensus, much less a revolution. At
the same time, the persistence of Lockean-Alger values did not
entail aversion to change, but the message sent by the electorate
in 1972 was not to take a great leap forward. Nor was it to go
back. It was to go slow. If one sees this message as being determined by a mood, and points out, as we have here, that moods
are more volatile than values, one has to consider Watts' and
Free's findings which merge mood and value:

> In the United States, the country of individualism *par excellence,*
> there is a sharp distinction in people's minds between their own
> personal lives and national life. Believing that individuals not
> only should but can take care of themselves and stand on their
> own two feet, Americans appear not to make a direct connection
> between their individual situations and the conditions of the
> nation—except in the case of war or severe national calamity. As
> a result, they find it possible to feel that they as individuals can
> fare well, even though they perceive the country to be faring
> poorly.[36]

If the electorate wants to go slow, the activist who wants to
win elections and move forward must go slow in his appeal and,
if he is elected, in his actions. This advice is offered in many
quarters, sometimes eloquently:

> The American dream in its classical form was not merely a
> statement of America's innate goodness; it was, instead, an
> assertion of America's bestness. . . . Then what is wanted is not a

restoration of the dream. It lacks credibility. What is wanted is a new, more modest, more mature faith that will bind us together. To say that America is not the New Jerusalem is not to say that it cannot be a good place, a decent place, is not to say that we are lost. . . . [The new dream] will be less grand, less compelling, perhaps, but more credible, more proximate to its promise. . . . Let our distressed brothers . . . help us to renew our nerve and our purpose and our decency, and then, carefully, cautiously, with our pain intact but also our hopes, to try to dream again.[37]

If this is what we can expect, to moderates it will be about right, to conservatives too much, and to those who share Burnham's views, as I do, not enough.[38] But let us not overindulge in the joys of pessimism—if the pessimist is proved wrong, he can share in the happiness of all; if he is proved right, he can partake in the perverse pleasure of saying "I told you so." Capitalism will be with us for an indefinite time to come, and, barring the possible catalytic effect of a physical development such as the energy crisis (a causal equivalent of war?), those who share Burnham's views can try through democratic means to reduce inequities—to reduce lag. They will not accomplish even that much if they disregard the ideas and values of the majority of the people. Perhaps the outer limits of what they can achieve are suggested in this comment by Hofstadter:

> When one considers American history as a whole, it is hard to think of any very long period in which it could be said that the country has been consistently well governed. And yet its political system is, on the whole, a resilient and well–seasoned one, and on the strength of its history one must assume that it can summon enough talent and good will to cope with its afflictions. To cope with them—but not, I think, to master them in any thoroughly decisive or admirable fashion. The nation seems to slouch onward into its uncertain future like some huge inarticulate beast, too much attainted by wounds and ailments to be robust, but too strong and resourceful to succumb.[39]

PART FOUR

Departure from

the Consensus View

Chapter Seven
Consensus and Losers:
The New Left

America since the 1890s

The significance of conflict and violence in the American past is a main theme in the writings of the New Left school of historians which emerged in the 1960s as the complacency, national self-confidence, and moral composure of the 1950s faded amid greater polarization in American society, increasing militancy on the part of blacks and other groups, more frequent resort to violence, rising opposition to American policy in Vietnam, growing campus unrest, and a new awareness of the problems resulting from racism, urbanism, and poverty.[1] Observing that the New Left has yet to work out a basic interpretation of all of our past, Grob and Billias surmise, on the basis of available writings, that such an interpretation might include these components:

> The Puritans being pictured as radical activists who hailed from the lower socio-economic classes; the American Revolution as a radical movement whose causes were rooted in genuine lower-class grievances; the Revolutionary War as a cataclysmic event characterized by great violence between Patriots and Loyalists; the Constitution as a divisive document with racism as the main issue as the founding fathers split over slavery; the Jeffersonian and the Jacksonian eras as periods of radical reform with anti-slavery men emerging as demigods; the denigration of the Civil War because of the failure to achieve a just and egalitarian society; the changed image of Lincoln as a great man because he was a trimmer and compromiser in his

stand on slavery; the continued rehabilitation of the Radical
Republicans as heroes of the Reconstruction era; the
denigration of American businessmen in the post–Civil War
era because they shaped the nation's imperialist ideology to
expand overseas as they sought to find more markets
for American goods and money; the revival of the old
"merchants of death" thesis regarding the causes for America's
intervention in World War I; the interpretation that America
entered World War II primarily to protect its economic interests
and not to further the cause of freedom; and the discovery
that violence has been a major means of settling conflicts
throughout American history.[2]

The inner dialectic of ideas as well as change in the climate
of opinion undoubtedly influenced the New Left historians.
Needless to say, they reject the consensus view of American history. As David Donald writes,

They accuse their predecessors of contributing to our present
crisis by promulgating a cheerily optimistic view of the American
past. Their chief enemies are the "Consensus" historians —as
they label the middle-aged leaders of the profession—whose
writings minimize political, social, and economic conflict in
American history and stress the beliefs and experiences which
most of our people have shared. . . .

The new generation of historians sweepingly condemns all
Consensus scholars for accepting, and even eulogizing, a society
where poverty is tolerated because it is presumed to be transient;
where racial discrimination is permissible because it too will pass
away; where political conflict is muted, since everybody agrees
on everything; and where foreign adventurism is acceptable
since politics stops at the water's edge.[3]

In leveling these charges against consensus historians, the New
Left draws on the legacy of the consensus historians' Progressive predecessors. The New Left interpretation of America's
past, Clifford Solway writes, is at the end of a straight historiographical line running from Turner and Beard.[4] Turner's
copaternity derives not from his frontier thesis but from his attack on the geographic bias of Establishment historiography.[5]
Beard's status as a New Left patron saint rests not on his
specific interpretations of the Revolution and the Constitution

but his general anti-Establishment views: his call for democratic collectivism and his advocacy, especially in *The Open Door at
Home* (1934), of isolationism.[6] The New Left approach to our
past has not only been labeled "Neo-Progressivism"[7] but also
"Neo-Marxism"[8] and both—"the latest expression," as Solway
puts it, "of a hybrid tradition of dissent within American historiography: Progressive idealism, native and utopian, fused
with Marx, but having no parallel in the forced application of
Stalinism to the America of the 1930's."[9]

In view of the New Left historians' concern with contemporary problems, we may add the name of James Harvey
Robinson to the roster of their Progressive predecessors.[10] We
should also consider basic similarities and differences between
the Old and the Neo-Progressives before examining New Left
historiography at some length. Gene Wise compares the basic
views of Progressive and New Left historians, pointing out several similarities: both groups focus on injustice in American
society, both are primarily concerned with politics and
economics, both depict a society divided into classes, and both
see more conflicts than unities in American history. Wise also
specifies a number of important differences. Regarding change
in the past, the Progressives assumed that everyone had benefited from reforms, that new frontiers had provided opportunity while serving as a safety valve for socioeconomic discontent.
The New Left holds that only the most organized groups have
obtained power—by reducing their goals and being coopted
—that new frontiers have been an escape hatch or a means of
evading effective confrontation with basic socioeconomic problems. With respect to the extent of change which they saw as
needed in their time, the Progressives worked for more liberalism, their heroes were system-reforming liberals, they
believed that Americans "could get a fresh start toward restoration of the really American part of the nation's heritage if they
could only rearrange this or that." They wanted to reform the
structure of American experience. The New Left, on the other
hand, sees liberalism and its system as America's problem and
its heroes are "losers" and system-changing radicals. It has
abandoned the national covenant with its sense of mission and
progress, and it wants to replace the structure of American experience. Concerning the role of ideas in history, the Progres-

sives believed that some ideas reflected interests while other ideas—progressive ones—were self-generating and transcended interests, that the idea of progress could right the system. The New Left has little faith in the idea of progress and believes that ideas reflect the system and will change only when the system changes.[11]

If the New Left historians have not had time to treat all aspects of our history and to spell out a comprehensive interpretation, their writings do reveal an intellectual frame through which they view the past, a context which Solway synthesizes brilliantly and, in the opinion of a leading New Left historian,[12] accurately. The New Left view of American history, Solway writes, requires that one "see recent American history in a perspective *not* formed by the New Deal." This is an agonizing mental exercise for those who felt the effects of the Great Depression and cannot detach "mind and emotions from the trauma of the 1930's and an almost personal identification with the father figure" and his fireside rhetoric.[13] The place to begin is with Populism, which was basically different from subsequent reform movements: "bruised and frustrated" farmers angrily demanded drastic reform—socialism. Populism, however,

> is put down, but the economic oligarchs have seen chaos, and it frightens them half to death; to save the system, they must correct its worst abuses. This overhaul job, otherwise known as reform capitalism, is the *real* frame of twentieth-century American history, that which makes sense of it. The personalities up front, Presidents and their claques, are mere stand-ins for the oligarchs: Progressive aristocrats moved by the spirit of *noblesse oblige* and deputized to manage the job. The first is that somewhat addled imperialist Teddy Roosevelt, who launches both the politics of reform and the American Empire—each of them agents in rationalizing the economy. By the 1930's this process of saving the nation for the status quo is so completely institutionalized hardly anyone acknowledges it anymore. FDR's cloudy, patronizing rhetoric merely adds layers to the disguise, hiding his own innate conservatism and the failure of the New Deal to lick the depression as well.[14]

The New Left historians carry down to the present their theme that the recent national experience is "so many footnotes to Populism." They concede the success of the welfare- or corporate-liberal state "on the state's own terms": millions enjoy an "institutionalized middle-class way of life . . . the rest aspire to it." But the triumphant system embodies two contradictions that "limit and impugn it drastically": it is based on exploitation of "blacks, the faceless poor, floaters, losers, and, finally, the world's helpless, underfed billions"; it is a "hollow success, cheapened, overcommercialized, consumerized, tranquilized . . . a life made pointless because its price is the social impotency of the individual." Classic Marxism identifies the exploitative foundation of the system—an informal economic empire providing raw materials and markets for the corporate economy's surpluses—and a native utopian idealism indicates the vacuity of middle-class success while offering a "dazzling new version of the good life."[15]

The historian who has "really put together the counter-tradition in its modern form" is William Appleman Williams. The basic theme that emerges from his work is that an undisciplined, hopelessly self-centered, uncontrollably acquisitive nation was never able to work out what it wanted to make of itself and get its priorities right. Ironically, the devil in this interpretation is Turner's frontier, a lure that has always pulled Americans away from reality and social responsibility, and led them, in Williams' words, to "substitute motion for structure" and fostered an expansionist frame of mind that has created what he calls an "unrestrained, anti-intellectual individualist democracy." Foreign policy since the 1890s, Williams holds, has been essentially the application of the frontier-expansionist theory to the rest of the world in order to rationalize an economy continually on the verge of stagnation. The result is an informal imperialism which preserves a global market for American business and, as a first principle, considers all revolutions anathema. The Cold War was the outcome of a later phase of the application of this principle to the Russian Revolution. In order to develop clear ideas and formulate programs for the future, America must abandon its policy of defining its welfare as a function of Russian conduct; it must learn to share a world with others not on its own terms exclusively; it must find a moral substitute for the market place in American society, responding to its own needs, knitting itself together, harmonizing its conflicting interests, redeeming its citizens from alienation, giving them a handhold on their destiny. Thus from historiography emerges a utopian prescription for America today, "an updated secular version of the feudal Christian commonwealth."[16]

The New Left historians move beyond deploring the fact of consensus in a general way for causing America's failure to get at the roots of modern problems—the kind of condemnation Hofstadter expressed in 1948 and Hartz in 1955. Their censure of consensus also extends further than denouncing the underestimation of conflict. Conflict has produced losers as well as winners and the New Left historians are engaged, to borrow Solway's title, in "Turning History Upside Down" by writing about losers past and present: rebellious slaves, abolitionists, freedmen then and now, radical Populists, the old Socialist Party, the Wobblies, those to whom the New Deal dealt no cards, the inarticulate, the poor, the socially impotent middle class. Having revised the old American Dream beyond recognition, they offer a new American Dream. They see their function, Christopher Lasch writes, as the creation of a "broad consciousness of alternatives not embraced by the present system."[17]

The New Left historians' call for changing the premises of American society in order to change and widen its options is rejected by Middle America, which clings, perhaps more tenaciously than ever before, to the old American Dream. But the establishment of radical goals for America, Solway states, appeals to "young people in the educated middle class [who] buy it, believe it, and to some extent act on it, because it seems to lend sense to their lives." The radical explanation of American history is "winning the support of the educated young and conditioning their view of the society and its politics." Thus the New Left historians, although they recognize that Middle America is now in charge of politics, feel time is on their side. They disqualify "liberalism," New Deal Democrats, and liberal Republicans as carriers of the reform impulse into the system, or as advocates of goals oriented to the needs and hopes of the young. Likewise, New Left historians feel time is on their side with respect to historiography. The process of "legitimizing and domesticating" the radical explanation of history within a native historical tradition is well advanced, and they expect it to advance further as the students of today become the historians of tomorrow. In 1969, for the first time in the history of the American Historical Association, there was a contest for the presidency as the Radical Caucus presented a nominee at the annual meeting. This convention, Solway writes, "showed the counter-tradition to be dug in, poised to infiltrate the textbooks of the seventies. This is what the exercise was all about: Who had the right to control the assumptions of history in the 1970's."[18]

Present-Mindedness

The New Left historians' view of American society today, prompted by the racial, urban, and martial developments which were the "chief precipitants of discontent" of the 1960s,[1] no doubt determines the themes they stress in American history: "incessant conflict . . . violence and racism welded into the character of the American people, Afro-American cultural continuity, the view from the social bottom, the persistence of a native radical tradition, these corporatist life and times."[2] Hence the charge against the New Left of present-mindedness, which refers not only to their selection of themes but, more importantly, to their treatment of them. Irwin Unger, who himself objects to the overworking of the consensus approach and is by no means unsympathetic to the New Left's contribution to historiography, finds that the New Left historians, "as scholars and social critics, simultaneously," are guilty of "exaggerated present-mindedness," of partisan and propagandistic distortion in order to create a "usable radical past to provide direction for the new radical community."[3] The New Left historians, for their part, charge consensus historians with yielding to contemporary pressures, with timorously abandoning, in response to McCarthyism, the Jeffersonian view of the common man for a "safe" elitist, aristocratic, New Conservative view of society.[4] Solway presents their indictment:

> Inured to *Realpolitik,* proud of their realism in coping with past and present, they exude . . . an Establishment's perfect certainty about how things were, are, and should be, not to mention the

galling complacency about the "objectivity" of their own account of recent events. . . .

The consensus school['s] complicity in the gaffes of recent foreign policy, from the Bay of Pigs to Vietnam, makes it a choice target, and its rather lofty contempt for "committed" history, the kind in which the past is enlisted in the service of the present, merely provokes radicals to holler hypocrisy. . . .

By now no more than an apology for the system, the consensus viewpoint was riddled with present-mindedness (the very thing radicals were accused of), and was trapped by its own profitless cold war assumptions; it was a last hurrah for the status quo.[5]

Although the historiography of the American Revolution is not our direct concern here, it merits citation since it has occasioned the firing of missiles marked "present-mindedness" at both consensus and New Left targets. The 1950s saw the emergence in this field of a neo-Whig view, which conceded the existence of social, economic, and sectional divisions in American society but stressed the colonists' "attachment to principle" and maintained, to quote Edmund S. Morgan, that "to magnify the internal contest to the same proportion as the revolt against England is to distort it beyond recognition."[6] Max Savelle, perhaps an old Populist but not a New Left historian, in a review of Morgan's *The Birth of the Republic 1763–89,* declared that "this little example of revisionism, written in the flush times of mid-twentieth century capitalism and of chaste and dedicated patriot-businessmen, has taken on the hue of Eisenhower prosperity."[7] Jack P. Greene responded, as it were, to Savelle's assertion. Although the Progressive historians responded to the spirit of their times, the "neo-Whigs," Greene wrote, were not influenced by the spirit of the 1950s. He held that in the years after the Second World War "the absence of serious internal economic problems and the general leveling of society . . . have made possible an increasing detachment among historians of the Revolution."[8] Merrill Jensen called this a "rather remarkable" assumption.[9] Greene, it is true, conceded that "social determinants" do affect historians' work, but his conclusion was unqualified: "Some commentators have associated a few writers, in particular Boorstin, Hartz, and Rossiter, with the new conservatives, who may well find the neo-

Whig interpretation of the Revolution congenial, but all of the neo-Whig writings are decidedly apolitical."[10] With respect to Boorstin in particular, this statement is indeed remarkable.

Meanwhile, the New Left historian Jesse Lemisch attacked the consensus interpretation of the Revolution:

> those who, like Daniel Boorstin, have asserted that the Revolution aimed only at a separation from Great Britain and not at social revolution are quite right, but only insofar as they have described the attitudes of the elite: what the common people and articulate radicals made of the Declaration of Independence may have been quite a different matter.[11]

Lemisch asserted that existing evidence concerning "the place of the inarticulate in the political thought and practice of the colonial elite and . . . the thought and conduct of the inarticulate themselves" indicated that "there was, from the very beginning, something of a struggle over who should rule at home." In his essay, meant to be suggestive, Lemisch stated that "a radically new view is just now becoming visible" and he called for the gathering of additional evidence in the history of the inarticulate.[12] This expression of the New Left historians' concern with history, "from the bottom up" provoked, in turn, an adverse response by Eugene Genovese: "History written from the bottom up is neither more nor less than history written from the top down. It is not and cannot be good history."[13]

Present-mindedness on the part of historians is, of course, unavoidable. Nor should it be shunned. "Every true history," Croce insists, "is contemporary history"—meaningful to contemporaries with respect to their own problems.[14] Merton L. Dillon, in a survey of recent historiography on the abolitionists, states:

> It was easy for an advocate of civil rights in 1965 to feel kinship with the historical abolitionists and to identify their public activity with his own. For that reason the antislavery movement could be studied with greater perception and depth of understanding than had generally been possible before.[15]

Lawrence W. Levine insists that it is possible for the historian to bridge the gap between his own cultural conditioning and expectations and those of his subjects by "painstaking historical

reconstruction and a series of imaginative leaps that allow him
to perform the central act of empathy—figuratively to crawl
into the skin of his subjects."[16] Taken together, these comments
call for simultaneously turning present-mindedness to advantage and transcending it. The problem is not present-
mindedness but exaggerated present-mindedness, a pit into
which the historian can easily plunge if he abandons, consciously or inadvertently, the controlled approach implicit in
Dillon's and Levine's remarks. One need only turn to Dillon's
area of interest to encounter a heated debate arising from the
charge that in their treatment of the abolitionists the New Left
historians romanticize American radicalism.[17]

A Usable Past and a New American Dream

The exchange of charges of exaggerated present-mindedness
by consensus and New Left historians amounts to a tale of pots
and kettles, but two historiographical wrongs do not make a
right. Undue present-mindedness, of course, is neither a problem nor a pit if one's aim is to make the past speak to the present regardless of the integrity of history, the past as past. Nor
do the study, teaching, and writing of history, in the view of
many New Left historians, afford sufficient means for making
an impact on the present. This attitude raises the question—a
corollary of the matter of inappropriate present-mindedness in
historiography—of the historian as social critic and social activist and the relationship of these roles to his writing.

Howard Zinn maintains that historians' social thought is
usually humane, but only in an ineffectual private sense because, as Skotheim puts it in a commentary on Zinn's *The Politics
of History* (1970), "the careerism of most historians turns them
into passive spectators of society's ills. Their conception of
scholarship as a detached and disinterested inquiry provides
theoretical grounding for their narrow professional
ambitions."[1] Deciding that the activities of a historian as historian actually retard the attack on present problems by stressing their intractability, Zinn became an activist in the civil
rights and peace movements while publishing *The Southern Mystique* (1964), *SNCC: The New Abolitionists* (1964), and *Vietnam:
The Logic of Withdrawal* (1967). Needless to say, the variety of
backgrounds of the participants in these movements shows that

one does not have to be a historian to be a social activist. At the same time, a historian can be a social activist without integrating his personal and professional lives. Hofstadter deftly makes this point: "If the essentially political revulsion from consensus history has some warrant, it is still no more than a marginal consideration. . . . To take a strong stand for Negro rights today, for example, it is not necessary to find a long history of effective slave rebellions."[2]

Zinn disagrees with Hofstadter. He would have historians write the way they act. The cause in which the historian enlists as a social activist becomes a moral absolute, and his written history or historical truth becomes merely instrumental, subordinate to moral truth.[3] In sum, as Skotheim says, "Zinn's own writings on the past and the present, if consistent with his theory of action scholarship, would have to be considered intentionally propagandistic."[4] Meanwhile, in urging historians to "write propaganda for good causes, Zinn was apparently not worried by the uses to which others might put actively propagandistic histories."[5] His plea can be "answered by activists on the John Birch Right as well as the Howard Zinn left."[6] Surely the authors of "Marxmanship in Dallas," the *American Opinion* version of the assassination of John F. Kennedy, and *None Dare Call It Treason* are, like Zinn, sincere in their espousal of a cause as a moral absolute. Zinn, to be sure, would, as Skotheim notes, reply that "dominant ethnic, economic, and military groups in America already use scholarship and universities for their own purposes."[7] There is, in Zinn's view, no "objective" history concerning current problems; and "disinterested" scholarship which does not address itself to present social ills is "propagandistic" in that it contributes by default to the perpetuation of the status quo.[8] All history—left, right, center, and "neutral"—about all eras is propaganda.

Conceding to Zinn that no one writes wholly nonsubjective, non-present-minded history, one can reply that some historians are more objective than others. In addition to the question whether the ideal of pure objectivity is attainable, a question relevant to Zinn's argument may be raised within the limits he lays down: Does historiography make history? If historiography is made by the times, including the climate of opinion as well as the inner dialectic of ideas and the historian in his indi-

viduality, does historiography make the times? Warren Susman
attempts to "show that the *ways* in which the past is treated, the
structure and form of historical thought, *are* of consequence
for the development of a culture,"[9] and Skotheim states that
"the relation between the historian and the climate of opinion
in which he works is reciprocal."[10] Tillinghast believes that
"more than most other fields, historiography reflects the general attitude of the society in which it is written."[11] In any event,
if one holds that historiography affects the present and
future—second by second the present becomes the future—to
some extent, does one thereby yield to Zinn? Not at all if one
rephrases the question: What kind of history, propagandistic or
"objective," is most likely to influence the present and the future?

　　By way of introducing a discussion of this question I present two sets of questions posed by Tillinghast, who asserts that
the New Left historians, despite their occasional shrillness and
frequent dogmatism, have a good deal to say to us. "The first
comprises the questions they are asking and the second includes some of the questions they are *not* asking":

> 1. To what end are historians now carrying on their
> indefatigable researches?
> 2. In relation to what is a historian objective? Is it possible to
> distort the past by claiming one is being objective about it? Is
> subjective history valid or not?
> 3. Why do we tend to be more suspicious of historians who
> excite us than of those who bore us?
> 4. Are historians bound in conscience to confront something
> besides documents dealing with the past?
> 5. Is history a private or a public enterprise?
> 6. Can historians use knowledge of the past to help bring about
> a juster society in future without being intellectually dishonest?
> Is it possible *not* to do so without being morally dishonest?
>
> 1. Should all past problems be judged strictly by their relevance
> to present ones?
> 2. Has a historian the right to manipulate his readers in the
> direction of even a millenially just society?

3. Can moral passion and social involvement be used to cover a lack of technical expertise in handling immensely complex historical situations that may or may not parallel our own?
4. Do not all questions have two sides? In other words, can anything be said in *favor* of the Viet Nam involvement, majority rights, or male chauvinism?
5. Is concern for the future of a society in deep trouble a legitimate part of scientific study of the past, is it identical with that study, or are the two altogether different? If different, in what order do they stand, and who is to decide? [12]

I would take exception to Tillinghast's query, "Do not all questions have two sides?" More to the point is Cromwell's plea, "I beseech you . . . think it possible that you may be mistaken." What can be said in favor of male chauvinism, for instance? That it gives a comfortable life to some men. But if we widen the context, we see that it rests upon the suppression or exploitation of half the human race, and it can be defended only by asserting the inferiority of women, for which there is no evidence, or the right of the strong to exploit the weak, which goes against everything we profess to believe about human freedom and individual opportunity and responsibility.

If one sees any kind of relationship between the study of the past and America's future, one might also ponder the last three sentences of Tillinghast's book:

As there is no knowledge of the past that is unconditioned by hope or fear for the future, so there is no knowledge of the future that is not based on past experience. If knowledge of the past dies, there will be no possibility of either a rational or humane future. Those whose lives are spent digging out its various meanings have less need to lose heart than we are often told.[13]

In specifying a rational future as a desideratum while linking the future to the past, Tillinghast implies a preference for rational over propagandistic knowledge of the past as a guide to building a better future. Blueprints for such a future will undoubtedly have to go back to the drawing board if they are laid out hazily and only with reference to a particular conception of what the future *should* be. The blueprinter must consider others' attitudes toward his dream.

The new American dream which the New Left historians offer is not only anathema to the right and to Middle America, but it is also rejected by the Old Left and treated skeptically by liberals. Gil Green, a veteran Communist leader, emphatically rejects the anarchistic trends in the New Left rebellion,[14] while the liberal George Mowry is puzzled as to the precise nature of the New Left version of the American dream:

> The New Left is obviously in favor of socialism, but also antibureaucracy and antiestablishment. Its emphasis is a sort of combination of Emerson and Marx, if one can conceive of that fact. It reflects, I suppose, a paradox of the present generation of students one deals with daily: presumably they want to preserve the productiveness of modern society but destroy its social and political organization.[15]

Presumably, too, the New Left historians would vehemently reject Mowry's comment, but the relevant point here is that the vagueness of their dream by itself can evoke such judgments.

Without insisting on a detailed blueprint, one might expect New Left economists and writers on political economy to be more specific as to means than are New Left historians in their discussion of the new American dream. The 5 percent of college and university economists who belong to or sympathize with the Union for Radical Political Economics list the features of reality they are against—irrational resource allocation, poverty, pollution, waste, monopoly, unemployment, inflation, and imperialism—and they deplore the irrelevance to reality of prevailing ideology. The economic historian Douglas F. Dowd, for example, is very critical of social scientists who place too many things outside their framework, taking them as given, and find "ways of making the existing system work better" without considering alternatives that would be implied in a different set of questions: "How does the society work, where 'work' means who gains and who loses? What is gained and lost? What are the dynamics at work, and how and why?" Economists, Dowd charges, "have come to conclusions that are not only innocuous to the status quo but frequently useful—to the status quo, as distinct from social understanding":

The New Economics, in short, has been housebroken. However, just as pre-Keynesian economics was irrelevant to the crisis of the interwar years, so too is contemporary economics largely irrelevant or misleading for the social crisis of today.[16]

Yet New Left literature on political economy fails to make explicit the New Left vision of the liberated community—a community in which, as Greg Calvert and Carol Nieman write in the preface to *A Disrupted History: The New Left and the New Capitalism* (1971), "each individual could say: 'I am a lover in a society of friends.'" Reed Whittemore, a liberal critic of this book, asserts that "A long term program must be developed —but what program? . . . while solutions admittedly come hard, imagining non-solutions to be solutions will only make them come harder."[17] This theme recurs in the liberal economist Melville Ulmer's review of Howard Sherman's *Radical Political Economy: Capitalism and Socialism from a Marxist-Humanist Perspective* (1972), which Ulmer describes as the "first full-dress statement available of the new radical creed." Ulmer concludes that "Sherman's new radical creed turns out to be little different from the cruder Marxist analyses of the past."[18] I agree with Ulmer's judgment as far as it goes, but Sherman's volume is not a strident tract, and he carries on a thoughtful dialogue with those who disagree with him.

In *The Political Economy of the New Left: An Outsider's View*, the Swedish social democratic economist Assar Lindbeck distills the essence of the New Left arguments against neoclassical or conventional economics. This summary, further condensed by Robert L. Heilbroner, echoes Dowd's charges: conventional economics (1) tends to underestimate the importance of the question of income distribution—the division of income among classes—dealing instead with marginal issues such as wage differentials arising from various causes; (2) analyzes resource allocation with respect to consumer preferences while taking these preferences as "given"; (3) concentrates on quantitative problems to the neglect of qualitative ones; (4) studies the variables of a given system or changes at the margin rather than the parameters of the system or changes in the totality; and (5) neglects the interaction of economic and political processes.

Lindbeck grants that there is some truth in these charges,

and sometimes more than that, but he does not agree with the New Left that neoclassical economics is a sterile apology for the prevailing system. It possesses adequate tools to analyze major economic problems, he believes, but the profession has been diverted from them by various social processes or pressures. Heilbroner disagrees with Lindbeck, insisting that conventional economics cannot deal adequately with these problems. At the same time, he agrees with Lindbeck that the New Left's explanations of a number of aspects of socio-economic reality are doctrinaire or simply incorrect. But the New Left, Heilbroner avers, deserves credit at least for facing problems which the conventional economists overlook. Regarding Lindbeck's discussion of the New Left's criticism of the economy, Heilbroner has reservations about the effectiveness of Lindbeck's counterarguments, but sees a "powerful indictment" in the Swedish economist's challenge to the New Left to discuss the methods of solving the major economic problems. As Heilbroner puts it, "the New Left is almost entirely concerned with criticism, not program."[19]

Ulmer points out that the "gut feeling" of students and younger professors which accounts for their favorable response to the Union of Radical Political Economics is "most effectively translated into specific, understandable propositions not in any of the new left's own literary efforts, but in works now several decades old of the generally unrecognized father of modern new left economics, the prolific, iconoclastic British economist, G. D. H. Cole."[20] One may also note that many of the younger economists applauded loudest when Leon Keyserling, whose writings contain many specific proposals for fighting poverty, exhorted the American Economic Association to move, so to speak, beyond Keynesianism,[21] but the New Left economists cannot claim this alumnus of the New Deal as one of their own. Nor can they claim Ulmer himself, who emphasizes the failure of Keynesianism evident in the ineffectiveness of the "trade off" (until the 1970s it was possible to bring inflation down to about 3 percent by allowing unemployment to rise to about 6 percent; now only an intolerable 12 percent inflation can be obtained by allowing unemployment to rise to about 6 percent). Instead of making a minimal dent in unemployment by creat-

ing a limited number of jobs for the unskilled through over-
heating of the economy, Ulmer proposes that we have another
WPA.[22]

Merely offering the new American dream will not bring it
about; and, as our comments in chapter 6 suggest, time is not
necessarily on its side regardless of a growing counter culture
and electoral realignments due to changes in the age structure
of the population. Nor will time inevitably increase the number
of those who teach and those who respond to a radical version
of the American past—a presumed trend which the New Left
historians are counting on. True, before the college-educated
counter culturalists drop out, they are exposed to an increasing
number of professors who espouse a radical view of the American past. More importantly, so, too, are young people who do
not drop out. There are indications, however, that the New
Left historians' optimism about trends in the sociology of the
profession and in the attitudes of college students in general
may prove unwarranted. Even now radical growth is confined
by the cruel contradiction in employment of historians by colleges. Meanwhile, in the early 1970s, as noted in chapter 6,
radicalism among undergraduates—the source of future doc-
toral candidates who will be entering programs enrolling fewer
students—appears to be waning. Before the 1970s the institutions which produced the most Ph.D.'s in history, and the
greatest number of radical historians, also had the most radical
undergraduate student bodies—as the Bergers point out, Yale
is not Fordham or Wichita State[23]—but the undergraduates in
these institutions, too, as we have indicated in chapter 6, are
much different from their radical predecessors of the late
1960s.

These trends among college students have long-term implications for the New Left historians' optimism regarding
politics. Meanwhile, there are no grounds for New Left hope-
fulness in the short run. The neo-Marxist Eugene Genovese,
writing in the conservative *National Review* in 1969, declares:

> The chances for an electoral victory by an opposition to the left
> of liberalism are nil and receive no attention within any section
> of the left wing movement; the chances for a seizure of power by
> one or more sections of the Left are slightly inferior to the

chances of a seizure of power by a coalition of the Campfire
Girls and the Gay Liberation front under the leadership of
Ti-Grace Atkinson.[24]

Even with respect to the long run, the New Left historians
have little reason to be sanguine about the eventual demise of
the political dominance of Middle America, or the outcome of
such a dissolution. In fact, in their approach to Middle America
they have assigned themselves an extremely difficult task. The
matter of various kinds and degrees of "winning" and "losing,"
which we discussed in chapter 3, is in a sense irrelevant to the
New Left historians since from their perspective even winners
are losers, for the institutionalized middle-class way of life
which they enjoy and to which others aspire is empty. In order
to convince Middle America of the validity of this Marcusean
judgment, the New Left historians must persuade millions of
people that they should not like what they like. Only then will
Middle Americans demand basic change not only for themselves but also for those Americans whose status as losers is
widely agreed upon.

The New Left historians and spokesmen are prone to underestimate the difficulty of their chosen task. To the frequent
comment that there is nothing startling or new about their prescription of socialism they might reply that the adoption, not
the proposing, of such a prescription would be new. They are
right, and that is why their political counsel often appears to be
unrealistic. Michael Lerner, for example, in *The New Socialist
Revolution,* calls for the formation of a new Socialist party which
will engage in independent electoral activity and trade union
organizing.[25] In view of the failure of the radical tradition to
make significant headway among the working, as well as the
middle and upper, classes throughout American history,
Lerner and like-minded social critics and activists need all the
help they can get, but they bitterly flay the liberal advocates of
piecemeal rather than comprehensive change, although they
are the most likely source of recruits to a new socialist party.

In order to affect the attitudes of Middle America, white-
or blue-collar, one must know the history of middle, as well as
upper and lower, America. This axiom applies as well to race

relations, for example, despite Zinn's declaration in *The Southern Mystique* that "I will not tangle with *cause*, because once you acknowledge cause as the core of a problem, you have built something into it that not only baffles people, but, worse, immobilizes them."[26] Teachers of history may infer from this that students who become aware of complexities and of obstacles to change in the past will become discouraged about or uninterested in improving life in the present and future. But can we follow Zinn and ignore cause while concentrating on results? In other words, can we dismiss past causes of present results as being irrelevant to the achievement of present and future results?

A historian's "plan" for the future must embrace means as well as ends, and the most objective knowledge of the past that is obtainable would appear to be one means of bringing about a better future. To deny this, to claim, as Staughton Lynd and Zinn do, that the historian should search the past as a source of alternative models for a potentially better future, of visions of what can be rather than what will be,[27] is to use the past as myth. "The function of myth," Susman writes, "is largely utopian: it provides a vision of the future without providing in and of itself any essential dynamic element which might produce the means for bringing about any changes in the present order of things."[28]

In the end, disinterested historiography and the attainment of social goals converge. "Existential freedom to choose," Kraditor states,

> can imply real power or total powerlessness, depending on whose interests are served by the choices made. . . . If autonomy is largely dependent on one's understanding oneself—and that implies understanding one's culture—then a radical historiography that obscures that understanding helps to empty of meaning a current radical's own existential freedom to choose.

If one's response to present realities obscures the historical roots of these realities, one surrenders one's freedom to choose an alternative likely to produce change in the present order. Kraditor, whose caution applies to all historians, urges radical historians to adopt a "new, non-mythic approach to their own society, their place in it, and their task of changing it—in short that they become relevant to history."[29]

A possible interpretation of Kraditor's commentary is that if the New Left historians ignore her stricture, they will replace one set of myths with another. In fact, the myths which have marked the teaching of American history, particularly in the elementary and secondary schools, will persist indefinitely in the minds of many, perhaps most, Americans. Ideally, historians would change this by revealing the facts behind myths, both to test them as truth and to understand their force as myths. This would presumably prevent the popular perpetuation of myths as unexamined imagery as well as the replacement of one set of myths by another. If this ideal situation is not to be realized, there is something to be said for balancing myths: "The Founding Fathers Against Tyranny" and "The Founding Fathers as Slave Owners," "The March of Western Civilization Across the Continent," and "The Destruction of Ancient Native Civilizations by Ignorant Hordes," the happy ending myths like The Success of Alger and VE Day and the tragic myths of losers. This would amount at least to recognition, however fanciful, of winners and losers at the same time, if not to the close, hardheaded study of them together or in interaction which Kraditor calls for.

The Reform Tradition

In the end, too, one must judge the New Left historians' history as history. "The historian and his readers," Skotheim writes, "demand obedience to the integrity of the past, even though they recognize the necessity of viewing the past through the lens of the present."[1] Nor is the allegation of present-mindedness relevant to a final assessment. New Left historian Barton J. Bernstein is correct in emphasizing that the influence of the times on the New Left historians "is not to discredit them nor necessarily to invalidate their efforts. To repudiate them on this basis could be to confuse concept formation (how one gets an idea) with judgment formation (how one determines validity)."[2] Thus, despite all that has been said here about the New Left historians' unwarranted optimistic assumptions about the climate of opinion, the most demanding test their history must undergo does not involve the attitudes of college students, developments in the alignment of the electorate, or the sociology of the historical profession. This test arises from the inner dialectic of ideas, the probing and testing which their work generates. With this in mind, we may turn to a consideration of the New Left historians' treatment of certain aspects of American history. Although there are still gaps in their coverage, Solway has been able to sketch in their perspective on twentieth-century America from their writings on Populism, Progressivism, and the New Deal. Solway's synthesis of the New Left view is perceptive as a summary. Whether the New Left analyses of Populism, Progressivism, and the New Deal are valid or convincing is another question.

With respect to Populism, the New Left assessment is in accord with the more credible of the two main opposing interpretations: Populism as a retrogressive and as a progressive movement. Hofstadter, using status-anxiety theory, and others have argued that the Populists were romantically nostalgic, given to conspiratorial views, anti-intellectual, anti-Semitic, xenophobic, chauvinistic, and proto-fascistic—the source of McCarthyism in the 1950s.[3] Taken together, studies by Norman Pollack (1962), Walter T. K. Nugent (1963), and Michael Paul Rogin (1967), and others have drastically weakened this argument.[4] The principal point of disagreement now is over how progressive or radical the Populists were.

In Pollack's New Left view, Populism

> accepted industrialism but opposed its capitalistic form, seeking instead a more equitable distribution of wealth. But Populism went further in its criticism: Industrial capitalism not only impoverished the individual, it alienated and degraded him. . . . Is Populism, then, a socialist movement? Here labels become unimportant; it was far more radical than was generally assumed. Had it succeeded, it could have fundamentally altered American society in a socialist direction.
>
> Its critique was neither partial nor superficial; higher crop prices and lower interest rates were not the answer. The issue at stake was nothing less than human dignity.[5]

Nugent, in his study of the Kansas Populists, concedes that they were anti-intellectual but otherwise acquits them of the various charges arising from the view that they lived in "some neurotic agrarian dream world." They sought the "solution of concrete economic distress through the instrumentality of a political party." Their comprehensive, idealistic platform of 1892 bore "no more nor less relation to the practical operations of the party than platforms usually do," and they directed their attack from start to finish on landlordism, transportation monopoly, and money shortages. They brought to "radical social changes a radical response," but their protest, Nugent holds, occurred within the context of democracy *and* capitalism: "it was usury, irresponsible economic power, and minority rule that they were opposing and not the industrial revolution, urbanism, or capitalism and banking as such."[6] Sheldon Hackney, in his study of Populism in Alabama, agrees with Nugent's view of the relationship between platform and campaign: "In their campaign propaganda they did not stress nationalization of transportation and communications, nor the subtreasury scheme, nor the income tax, nor their other advanced proposals." The Alabama Populists, Hackney concludes, were "neither backward-looking nor revolutionary; they were merely provincial." They believed that "Power, not a new system, was what the people required."[7]

If one leaps ahead to the New Deal, one finds some farmers still advocating Populist measures: inflation of the currency and a guarantee of cost of production as a panacea, a single measure that would by itself create prosperity and happiness for all Americans. In "Populism in the Nineteen-Thirties: The Battle for the AAA," John L. Shover shows that it took a firm stand by the Roosevelt administration to prevent the enactment of a guarantee of cost of production in its panacea version.[8] If the Populist proposals of the 1930s were impractical, however, they were conceived within the framework of capitalism. That the radical farmers of the 1930s were not unshakably committed to any particular means of dealing effectively with their problems as capitalists is evident, moreover, in their abrupt abandonment of Communist radicalism when their plight was only partially alleviated by the

AAA and when the Communists moved from espousing programs dealing with the farmers' immediate economic needs to "showing the face of the party."[9] The rank and file of the Farm Holiday movement, the most active protesters among farmers, were concerned, Shover writes, "only with immediate goals such as raising prices in thirty days or stopping a forced sale today." Holiday Association leaders detested the domestic allotment plan of the AAA and bitterly denounced Roosevelt and the whole New Deal, but the vast majority of the farmers participated in the program: "The promise of amelioration had undercut the Holiday movement."[10] To be sure, 1933 was not 1896, and in the American political spectrum of the Gilded Age the Populists were definitely radical. Nor ought we to question the genuineness of their concern, underlined by both Pollack and Nugent, for human dignity. But the failure of agrarian radicalism in the early 1930s to survive even the promise of better times suggests the absence of deeply rooted anticapitalist convictions in the Populist tradition.

Still, a New Left historian could argue, the Populists were radical, and to the industrial capitalists and workers who did not scan Bryan's campaign speeches, which were by no means severely critical of the capitalist system in its essentials, the Populists appeared to be more radical than they actually were. This argument leads to the New Left view of twentieth-century American history as "so many footnotes to Populism." A historian would like to know how we moved from the Populism of the late 1890s to Teddy Roosevelt's Progressivism. Did Populism, as a part of a continuous liberal tradition or stream, simply go underground for a time and re-emerge as Progressivism? Arthur Mann points out that recent scholarship has corrected this notion.[11] Did fear of the radical Populist spectre dictate the strategy and tactics of corporate capitalists in the Progressive era? It is striking that this is not the explanation offered by Gabriel Kolko, the author of the most important New Left studies of the Progressive era.[12] According to Kolko, as noted in chapter 1, increasing competition and decentralization moved big businessmen to engineeer progressive federal legislation in order to assure their control over the economy. They did recognize popular discontent, but one cannot conclude from Kolko's account that they "have seen chaos, and it frightens them half to death":

> If economic rationalization could not be attained by mergers and voluntary economic methods, a growing number of important businessmen reasoned, perhaps political means might succeed. At the same time, it was increasingly obvious that change was inevitable in a political democracy where Grangers, Populists, and trade unionists had significant and disturbing followings that might tap a socially dangerous grievance at some future time and threaten the entire fabric of the status quo, and that the best way to thwart change was to channelize it. If the direction of that change also solved the internal problems of the industrial and financial structure, or accommodated to the increasingly obvious fact that the creation of a national economy and market demanded political solutions that extended beyond the boundaries of states more responsive to the ordinary people, so much the better.[13]

Kolko arrives at a valid conclusion regarding an aspect of the Progressive movement through an incomplete, selective argument. That is, things sometimes turned out the way he says they did in one area, but this outcome was by no means always the result of the process which he says produced it. There is no doubt that some important businessmen promoted some regulations in order to fend off ruinous competition which they could not control by themselves, but some big businessmen were not all big businessmen, some regulations of corporation activities were not all regulations of this kind, and regulations of this kind were not the only significant laws enacted in the Progressive era.

In "The Progressive World of Gabriel Kolko" Fred Greenbaum notes that none of the four major pieces of railroad legislation of the Progressive era included the legalization of pools, the provision the railroads wanted most, or the elimination of rebates, which they also greatly desired. Greenbaum also questions Kolko's contention that the railroads did not oppose the Hepburn bill. If this was so, Greenbaum asks, why did Teddy Roosevelt have to maneuver so adroitly to obtain passage? Greenbaum gives other examples of legislative objectives which the railroads were unable to realize while remarking that the large corporations were unable to achieve their goals of federal licensing and approval of mergers and pricing arrangements. While Kolko stresses Roosevelt's detente with U. S. Steel and International Harvester, Greenbaum maintains that these detentes were on Roosevelt's terms, "for when Standard Oil attempted a similar arrangement it found itself in a court of law for not obeying the laws." Greenbaum states that in the area of regulation of meat packers, the Act of 1895 accomplished the purpose of limiting competition, the purpose which, Kolko says, the large packers pursued in supporting the Meat Inspection Act of 1906. The important difference between the Acts of 1895 and 1906 was the provision in the latter for inspection of meat produced for domestic consumption. In his analysis of the passage of the Federal Reserve Act, Kolko, Greenbaum writes, dismisses differences of opinion as technical and tactical matters and emphasizes bankers who supported the measure while discounting significant opposition.[14]

In sum, Greenbaum charges Kolko with selectivity which distorts reality: Kolko discounts significant differences between pieces of legislation, he fails to show that legislation was enacted in the form which the trusts desired, and he ignores laws that do not fit his thesis: the Expedition Act, the Underwood Tariff Commission, and all of Wilson's social legislation. He focuses on proponents of certain measures and discounts opponents, ignoring the disunity of the business community in the Progressive era which Wiebe demonstrated in 1958 with respect to banking and currency reorganization, railroad rate regulation, and the control of trusts. He ignores the necessity for Roosevelt and Wilson constantly to reassure big businesses that they did not want to destroy them. Finally, he ignores the drive for political democracy. This selectivity accords with Kolko's apparent ideological premise: "he seems to indicate that anything short of a drive to revolution is conservative."[15]

Yet Kolko underlines a significant outcome of regulatory legislation—the dominance of the regulators by the regulated, the "co-optation" discussed in chapter 3. Still, if he is correct concerning consequences, he is not always convincing concerning causes. As Greenbaum notes in regard to the Hepburn Act, "To show, as Kolko does, that the railroads felt they could live with the legislation, does not mean that they wanted it; nor does it mean that they had no intention of undermining it."[16] Kolko would concur with the contention that the railroads intended to undermine the legislation, but to undermine legislation if you cannot prevent its passage is not the same as wanting that legislation in the first place.

This distinction between original desires and eventual manipulation is evident in Stanley P. Caine's *The Myth of a Progressive Reform: Railroad Regulation in Wisconsin 1903–1910*. In his preface Caine states that his study is a test in Wisconsin of the Kolko thesis, the argument that "the carriers themselves were responsible for most of the agitation for regulation, since they viewed regulation as a way of rationalizing their industry and dampening competition." In fact, Caine's excellent book substantiates half of the Kolko thesis, the half having to do with consequences. Caine shows that as the result of their notion that commission rule was "good in and of itself," the reformers lost the game which they thought they had won with the creation of a Railroad Commission in 1905—in fact, the game had only then begun. The outcome was the kind Kolko specified. As to causes, however, Caine's findings do not accord with Kolko's thesis. Describing in detail developments in the years 1903–1905 out of which a law representing half a loaf emerged, Caine concludes:

> Only the railroads interpreted the regulation bill as a defeat. There can be little question that the Wisconsin carriers had no desire to be regulated by a state regulatory commission. Even after a moderate commission bill was passed, railroad executives were quite candid in admitting their distaste for the new order of things.[17]

Since the outcome was what Kolko says it was, one may inquire in his behalf, is it not the outcome that counts? There are at least two possible replies: as recreator of the past, the historian must strive for an accurate account of the developments leading to the outcome; and such an account, like Caine's, will be instructive to those who wish to regulate business while averting the co-optation outcome as well as to those who, like

Theodore Lowi, wish to eliminate co-optation where it exists.
Lowi makes some trenchant, concrete proposals, under the
heading "juridical democracy," for combating co-optation by
reviving the prohibition in the famous NRA or Schecter case
decision of 1935 against vague delegation of authority by the
Congress to the executive branch.[18]

Reviewing the historiographical controversy over Kolko's
Railroads and Regulation 1877–1916 (1965), Robert B. Carson
recognizes the distinction between prelude and denouement,
intentions and outcome, but he does not attach basic importance to it. In essence, the "Kolko controversy," Carson holds, is
an ideological controversy involving value judgments, based on
a radical bias or comfortable pragmatism, about American
economic development, business–government relations, and
the basic social organization of America. The historical
profession's response to Kolko has been to "paper over the
ideological division by shifting the controversy to matters of
method and scholarship . . . internal matters of research and
factual interpretation" in order to destroy a challenging argument. Carson concedes that Kolko's discussion of rail rate-
making problems is careless, neglecting the roles played by
shipping interests, unions, and others in the origins of rail regulation, but he objects to critics' making Kolko into a straw
man: "Either pro-railroad means anti-shipper or anti-other interests or it doesn't; and if it doesn't [if other groups benefited
from railroad regulation] the whole study is nonsense," or "If
other business groups supported regulation of the railroads
there is no reason to believe that the regulation was especially
pro-railroad." None of the criticism he reviews, Carson maintains, is an important challenge to Kolko's "basic thesis that the
outcome of Progressive Era rail regulations was largely in the
interest of the industry rather than the public." The full meaning of this thesis becomes apparent only when we recognize the
difference between the Smithian classical faith or progressive
liberalism, both of which "assume that the working of private
interest, in this case meaning the maintenance of private property relations, leads to the maximization of public interest," and
Kolko's "implicit" radical perspective: "By determining public

interest through the acceptance and maintenance of private
property relations, a society necessarily puts itself at the mercy
of those who control property."[19]

In characterizing Kolko's basic thesis, Carson stresses the
prorailroad outcome of railroad regulation. This thesis, he continues, is grounded in a radical perspective which views such an
outcome as inherent in capitalism, as inevitable in a capitalist
society, but this radical perspective is only "implicit" in *Railroads
and Regulation*. If Kolko had made this perspective explicit, he
would have rendered much of his research superfluous and
many of his critics' comments irrelevant. If those who control
property necessarily control government—if the state is the tool
of the bourgeoisie—the co-optation outcome follows from a deterministic course of development, and the identity of the original advocates or supporters of regulation is of only secondary
significance since the bourgeoisie can subvert any measure
which they allow to be enacted. To devote considerable attention to this matter of identity is implicitly to assign causal weight
to antideterministic factors—an attribution that conflicts with a
deterministic explanation of the outcome.

In fact, at the time Kolko wrote *Railroads and Regulation*
(1965) he made no claim that the state was the tool of the
bourgeoisie. In the concluding chapter of *The Triumph of Conservatism* (1963) he referred to Marx's formal theory that the
capitalists controlled the state but noted that Marx did not expect the capitalists to use the state in the economic sphere
—Marx neglected "political capitalism." In *The Roots of American
Foreign Policy* (1969), however, Kolko, as we have seen in chapter 5, although he did not refer to the state as the "tool of the
bourgeoisie," might just as well have used this phrase. If by
then he was not a Marxist in some strict sense, his view of history was materialistic and deterministic. Perhaps if he had written *Railroads and Regulation* six years later, he would have focused on outcome and made his challenge to classical and liberal thinkers manifest: Can you disprove my thesis that the
domination of the regulators by the regulated is inherent in
capitalism by eliminating the co-optation of the regulatory
agencies, by means of Lowi's device or any other? There would
be little consolation for the mass of Americans if one had to

reply that one rejects inevitability in history but must concede that co-optation cannot be eliminated. In any case, it is not necessary to dwell on the question of inevitability in testing even a deterministic thesis, although one would expect the exponent of such a thesis to be consistent in his determinism. In the next section of this chapter, I reject the Marxist model for capitalist imperialism not because it is deterministic but because capitalists' behavior does not appear to support it. In this light, although I do not share Kolko's radical perspective but am familiar from my study of the New Deal with the AAA's becoming the big farmers' agency and the NRA's becoming big business' agency, I take Kolko's challenge, as restated here, quite seriously.

Yet this recognition of Kolko's contribution, despite his making a chapter of Progressivism the whole story, must be accompanied by two additional qualifications, one partly historiographical and one referring to work in another discipline. The Old Left of the 1930s provided a precedent for Kolko's thesis, and Robert Wiebe, in *Businessmen and Reform: A Study of the Progressive Movement* (1962), with balance and care spelled out the proposition that businessmen played an important role in the Progressive movement. In the field of sociology, Philip Selznick has published *TVA and the Grass Roots: A Study of the Sociology of Formal Organization* (1949), a book which prompts one to ask a question that both Kolko and his critics, including this one up to this point, fail to raise: Is cooptation confined to capitalism? In *The Triumph of Conservatism* Kolko criticizes Max Weber for his overschematized treatment of an uncommitted, objective, impersonal bureaucracy without reference to concrete historical political and economic forces and their impact on bureaucracy. Weber, Kolko contends, does not allow for the kind of "political capitalism"—Weber's own term —which has arisen in the United States.[20] Selznick's analysis of a concrete historical development suggests that Kolko himself does not allow for cooptation, for bureaucracy's becoming an instrument of special rather than general interests, as a process transcending capitalism. Selznick observes:

> words like democracy and socialism might be useful as utopian
> calls to action, and as cementers of solidarity, but they do not

serve well as guides to policy. They do not contain the specific criteria needed to assure that the contemplated end is truly won and that the cost of winning is acceptable. They also become readily available as protective covers behind which uncontrolled discretion can occur.[21]

The emergence and nature of the New Left treatment of the New Deal are described and analyzed judiciously and with discernment by Otis L. Graham, Jr. Early attacks on the New Deal came from both the right and the left—now called the Old Left—but of the two assaults the one from the right, which in broad terms condemned the New Deal for going too far, evoked the greater response. Meanwhile, by the late 1950s the liberal defense of the New Deal as a workable response to crisis, a democratic "middle way" between totalitarian extremes, became the dominant assessment. If the right no longer posed a political or scholarly threat to the New Deal, however, the left launched an attack in the 1960s, rejecting New Dealish solutions to present problems and downgrading the New Deal itself for having failed to prevent the emergence of these problems. The new critics of the New Deal, Graham writes, asked "hard questions about the actual degree of social change it had brought." They showed a deep interest in the location of money and power and the conditions of life for marginal and working economic classes. They asked questions which the conservatives, who had assumed that the New Deal was socialist, had not asked, and they gathered the data to fill out the broad picture which their Old Left ancestors had only sketched. William E. Leuchtenburg's *Franklin D. Roosevelt and the New Deal 1932–1940* (1963), which candidly discussed the limited impact of recovery and reform measures in the 1930s, was the first omen of a critical examination of the New Deal by critics less moderate than its liberal author. By the end of the 1960s important attacks from the left, compared to which Leuchtenburg's criticism appeared mild, were mounted by Howard Zinn (1966), Paul K. Conkin (1967), and Barton J. Bernstein (1968)[22] (although none of Conkin's other works can be called New Left).

One of the virtues of the New Left historians of the New Deal, Graham concludes, is that they have "helped clarify how much more modest than we thought were New Deal attainments in income redistribution, in power restructuring—industrial and even political—and in relief of suffering." They have shown that "New Deal achievements were disappointing even to some candid New Dealers themselves." The accomplishment of the New Deal—"barely measurable advances toward economic recovery and racial justice . . . moderate steps in organizing industrial labor in the northern cities, in underwriting the economic security of landowning farmers and the unemployed, in liberalizing the Democratic party, in restoring 'faith' in ailing political and economic institutions"—is, Graham states, now apparent, at least in a general way. The main debate at present is over the question whether this accomplishment was "a credit to the men who managed it or a permanent indictment of them and their ideas." Those who maintain that it was creditable cite the virtues of the New Deal as a viable democratic "middle way" amid economic and spiritual crisis and, like Jerold S. Auerbach, insist that it was about all that was possible under the circumstances. The radical historians aver that Roosevelt's middle way was not the only possible middle way, that the historical function of the New Deal was "to put down pressures for real reform and inadvertently perpetuate, perhaps even strengthen, an intolerable social system." They insist that "the New Deal performance could and should have been better." Thus the main controversy in New Deal historiography is now between the center and the left.[23]

In assessing this debate, Graham considers some of the guidelines which Kraditor lays down in her commentary on New Left historiography. Three of the analytical errors she ascribes to exaggerated present-mindedness are: the emphasizing of the heroism and love for The People displayed by Our Side (the treatment of adversaries, so to speak, as Good Guys and Bad Guys); the lifting of movements out of their historical contexts, which results in the mistaken application to past developments of terms like radicalism in their current sense; and the neglect of the circumstances that surround a movement as it strives to realize certain abstract ideals, circumstances which dictate reformers' strategies and tactics, which enhance or limit reformers' achievements, and which determine whether their accomplishments weaken or strengthen the established order. An account that stresses the reformers' struggle "to wring concessions from politicians and bosses . . . tells only half the truth," Kraditor writes, "for it ignores the system's power structure and capabilities."[24]

Graham recognizes that present-mindedness can sharpen sensitivity to new issues and reveal new perspectives, but he emphatically condemns the deliberate use of history to serve contemporary ends. Like Kraditor, he declines, in effect, to analyze the New Deal in terms of Good Guys and Bad Guys when he rejects the proposition, implicit in the New Left appraisal, that the New Dealers were "indefensibly cautious, insensitive to misery and injustice." He also declines to judge the liberals of the 1930s by the criteria of the 1960s: "Let us add [to the context] the total range of social and political ideas in America in the 1930s and before, and the New Dealers appear well toward the innovative and daring end of the spectrum, with stronger democratic instincts and a more steady humanitarianism than all but a scant minority of their contemporaries." Finally, Graham, like Kraditor, deplores historians' neglecting one of these two sets of factors: forces making for change and forces working against change—Graham refers to opportunities and obstacles, forces of movement and forces of resistance. Radical, liberal, and conservative historians, he asserts, have all failed to study "the relation between opportunities and obstacles with any real dedication." The radical historians have tended to maximize the forces of movement and minimize the forces of resistance. Offering impressionistic judgments which neglect the advantages of the defenders of existing arrangements and underrating obstacles, they have failed to define conclusively how much more was possible.[25]

The productive question which radical and other historians have not addressed, Graham maintains, is "why have we had such stability in our basic economic and social institutions, even during the deepest economic crisis in our history?" Graham himself offers a preliminary, tentative response in the form of a list of forces of movement—Huey Long, Father Coughlin, Governor Floyd Olson of Minnesota, Upton Sinclair, the progressive bloc in Congress, the third-party movement in Wisconsin, the radicalism of the intellectual classes—and the forces of resistance, which included the persistence of old ideas and habits, the durability of class structures, the inadequacy of economic knowledge, economic ambivalence as between individualism and concentration, the lack of competent personnel to carry out immediate and drastic reforms like the nationalization of the banking system, "co-operation" with business during the Hundred Days in accordance with the analogue of war which prevailed in a national emergency, the threat of unconstitutionality, the organization of Congress, party organizations, the Second World War, the media, public ignorance, the political apathy and impotence of the under classes, Roosevelt's orthodoxy, reactionary and unrepresentative state governments, and liberal ideology. The New Left historians, Graham notes, underrate these obstacles, with one important exception. They argue that the New Deal was restricted by its ideology. "How important in the final summation," Graham asks, "will be the inadequacies, preventable and inexcusable, of liberalism as an ideology?" A safe guess is: "not as important as the New Left historians have said." The answer to the question as to why there was not more reform in the 1930s, Graham concludes, is "mostly structural, not ideological."[26]

Foreign Policy

In the area of foreign policy, New Left historians have produced a considerable body of literature which in varying degrees follows the lead of William Appleman Williams' "Open Door" thesis: the main moving force behind American foreign policy has been the desire to create the worldwide trade and investment opportunities for American capitalism that it requires in order to survive.[1] There is no question that this literature has at least three major virtues: it emphasizes factors which diplomatic historians tended to neglect during the two decades of intense Cold War antagonism; it underlines the discrepancy between altruistic rhetoric and the self-interested nature of American foreign policy; and it makes a substantial research contribution. The basic flaw in New Left historians' writings on foreign policy is, broadly speaking, selectivity—conceptual and methodological: they make a part of the story the whole story, and they marshal evidence selectively in order to support their central thesis.

This thesis is not as simple as it may appear at first glance. While most New Left historians of American foreign policy attribute American expansionism or imperialism to the nation's socioeconomic structure or, more precisely, the institutional structure of American capitalism, Williams himself identifies as the basic source of expansionism not the institutional needs of capitalism as such but, rather, what Americans have mistakenly thought these needs to be.[2] This view raises the extremely complex question of the role of ideas in history, a question which a historian who draws on Marxist thought, as Williams does, must confront in the form of Marx's combination of material base and Idealist or intellectual superstructure. Genovese, who in a general way is sympathetic toward Williams' efforts, finds that the Idealist Williams, in rendering the materialist Marx as an Idealist, shifts back and forth between conditions and ideas as primary historical causes.[3] Robert W. Tucker, who is far from sympathetic toward the New Left interpretation of American foreign policy, believes that judgment of the basic New Left thesis can be undertaken without solving the related problem of the role of ideas in history, since the gap between a materialist or economic determinist like Kolko and the Idealist Williams can be bridged when one sees that Williams' "psychic necessity is still, at bottom, an institutional necessity."[4] In other words, whether capitalism itself has certain needs or whether capitalism inevitably produces a widespread though erroneous belief that it has these needs, the society will be expansionist so long as it is predominantly capitalist.

In making a part into a whole the New Left historians have neglected at least two kinds of diversity in the capitalist world: differences between American capitalists and differences between American capitalism and that of other nations. Although it would be unreasonable to insist that the New Left thesis account for the attitudes and behavior of all American capitalists at all times, it implies a closer relationship between capitalism and capitalists' preferred policies than the one which a number of studies of capitalists' policy positions depict. On domestic issues one may cite such studies as Wiebe's portrayal (1958), mentioned above, of business disunity during the Progressive era and Stanley Coben's description (1959) of deep divisions among northeastern businessmen during the era of Radical Reconstruction,[5] but our concern at this point is foreign policy. In a recent relevant study of foreign policy in the Gilded Age, Paul S. Holbo points out that in that era "economic interests were divergent and often conflicting."[6] In another recent study, Joan Hoff Wilson's *American Business and Foreign Policy, 1920–1933*, she shows that business opinion divided along occupational, sectional, political, and organizational lines on the leading foreign policy issues of the time: disarmament and peace, commercial and foreign loan policy, war debts and reparations, Latin American and Far Eastern policy.[7]

The differences between American capitalism and that of other countries—"polycentrism" in the capitalist world—must also be taken into account in assessing the radical view of capitalist dynamics: that the inherent incompatible tendencies of capitalism inevitably give rise to imperialism, racism, sexism, and widespread alienation. Heilbroner considers several nations which have had the same basic economic structure based on private property and the market mechanism but which differ in their social, political, and economic institutions:

> Japan, where the large corporations guarantee lifetime employment to their workers—and the Republic of South Africa, where something very close to indentured labor is an essential part of the system; New Zealand, with its virtual absence of unemployment—and the United States, with its nagging problem of unemployment; Norway, with its severe taxation of upper incomes—and Italy with its *dolce vita;* Denmark, with its long tradition of political security—and France with its equally long tradition of insecurity. . . .
>
> It is difficult to maintain in the face of this diversity that imperialism (Norway?), racism (Denmark?), a widening gap between rich and poor (Sweden?) or other such problems are inherent in "capitalism." To put it differently, it is hard to explain how capitalism can assume so many shapes and forms unless we admit that factors of a noneconomic

kind—geographic positions, size, racial mixtures, political institutions, "national character" or whatever—are critical in determining the outcome of capitalist dynamics in each case.

In sum, the radical thesis concerning capitalism fails the comparative test. This failure, Heilbroner notes, suggests that the long-run fate of American capitalism will depend, and one may add, scholars should focus, "less on those elements in America that are capitalist than on those elements in capitalism that are American."[8]

In addition to citing the differences between nations within the sphere of capitalism, Heilbroner points to similarities between capitalist America and the socialist Soviet Union. If capitalist America is imperialist, racist, sexist, and alienated, the socialist Soviet Union is also imperialist, racist, and alienated. How, then, can we say that these evils (and we can add polution and resource depletion since Lake Baikal is nearly dead and resource conservation is almost unknown in Russia) are inherent in either capitalism or socialism? If the radical maintains that the Soviet Union is not the archetype of socialist society because of the special circumstances of its national heritage and traditions, how can we maintain that the United States is the archetype of capitalist society while disregarding *its* national heritage and traditions? Why not, Heilbroner asks, make Norway or Sweden the model of "pure" capitalism and dismiss the United States as "only a sorry case of capitalism come to maturity in a land cursed with slavery (not a capitalist institution) and formed in the peculiar mold of an exacerbated frontier individualism?"[9]

Relevant to Heilbroner's comparative analysis is Tucker's discussion of the radicals' belief that a socialist America would pursue a foreign policy fundamentally different from the foreign policy of capitalist America. This belief, Tucker holds, rests on the equating of the "ways" of great powers with the "ways" of capitalism when, in fact, from time immemorial great powers have almost always manifested certain pretensions. If history has any relevance here,

> there is no apparent reason to assume that the new America would refrain from identifying the collective self with something

larger than the self. If this is so, the nation's security and well-being would still be identified with a world that remained receptive to American institutions and interests. No doubt, a Socialist America would define those institutions and interests in a manner different from the definition of a Capitalist America. But this difference cannot be taken to mean that we would refrain from attempting to influence the course of development of other peoples.

Elaborating his dissent from the radicals' belief about a socialist America, Tucker questions their assumption that the necessity to preserve access to sources of raw materials is one unique to capitalism. He also questions their assumption that in a world of the strong and the weak, the rich and the poor, a socialist America would act justly toward the weak: "It is, after all, not only the Capitalist states that have sought to take advantage of their strength when dealing with poor and weak states." Finally, he questions their assumption that "the world as we know it today is America's special creation." Would a socialist America, for example, be able to resolve the conflict between China and the Soviet Union? Would this conflict hold no dangers for a socialist America? In the end, Tucker writes, the radicals' belief about a socialist America's foreign policy "rests on the assertion—a tautology—that if men are transformed, they will then behave differently . . . . But this is to resolve the problem of how a Socialist America would behave by defining the problem away."[10]

Finally, the exponents of the Open Door thesis fail systematically to apply to their data the Marxist model from which their thesis is derived. Robert Zevin does attempt such an application. Surplus, he explains in a summary of the Marxist-Leninist theory of imperialism, is the difference between the labor value and the market value of national product. "The dynamic process, which leads to imperialism, begins when the flow of surplus value to capitalists exceeds their consumption requirements." Over time, if the "subsistence" wage does not increase at the same rate, there will be increases in the stock of capital per worker, flow of real product per worker, and the absolute and relative flow of surplus value per worker. Eventually, under the law of diminishing returns, each addition to

capital will yield progressively smaller additions to product,
to capitalists' surplus value, and to profit (with the average rate
of profit as well as the marginal rate eventually declining).
Investments of surplus, unlike workers' consumption expenditures, are comparatively volatile and inevitably produce cyclical downturns of increasing frequency and severity. Such a
downturn or "crisis"

> is alternatively described by Marxist and semi-Marxist writers as
> a growing surplus of production in search of a market or a
> growing surplus of savings in search of investment
> opportunities. For purposes of the Marxist analysis, a solution to
> one problem is essentially equivalent to a solution to the other.
> By the logic of the case, less-developed countries appear to offer
> such solutions since . . . marginal increment of product per
> worker to each increment of capital per worker is large relative
> to the mother country.[11]

Zevin relates this Marxist model to two waves of American
imperialism, one "reaching a climax between 1898 and 1918;
the other beginning in World War II and accelerating at least
until the very recent past." He finds that investment and sav-
ings were a rising proportion of national product and income
through the nineteenth century, that they have been a constant
or declining proportion since. "This is consistent with the
Marxist hypothesis for the first wave of American imperialism
but not the second." Zevin then notes that capital per worker
and national product per worker grew throughout the period
1869–1955. "These data are consistent with the Marxist model
or indeed with almost any other." The test of the Marxist
model, however, is whether there was an increased rate of
exploitation—an increase in profit as a percentage of national
income—and a decrease in the marginal rate and then the average rate of profit. The averate rate of profit (the ratio of
national product per worker to capital per worker) was flat to
slightly downward in the period 1869–1955. This absence of a
secular trend does not square with the Marxist assumption of a
fixed level of subsistence wages and a sharp rise over time in
the average profit rate. The marginal rate of profit (the ratio of
change in product per worker to change in capital per worker)
declined very slightly from the late nineteenth century through

the early twentieth century, then rose sharply after 1929: "Although it may have declined slightly around the first wave of nineteenth-century imperialism, we cannot avoid the conclusion that it has moved dramatically higher in the mid-twentieth century." Commenting on his findings up to this point, Zevin states, "Thus these statistics are neutral at best and often sharply in contradiction with the Marxist expectations for a period of growing capital per worker and imperialist activity."[12]

Zevin next considers "the most directly relevant statistics, those dealing with American foreign trade and international capital accounts." Annual gross export figures as percentages of gross national product rose from 6.2 percent for the decade ending in 1878 to 6.8 percent for the decade ending in 1908, and after the First World War, "when the fruits of imperialism should be plucked," the percentage dropped to 5 percent by the end of the 1920s and 3 percent in the 1930s, fluctuating around 4 percent after the Second World War. "These figures can only be called a decisive contradiction to the Marxist interpretation." Analysis of the surplus of commodity exports over imports and of the surplus of merchandise exports is "no more favorable from the Marxist point of view." A balance sheet analysis of American international accounts—United States public and private claims against foreigners and public and private claims of foreigners against the United States—

> also yield unimpressive results in terms of Marxist analysis. . . . Both the relative magnitudes and the lack of trend in these figures would seem to decisively contradict the Marxist predictions for a major capitalist country entering its second century of modern imperialist activity. We are thus forced to reject the Marxist model as an explanation for United States imperialism. The evidence does not provide any support, either for the proposition that United States imperialism was a response to a growing need in the economy to export surplus product and invest surplus savings, or that United States imperialism had the result of making such increased exports and foreign investment possible.[13]

Zevin does point out that aggregate statistics which indicate the magnitude of foreign trade or investment relative to gross national product conceal absolute changes. "In actual fact, the onset of major United States imperialist activities in the 1890s was accompanied by a major expansion of United States overseas investments." This does not confirm the Marxist interpretation, however. Examination of international economic relationships shows that from the 1890s to 1929 the United States was a net investor in Western Hemisphere and other undeveloped countries and, through 1914, a net borrower from Europe. Trade in this period was of a triangular sort: the United States was a net importer from Western Hemisphere and other underdeveloped countries but a net exporter to Western Europe; the underdeveloped countries were net importers from Western Europe but net exporters to the United States: Western Europe was a net importer from the United States but a net exporter to the underdeveloped countries. With respect to the United States, "These results are hardly consistent with the Marxist view of the foreign economic relations of a great imperialist power." Moreover, Zevin notes, making a point which we shall refer to again, percentages which have hardly changed from the First World War to the present show that 60 percent of United States direct and portfolio investments and over 75 percent of United States trade are in the developed or industrial world: Western Europe, South Africa, Canada, Australia, and Japan.[14]

If the Marxist model were to apply to the first wave of American imperialism but not the second, it would not be viable as a theoretical explanation. Zevin, of course, does not believe that the Marxist model explains even the first wave. Still, he concedes that on "the question of crises, the nineteenth-century [although not the twentieth-century] American experience is . . . consistent with a Marxist viewpoint," and he notes that "Walter La Feber and others have seized upon the terrible economic difficulties of the 1890's as a convenient explanation for the accelerated pace of United States imperialist activity in the decade." Zevin, however, does not accept an explanation which hinges on the presence of a growing surplus which had no place to go without imperialism (either in its annexationist or economic-penetrative form):

> A closer analysis [than La Feber's] would seem to indicate, however, that the fluctuations in American investment in the

late nineteenth and early twentieth centuries were caused not so much by the inertia of the swelling surplus of capitalists as by the sensitivity of the American economy, and particularly the railroad section, to economic fluctuations in Europe.[15]

In rejecting the Marxist-model explanation, Zevin does not drain imperialism of economic motives or content. On the contrary, he concludes that individual, as distinguished from class, capitalist interests have promoted and benefited from imperialist policies—in some cases but not in others. In general,

> there is no vital economic self-interest of the American capitalist class or the American economy in the aggregate which has been, is, or could be served by imperialist policies. Much of America's imperialist behavior can still be explained by the fact that *individual* economic interests can be decisively advanced by a government policy whose costs or consequences are relatively unimportant to the disinterested parties.

In regard to the numerous cases of this kind, Zevin states, an economic interpretation of imperialism is justified, but such an interpretation does

> not appear sufficient to explain American involvement in major and costly imperialist efforts such as the war in the Philippines and the war in Indochina. Nor do [such cases] explain other actions which carried equally grave potentials such as the intervention in the Dominican Republic or the Bay of Pigs invasion.

Students of American imperialism, Zevin writes, often dismiss expansionists' ideological and moral arguments as a facade while accepting their appeals to national economic self-interest as genuine. He suggests that it may be the other way around, that the expansionists' ideological statements might have expressed their true motives while their economic arguments were disingenuous. Hubert Humphrey might really have meant it when he said the purpose of American involvement in Vietnam was "simply to take the Great Society to Southeast Asia."[16]

In *Toward a Democratic Left*, Michael Harrington presents conclusions concerning American foreign-economic policy in the post–Second World War period that are essentially like

Zevin's—a reminder to New Left historians that their view is not the only one on the left. Harrington tests Lenin's belief that capitalism is compelled to export its capital because it cannot be invested profitably (or profitably enough) within the confines of the metropolitan economy. In Lenin's own terms, Harrington maintains, imperialism is not the inevitable policy of the United States because there is "a general American commitment to government intervention against depressions and capitalism has developed agriculture, raised the living standard of the masses, and remained capitalism." Nor has imperialism as defined by Lenin been the actual policy of the United States since 1945. True, material self-interest was involved in our political and military commitment in Europe after the Second World War but "once one leaves the initial, European period of the Cold War and turns to the Third World, the disparity between economics and foreign policy becomes manifest." In Asia ideological hostility "took on a life of its own." The Cold War became a conflict between good and evil, and the United States felt compelled to meet any challenge, anywhere. In the economic sphere, meanwhile, American policy "escape[d] from economic determinism." Since 1945 Lenin's assertion has been "less true with every passing day." In the postwar period most overseas capital investment by the affluent powers as been in each other, and for the American economy as a whole "the raw materials and capital export markets of the Third World have become less and less important." Harrington refers to several sources of statistical data on international trade and cites Heilbroner's estimates that total American capital in Asia, Africa, and Latin America is $16 billion while total corporate assets in the American economy amount to $1.3 trillion. Harrington also considers Paul Baran's and Paul Sweezy's attempt in *Monopoly Capital* to adapt Marxist theory to new mid-century realities. Their thesis is a kind of iron law of military Keynesianism: enormous military expenditures are the only form of social spending which can prevent a depression and, regardless of whether overseas profits are vital to the American economy, domestic needs force the United States to pursue a Cold War policy. Harrington believes Baran and Sweezy are wrong.[17]

Although we do pursue policies that help to shore up an international economy which exploits impoverished peoples and we do have a huge military budget, Harrington insists that neither is economically necessary, an inexorable expression of our social and economic structure. We could get along well without them—at least in theory: "In practice, everything depends on politics." Harrington believes that it is possible for the United States to adopt new international and domestic expenditure policies without undergoing a drastic domestic transformation, although such a shift would require "a considerable radicalization of political life." In any event, he is not overly optimistic: "progress is certainly not inevitable and perhaps not even possible." There are formidable "non-economic" obstacles to sweeping change in either foreign-economic or domestic policy. America must overcome special institutional interests (especially those of the politically powerful oil industry), myths (such as that of a world market based on reciprocity), and imperialist and racist psychology if it is to help the world's poor or acquire the ability politically to tolerate, through a policy of watchful waiting, the turmoil and violence inherent in the developmental process in the poorest nations. Dramatic change in domestic policy, Harrington asserts, would require overcoming ideological attachments which make the "socialization of death . . . much more generally popular than the socialization of life."[18]

The New Left historians of foreign policy are thus selective in making part of the story—economic factors—the whole story. As Holbo puts it, their "thesis has the compelling appeal of simplicity. But its authors misread American political history and fail to note emotional and ideological ingredients that affected foreign policy."[19] They are also selective in marshaling evidence. "Too frequently," Holbo writes, "only those parts of statements are quoted that seem to support the interpretation, and they appear without the context necessary to understand them."[20] He gives a number of specific examples. Two will suffice here. In 1894 Secretary of State Walter Q. Gresham, as La Feber points out,

> wrote of the nation's seeming inability to "afford constant employment for our labor." However, La Feber failed to quote the next sentence, in which Gresham said, "This is owing, in

part, to the rapid increase in labor-saving machinery, but in greater measure to high protective tariffs. . . ."

La Feber also cited a lengthy *Harper's* article by Carl Schurz in October, 1893, and his correspondence with Gresham. But this material in fact focused overwhelmingly on the great foreign policy question of Hawaii, which was Gresham's immediate responsibility and growing concern. Only one paragraph dealt with foreign trade. Thus it is misleading to claim that Gresham was "obsessed" by the problem of "glutted wealth" or that he "concluded that foreign markets would provide in large measure the cure."[21]

Arthur M. Schlesinger, Jr., refers to "the anxiety with which Professor Williams seeks to press recalcitrant evidence into the service of his thesis. Again and again, he overstates and manipulates his case in order to insert overseas-market preoccupations when they existed only feebly or not at all"—and Schlesinger, too, offers several illustrative examples.[22]

The New Left historians of foreign policy allow themselves the license to indulge in these two kinds of selectivity because the details of their specific revisionist arguments rest on what Charles S. Maier calls "implicit conceptual models and underlying assumptions about the decisive factors in American foreign relations."[23] The key word here is *implicit*. We have presented Zevin's explication of the Marxist model of imperialism at some length in order to show that a Marxist model is nothing to play with. A writer who uses it implicitly permits himself to engage in unrestrained selectivity while making it difficult, although by no means impossible, for critics to pin him down. The context of the Marxist model of imperialism, moreover, is a deterministic view of history. If the writers who use this model implicitly were to use it explicitly and in a manner consistent with its deterministic context, they would not in effect contradict themselves by devoting so much attention to and placing so much emphasis on the identification of the supporters of imperialistic policies. Nor would they have to resort to unsatisfactory distinctions between a capitalist system's inherent needs and what capitalists think the system needs.

Consider the orthodox Marxist Plekhanov on *The Role of the Individual in History:*

> Saint-Beuve thought that had there been a sufficient number of
> minor and dark causes of the kind that he had mentioned, the
> outcome of the French Revolution would have been the opposite
> of what we now know it to have been. This is a great mistake. . . .
> The causes of the French Revolution lay in the character of
> social [or economic] relations; and the minor causes assumed by
> Saint-Beuve could lie only in the personal qualities of
> individuals. The final cause of social relationships lies in the
> state of productive forces. . . . No matter what the qualities of the
> given individual may be, they cannot eliminate the given
> economic relations if the latter conform to the given state of
> productive forces.

Plekhanov asks what would have happened if Mirabeau had
lived longer or if Robespierre had been accidentally killed by a
falling brick in January 1793. Events would have taken the
same course, although the timing might have been different.
"Owing to the specific qualities of their minds and characters
influential individuals," Plekhanov writes, "can change the individual features of events and some of their particular consequences, but they cannot change their general trend, which is
determined by other forces."[24]

Bearing in mind Marxist determinism, we may turn to a
consideration of La Feber's analysis of United States entry into
the Spanish-American War. We shall see that he emphasizes a
last-minute switch in businessmen's opinion as a determinant of
American policy while relating that policy to a 50- or 150-year
trend. This approach raises at least two questions, one empirical and one interpretive: Was the relationship between business
and government what La Feber says it was? Does he give due
consideration to the deterministic context of the Marxist model
implicit in his Open Door view?

In *The New Empire*, published in 1963, La Feber refers to
Julius W. Pratt's *Expansionists of 1898*, published in 1936. Pratt
concluded that while those who were directly or indirectly concerned in the Cuban sugar industry clamored for intervention in
Cuba, others whose businesses would suffer direct injury from
war, and the overwhelming preponderance of businessmen in
general, were opposed to intervention until the last minute
—March 1898.[25] Pratt, it is true, also concluded that American

businessmen, after finally yielding reluctantly to the necessity of a war with Spain, then built "high hopes upon the supposed opportunities for trade and exploitation in a string of dependencies stretching from the Philippines to Puerto Rico."[26] In view of the prevailing attitude of businessmen until the last minute, however, these hopes cannot be read back into the prewar period. La Feber agrees with Pratt on the chronology of businessmen's attitudes toward entry into war with Spain:

> Perhaps the business community exerted the most influence on the administration during the last two weeks in March when influential business spokesmen began to welcome the possibility of war in order to end the suspense which shrouded the commercial exchanges. Although other historians have touched briefly on this important change, it should be noted that some important business spokesmen and President McKinley apparently arrived at this decision at approximately the same time.[27]

La Feber's footnote 93 cites *Expansionists of 1898*. On the next page, and again near the end of his concluding chapter, La Feber stresses the impact on antiwar business journals of an interventionist speech by Senator Redfield Proctor of Vermont on March 17, 1898[28]—five weeks before war was declared on April 25.

In an essay on "That 'Splendid Little War' in Historical Perspective," published in 1968, La Feber again pointed to the last-minute switch in business sentiment. There were three "chains" of causes—the economic crisis of the 1890s, opportunities in Asia after 1895 and in the Caribbean and the Pacific beginning in 1898, and a partnership between business and government—which in 1898 "had a 'valuable collision' [J. B. Bury's phrase] and war resulted." In January 1898, new revolts took place in Havana, and in February the "Maine" incident occurred. "McKinley confronted the prospect of immediate war. Only two restraints appeared": the possibility that war could lead to the annexation of Cuba, and the business community. By mid-1897 increased exports had relieved twenty-five years of domestic strain, and "businessmen did not want the requirements of a war economy to jeopardize the growing prosperity." The removal of these two restraints "indicates why war occurred in April 1898." McKinley had no desire to acquire a colonial empire in the Caribbean, and he devised a "classic solution" whereby the United States would retain a veto power over the more important Cuban policy decisions. "The second restraint disappeared in March 1898, exactly at the time of McKinley's decision to send the final ultimatum to Madrid." The businessmen, however, did not manipulate the President: "McKinley was never pushed into a policy he did not want to accept." Emerging from the depression of the 1890s and having witnessed European powers granting themselves trade preferences in Asia which would shut out competition, businessmen and the President shared

> a common conclusion: the nation's economy increasingly depended upon overseas markets, including the whole of China; that to develop these markets not only a business-government partnership but also tranquility was required; and, finally, however paradoxical it might seem, tranquility could be insured only through war against Spain.[29]

The year 1968 also saw the publication of Marilyn Blatt Young's essay on "American Expansion, 1870–1900: The Far East." Although she is a revisionist, she offered a highly qualified version of the Open Door thesis in which she presented a picture different from La Feber's of "the system of cooperation between businessmen and politicians which began to emerge in the 1880s and reached fruition after the turn of the century." She saw the causes of American entry into war with Spain as religious, political, nationalist, and racist as well as economic, all of them contributing to a "national neurosis [which] was acted out in the fantastic fervor which preceded the war and perhaps made it inevitable." Of particular interest here, since La Feber sees the war with Spain as a consciously chosen means of achieving the tranquillity required to develop "overseas markets, including the whole of China," is Young's analysis of America's China policy. The scramble for concessions in China, she wrote, "turned America's attention to China as never before. Although the air was filled with demands that America do something, what precisely should be done was left almost entirely up to the government." Both businessmen and government were vague about what should be done. McKinley could be sure that "*some* action in regard to China would be favored by the business community [but] it was not clear how much action they were willing to countenance." Actual government policy in asserting American interests in China, "despite the tedious reiteration of the importance of Chinese markets, despite the ultra-nationalists' boasts and the frequent opportunities for action . . . was cautious in the extreme."[30]

If, as in La Feber's account, concern for the Chinese market produced close cooperation between business and government and agreement between them on the necessity of declaring war on Spain, in Young's analysis such close cooperation, which would presumably entail *specific* recommendations by business to government, did not exist, and the boldness of the policy agreed upon in 1898 virtually evaporated in two years. The sledgehammer in Cuba of 1898 became a flyswatter in China by 1900. Thus Young holds that the relationship between business and government was not what La Feber says it was. She also criticizes La Feber for "a certain flattening out of history" from 1850 to 1889 and beyond: "One loses sight of the unique situation that each politician faced and the impact on his actions of day-to-day problems. Moreover, distinct changes are blurred as we follow the line of continuity."[31]

While Young implies that La Feber's approach is too deterministic to do justice to details, I maintain that his treatment of certain details does not jibe with the deterministic context of the Marxist model of imperialism implicit in his Open Door view. Although La Feber accepts Pratt's account of an eleventh-hour switch in businessmen's opinion, chronology is implicitly not crucial in his analysis, which seems to imply that the last-minute switch followed from a long-term trend. The last sentence of La Feber's final chapter reads: "A new type of American empire, temporarily clothed in armor, stepped out on the international stage after half a century of preparation to make its claim as one of the great powers."[32] In the last paragraph of his book, at the end of his "Epilogue," La Feber writes, "By 1899 the United States had forged a new empire. American policy makers and businessmen had created it amid much debate and with conscious purpose . . . one hundred and fifty years of American history had suddenly fallen into place."[33] If businessmen's last-minute switch followed from a long-term trend—an accumulation of a surplus and/or the belief that there was a surplus—why was there a last-minute switch at all? Why did not most businessmen, in accordance with the trend, favor intervening in Cuba when the possibility of doing so first appeared? This question may, in effect, demand of human beings more consistency than a historian can reasonably expect. Long-held beliefs, as Edmund S. Morgan notes, can be sincerely held although the men who espouse them express them explicitly only when the need for their defense or the opportunity for their advancement is especially evident.[34] Still, to argue from "human nature" is to depart from the determinism implicit in the writings of the Open Door historians. Why not avoid the pitfalls of the chronology of advocacy and the identification of advocates by explicitly adopting a deterministic approach?

When La Feber turns from advocates to economic facts, he also runs into trouble. On the second page of his "Epilogue" he restates the long-term economic fact which is central to the Open Door thesis:

> One striking characteristic tied these acquisitions [Alaska, Midway, Pago Pago] to the new territory brought under American control in 1898 and 1899, immediately after the war with Spain. The United States obtained these areas not to fulfill a colonial policy, but to use these holdings as a means to acquire markets for the glut of goods pouring out of highly mechanized factories and farms.[35]

This statement would satisfy a Marxist for its deterministic assumption regarding capitalist imperialism, but La Feber also dwells on *occasions* which triggered vigorous advocacy of the Open Door—short-term economic facts. The nation, La Feber writes, had emerged from the severe depression that had begun in 1893: "During the first two months of 1898 the nation began to enjoy prosperous conditions for the first time in five years." But in mid-March "financial reporters noted that business in commodities as well as stocks had suddenly slowed."[36] Near the end of his concluding chapter, La Feber again refers to "the uncertainty that plagued the business community in mid-March." This uncertainty, which arose out of concern over the government's policy toward Cuba, "was exemplified by the sudden stagnation of trade on the New York Stock Exchange after

324

March 7. Such an unpredictable economic basis could not provide the springboard for the type of overseas commercial empire
that McKinley and numerous spokesmen envisioned."[37] In this
manner La Feber leaps from a slow-down in business activity,
beginning in March and converting business to a prowar attitude
within a month, to the long-term Open Door position.

Plekhanov allows for short-term facts which do not, as well
as those which do, accord with the deterministic, long-term main
course of historical development. Why not avoid the pitfalls of
the analysis of short-term facts and focus on the facts which do
not emerge or vanish from month to month or year to year—the
"glut of goods"? If Zevin's views on the causes of fluctuation in
American investment in the late nineteenth and early twentieth
centuries create doubt as to whether the glut of goods played the
crucial role which Open Door historians assign to it, why not
focus on capitalists' beliefs rather than capitalism's problems? La
Feber, in fact, does this in the last paragraph of his "Epilogue,"
with emphasis:

> The movement of this empire could not be hurried. Harrison
> discovered this to his regret in 1893. But under the impetus of the
> effects of the industrial revolution and, most important, *because of
> the implications for foreign policy which policy makers and business men
> believed to be logical corollaries of this economic change,* the new empire
> reached its climax in the 1890's.[38]

Let us assume for purposes of discussion that most
capitalists did believe there was a glut of goods. This belief led to
concern for markets which might absorb a significant portion of
this surplus, giving rise to the belief that the China market would
afford substantial relief from surfeit. In fact, as Paul Varg,
among others, has shown, the China market was limited—it was
an illusion.[39] Most Open Door historians concede that in actual
importance the China market ranked low, but, they maintain,
what it lacked in reality it made up for as a historical force since
Americans, reality notwithstanding, had faith in the potential
of the China market. There is no question, as we have held in
chapters 2 and 6 in regard to the Alger ethic, that a belief which
has little basis in fact can nevertheless be an important causal
factor in history. We may thus inquire as to the behavioral
consequences of the myth of the China market.

Young, as just noted, emphasizes businessmen's failure to make specific policy recommendations to government and extreme government caution. She also cites a study which shows, as she puts it, that "exporters in the period 1895–1905 concentrated not on Asia or Latin America but on Europe. It was only in the following decade that underdeveloped nations became the focus of attention. . . . Despite the urgings of consular officials, business leaders, and politicians, American manufacturers in the period under discussion . . . made little effort to adjust their products to Asian needs."[40] La Feber's interpretation of American policy at the end of the nineteenth century, however, does not depend on the development of the China market after 1905. In his essay of 1968 he writes, "United States trade in China jumped significantly after 1895, particularly in the critical area of manufactures; by 1899 manufactured products accounted for more than 90 percent of the nation's exports to the Chinese, a quadrupling of the amount sent in 1895. In their moment of need, Americans had apparently discovered a Horn of Plenty."[41] Now ninety cents is 90 percent of a dollar, and what percentage of the value of exports to all nations does a dollar represent? This is not meant to be facetious; the point is that La Feber's figures in this case are meaningless. In Varg's study the Horn of Plenty was more like Mother Hubbard's cupboard.

Nowhere in *The New Empire,* including his chapter on "The Economic Formulation," does La Feber systematically apply the Marxist model of imperialism to the economic facts he cites. If he had done so, he would have had to abandon his thesis. One cannot even ask, "If New Left diplomatic historians are Marxists, why are they Marxists?" Williams, for example, in Schlesinger's view, "is not really much of a Marxist, except in the *epater-l'academie* sense. He is rather a native American radical, somewhat in the school, although without the grandeur, of the earlier Charles A. Beard."[42] The appropriate question here is, "Why do they treat foreign policy the way they do?" Schlesinger answers this question in regard to Williams:

> In his case, his theory of American imperialism evidently performs a political function. As he explains in a long, personal, and not unappealing preface to his book [*The Roots of the Modern*

American Empire], his hope is to establish the "relevance of history." The overseas-markets thesis thus hands him history as a weapon to wield against the marketplace. It enables him to argue that the United States can cure itself of the imperial psychosis *only* by abolishing capitalism. Hence the need to prove that imperialism is economic in nature and derives from capitalism—and hence the unconscious rejection of all evidence showing other motives and bases for expansion and dominion. Now Professor Williams may be right or wrong in espousing his brand of communitarian socialism. But this is a program to be considered on its own merits and not as part of an argument over foreign policy.[43]

Neither do I accept the New Left historians' explanation of our imperialism, and I feel an obligation to cite, if only briefly, an alternative interpretation—Ernest R. May's. In the first stage of the Cold War, May writes, the United States "simply opposed the imperialist spread of another power. It sought to prevent the Soviet Union from establishing control over neighbor states. Imperceptibly, this stage merged into a second when it became the American aim to resist the spread of an alien ideology." This resistance led to the assumption of commitments to defend non-Communist nations around the world —the globalization of the policy of containment and the acquisition of an American "empire." This empire was not a political empire since its members retained their autonomy; it was not an economic or a strategic empire since in "cold-blooded economic or strategic terms" many parts of it were liabilities. Why, then, May asks, was this empire acquired? Underlying American policy was "the spirit of uplift, the mood of the secular missionary, the *mission civilisatrice*." In the view of most Americans the Cold War "was not a struggle for power. It was, like the two world wars, a contest for democracy. Underlying American policy was a vision, with deep historical roots, of a world in which all men would enjoy political, economic, and social institutions similar to those in the United States."[44]

The impulse to create an American-like world involves economics, but only as a part of a Way of Life, and it necessarily leads to anti-Communism. During the Cold War anti-Communism came to take precedence over spreading the American Way—that is, the United States supported a number of anti-Communist regimes even though they were not American-like or democratic. Commitments on this basis rested on a view of Communist regimes as metaphysical essences, parts of an evil worldwide monolith, rather than as "countries inhabited by ordinary human beings."[45] Not only does indiscriminate anti-Communism thus overlook nationalism, but when it results in the support of narrowly based regimes it also ignores the internal structures and relationships of the societies which these regimes claim to govern. The maintenance of narrowly based regimes requires an astronomical investment in men and resources. This would have been the case in China after 1945 because, as John Carter Vincent, John Paton Davies, and John Stewart Service informed American officials, we were putting our money on the wrong horse—the narrowly based Kuomintang regime whose unexpectedly rapid collapse in the years 1946–1949 resulted not from the Chinese people's dedication to Communism but from their unwillingness to lay down their lives for a regime in which all but a few had little or no stake. Vincent, Davies, and Service were hounded out of the State Department because the United States had "lost" China to Russia. Meanwhile, in 1949 the Soviet regime arrested its China experts, including Mikhail Borodin, for "losing" China to China—that is, the few experts who had not been purged after Russia "lost" China in 1927 and "lost" it again in the mid-1930s.[46]

The expression here of a preference for the mission view over the Open Door thesis ought not to end without specifying at least a few important qualifications. May's analysis does not settle the controversy over the origins of the Cold War. One can leave open the question of the emergence of the Cold War at a time when containment applied to the Soviet continental empire while subscribing to May's view that America's sense of mission underlay the globalization, with few limitations, of containment. True, anti-Communism has been an integral part of America's attitude toward the Soviet Union since 1917, but one can safely assume that the United States would have reacted negatively to Russian expansion into Eastern Europe and what was perceived as a Russian threat to Western Europe even if Russia were still under Romanov rule. There is a difference, as George Kennan believed—although this certainly was not ap-

parent in his famous "Mr. X" article of 1947 which presented
the rationale for the containment policy—between opposing
the actual or potential encroachment of Communist Russia on
Eastern Europe and the industrial areas of Northwestern
Europe and the United Kingdom (two of the five key industrial
areas, the others being the United States, Japan, and the Soviet
Union), and opposing Communism everywhere.[47]

It is appropriate to point out here that in his essay of 1968
on "That 'Splendid Little War' " La Feber summarizes explanations of United States entry into the Spanish-American War but
neglects the *mission civilisatrice* view. He lists four general interpretations: (1) mass opinion, an irrational "general impulse
for war on the part of American public opinion," presented in a
sophisticated version by Hofstadter, according to whose
"psychic crisis" thesis, La Feber writes, "the giddy minds of the
1890's could be quieted by foreign quarrels"; (2) humanitarianism, a resort to war "to free Cubans from the horror
of Spanish policies and to give the Cubans democratic institutions," a measure which had the unanticipated consequence
of the acquisition of an empire in a moment of "aberration";
(3) "Large Policy" advocates, a few shrewd, conspiratorial,
imperialistic maneuverers, especially Lodge, Mahan, and
Roosevelt; (4) economic drive, acceptance of war in order to
open overseas markets as an outlet for an oversupply of goods
which had caused domestic distress. Regarding the first three
interpretations, La Feber states that each "deals with a superficial aspect of American life; each is peculiar to 1898, and none
is rooted in the structure, the bed-rock of the nation's history."[48] The economic interpretation, on the other hand, involves not "irrational factors or flights of humanitarianism or a
few stereotyped figures, but . . . the basic structure of the
American system." La Feber defines American diplomatic history as "the study of how United States relations with other nations are used to insure the survival and increasing prosperity
of the American system. . . . Turning this definition around, it
also means that domestic affairs are the main determinant of
foreign policy."[49]

La Feber maintains that in light of the first three interpretations, since they refer to superficial factors, the distasteful and
disadvantageous results of the war ("and on this historians do

largely agree") were "endemic to episodes unique to 1898."[50] Without arguing this point for the moment, one may agree with La Feber that economic motives for American imperialism were not unique to 1898, but the question that his Open Door thesis raises is: Were economic motives the main force behind all, or even all major, American imperialistic activities? Finally, if La Feber, in accordance with the deterministic implications of his central thesis, dismisses the "Large Policy" interpretation as one of those "conspiracy theories [which] seldom explain history satisfactorily," why does he devote so much attention to and place so much emphasis on the last-minute switch in attitude of "pivotal businessmen"?[51]

La Feber comes close to specifying the *mission civilisatrice* view when he cites the humanitarian impulse, with its concern for democracy. Certainly the mission view embraces humanitarianism and democracy, but it is, so to speak, a fifth interpretation. If one sees its basic quality as a desire for an American-like world, one can see that its humanitarianism and concern for democracy can, and have, become distorted. The very desire to create a world of little United States involves, as Snowman points out, moralism or self-righteousness, and certainty of the superiority of one's own system produces xenophobia and anti-Communism.[52] Where other ways of life are, ours is not, and, as noted above, we have succumbed to the impulse of containing un-American-like systems to the extent that we have supported un-American-like regimes to achieve this end.

Now an explanation is not necessarily a justification since it can account for an irrational as well as a rational policy. Indeed, the Open Door advocates would do well to consider the views of Hartz, the theorist of fragmentation and *irrational* Lockeanism. The Whig or Lockean fragment, part of the European world, moved to a distant shore where it became the whole of the American world and extended that world to the Pacific shore in accordance with its Manifest Destiny—its mission, which involved not just creating a better life for Americans but also providing for the world an example, a laboratory-like demonstration, of a better way of life. True, brushing aside the Indians and the Mexicans, to put it euphemistically, was not reliance on example, but the Old Manifest Destiny was

nevertheless confined to contiguous areas which, it was assumed, would eventually be incorporated into the nation on
equal terms with the original states. When the unitary fragment, now the whole, experienced the impact of other nations
in a shrinking world, it oscillated between withdrawal and
spreading the American Way of Life—and not just by example.
It did not react realistically by viewing other systems or nations
as representatives of interests to be dealt with as interests; instead it saw them as entities to be shunned or remade in
ideological fervor. Thus the theme underlying both withdrawal
and imposition and deriving from predominant Lockeanism is
insistence on uniformity or inability to tolerate diversity.

Is the sense of mission fundamental rather than superficial, part of the structure of the nation's history, part of the
basic structure of the American system, part of domestic affairs? It is evident in the Puritans' City on a Hill, in Manifest
Destiny, in Lincoln's "great war testing whether that nation or
any nation so conceived and so dedicated can long endure," in
Albert J. Beveridge's declaration of the "divine mission of
America," in Woodrow Wilson's effort to instruct the Mexicans
in good government, in a World War to "make the world safe
for democracy," in another to establish the Four Freedoms, and
in Hubert Humphrey's desire to take the Great Society to
Southeast Asia. And it was evident in 1898 when the Old Manifest Destiny gave way to the New Manifest Destiny embracing
acquisition of ethnically and culturally remote overseas ter-
ritories. As Norman Graebner points out:

> What mattered in the events of 1898 was not that the United
> States had become a world power or an imperialistic nation but
> that, in acquiring the Phillippine Islands, it had deserted those
> principles of statecraft which had determined important
> decisions throughout the previous century. The defiance of
> diplomatic tradition lay in the determination of American
> officials to anchor the nation's behavior to abstract moral
> principles rather than the political wisdom of the past. Neither
> war against Spain nor acquisition of the Philippines resulted
> from any recognizable or clearly enunciated national interest.
> They emanated, rather, from a sense of moral obligation. In a
> large measure the critical decisions of 1898 were totally
> incompatible with the assumptions and methods upon which

earlier generations of Americans had attempted to defend the
national interest abroad. For this reason, they inaugurated a
new age for the United States in world affairs.⁵³

In 1795 and 1796 President Washington had laid down the
precepts of the realistic tradition which prevailed before 1898.
It had been challenged by "those who believed that American
policy abroad should seek fulfillment of the nation's democratic
mission." The challengers, however, had not been in policy
making positions, and every administration, including
Cleveland's "countered all pressures to involve the nation in
humanitarian movements abroad." The nineteenth-century
realistic tradition of diplomacy was shattered by the Spanish-
American War. The great ease and small expense involved in
attaining the original objective of liberating Cuba, moreover,
"merely confirmed the growing conviction that policy anchored
primarily in national interest was no longer legitimate for a
nation so fortunate in its institutions and so militarily and
economically powerful."⁵⁴

One ought to note that the consensus historians, Boorstin
and Hartz, whose work is so often associated with the Cold
War, did not stress America's mission. On the contrary, they
explicitly emphasized the nonexportability of the American
way of life. Withdrawal from Vietnam represents, as it were,
belated recognition of the validity of their warning. A sign of
such recognition was President Kennedy's famous speech at
American University in June 1963, in which he said, in effect,
that no one was going to conquer the world, that it would be a
world of diversity—a dramatic contrast to the Cold War-as-
holy-war theme of his inaugural address. We do not know what
policies President Kennedy would have pursued had he lived
longer than five months after the American University speech.
We do know that President Johnson was going to "nail that
coonskin to the wall," and that President Nixon, in visiting
Moscow and Peking and in withdrawing from Vietnam, pre-
sided over the putting aside of an impossible mission, one
which had enjoyed acceptance by Americans in all walks of life:
capitalists and workers; statesmen like Dean Acheson who in
late 1964 said, in a Cold War-as-holy-war context, that the goal
of American foreign policy has been to "preserve and foster an

environment in which free societies may exist and flourish,"[55] and ordinary citizens like the Vietnam veteran who, when asked whether our presence in Vietnam was justified, replied, "As far as fighting communism, yes. As far as helping the South Vietnamese, no."[56] Since parts of Acheson's "free" world are not so free, his views and the veteran's are complementary.

In view of the enormous impact of our Vietnam commitment on American society, additional comment on it may be warranted. Paul A. Samuelson, like Zevin, asserts that there was no economic basis for our involvement in Vietnam:

> There are negligible deposits of oil, copper, bauxite, uranium or other resources that could tempt an ITT or Exxon, in the pursuit of exploitative profit, to lean on Congress or propagandize the American public to start the war or to continue it.
>
> The Kennedy-Johnson mid-1960's prosperity had no need for a new war to keep the American GNP growing. On the contrary. As Johnson's economic advisers told him at the time, our 1965 escalation of defense spending jeopardized the smooth approach to full employment with reasonable price stability that was then taking place.[57]

It appears that we have here an important empirical test of the proposition that American capitalism must follow a policy of expansion or succumb to inner decay. In early 1965, when the escalation of our commitment in Vietnam began, did the American economy objectively require expansion in order to remain healthy, or, if one prefers to stress the psychic rather than the institutional needs of capitalism, did American policy makers decide that the American economy required overseas expansion? Samuelson replies in the negative. We must bear in mind, moreover, that when we test a thesis, all cases are not of equal importance. If it is too much to expect of the Open Door thesis that it explain all cases, one can insist that it explain a great deal about one of the very largest overseas commitments of men and resources in American history. Yet, La Feber declares, referring to the Open Door, "The line of conquest from the Philippines in 1898 to the attempted pacification of Vietnam in 1968 is not straight, but it is still quite traceable."[58]

In response to Samuelson, one might offer a "domino theory" version of the Open Door thesis: American policy makers' concern over Vietnam derived not from the importance of that nation's resources as such but from the assumption that if Vietnam fell to Communism, the other nations of Southeast Asia, with their resources, would not be accessible to the United States. This argument raises a basic question about a theme of the Open Door thesis itself: the Marxist view of the relationship between policy makers and businessmen. Schlesinger states, "Let us take the case of the escalation in Indochina. Has the clamor of American business for foreign markets been responsible for the widening of the war? To ask the question is to expose the fatuity of the Williams thesis."[59] If the advocate of the Open Door thesis were to reply to Schlesinger that the key factor was the attitude of policy makers, not businessmen, he would abandon the concept of the state as the tool of the bourgeoisie. This Marxist tenet is one which Kolko, dismissing his own analysis of the backgrounds of policy-makers as irrelevant, emphasizes in *The Roots of American Foreign Policy*.[60]

Withdrawal from Vietnam does not mean that America can withdraw from the world in a general way or that international relations is no longer a rough game in which self-interested nation-states play for keeps. Since the world is not an American creation, it will not become a dramatically different world as the result of changes, however drastic, in American policy. The mission interpretation is not offered here as the sole or main explanation of all American imperialist activities. It is offered as having wider application than the Open Door thesis. In the end the error in selectivity which the Open Door exponents make is their underestimation of the role of ideas in history—in this case the American consensus which underlay the missionary impulse. There is no desire here to repeat this mistake in its opposite form, but of the seven deadly sins, the age-old vices of mankind, I consider avarice no more important than pride.

Finally, one cannot ignore Williams' charge of a Great Evasion[61]—the failure of this society to attack with vigor and substantial impact many of its major domestic problems. But literally millions of people have made this point. The relevant question here is whether this evasion has resulted, as Williams maintains, from Americans being diverted from an all-out assault on vital domestic problems by the exploitation of continental and world frontiers. I am more impressed by the explanation of Hartz and Burnham, who stress the grip on American minds of an outdated ideology.

Unfulfilled Promise

Returning to domestic matters, I remind the reader of my conclusion that the New Left historians' treatment of the New Deal illustrates both one of their main virtues and one of their main shortcomings. Their demonstration of the limited extent of the New Deal's attainments relates to their concern with losers, and, Gerald W. McFarland writes, they

> make their strongest scholarly contribution as dissenters and historical muckrakers when they write about the seamier side of the American past. Lest we be too smug about our special superiority to other nations economically, it is well to be reminded by a Howard Zinn or a Jesse Lemisch that America has had an unhappy and largely invisible lower class from colonial times to the present.[1]

At the same time, in neglecting the obstacles in the 1930s to greater reform on behalf of losers, including the passivity of the under classes themselves, the New Left historians lose sight of winners—among whom one finds the forces of conscious or active resistance to change.

Or perhaps we should not say that the New Left historians lose sight of winners but rather that they often fail to analyze them. William E. Leuchtenburg finds the New Left attack on consensus history somewhat ironical since "their own approach homogenizes American history to a far greater degree by making it appear that nothing important really ever happened. Since socialism was not attained, they seem to suggest, no other development really had much significance."[2] David Donald remarks that the New Left historians "leave unshaken the consensus historians' argument that most Americans throughout our history have been contented participants in the capitalist system."[3] In fact, the New Left historians do not try to shatter this argument. Putting aside their Marcusean contention that even winners are losers, we can see that they are quite aware of the existence of winners—a historian of the poor or blacks or women might say that in his study of Progressivism Kolko focuses on well-to-do white males seeking power, which is his prerogative—but they are often concerned with the system's nonparticipants and the nonbeneficiaries whom the contented participants or beneficiaries, including many historians, have failed to discover or have disregarded. In expressing this concern they fail, as Kraditor points out, to study losers and winners together in order to ascertain the limitations on change which might have benefited losers. Their focusing on losers rather than winners amounts to "Turning History Upside Down," the exercise which Solway seems to commend. Higham, however, takes a different view of this approach: "Of a major scholarly movement that claims the function of moral judgment we are entitled to ask for a widening, not a mere reversal, of perspectives."[4]

General assessments of New Left historiography run the gamut from Solway's and McFarland's commendation through Tillinghast's weighing of pluses and minuses and Donald's and Higham's disappointment to Henry Fairlie's condemnation. In 1968 Donald was harsh in his judgment.[5] In 1970 he was impressed with the New Left historians' stimulation of new attention to American intellectual history, their endowing of diplomatic history with new importance, and their arousing of new interest in the reading and writing of American history in general, but he was not impressed with the substance of their work.[6] Higham writes that the New Left historians have not yet produced the valuable interpretations of our past that it was commonly assumed their radical criticism of American society would yield. As a group "the radical scholars have found no distinctive approach to American history. Their books and articles have little in common except hostility to liberalism." The New Left cast of mind, with its lack of patience for weighing historical alternatives, "has tended to be casual or superficial in accounting for social change." Only Eugene Genovese and Gabriel Kolko, Higham states, "have contributed significantly to the flourishing analysis of social structure, which also engages historians with more moderate views."[7]

The position and tone of Fairlie's appraisal are apparent in his title, "Years of Intellectual Havoc." He reviews the well known controversy between Staughton Lynd, who shares Zinn's views on the historian as activist and as user of the past for present purposes, and Genovese, who insists that no present cause will benefit from the bad history which the unduly present-minded activist-historians write. Fairlie concludes that the New Left historians threw away their opportunity to meet the real need for historical revision which the consensus historians had failed to meet, while he praises Genovese as a powerful self-critical voice on the American left, a good historian who has "sought to use Marxism to assist him as a historian, and not to use history to justify him as a Marxist."[8] Is Genovese thus a good historian among bad New Left historians, is his clash with Lynd internecine warfare among New Left historians, is Genovese really a New Left historian? Is the holding of a "left" view of the present the hallmark of a New Left historian, or are social activism and the creation of a usable past for radical purposes the additional, crucial elements in a definitional guideline? If the latter is the case, Genovese is American Left, neo-Marxist, or new left, but he is not New Left. This view of the matter also deprives the New Left "school" of historians of another scholar who is often assigned to this category —Christopher Lasch, who writes:

> The worst features of progressive historiography reappear under the auspices of the "new left": drastic simplification of issues; synthetic contrivance of political and intellectual "traditions" by reading present concerns back into the past; strident partisanship. Worse still, the new emphasis on conflict has given rise to demands that historians cultivate an "activist outlook" and that history be subordinated to the needs of the "movement."

Lasch also expresses disappointment:

> Our generation has seen too many brave beginnings, too many claims that came to nothing, too many books unfinished, and even unbegun, too many broken and truncated careers. As activists, we have achieved far less than we hoped; as scholars, our record is undistinguished on the whole. It is not too late to achieve something better, but it is no longer possible to be complacent about our accomplishments or the superiority of our own understanding of American society to that of the generation before us.[9]

Chapter Eight
Conflict and
Consensus and Change

The Role of Ideas in History

Inexorable change in conditions and adjustment to this change—timely or belated, adequate or inadequate to the maintenance of stability—is society's problem and grist for the historian's mill. Tillinghast writes:

> Written history, like our lives, is based on the assumption that social patterns, like individual ones, continue to change, so that while they are never quite the same, they always retain some elements from other patterns out of which the present ones have developed. . . . If successive situations were either totally different or exactly the same, reading about the past would be a waste of time. This kind of movement—change within likeness and likeness within change—is what gives history its value for us.[1]

It goes without saying that the assessment of the role of ideas in history is one of the most difficult problems that the historian encounters in studying change. This certainly becomes clear when one examines consensus history.

At the most elementary level of analysis, as Carl Gustavson points out, it is obvious that "Organized social movements cannot appear and institutions cannot function without ideas. They are the threads which bind the minds of men together sufficiently for joint action to occur."[2] Gustavson also asserts, "To ask the proportionate weight of ideas in the framework of social events is to enter a long and fruitless discussion."[3] This may be a case of damned if you do and damned if you don't. Skotheim divides American intellectual historians into two main groups: those who assign ideas a primary or independent causal role and those who assign them a secondary or derivative one. In a generally favorable review of Skotheim's book, John William Ward writes concerning the question of the consequences of ideas, "But one would like finally to have Mr. Skotheim's judgment."[4] Skotheim's judgment would undoubtedly provoke considerable dissent since there is nothing like a consensus among historians, of the consensus persuasion or any other, on this question. For example, the year 1913 saw the publication of Ephraim Douglas Adams' *The Power of Ideals in American History* as well as Beard's *An Economic Interpretation of the Constitution of the United States*, and Beard later changed his views on causation.[5] In any case, damnation, for an act of commission rather than omission, seems unavoidable here. The nature of the subject compels a commentator on consensus historiography to say something about its treatment of the role of ideas in history, and it seems incumbent on him first to indicate his own views on ideas and historical causation.

Essentially, I agree with Gustavson, who presents a brief but rewarding "elementary sketch" of the role of ideas in social processes, the role which John Dewey emphasized more than sixty years ago and which Merle Curti has stressed for more than thirty years.[6] In the end, Gustavson assigns the preponderant causal role to changes in conditions rather than to ideas. Each idea which has had major historical significance has been "the product of certain distinctive conditions, changes, and prominent features of life that called for explanation and enunciation." "Cultural lag" denotes the failure of ideas to keep pace with physical change, the "maladjustment between ideology and human reality." Not only is there lag in formulation by great thinkers, "the sensitive antennae of society," of new concepts to explain new realities, but it takes time for these new concepts to attain general acceptance. As an idea attracts widespread assent, "it may be so modified as to become quite different from the original concept," and it loses its "atmosphere of speculation, of philosophical meditation, and tends to become dogma." Finally, Gustavson holds, "an idea which is not adopted by a group which is also motivated by other drives as well is not likely to rise to first-rate importance." In other words, the idea itself represents a response to reality, and the response to the idea is rooted in reality.[7]

My basic agreement with Gustavson derives especially from inquiry into the era of the Great Depression and the New Deal, with study of the career of Rexford Tugwell serving as my point of entrance into this period. It was evident to Tugwell in the 1920s that the conventional wisdom in the areas of economics and political economy had become divorced from reality, had lost its explanatory power. Tugwell identified this gap, and in 1926 he predicted dire consequences in the absence of appropriate adjustment while specifying preventive measures based on an alternative conceptualization or explanation of how the world worked. The ideas which he articulated were neither "new" nor "his" in any strict sense. Other economists, (comparatively few, to be sure) held them, and their origins went back at least to Thorstein Veblen's writings at the turn of the century. Tugwell's ideas did not gain widespread acceptance in view of the grip on Americans of old ideas. Preventive measures were not taken and the nation suffered economic collapse. Then the nation, to succumb to the American penchant for finding analogues for social developments in sports, played "catch-up ball" through the mechanism of its democratic politics which permitted belated, critical—but nonviolent —adjustment to overcome lag. The in party became the outs, and the former out party became the new ins, acquiring normal majority status as the result of the response to its acts—"the politics of the deed"—and the ideas associated with them. These ideas did not originate with the Democratic party, and they were not new, although their implementation was new; from Tugwell's standpoint they still lagged thirty years behind the times. In accordance with Gustavson's scheme, it took some time for these ideas to gain widespread acceptance, they became so modified as to become quite different from the original concepts, and they became dogma.

Widespread acceptance, of course, did not mean anything like near-unanimity. Not everyone approved or went along with the ideas of welfare statism and deficit spending—Landon, after all, received nearly seventeen million votes. Over a longer time span, it is true, the Republican party accepted the New Deal. The New Deal itself, however, had been significantly affected by lag—not only in the form of opposition to its programs but also in the form of ambivalence between the old and the new, between individualism or antitrustism and collectivism or concentration-and-control, for example, on the part of the New Dealers themselves. Lag thus contributed to the substantial modification of the relevant ideas in their original state, and it was in this altered form that these ideas became dogma. Now we can discern lag compounded, for the new conventional wisdom of Keynesianism, which was modified by lag as it emerged, is itself identified as a source of lag, as being outdated but still having a grip on American minds and policies.

We shall not burden the reader with an account of what happened in the crucible of politics to Tugwell's ideas on "planned capitalism," a subject which I have discussed at undue length, concluding that even in the crisis of the 1930s the historical, institutional, ideological, and political obstacles to the acceptance of unorthodox ideas were formidable.[8] For present purposes a brief reference to Keynes is more appropriate. Some of his observations on the role of ideas in history are relevant, and they are illuminated by the fate of the ideas which he himself advanced in the 1930s. This statement by Keynes has become an aphorism in scholarly circles:

> The ideas of economists and political philosophers, both when they are right and when they are wrong, are more powerful than is commonly understood. Indeed, the world is ruled by little else. Practical men, who believe themselves to be quite exempt from any intellectual influences, are usually the slave of some defunct economist. . . . I am sure that the power of vested interests is vastly exaggerated compared with the gradual encroachment of ideas.

But Keynes also said, in 1949, "It is, it seems, politically impossible for a capitalist democracy to organize government expenditure on the scale necessary to make the grand experiment which would prove my case—except in war conditions."[9] New

Deal fiscal and monetary policies embodied neither practical
nor intellectual acceptance of Keynes's ideas. Even the testing
of his ideas which the Second World War occasioned was a
practical rather than an intellectual matter. Eventually, the tax
program of 1964, advocated earlier by President Kennedy
under the tutelage of neo-Keynesian Walter Heller, represented a major, conscious application of Keynes's ideas
—precisely thirty years after the British economist had personally presented his views to President Roosevelt. Now at least
a minority of economists besides neo-classicists, who never
accepted Keynesianism, urge us to move away from Keynesianism. Taken together, Keynes's two statements suggest how
lag blends the roles of conditions and ideas in history.

A historian who holds that changes in conditions are the
source of changes in ideas may be classed with the philosophers
who subscribe to the "mind-brain identity" thesis—that is, with
those who reduce mind to matter. A historian, however, who
sees ideas as the primary cause in history may be compared
with the British Empiricist philosophers who see the physical
world as merely a construction of the mind—thereby reducing
matter to mind. It must be recognized that philosphers and
psychologists are still wrestling with the epistemological question, How do we know what we know? Psychologists and other
behavioral scientists are still grappling with the relationships
between material and psychic components of human motivations. Researchers in medicine and psychiatry have discovered
that the chemical content of the brain changes when a person
becomes depressed; but they don't know if the change is a cause
or a result of the depression. To take a definite position on the
side of ideas or of events at this point is to get ahead of our
knowledge.

To a historian who is no nearer than scholars in other
disciplines to resolving these dilemmas, the phenomenon of lag
is an impressive explanation of the development of societies. It
enables one to assign ultimate causal priority to changes in
conditions, as Gustavson does, while refusing to be categorized
on one or the other side of a dualism. Declining to go back to
Adam and Eve or the first human intellectual response to physical changes in order to determine first causes, one can hold

that once an idea comes into existence, it has a life of its own as a causal factor. This life is evident in lag: the grip of the old ideas delays recognition of new realities, delays the formulation of new explanations of the new realities, delays acceptance of the new explanations, and compels modifications of the new explanations as the price of widespread acceptance. Existing ideas always play an important part in a society's response to changing conditions, whether that response takes the form of a steady adjustment or, as is more often the case, periodic, spasmodic, and partial accommodation.

A Comparison of Boorstin and Hartz

The foregoing discussion of the role of ideas in history is routine, but it is presented here as a frame for some concluding comments on the work of Boorstin and Hartz. In a word, Boorstin's interpretation of American history does not fit into this scheme, while Hartz's, with a little wedging or extrapolation, does. Boorstin's identification of the nonideological causes of consensus in *The Genius of American Politics* essentially deprives inheritance—the legacy of European thought—of causal force. Is Boorstin a metaphysical materialist? Not really, "For the Puritans," he writes, "were the first, and perhaps the last, sizeable community in American history to import from Europe a fully developed and explicit social dogma, and try to live by it on this continent."[1] The Puritans had acquired their ideas in Europe, and they lost them in America. Ideas have thus had a role in history, but *not in American history*. There was lag, since the decline of Puritan dogma took place over several generations, but this dogma "was not so much defeated by the dogmas of anti-Puritanism as it was simply assimilated to the conditions of life in America."[2] At this point the ongoing historical process involved in intellectual lag becomes irrelevant.

As one of Noble's *Historians against History*, Boorstin severs American society from its European past. The Puritans, he maintains,

> became more and more responsive to the values which seemed to emerge from their daily lives. The Puritan experience thus shows some persistent characteristics of American history which have encouraged belief in the implicitness of values. Already in

that earliest age we see a growing sense of "givenness."

There is a subtler sense in which the Puritan experience symbolizes the American approach to values. For the circumstances which have nourished man's sense of mastery over his *natural* environment have on this continent somehow led him away from dogmatism, from the attempt to plan and control the *social* environment.[3]

When Boorstin says that the environment had an impact on the development of Puritan society, one cannot quarrel with him. When he writes of "givenness' as "Values Given by the Land-scape" or "the gift of the present," however, one must ask, as Pole does: How did the land itself put values into American heads, and why did Americans choose the social organization they did? Blueprints to plan and control the social environment such as the Nazi and Communist schemes, which Boorstin cites in his discussion of the Puritans, are not the only approaches to the social environment that are planned—according to Boorstin's analysis. He equates planning with ultra-planning, and he lays down a planning–nonthinking dualism. The dictionary tells us that a plan is "any detailed method, formulated beforehand, for doing or making something." In this sense, the planning of an unplanned society is a contradiction, but an unplanned or unregimented society is "planned" in that rejection of regimentation must arise from ideas held before-hand—"must" in the case of America because different frontier societies have developed in different ways, and some have become regimented while others have not. In other words, Boorstin, given his emphasis on nonideological sources of values, claims, as it were, that because Americans did not draw up a blueprint, a plan for their social environment, their heads were empty of ideology.

This witlessness ascribed to Americans by Boorstin also rests on his very unsatisfactory treatment of the role of ideas in history involved in his other, nonenvironmental form of "givenness": "Values Given by the Past: The Preformation Ideal." According to this concept, Americans believed that explicit political theory was superfluous because they already possessed a satisfactory equivalent. What they possessed, Boorstin continues, was not in fact the equivalent of a theory—but they thought it was. Pole disagrees, insisting that what Americans thought was a theory, *was* a theory. This distinction is important because Boorstin's contention that what Americans thought was a theory really was not a theory renders the "gift of the past" as well as the "gift of the present" readily assimilable into an environmentalist interpretation of American development.

"Givenness" in the form of "Values Given by the Past" is the belief that a "perfect and complete political theory, adequate to all our future needs," was provided by "the earliest settlers or the Founding Fathers." This theory, Boorstin writes, "the ideas of the earliest settlers—the Pilgrim Fathers or the Founding Fathers—[was] the perfect embryo of the theory by which we now live."[4] It grew, according to our theory of society, into "a kind of exoskeleton, like the shell of a lobster," and we, in turn, grew "*into* our skeleton, filling it out with the experience and resources of recent ages. But we always suppose that the outlines were rigidly drawn in the beginning."[5] With considerable effort, required by Boorstin's confusing use of the word *theory*, one derives from his argument a theory of nontheory: the exoskeleton involved in the theory of embryo-to-exoskeleton is, despite Americans' belief to the contrary, a nontheoretical exoskeleton; therefore, the nature of the exoskeleton was never debated ideologically. In disagreement a host of historians point to the ideological conflict of the revolutionary generation, which, in Boorstin's view, carried out a "Revolution without Dogma." One cannot say in Boorstin's behalf that he may be wrong about the Founding Fathers in the late eighteenth century but still be right about the Puritans in the early seventeenth century because his third component of "givenness," continuity, does not permit such a distinction.

In Boorstin's analysis the experiential filling out of the nontheoretical exoskeleton involves by definition no interaction between developmental process and previously existing ideology—or, for that matter, any other kind of ideology. The inadequacy of this analysis becomes evident when one compares Boorstin's treatment of antebellum Southern political thought with Hartz's. Both historians assert, in quite different ways, continuity in American thought. Boorstin writes, "One of the remarkable characteristics of our Civil War, as contrasted with civil wars of recent European history (excepting possibly the English Civil War), is that ours did *not* significantly interrupt the continuity of our thinking about institutions."[6] Hartz sees continuity in the persisting dominion of the Lockean liberal idea, but this sway was interrupted in the form of a challenge, "The Reactionary Enlightenment" of the South. In Boorstin's view, no such discontinuity was involved in the Southern position.

In Boorstin's analysis slavery emerged in the Southern environment, and Southern thinkers advanced a twofold rationale: a sociological argument and a view within a "working federal system" with a different constitutional emphasis. The sociological argument embodied "givenness" as the "gift of the present": Southern thinkers "were assuming that the values would emerge from the facts . . . the good and the bad would emerge from the facts themselves."[7] Ideas—sociology—thus represented a response to reality. The Southerners also responded to reality by emphasizing, in addition to sociology, the federal as opposed to the national character of the Constitution. This view, they maintained, was based on "the ideas of the Founding Fathers."[8] Their argument with the Northerners who held the opposite view, however, occurred within an *institutional* context, for the Founding Fathers' constitutional contribution had been institutional: "The Civil War secessionist argument [was] like that of the Revolution . . . because both events were, theoretically speaking, only surface breaches in the federal framework."[9] The institution of federalism thus extended back, beyond the age of the Founding Fathers, into the colonial period. If we extend it, in accordance with Boorstin's emphasis on continuity, to the beginning of settlement, we arrive at a point where we must pose some questions for Boorstin.

Did the earliest settlers bring with them no ideas which might contribute to a theoretical rationale for the institution of federalism? Did they bring both such ideas and the institution with them, only soon to discard the ideas while retaining the institution? If either of these possibilities was the case, did Americans subsequently fail, in the face of the persistence of the institution of federalism, to formulate associated ideas, a theoretical rationale? Has any society ever discussed its institutions of long standing essentially and only in institutional-constitutional terms? Certainly societies with different institutions and constitutions have developed in different ways. If one stresses the causal impact on societal development of institutions and constitutions, however, one may neglect the prior question: Why did different institutions and constitutions develop in different societies? Can we exclude ideology from this development? In assessing Boorstin's analysis one always returns to his omission of previously existing ideology as a factor influencing the response—in this instance the antebellum Southern thinkers' reaction—to reality.

Hartz, on the other hand, not only shows that previously existing ideology influenced the Southern thinkers' response to reality, but he also underlines the general limitations of analysis at the institutional-constitutional level when he points out that the Constitution has survived so long because the men who devised it, " 'realists' in dealing with the stark facts of social conflict," were mistaken in their assumption of disunity in American society: "The Founding Fathers devised a scheme to deal with conflict that could survive only in a land of solidarity. The truth is, their conclusions were 'right' only because their premises were wrong."[10] Does Hartz's emphasizing the impact of the previously unifying ideology on the Southern thinkers' response to reality make him a metaphysical idealist? Hardly, for he calls "The Reactionary Enlightenment" a feudal facade for slavery—ideas representing a response to the reality of the "peculiar institution" and the culture attending it. At the same time, in formulating this rationale, the Southern thinkers, enormously creative as they were, could not wriggle off the Lockean hook—the South could not break "the ties it had to the liberalism it sought to defy." Although the Southerners duplicated the argument of Europe's feudal reaction, what lay beneath their ideas was not feudalism but slavery. They reproduced the argument of a feudal world which they had never seen because America had skipped the feudal stage of history, and "a feudalism which has once been liberal can never really be feudal." In America the establishment of liberalism without destroying feudalism "transformed the rationalist doctrine of Locke into the traditionalist reality of Burke." In using Burke to refute Locke, the Southerners thus refuted themselves. To have their citation of Burke's conservative traditionalism constantly reaffirming their ancient allegiance to America's traditional liberal-Lockean idea was for the Southerners "as keen a torture as the devilish brain of history could devise." Right down to the Civil War their theory was "shot through with the Lockean principles they destroyed . . . the old liberal and the old bourgeois preoccupations kept betraying it, contradicting it." In the end Locke was "too real, too empirical, too historical in America to attack."[11]

Hartz's treatment of the "Reactionary Enlightenment" is only one instance in which he allows for unusual responses to changing reality—within a Lockean framework. At the beginning of *The Liberal Tradition in America* he states that the liberal faith means that "all problems emerge as problems of technique. Not that this is a bar in America to institutional innovations of highly non-Lockean kind. Indeed, as the New Deal shows, you can depart from Locke with a kind of inventive freedom."[12] It was not easy, to be sure, for Locke to maintain his grip on the New Dealers amid economic collapse, but they did not escape him—indeed, with a few exceptions, they did their best not to. In spelling this out, Hartz offers an analysis far superior to Hofstadter's estimate of 1948, which saw the New Deal as an old deal, and Hofstadter's estimate of 1955, which saw the New Deal as a new deal. Hartz traces the past in the present, the interaction of the old and the new. Ultimately, as Hartz asserts toward the end of his book, the New Dealers' rejection of the doctrinaire pleas of both left and right revealed "the desperate ingenuity which a liberal community will use to maintain its link with the past . . . the handy pragmatism and submerged Lockeanism which governed the New Deal era."[13]

Does Hartz's argument for innovation, ingenuity, and handy pragmatism within a framework of submerged Lockeanism leave Locke supreme or does it leave Locke so submerged as to separate him from reality? Does experience have more explanatory power than ideology? Is Boorstin right and

Hartz wrong? No, for Boorstin's "experience" is environmental or geographical, and he fails to relate it to the cultural experience in its various ramifications; nor does explaining the American Way of Life as a creature of the environment or of experience as an environmentally derived phenomenon stand the comparative test. It is this test that provides the key to Hartz's saving Locke from the kind of submergence which would eliminate him as a factor in American development.

It was America's talent, Hartz maintains, as noted in chapter 2, to take a single idea, brought here by a Whig fragment, "out of the conscious intellectual struggles of Europe and plunge it deep into unconscious behavior where it reigns, without philosophy, without criticism, as an operational absolute." Other fragments or parts took other ideas out of Europe and carried them to other places, where these ideas became the unchallenged ideological whole, with other results. Does this scheme not rest on metaphysical idealism? No, because the ideas—feudal, liberal, and radical—which Europe exported at different times or from different places to different places —Canada, Latin America, South Africa, Australia—emerged from European realities. Conceding this point, one may still ask whether the ideological immobility of the fragment, the continuing dominance of the liberal idea—as seen in the cases of the "Reactionary Enlightenment" and the New Deal—involves a kind of metaphysical idealism, at least from the time of settlement onward. No, because Hartz, as we shall see in the next section, discerns the end of liberal immobility in the 1950s in response to international developments. In sum, Hartz's interpretation of American history does not divorce ideas from experience. Rather, as is pointed out by Burnham, who has a very high opinion of Hartz's work, it encompasses a 350-year lag.[14]

Hartz and His Critics

Consideration of Boorstin's and Hartz's interpretations of American history has led me, in the light of my own views on the role of ideas in history, to conclude that although Boorstin had a grip on an important insight, he lost it when he drained the concept of "givenness" of ideological content, and that he never should have written *The Genius of American Politics*. The two volumes of *The Americans* which have appeared do not systematically develop the didactic purpose of *The Genius*—in fact, the treatment of the coming of the Civil War in *The Americans: The National Experience* virtually gives away the basic interpretation of American history presented in *The Genius.* At the same time, the first two volumes of *The Americans,* as histories of social texture, by themselves have earned for Boorstin a place among the very first rank of American historians.

Hartz, on the other hand, is very impressive as a general theorizer. Perhaps his prowess in this regard would be more widely recognized if he had written *The Founding of New Societies* before *The Liberal Tradition in America,* since *The Founding* brings his analysis to the point where he takes up developments in America in *The Liberal Tradition.* The analysis in *The Founding* is consistent with that in *The Liberal Tradition,* and it is not an *ex post facto* construction since its essence appears in *The Liberal Tradition.* Someone has said that Marx had the ability to boil a simple idea down to three hundred pages (a talent one can appreciate when one compares Marx's and Lenin's explanations of surplus value). Perhaps Hartz should have made a virtue of such a fault by elaborating his fragmentation theory at greater length in *The Liberal Tradition.* This may not have been possible, however, since as of 1955 Hartz had apparently not yet worked out this theory in detail.

Even so, the basic components of the fragmentation theory are specified in *The Liberal Tradition,* pages 20–27, where Hartz, as noted in chapter 2, states that the absence of feudalism and the presence of liberalism are both results of the process of fragmentation, pointing out that his theory is derived from his study of comparative history. In a footnote on page 21 he calls for the kind of comparative study of new societies which he later pursued, and on pages 23–27 he discusses the "Implications for Europe" of his analysis while noting, "I have not tried in this book to explore the European pattern in special detail." He does toss out some examples which indicate how challenging and fruitful such an exploration could be. One is particularly appropriate here:

> . . . take the explanation from capitalist growth of the national
> Alger ideology after the Civil War. Capitalism was surely related

to Alger, but if it produced him, why did it not do so in Germany where it was booming at the same time or in England where it boomed earlier? Actually the Alger spirit is the peculiar instinct of the Lockean world, and what capitalist growth did, once the Whigs began to articulate it, was to fortify their case.[1]

In spelling out his fragmentation theory Hartz answers the criticism by Krieger and Hartshorne of the causal role assigned in *The Liberal Tradition in America* to the absence of feudalism and other criticism as well. In his brief exposition of this theory, published in 1963, he explains how in *The Liberal Tradition* he referred to "Locke" only as a symbol, replying, as it were, to Bartlett's and Meyers' contention that he uses "Locke" too broadly. Hartz is well aware that there is much in Locke that differs from certain intellectual developments in America and he concedes the great variety existing in American political thought within the context of "Locke," although he does not concede that this variety invalidates his basic generalization. The same may be said of his use of "Whiggery" which Gatell questions. In asserting the submergence of the Lockean idea into unconscious behavior while rescuing it—by means of the comparative test of the fragmentation theory—from sub-mergence which divorces it from reality, Hartz reconciles thought and behavior. He thus responds, in effect, to Kristol's doubts about his treatment of the relationship between them and to political scientists who relegate ideas to a relatively minor role in preserving democracy. In *The Founding of New Societies* and in "A Comparative Study of Fragment Cultures" (1969)[2] Hartz discusses the attitude of the fragment towards the non-European, answering, so to speak, Newby's criticism of his failure in *The Liberal Tradition in America* to qualify his generalizations about American history to take into account Afro-American history. To Reimer, who, it will be recalled, does take the fragmentation theory into account, one can pose questions derived from a reading of Hartz. If inheritance, envi-ronment, and American genius all contributed to American political thought and development, where did that genius come from or, to put it another way, why did America produce geniuses when it did? Perhaps the key question for Reimer, suggested in part by his remark that Jefferson refined Locke, is Why did these geniuses take Locke as their framework or, as Reimer would probably prefer since he discusses Locke literally rather than in Hartz's symbolic sense, Why did these geniuses take Locke as their point of departure?

In *The Founding of New Societies* Hartz makes an observation that pertains both to certain criticism of his views and to the assessment of them here: The United States, having experienced "over three hundred years of liberal immobility . . . now confronts on the world plane, thrust back at it from places as distant as Russia and China, the very alien ideologies it managed to escape."³ This description of the liberal tradition in America as being at the end of a phase has been cited above as an indication that Hartz is not a metaphysical idealist, that the monolithic state of the liberal idea is changing in response to reality—after a lag of 350 years. Hartz's observation amounts to a denial of his own admission, in the course of elaborating his fragmentation theory, that his thesis is deterministic as well as McNaught's charge of determinism. Three hundred years, to be sure, is a long time (to a historian if not to a geologist), but world events have at last affected the hold of the liberal idea on the American mind. Hartz's observation also pertains to Crick's assertion that in the developments of the 1960s, the tragic fate of the liberal society thesis was to be that of a theory killed by a fact. Actually, *The Founding of New Societies* aside, in *The Liberal Tradition in America* Hartz incorporated the death of consensus into his theory of consensus:

> one can easily wonder whether any purely domestic crisis could shake the national faith, whether innovations larger than those the New Deal dreamed of could not be made on the basis of the mechanism it used. But for better or worse that is not the issue we face, since the age of purely domestic crisis is apparently over. America's new world involvement explodes at once the handy pragmatism and submerged Lockeanism which governed the New Deal era.⁴

In view of developments since the appearance of *The Liberal Tradition in America* in 1955, one may wonder whether domestic factors in a relatively isolated America would themselves have been sufficient to produce the disunity of the 1960s, but as Hartz's statement suggests, such speculation is academic. What he was saying by means of the theory of fragmentation was that the liberalism of the Lockean fragment was no longer unchallenged in a shrinking world. This called not only for recognition that there were other peoples to whom Lockean liberalism did not apply but also for awareness that our traditional way of looking at ourselves needed to be reexamined. At the end of *The Liberal Tradition* Hartz wrote:

> the larger forces working toward a shattering of American provincialism abroad as well as at home lie of course in the world scene itself. . . . But surely, whatever the outcome, this is the largest challenge the American liberal world has faced, and the payment for meeting it effectively is more than mere survival in a world of turmoil. It holds out the hope of inward enrichment of culture and perspective, a "coming of age," to use the term of the 'twenties again, which in its own right is well worth fighting for. What is at stake is nothing less than a new level of consciousness, a transcending of irrational Lockeanism, in which an understanding of self and an understanding of others go hand in hand. . . .
>
> Can a people "born equal" ever understand peoples elsewhere that have to become so? Can it ever understand itself? These were the questions which appeared at the beginning of this book: inevitably also they are the questions which appear at the end.[5]

In other ways, besides referring to the fragmentation theory and cracks in the American consensus, *The Liberal Tradition in America* provides answers to various criticisms leveled at it. Morris' objection to Hartz's use of the term *feudalism* is not quite fair in view of Hartz's recognition of the differences between medieval and later feudalism and his acknowledgement that vestiges of feudalism—primogeniture, entail, and quitrents—existed in America in the eighteenth century.[6] It is not accurate, as noted in chapter 2, to contend that Hartz allows no role in American development for the environment, the material setting which he judged so favorable for the flourishing of the liberal idea. Nor does Meyers, in holding that Hartz assigns insufficient causal force to a "wise constitution," or Reimer, in praising Madison while deploring Boorstin's and Hartz's neglect of American geniuses, address themselves to the implications for their argument in Hartz's conclusion, cited above, that the Founding Fathers' claims of probable durability of the Constitution were right only because their analysis of social conflict in America was wrong. It should also be pointed out that Hartz's failure to discuss Americans' being "born equal," meaning equality of condition, an omission with which Meyers finds fault, turns out to be a virtue in the light of the findings of Pessen and others on the distribution of wealth in *ante bellum* America.

Above all, in *The Liberal Tradition in America,* Hartz does not shrink domestic conflict into insignificance:

> one cannot say of the liberal society analysis that by concentrating on national unities it rules out the meaning of domestic conflict. Actually it discovers that meaning, which is obscured by the very Progressive analysis that presumably concentrates on conflict. You do not get closer to the significance of an earthquake by ignoring the terrain on which it takes place. On the contrary, that is one of the best ways of making sure that you will miss its significance. The argument over whether we should stress solidarity or conflict in American politics misleads us by advancing a false set of alternatives.[7]

Hartz restated this position in 1962, reinforcing it by stressing the comparative nature of his approach. He characterized the comparative liberal society analysis as being indifferent to the "bias toward conflict which the Progressive history had." It errs if it trivializes or exaggerates conflict, but it sees no "issue of 'greater' or 'lesser' conflict." It provides a setting in which "a battle has the quality it has because of its relationship to other battles and because that quality explains its outcome." The comparative society analysis

> does not permit us to choose between "conflict" and "consensus" in American history as a man votes for a political candidate or develops an artistic preference. American history contains both of these elements in the proportions which make it, in relation to other national histories, explicable.[8]

A False Dichotomy

It is true, as Mann and Hofstadter comment, that in showing what has been missing from conflicts in America, Hartz does not tell us in detail what has been present in our conflicts. He

does, however, tell us about something very fundamental regarding conflicts in America—the containing, triumphant consensual framework. Broadly speaking, he tells us half the story,
but he does not claim—indeed he explicitly denies—that that
half is the whole story. Just as Wallace recounts the neglected
conflicts in American history while noting briefly that they
must be viewed in the light of the consensus which Hartz delineates, so Hartz discusses at length the sources and nature of
the consensus while noting that such an emphasis neither precludes nor is intended to minimize conflict.

Neither Wallace nor Hartz separates consensus and conflict in the manner of Zinn, who believes that the "consensus"
interpretation of American history holds

> a profound truth about our society, that its great "progress" and
> its political clashes have been kept within severe limits. What is
> missing in the consensus analysis is the persistent strain of
> protest that shows up repeatedly in American history. . . . The
> existence of this strain justifies the work of the "conflict" school
> of American history, which insists that Americans not forget the
> black abolitionists, the Wobblies, the Socialists, the anarchists,
> that we keep in mind Tom Paine, John Brown, Emma Goldman,
> Eugene Debs, Malcolm X.[1]

The designation of "schools" in this way results in historians'
missing the point which Hartz makes in *The Liberal Tradition*.
Denying any intention of obscuring or minimizing the nature
of internal conflicts, he asserts, "We can hardly choose between
an event and its context, though in the study of history and
politics there will always be some who ask us to do so."[2] This is
the point, of course, which Kraditor makes so convincingly
when she observes that "both liberal and radical historians can
use the same 'conflict' paradigm with such similar results"—the
reinforcement of their present political views—when they fail
to recognize that

> the conflict-consensus framework for looking at the American
> past can be made meaningful only if the contents of the conflicts
> and the contents of the consensual ideas and values are included
> as a necessary part of the framework. To do that is to shift the
> focus from the ahistorical *fact* of conflict or the *fact* of

consensus, to the historically conditioned contents of the
conflicts or the shared values and opinions that constituted the
consensus. But to do this is to discover at once that the
opposition between "conflict" and "consensus" is spurious.[3]

Hartz, to be sure, devotes far greater attention to the contents of consensus than to the contents of conflict. At the same
time, he deals with interaction: in showing how Locke does not
break, he considers developments that cause Locke to bend. He
engages in a perfectly legitimate intellectual enterprise because,
to repeat, he insists that the part of the story he tells is not the
whole story. His general history of political thought, moreover,
cannot be equated with a whole series of special consensus
studies which Hofstadter, as noted in chapter 3, regards as "a
related and convergent but quite independent development."
A monograph which presents a part of the story as the whole
story—whose author fails to understand, as Kraditor points
out, that the study of a protest or reform movement will illuminate the consensus of a given period and vice versa—is quite
different from Hartz's contribution. This legitimacy and distinctiveness of Hartz's work were obscured as the term *consensus
school* was widely adopted.

Such categorization also concealed the difference between
Hartz's and Boorstin's interpretations. In two examples of this
kind of distortion, one from a textbook and one from a scholarly journal, historians lump Hartz's and Boorstin's work together. The author of the textbook inadvertently, it seems,
simultaneously indicates Hartz's and Boorstin's contrasting
portrayals of a uni- and non-ideological American society:

> It has been argued that there is in progress a search for
> "consensus" in the American past, which has softened
> ideological conflicts too generously, has undervalued our
> radicalism, and has painted the landscape in the moral gray of
> value-neutralism. A book that seems to illustrate this tendency is
> Louis Hartz's *The Liberal Tradition in America.* In it, the author
> stresses the absence of genuine conservatism in American
> thought and the almost universal faith among all classes in
> progress, individualism, and nationalism. Daniel J. Boorstin's
> *The Genius of American Politics* explicitly hails the freedom of

American political life from ideology; and other works could be
cited that also stress what Americans have held in common,
rather than what they have debated.

In a sense the example from a scholarly journal represents
greater distortion:

> In accepting the revisionists' assessment that class conflict was
> not the appropriate ideological framework in which to view the
> colonial political experience, Boorstin and Hartz thus concluded
> that Americans have generally disdained all forms of ideology.
> They accept the Browns' [Robert E. and B. Katherine] notion
> that America was basically democratic by the 1770's, but they
> stress that it was a democracy born of practical experience, from
> the character of the American "landscape," rather than from a
> theoretical system of beliefs or ideas.[4]

It would seem that a simple comparative exercise would rule
out yoking *The Liberal Tradition* and *The Genius.* One need only
compare their treatments of the greatest single conflict in
American history—physical conflict with ideological conflict in
one case and without ideological conflict in the other—to see
the basic difference between them.

When one moves beyond direct comparison of the two
books to an examination of the critical literature, one encounters far less probing adverse criticism of Hartz than of
Boorstin—another reason to speculate about the widespread
practice of referring to their works without differentiation.
Such pondering suggests that if the climate of opinion of the
1950s had something to do with these works, it had as much to
do with the way they were assessed as with the way they were
written. That is to say, while Boorstin wrote *The Genius* to combat the Communist Party in one nation, Hartz's interest in
international or comparative political theory, stimulated by
Benjamin F. Wright, led him to react to Progressive history
—"ideas have an inner dialectic of their own." In a book published in 1931, Wright cited a number of political thinkers as
sources of American theories of natural law—especially Blackstone, Burlamaqui, Coke, Milton, Plato, Pope, Pufendorf, and
Sidney—but he referred to Locke more than any of the others.[5]
In 1937 Merle Curti challenged the widespread assumption

that Locke's influence on American thought faded in the first half of the nineteenth century.[6] In any event Hartz's approach has had a persistence, consistency, and growth of its own. Ten years passed before Fred Shannon dissected the bluntly stated, simplistic geographic determinism of Walter Prescott Webb's *The Great Plains,* but there was an immediate skeptical response to Webb's *The Great Frontier.*[7] One would not expect that a decade and a half would pass before a Pole or a Diggins, following Noble's 1965 lead, identified the inadequacies of Boorstin's geographic determinism—despite the subtlety with which it was expressed—or even that decade would pass before a Reimer, a Handler, or a Kristol specified the basic differences between Boorstin's and Hartz's interpretations. Since Reimer, Handler, and Kristol are not historians, and since some historians continue to overlook this difference,[8] one wonders whether the limited extent of historians' interdisciplinary interests contributes not only to their failure to ask certain questions but also to the failure of some even to take into account findings relevant to their field presented by nonhistorians.

Our basic purpose here is not to defend Hartz but to suggest that unqualified references to "schools" of historians can impede our efforts to gain a better understanding of American history. For some historians, it is true, "consensus" became an abstraction, a shibboleth, and a substitute for direct probing into some unpleasant matters, but labels can mislead not only historians but the critics of their works as well. We should adopt labels with due deliberateness. Regarding the American past, as distinct from "schools" of scholars who have written about it, the phrase *conflict within consensus* has some utility, but it also has limitations. It is applicable to the violence resorted to by those who want a piece of the action or participation in the American system, and to American politics—provided one is dealing with politics in the narrow sense that Bogue delineates. In the neglected preface to *The Age of Jackson,* Schlesinger saw conflict as occurring within consensus—agreement on capitalism and democracy—but some critics hold that he exaggerates the importance of conflict in American history while others refer to him pejoratively as a consensus historian. The phrase *consensus or conflict* is also unsatisfactory. It sets up a false dichotomy, implying that at a given time one or the other condition must prevail, that conflict always involves visible strife, that the absence of visible clashes indicates the presence of consensus. If visible conflict can be absent because of the presence of consensus, however, it can also be absent without consensus, as Wiebe suggests when he points out that the absence of visible conflict is a result in some cases of the dissenting minority's powerlessness. The editors of an anthology of readings in American history, in a prefatory remark to the third edition, refer to phraseology in such a way as to indicate that departure from the consensus view cannot validly entail a departure from consensus or denial of its reality—as a principal although not the only fact—in American history. Responding to recent developments in scholarship, they offer a better phrase than *conflict within consensus* and *consensus or conflict*: "Our title change (from *Conflict or Consensus* to *Conflict and Consensus*) reflects the changing approaches to the study of American history in recent years."[9]

The conflict–consensus dichotomy does not designate two truly independent elements. When it is doubled by the addition of the factor of discontinuity to the first half and the factor of continuity to the second half, the dividing line becomes even more hazy. Cushing Strout declares that conflict itself represented continuity in the view of the Progressive historians, who saw the same conflict repeating itself through the course of American history.[10] Richard S. Kirkendall, writing about the New Deal era, maintains that conflict resulted in continuity when the clashing forces were stalemated.[11] He also points to the changes which took place in some areas—especially in the size and power of the federal government—while deadlock prevailed in other areas.[12] In his analysis, conflict thus simultaneously produced both continuity and discontinuity. At the same time, one may add, consensus gave rise to discontinuity when the Wagner Act passed in the House without a roll call and in the Senate by a vote of 63 to 12. Does this undermine Kirkendall's association of discontinuity (as well as continuity) with conflict? Or does it suggest that the conflict preceding the voting was less deep than its rhetorical component seemed to indicate? In any case, it is apparent that the conflict-discontinuity vs. consensus-continuity dichotomy can break down, depending on one's perspective, definitions, and level of analysis. All of which underlines Kirkendall's insistence that the historian's "fundamental tasks . . . are the description, measurement, and explanation of change in human affairs."[13] Bearing that in mind, historians can more precisely delineate conflict, consensus, continuity, and discontinuity as promoters, retarders, or aspects—simultaneously—of historical change. The question which historians face, Wise writes, is not one "of choosing between broad categories such as 'consensus' v. 'conflict,' 'continuity' v. 'change.' It is rather that of more precise understanding of what is permanent and what is changing, and what in American history has caused change to take place."[14]

The description, measurement, and explanation of change—and the latter involves the question why there was not more change than there was—require open-mindedness as to methodology and approaches. There are frequently expressions of an either/or attitude in the work of both narrative and analytical historians. The former laud the works which add to the store of historical knowledge while deploring interpretive studies which allegedly substitute speculation for research. The historiographers among the latter implicitly pose the question: What do a hundred essentially descriptive monographs on a given subject add up to, what do they mean—in sum, do they enhance our knowledge by enabling us not only to describe but also to make sense out of the past? Any historian using almost any approach can make a contribution and, the strictures of such brilliant historians as Paul K. Conkin and Roland M. Stromberg notwithstanding,[15] it is essential that some historians utilize the methods and concepts of the social sciences. We cannot begin to answer Lane's question about the relationship between change in affluence and change in politics, for example, without quantitative analyses of electorates at the ward or precinct level which draw on cultural and demographic as well as economic data and encompass extended sequences of elections in given localities.[16]

Kraditor has provided us a valuable handle with which to grasp the interaction of conflict and consensus, but a historian of a sociological bent would object that her analysis of the leadership of protest and reform movements and their shaping of strategies and tactics in response to specific circumstances—the prevailing consensus at a given time—does not go far enough, does not accord due weight to the social forces at work in the context from which these movements arise. One can appreciate the cogency of this reservation on reading, say, Charles Tilly's study of the French Revolution, where he concludes that urbanization had more to do with the revolutionary or counterrevolutionary activities in various areas than the stated intentions of articulate individuals,[17] or Herbert G. Gutman's provocative exploratory essay on "Work, Culture, and Society in Industrializing America."[18] Gutman points the way to applying Kraditor's approach in its full implications. Employing the anthropologist's distinction between society and culture, he sees societal consensus in the business norms of order, obedience, discipline, industry, and material progress. He sees conflict arising when "cross-class but predominantly working-class ethnic subcultures" which are incompatible with the consensual society interact with that society. Gutman would modify Progressive and Marxist class doctrines and economic determinism as sufficient explanations of conflict, while combining conflict and consensus, by introducing an additional, cultural variable, "the arrangement," in anthropologist Sidney W. Mintz's words, "of persons in societal groups for whom cultural forms confirm, reinforce, maintain, change, or deny particular arrangements of status, power, and identity."[19]

At the same time, sociological historians and quantifiers must recognize that, although some questions can only be answered by quantitative methods, other questions can only be partially answered in this way, and still other questions do not lend themselves at all to quantified answers. Quantifiers, moreover, must resist the temptation to formulate questions "merely for their amenity to research techniques in favor."[20] They must avoid what J. H. Plumb calls a "penchant for the decorative statistic" and use their techniques to answer important questions.[21] And they must "set findings in useful and defensible theoretical frameworks."[22] Nor is there any reason, as Bogue writes, that behavioral history has to be consensus history.[23] Neither does behavioral history have to be conflict history. Hollingsworth points out that *consensus* in the exclusive, simplistic sense that gained wide currency in the 1950s and *conflict* in the exclusive, simplistic sense that gained wide currency in the 1960s led both consensus and New Left historians to view the past within the same methodological-conceptual framework:

> the method of analysis used by those of the New Left is hardly different from their predecessors of the 1950's. The difference between the groups results essentially from the fact that the New Left is engaged in ideological rejection of most of the American past and present. In other words, the two groups of historians seem to be analyzing the same phenomena from different ideological perspectives.

Hollingsworth urges historians to adopt a far more sophisticated methodological and conceptual approach, utilizing the social sciences in comparative study of political-economic-social cleavage in modernizing societies.[24]

In his essay on what he considers historians' unsatisfactory treatment of democracy, Kristol also expresses dissatisfaction with studies which look at the same things with different emphases:

> I should like to think that I am as good a democrat as the average historian, with as genuine an affection for the common man. But unlike the "consensus historians," I do not see that the condition of American democracy is such as automatically to call forth my love and honor, although I respect it enough to offer my obedience. And unlike the "conflict historians," I get no relief in discovering as many instances as possible of civil strife and mob disorder. Both of these schools of thought, it seems to me, perceive the common man—the one in his potential for merely self-centered activity, the other in his exclusive potential for resisting authority—in terms that remind me of Ortega's definition of the "mass man": the individual who is not capable of assuming responsibility for self-limitation, for a kind of self-definition that is both generous and self-respecting.[25]

Wise, too, urges historians to move beyond looking at the same things from different perspectives while emphasizing different categories. Changes in interpretation resulting from analyses utilizing categories such as *conflict* or *consensus*, he writes, usually amount to "a shift in pattern of organization, or paradigm."[26] In *American Historical Explanations* he proposes new approaches to the study of historiography and intellectual history which will uncover new things.[27]

The turning inward involved in extending Kraditor's approach will undoubtedly be accompanied by the turning outward that Hollingsworth calls for. Among historians whose history begins at home, the revival of local history which began in the late 1950s will probably continue.[28] Let us hope so, for, as I have found in reading the literature on the Great Depression in various localities, there is much that histories written at the national level do not tell us.[29] This also becomes evident when one compares the role of big businessmen in the promotion of Progressive reforms at the national level (discussed in chapter 7 in some comments on Kolko's work) with their activity in this regard in various cities as Samuel P. Hays has described it.[30] Meanwhile, as Higham suggests, other historians will look outward. In 1970 Higham found "all forms of general interpretation in short supply." Proposals ranging from Turner's frontier thesis to the consensus interpretation of the 1950s "now sell at a heavy discount." It was not at all clear to Higham where to find a "new set of coordinates for charting directions." He pointed to the possibility that they cannot be found specifically in American history, that the ordering of historical knowledge "may have to depend increasingly on a wider view of the nature and destiny of modern society."[31] It is in the light of this possibility that Hartz's work can be appreciated. There is no question that he writes at a high level of generalization, but he raises the kinds of questions that sociologists, political scientists, economists, and a small but growing number of historians attempt to answer in their detailed comparative investigations. Although the fragmentation theory is audacious, clever, and consistent, it may well falter upon careful testing. In this regard there is much that historians of Latin America, South Africa, Canada, and Australia can contribute.

As we have seen in chapter 2, McNaught, a historian of Canada and a Canadian, finds Hartz's theory overly deterministic—although in this case McNaught is writing about the United States rather than his own country. His criticism leaves us with a question: If "the decision of thousands of middle-class American socialists not to stay with their socialist party when the weather stiffened remains crucial,"[32] are "the great questions of free will and inevitability" closed? When thousands of individuals make the same decision at about the same time, the explanation may not lie wholly in inevitability, but, as McNaught recognizes, neither is it likely to lie wholly in free will without regard to social-intellectual forces. If Hartz, as McNaught contends, espouses an ideological determinism, A. L. Burt, another historian of Canada and a Canadian (who eventually became a naturalized citizen of the United States), asserts another kind of determinism. Although Burt does not refer to *The Liberal Tradition in America*, in effect he rejects Hartz's fragmentation theory. In an essay entitled "If Turner Had Looked at Canada, Australia, and New Zealand When He Wrote about the West," Burt concludes that the form and spirit of democracy in Australia differ from those of democracy in the United States, Canada, and New Zealand because of environment or geography. Absent in Australia but present in other countries was "a combination of soil and climate that was ideal for close agricultural settlement over most of the country."[33]

This explanation, however, would not satisfy Kenneth D. McRae, who, in an essay in *The Founding of New Societies* on "The Structure of Canadian History," emphasizes the differences between the French and English fragments.[34] Meanwhile, Lipset, in his review of *The Founding of New Societies*, writes that McRae neglects literature which both undermines and reinforces his dual fragment analysis of Canadian history.[35] Other reviewers of *The Founding of New Societies* judge the fragmentation theory to be pioneering and provocative while charging Hartz with adopting an exclusive, doctrinaire approach[36] and, alternatively, with spreading his "theoretical net so wide . . . that the theory becomes so complicated that it can explain anything."[37]

The need to test Hartz's theory which these comments suggest is met only indirectly by existing studies in frontier history. Students in this field who, like Burt, emphasize environmental factors in effect reject the fragmentation theory

with its virtually exclusive focus on ideology. Those who emphasize the role of ideas in the development of frontier
societies, as well as those who stress a causal combination of
environment and cultural-intellectual inheritance, allow for
but do not explicitly substantiate the validity of the fragmentation theory.

Dietrich Gerhard examines a substantial body of literature
on the settlement of frontiers in Canada, Australia, South
Africa, medieval Germany, and Russia in order to test Turner's
thesis concerning the main traits produced by the impact of the
frontier on institutions and society: "political democracy in the
form of self-government; tendency towards social equality;
mobility and the resulting 'breaking the bond of custom.' "
Gerhard prefaces his discussion of various frontiers with a
Hartz-like observation: "Amongst the societies chosen for comparative analysis basic differences of their origin have to be
emphasized." Overseas societies established by the British,
French, and Dutch in the seventeenth, eighteeenth, and early
nineteenth centuries originated in "a period when medieval
institutions crystallized throughout the whole of Europe." The
cultural heritage of the Russian frontier differed even more
from that of the British, French, and Dutch frontiers.[38]

Turning to French Canada, Gerhard finds only one moving or Turnerian frontier—the traders' frontier. It was not
followed by a settlers' frontier, and "geographical conditions
alone do not explain this phenomenon." Nor does lack of population. As Gerhard sees it, the tenacity with which the French
Canadians held on to their property was a socio-psychological
phenomenon—attachment to the land. While Burt finds
Turner's frontier on the banks of the St. Lawrence, Gerhard
disagrees. He concedes that there were profound differences
between the societies of New France and contemporary
France—that there was relatively less class distinction and
greater social mobility in French Canada—but he refers to "recurrent quarrels about privilege and procedure." In politics,
the French Canadians were "less concerned with self-government than with being left alone, and no representative institutions were transmitted by New France to British Canada."
Gerhard's conclusion concerning French Canada is essentially
environmental, but it is not Turnerian:

> To me the greater independence of the French farmer seems to
> be the result of structural changes in society caused by the
> distance from the mother country and by the poverty of the
> colony. As New France evolved she proved to have left a great
> deal behind in the mother country, but it is hard to demonstrate
> that this was the effect of the frontier in a specific sense.[39]

British Canada or Ontario of the late eighteenth and early
nineteenth centuries, with its leveling influences, more nearly
resembled Turner's frontier. English travelers experienced
shock at the "leveling system" of Upper Canada, but, Gerhard
asks, "to what extent can the frontier be held responsible for
such experiences?" He replies with a pro-Hartz, anti-Turner
reference to the transfer of culture: "Through numerous
channels—English, Scottish, but most of all American
immigrants—[was] transmitted the spirit of political action and
social equality to the new country." Still, Gerhard does not rule
out the influence of the frontier in the development of Ontario.
In fact, he states that Methodism, the decisive force in changing
control of church and school by traditional groups towards a
more flexible colonial society, was a "child of the Great
Awakening and of the frontier." At the same time he inquires,
"Who would dare to claim this [change] was exclusively the
effect of the frontier?" Referring to the emergence by the middle of the nineteenth century of "responsible government," a
momentous change, Gerhard writes, "Undoubtedly it would be
wrong to interpret this change as a victory of the frontier." On
the other hand, the frontier "had its share in the
development."[40]

Gerhard's conclusions about the Australian frontier are
decidedly Hartzian. He emphasizes the lasting imprint which
the miners, with their strong nonconformist and chartist elements, left on Australian society. But he asks whether the miners' frontier, which soon dissolved as the gold diggers turned to
agriculture and industry, lasted long enough to be considered a
frontier. In any event, Gerhard is certain that Australia, "still in
the process of formation when in the mother country the British radicals struggled for political and social reform, can be
called an outpost of this British movement, its Pacific Frontier,
if you like." Thus unionism was "a heritage from the miner's

period but hardly from the frontier." It was "a direct extension
of the traditions of British radicalism, with utmost use made of
Australian opportunities." Likewise, in regard to the development of an American-like school system, "All signs point in the
direction of a direct carry-over from England—with greater
and faster success than in the mother country—not by way of
the frontier." Gerhard mentions an environmental agent in
Australian development when he cites geography and climate
as among the causes of early urbanization (and some historians
of Australia, and Canada as well, have developed a "metropolitan" interpretation of national institutions). Needless to say,
emphasizing the importance of the cities is not a Turnerian
approach. In sum, the contribution of the frontier of
Australia's emergence as an advanced, strongly egalitarian
democracy can only have been of "auxiliary nature."[41]

Analyzing the inland trek of the Boers, Gerhard finds
Turner's moving frontier in South Africa only in a highly modified form. This spatially moving frontier, like Quebec's spatially static frontier, was a rather closed society of country
people—farmers in New France, ranchers in South Africa.
There was no continuous influx of immigrants as in America.
Above all, "only in its early phase did this frontier show the
basic prerequisite of Turner's frontier, free land." The Boer
frontier encountered a numerically superior movement, the
Bantu frontier, and "at an early time it had to transform itself,
much more permanently than the American frontier, into a
defensive organization." Gerhard, it is true, recognizes certain
Turnerian traits on the Boer frontier: "decentralization, self-
government, averson to officialdom—though by no means absent in the Netherlands—are easily discernible. They made the
Boer Republic a primitive democracy, with representative institutions which certainly cannot be called dynamic." Like New
France, the Boer frontier left a great deal behind in the mother
country but created "few institutions to offer fundaments for a
modern state."[42]

Having examined studies of the Canadian, Australian, and
South African frontiers, Gerhard poses two problems in
analysis. "In all of the European overseas settlements within
the later Commonwealth," he says, "the traditions of the

stratified society and of paternalistic government were considerably modified." New France and the Boer frontier, however, were transformed far less rapidly than the immigrant societies of Ontario and Australia. To what extent can changes in these immigrant societies be attributed to specific frontier influence? Gerhard's answer is, "Direct transfer from abroad—in Australia from the mother country, in Ontario even more from the United States—played at least as great a part as the frontier. The frontier actually accelerated and intensified the process." A second problem arises from the fact that while modification of social and political traditions was occurring in the overseas settlements, "Europe went in a similar direction, partly by way of revolutionary change." This raises the question: whatever promoted political democracy, mobility, and equality of opportunity, are these "specific features characteristic of a late phase in the Western development or [do] other moving frontiers show similar tendencies?" In response to this question, Gerhard devotes the remainder of his essay to the "historically more remote frontiers which Turner also refers to, those of medieval Germany and of Russia."[43]

In the case of medieval Germany, Gerhard concludes, the colonizing process was basically different in its main features from the American westward movement. With very few exceptions, there was no advance into open space; there was no sequence of frontiers; and there was no permanent establishment of democracy or social equality. "Everywhere the colonization, whether pushing into unsettled regions or into already thinly populated areas, transmitted to the East the constituent corporate and feudal features of medieval Germany . . . lock, stock and barrel." Gerhard compares this migration of the medieval corporate organization to the flowering overseas, five and six centuries later, of the emancipist elements of the West—an analogy which accords with Hartz's views. On the Russian frontier, except where it touched on Poland and Sweden, there was a Turnerian moving frontier. Geographical similarities, however, are outweighed by fundamental political differences. Unlike the settlers of Turner's frontier, the Russian colonists did not move ahead of the government: "The advance under an autocratic or military government was essentially gov-

ernment-directed." At times the Cossacks and other groups
were given special privileges, "yet in the long run all of them
had to be integrated into a society in the service of the state."
Colonists on the frontiers of European Russia enjoyed relatively less freedom than the early settlers in Siberia. There,
even after large-scale colonization with government assistance
got underway in the nineteenth century, the older structure of
society became greatly simplified, the pressure of government
was less demanding, and a class of wealthier, more independent peasants emerged. "Even so," Gerhard concludes, "what is
true for New France and for South Africa is also true for
Siberia: no institutions of national significance were created on
the Siberian or, apart from the Cossacks, on the European
frontier."[44]

In the end Gerhard stresses the inextricable intertwining
of the frontier and other changes of the old society as con-
tributors to the development of "features which are characteristic of American society and increasingly . . . of all modern
society. To what extent the frontier independently contributed
to this development, to what extent it only reflected forces
emerging from the old society will always remain a matter of
debate."[45] This keeps both Turnerian and Hartzian factors in
the combination of causes. If Hartz's theory of the ultimate
origin of dominant forces falls, shall we be able to deny the
existence and the impact of the social-intellectual agents which
he describes? I raise this question because of my concern with
politics and public policy. Historians are properly wary of
single themes which purportedly explain all of American history, and consensus by itself is by no means the entire American
story. There has been conflict and, in both the society as a
whole and each individual, as Kammen brilliantly demonstrates, profound ambivalence. But if Kammen were to follow a
reviewer's suggestion and "subsume the whole debate [over
conflict and consensus] within his scheme as merely another
biformity,"[46] the political historian, interested in the final outcome of public policy, would still want to know why, for example, the United States is the only industrialized country without
a national system of health insurance, and why a student of
political economy writes about "U.S. Ideology vs. European

Pragmatism."[47] Hartz helps us to answer these questions when he spells out the implications for American history of F. S. C. Northrop's observation in a sophisticated discussion of ideological-biological, theoretic-aesthetic man:

> human beings in society are reacting not merely to particular natural events occurring just once at a given time and place, but also to symbols, to socially determined symbols, which keep their meanings constant during the period of decades or centuries, as the case may be, in which a given normative social theory captures their faith and thereby serves as a norm for their social behavior and cultural institutions.[48]

Still, there is more to politics than political economy, and there is more to American history than the consensus which scholarly journeys abroad illuminate. At home we find consensus *and* conflict. If Hartz's delineation of consensus merits our acclaim, Lee Benson's stimulation of inquiry into ethnocultural and religious sources of conflict—along with his writings on methodology and conceptualization—has earned for him a very high place among heuristic historical thinkers of the past decade. We may hope that a future historian will have the opportunity of trying to explain why there was a benign elimination of losers of all colors, creeds, and national origins —something which, if it occurs, may or may not take place amid the domestic tranquillity the Founding Fathers sought to insure.

Notes

Each source is cited in full upon its first appearance in a chapter. The notes are numbered within sections of chapters.

Chapter One: The Consensus View: Ideology and Politics

Point of Entry

1. Gene Wise, *American Historical Explanations: A Strategy for Grounded Inquiry* (Homewood, Ill., 1973).
2. Ibid., 84−85, 90, 101−102, 107.
3. Ibid., 84, 89−90, 102, 104−105.
4. Ibid., 84, 90, 92, 100.
5. Ibid., 84, 92, 102−103.

Conformity: Uni-Ideological and Non-Ideological

1. Robert A. Dahl, *Pluralist Democracy in the United States: Conflict and Consent* (Chicago, 1967), 357.
2. Louis Hartz, *The Liberal Tradition in America: An Interpretation of American Political Thought since the Revolution* (New York, 1955), 11. Daniel J. Boorstin, *The Genius of American Politics* (Chicago, 1953, Phoenix Books edition), 9, refers to the "American Way of Life." See also Yehoshua Arieli, *Individualism and Nationalism in American Ideology* (Baltimore, 1966, Penguin Books edition), chapter 2, "Ideology and the American Way of Life," 15−28.
3. Arthur Mann, "The Progressive Tradition," in John Higham, editor, *The Reconstruction of American History* (New York, 1962), 170−71.
4. Daniel J. Boorstin, *The Genius of American Politics*, 9, 14.
5. Irving Kristol, "American Historians and the Democratic Idea," *American Scholar,* 39 (Winter 1969−70), 102. This essay is reprinted as chapter 4 in Kristol, *On the Democratic Idea in America* (New York, 1973, Harper Torchbook edition), 48−67.
6. Daniel J. Boorstin, *The Genius of American Politics*, 8.
7. J. R. Pole, "Daniel J. Boorstin," in Marcus Cunliffe and Robin W. Winks, editors, *Pastmasters: Some Essays on American Historians* (New York, 1969), 221.
8. Ibid., 224.
9. Ibid., 224.
10. Ibid., 221.
11. Daniel J. Boorstin, *The Genius of American Politics*, 71−95.
12. Ibid., 14.
13. John R. Howe, Jr., "Republican Thought and the Political Violence of the 1790's," *American Quarterly, 19* (Summer 1967, Part 1), 152, 152n.

14. J. R. Pole, "Daniel J. Boorstin," 211, 229.
15. David W. Noble, *Historians against History: The Frontier Thesis and the National Covenant in American Historical Writing since 1830* (Minneapolis, 1965), chapter 9, "Daniel Boorstin: Blackstone and the Conservation of the American Covenant," 164, 169, 171.

Internal and External Pressures on Historians

1. Gerald W. Grob and George Athan Billias, editors, *Interpretations of American History: Patterns and Perspectives*, Second Edition (New York, 1972), 1: 13–14.
2. Thomas L. Hartshorne, *The Distorted Image: Changing Conceptions of the American Character* (Cleveland, 1968), 159.
3. Ibid., 159–66.
4. Richard Hofstadter, *The Progressive Historians: Turner, Beard, Parrington* (New York, 1968), 439.
5. Samuel Eliot Morison, "Faith of a Historian," *American Historical Review*, 56 (January 1951), 273.
6. William J. Newman, *The Futilitarian Society* (New York, 1961), 301–302.
7. Ralph Gabriel, *The Course of American Democratic Thought* (New York, 1940). See also Robert Allen Skotheim, *American Intellectual Histories and Historians* (Princeton, N.J., 1960), 217–18, 241–43, and Robert M. Crunden, *From Self to Society 1919–1941* (Englewood Cliffs, N.J., 1972), 195–98.
8. Richard Hofstadter, *The Progressive Historians,* 452n.
9. Richard Hofstadter, *The American Political Tradition and the Men Who Made It* (New York, 1954, Vintage Books edition), vii, x, and chapter 3, "Andrew Jackson and the Rise of Liberal Capitalism," 45–67. Hofstadter also summarizes this estimate of American reform movements in *The Age of Reform: From Bryan to FDR* (New York, 1955), 303–304.
10. Lincoln Steffens, *Autobiography* (New York, 1931); John Chamberlain, *Farewell to Reform: Being a History of the Rise, Life, and Decay of the Progressive Mind in America* (New York, 1932).
11. Quoted in Louis Filler, "John Chamberlain and American Liberalism," *Colorado Quarterly*, 6 (Autumn 1957), 207.
12. James P. Young, *The Politics of Affluence: Ideology in the United States since World War II* (San Francisco, 1968), 4.
13. Richard Hofstadter, *The American Political Tradition*, 56–58.
14. Ibid., 58.
15. Bray Hammond, "Public Policy and National Banks," *Journal of Economic History*, 6 (May 1946), 79–84; "Jackson, Biddle, and the Bank of the United States," ibid., 7 (May 1947), 1–23.
16. Joseph Dorfman, "The Jackson Wage-Earner Thesis," *American Historical Review*, 54 (January 1949), 296–306.
17. Frank Otto Gatell, "Sober Second Thoughts on Van Buren, the Albany Regency, and the Wall Street Conspiracy," *Journal of American History*, 52

(June 1966), 29. Gatell's later view of Jacksonian politics is discussed below in chapter 4.

18. Robert V. Remini, *Andrew Jackson and the Bank War: A Study in Presidential Power* (New York, 1967), 179.

19. Lee Benson, *The Concept of Jacksonian Democracy: New York as a Test Case* (Princeton, N.J., 1961), 336. Gene Wise, "Political 'Reality' in Recent American Scholarship: Progressives versus Symbolists," *American Quarterly,* 19 (Summer 1967, Part 2), 310–16, makes a provocative comparison of Schlesinger's and Benson's views.

20. Walter T. K. Nugent, *The Tolerant Populists: Kansas Populism and Nativism* (Chicago, 1963). See also Nugent, "Some Parameters of Populism," *Agricultural History,* 40 (October 1966), 255–70. Kenneth Barkin, "A Case Study in Comparative History: Populism in Germany and America," in Herbert J. Bass, editor, *The State of American History* (Chicago, 1970), 373–404, supports Nugent's view.

21. Otis L. Graham, Jr., *An Encore for Reform: The Old Progressives and the New Deal* (New York, 1967), 230.

22. See Russel B. Nye, *Midwestern Progressive Politics: A Historical Study of Its Origins and Development, 1870–1958* (New York, 1965, Harper Torchbooks edition); David P. Thelen, "Social Tensions and the Origins of Progressivism," *Journal of American History,* 56 (September 1969), 323–41.

23. Gabriel Kolko, *The Triumph of Conservatism.*

24. Ibid. (Chicago, 1963, Quadrangle Paperback edition), 3.

25. Ibid., 280, 283, 302, 305.

26. Clinton Rossiter, *Parties and Politics in America* (Ithaca, N.Y., 1960), 108.

27. Clinton Rossiter, *Marxism: The View from America* (New York, 1960).

28. Merle Curti, *The Growth of American Thought,* Third Edition (New York, 1964), 772.

29. Clinton Rossiter, *Conservatism in America: The Thankless Persuasion,* Second Edition, revised (New York, 1962, Vintage Books), ix, 13.

30. Thomas L. Hartshorne, *The Distorted Image,* 166.

31. Gerald W. Grob and George Athan Billias, editors, *Interpretations of American History,* 1: 17–18.

32. John P. Diggins, *The American Left in the Twentieth Century* (New York, 1973), 145–48, discusses Hofstadter, Boorstin, and Hartz under the heading, "American History: From Marx to Locke."

33. Louis Hartz, *The Liberal Tradition in America,* 254–55, 305.

34. Benjamin F. Wright, *American Interpretations of Natural Law* (Cambridge, Mass., 1931); "American Democracy and the Frontier," *Yale Review,* 20 (December 1930), 349–65.

35. William J. Newman, *The Futilitarian Society,* 318; John Higham, "The Cult of 'American Consensus': Homogenizing Our History," *Commentary,* 27 (February 1959), 96; Thomas L. Hartshorne, *The Distorted Image,* 164.

36. Richard Hofstadter, *The Progressive Historians,* 451.

37. Richard Hofstadter, *The Age of Reform,* 12.

38. Quoted in Jesse Lemisch, "The American Revolution Seen from the Bot-

tom Up," in Barton J. Bernstein, editor, *Towards a New Past: Dissenting Essays in American History* (New York, 1969, Vintage Books edition), 31n.

39. Kenneth S. Lynn, "The Education of Daniel J. Boorstin," *Kenyon Review,* 28 (January 1966), 116.
40. William J. Newman, *The Futilitarian Society,* 332.
41. Conyers Read, "The Social Responsibilities of the Historian," *American Historical Review,* 55 (January 1950), 284–85.
42. Merle Curti, "The Democratic Theme in American Historical Literature," *Mississippi Valley Historical Review,* 39 (September 1952), 25.

The Historian as Individual: Daniel J. Boorstin

1. Marcus Cunliffe and Robin W. Winks, editors, *Pastmasters,* vii.
2. John P. Diggins, "Consciousness and Ideology in American History: The Burden of Daniel J. Boorstin," *American Historical Review,* 76 (February 1971), 100.
3. David W. Noble, *Historians against History,* 158–71. This summary does not do justice to Noble's analysis, a fascinating aspect of which is his identification, ibid., 164–66, 169, of the parallels between Blackstone's and Jefferson's views of reality and between Blackstone and Boorstin as political philosophers of conservatism.
4. Ibid., 173.
5. J. R. Pole, "Daniel J. Boorstin," 237.
6. Quoted in David W. Noble, *Historians against History,* 174.
7. Ibid., 175.
8. Ibid., 174–75.
9. Ibid., 175.
10. John P. Diggins, "Consciousness and Ideology in American History," 114–15.
11. Ibid., 114. The consensus view of the Civil War is discussed below in chapter 3.
12. Ibid., 117–18.
13. Ibid., 118, 118n.
14. J. R. Pole, "Daniel J. Boorstin," 211.
15. Ibid., 220, 237.
16. Ibid., 222.

The Similarity of the Major Parties

1. Charles G. Sellers, Jr., *Jacksonian Democracy* (Washington, D.C., 1958), 2.
2. Walter Adams, "Economics, Ideology, and Politics," *Diogenes,* 36 (Winter 1961), 55–58.
3. Van Beck Hall, *Politics without Parties: Massachusetts, 1780–1791* (Pittsburgh, 1972); Richard R. Beeman, *The Old Dominion and the New Nation, 1788–1801* (Lexington, Ky., 1972). On ideological conflict in the years 1797–1801, see Richard Hofstadter, *The Idea of a Party System: The Rise of Legitimate Opposition in the United States, 1780–1840* (Berkeley,

Calif., 1969), 102—21. In his paper on "Party and Faction in Congressional Voting, 1789—1801," Rudolph Bell maintains that a genuine party system could not develop until the ideological issues of the 1790s were settled; reported in Robert W. Johannsen, "The Sixty-Third Meeting of the Organization of American Historians," *Journal of American History,* 57 (September 1970), 371. Bell's full-length study is *Party and Faction in American Politics: The House of Representatives, 1789—1801* (Westport, Conn., 1973).

4. Richard Buel, Jr., *Securing the Revolution: Ideology in American Politics, 1789—1815* (Ithaca, N.Y., 1972).
5. Richard Hofstadter, *The American Political Tradition,* ix.
6. E. A. J. Johnson, "Federalism, Pluralism, and Public Policy," *Journal of Economic History,* 22 (December 1962), 442.
7. William D. Grampp, "A Re-Examination of Jeffersonian Economics," *Southern Economic Journal,* 12 (January 1946), 281.
8. David Hackett Fischer, *The Revolution of Conservatism: The Federalist Party in the Era of Jeffersonian Democracy* (New York, 1965).
9. Charles M. Wiltse, *The New Nation: 1800—1845* (New York, 1961), 92.
10. James M. Banner, *To the Hartford Convention: The Federalists and the Origins of Party Politics in Massachusetts, 1789—1815* (New York, 1970), 109, 118, 120.
11. Charles M. Wiltse, *The New Nation,* 92.
12. Marcus Cunliffe, *The Nation Takes Shape 1789—1837* (Chicago 1959), 181.
13. James M. Banner, *To the Hartford Convention;* Linda K. Kerber, *Federalists in Dissent: Imagery and Ideology in Jeffersonian America* (Ithaca, N.Y., 1970).
14. Norman L. Stamps, "Party Government in Connecticut, 1800—1816," *Historian,* 17 (February 1955), 172—90.
15. Carl E. Prince, *New Jersey's Jeffersonian Republicans: The Genesis of an Early Party Machine, 1789—1817* (Chapel Hill, N.C., 1967); Paul Goodman, *The Democratic-Republicans of Massachusetts: Politics in a Young Republic* (Cambridge, Mass., 1964). An excellent discussion of recent studies of parties is Jacob E. Cooke, "The Federalist Age: A Reappraisal," in George Athan Billias and Gerald N. Grob, editors, *American History: Retrospect and Prospect* (New York, 1971), 104—15. Prince's later study is "The Leadership of New Jersey's First Party System," *Proceedings of the Second Annual Symposium of the New Jersey Historical Commission* (Newark, 1971), 1—10.
16. Lee Benson, *The Concept of Jacksonian Democracy,* 336.
17. Richard P. McCormick, "Suffrage Classes and Party Alignment: A Study in Voter Behavior," *Mississippi Valley Historical Review,* 44 (December 1959), 409.
18. Richard P. McCormick, *The Second American Party System: Party Formation in the Jacksonian Era* (Chapel Hill, N.C., 1966). Glyndon G. Van Deusen, *The Jacksonian Era, 1828—1848* (New York, 1959), 26, 96, and Mark H. Haller, "The Rise of the Jackson Party in Maryland, 1820—1829," *Journal of Southern History,* 18 (August 1962), 307—26, express a similar view.

19. Lynn L. Marshall, "The Strange Stillbirth of the Whig Party," *American Historical Review,* 62 (January 1967), 445, 462n.
20. Michael Wallace, "Changing Concepts of Party in the United States: New York, 1815—1828," *American Historical Review,* 74 (December 1968), 470.
21. Richard Hofstadter, *The Idea of a Party System,* uses *consensus* as Wallace does.
22. Richard P. McCormick, "New Perspectives in Jacksonian Politics," *American Historical Review,* 65 (January 1960), 296.
23. Louis Hartz, "The Rise of the Democratic Idea," in Arthur M. Schlesinger, Jr., and Morton White, editors, *Paths of American Thought* (Boston 1963), 47—48. See also Hartz, *The Liberal Tradition in America,* 16.
24. Henry Bamford Parkes, *The American Experience: An Interpretation of the History and Civilization of the American People* (New York, 1959, Vintage Books edition), 154, 164—65.
25. Clinton Rossiter, *Parties and Politics in America,* 108.
26. John Higham et al., *History: The Development of Historical Studies in the United States* (Englewood Cliffs, N.J., 1965), 221.
27. Clinton Rossiter, *Parties and Politics in America,* 198n., cites a number of these studies.
28. Daniel J. Boorstin, *The Genius of American Politics,* 3.
29. Andrew Hacker, "America Follows the Middle of the Road," *New York Times Magazine,* May 5, 1963, 21, 112.
30. Marshall Dimock, *The New American Political Economy: A Synthesis of Politics and Economics* (New York, 1962), 209—10.
31. Paul W. Glad, *McKinley, Bryan, and the People* (Philadelphia, 1964), 208.
32. Richard Jensen, *The Winning of the Midwest: Social and Political Conflict, 1888—1896* (Chicago, 1972), xv.
33. Ronald Lora, *Conservative Minds in America* (Chicago, 1971), 197.
34. James MacGregor Burns, "Goldwater Challenges the '4-Party' System," *New York Times Magazine,* June 28, 1964, 57.
35. Ibid., 62. Burns' full-length study is *The Deadlock of Democracy: Four-Party Politics in America* (Englewood Cliffs, N.J., 1963), which identifies a liberal "presidential" and a conservative "congressional" wing in both major parties.
36. Philip E. Converse et al., "Electoral Myth and Reality: The 1964 Election," *American Political Science Review,* 59 (June 1965), 328.
37. Paul T. David, *Party Strength in the United States 1872—1970* (Charlottesville, Va., 1972) 45, Figure 5.3.
38. A. E. Keir Nash, review, William Nisbet Chambers and Walter Dean Burnham, editors, *The American Party Systems: Stages of Political Development* (New York, 1967), in *American Political Science Review,* 62 (December 1968), 1276; Allan C. Brownfield, "The Irrelevance of American Politics," *Yale Review,* 60 (October 1970), 1—13; Theodore J. Lowi, "The Artificial Majority," *Nation,* 211 (December 2, 1970), 591—94; David Broder, *The Party's Over: The Failure of Politics in America* (New York, 1972).

39. Elizabeth Drew, "Contemplating the National Navel," *New York Times Book Review,* June 4, 1972, 57–58.
40. Jorgen S. Rasmussen, "Party Responsibility in Britain and the United States," *Journal of American Studies,* 1 (October 1967), 233–56.
41. George Jenks, "Party Lines Breaking Up," *Toledo Blade,* March 21, 1973.
42. Editorial, "Choosing Up Sides," *New York Times,* March 11, 1973.

Chapter Two: Causes of Consensus

Social Scientists on Causation

1. Bennett M. Berger, review, Alvin W. Gouldner, *The Coming Crisis of Western Sociology* (New York, 1970), in *New York Times Book Review,* October 25, 1970, 60–61. Gouldner, also available in an Equinox Books paperback edition, discusses Positivism, Marxism, classical sociology, and Functionalism in chapter 4 and "The World of Talcott Parsons" in chapters 5–8. Robert F. Berkhofer, Jr., *The Behavioral Approach to Historical Analysis* (New York, 1969), 169–210, discusses the ideas of Parsons and some of Parsons' students: Marion J. Levy, Jr., Robert Merton, and Neil Smelser.
2. Talcott Parsons, "The Distribution of Power in American Society," *World Politics,* 10 (October 1957), 128–39.
3. See, for example, V. O. Key, Jr., "Secular Realignment and the Party System," *Journal of Politics,* 21 (May 1959), 198–210; Kay and Frank Munger, "Social Determinism and Electoral Decision: The Case of Indiana," in Eugene Burdick and Arthur J. Brodbeck, editors, *American Voting Behavior* (Glencoe, Ill., 1959), 281–99.
4. Seymour Martin Lipset and Stein Rokkan, "Cleavage Structures, Party Systems, and Voter Alignments: An Introduction," in Lipset and Rokkan, editors, *Party Systems and Voter Alignments: Cross-National Perspectives* (New York, 1967), 1, 26.
5. Ibid., 27–29.
6. Ibid., 26.
7. Dan Nimmo and Thomas D. Ungs, *American Political Patterns: Conflict and Consensus* (Boston, 1967), 33–35, 54.
8. Ibid., 55.
9. Ibid., 56–57.
10. Louis Hartz, "Comment," *Comparative Studies in Society and History,* 5 (April 1963), 279–81, 284; Hartz, *The Liberal Tradition in America: An Interpretation of American Political Thought since the Revolution* (New York, 1955), 28.
11. Robert A. Dahl, *Pluralist Democracy in the United States: Conflict and Consent* (Chicago, 1967), 56–62, 71–76.
12. Ibid., 302–24. On the Civil War and consensus history, see below, chapter 3.
13. Ibid., 334–37, 357. On causation see also Dahl, section entitled "Consensus," in Dahl, editor, *Political Oppositions in Western Democracies* (New Haven and London, 1966), 35–48.

Hofstadter, Boorstin, and Hartz on Causation

1. Richard Hofstadter, *The Progressive Historians: Turner, Beard, Parrington* (New York, 1968), 454–55.
2. Frank M. Albrecht, Letter to the Editor, *Reporter* (November 27, 1958), 5.
3. Daniel J. Boorstin, *The Genius of American Politics* (Chicago, 1953, Phoenix Books edition), 7.
4. Ibid., 5.
5. Ibid., 8, 11, 14, 16, 20, 26.
6. Ibid., 8–22.
7. Ibid., 22–35.
8. Ibid., 9.
9. J. R. Pole, "Daniel J. Boorstin," in Marcus Cunliffe and Robin W. Winks, editors, *Pastmasters: Some Essays on American Historians* (New York, 1969), 221–22.
10. Ibid., 212, 221.
11. Ibid., 216–21.
12. Ibid., 226–27.
13. Ibid., 220–23.
14. Ibid., 220–21.
15. Ibid., 217, 221, 222. Boorstin, *The Genius of American Politics,* 26, considers Turner's frontier thesis a sociological expression of the "golden land" idea, and, ibid., 36–65, discusses the development of the Puritan settlement as a frontier experience.
16. J. R. Pole, "Daniel J. Boorstin," 235.
17. Louis Hartz, *The Liberal Tradition in America,* 6.
18. Ibid., i.
19. Charles M. Andrews, for example, earlier made this point, as Ralph H. Gabriel notes in "History and the American Past," in Robert E. Spiller and Eric Larrabee, editors, *American Perspectives: The National Self-Image in the Twentieth Century* (Cambridge, Mass., 1961), 13.
20. Arthur Mann, "The Progressive Tradition," in John Higham, editor, *The Reconstruction of American History* (New York, 1962), 171.

Criticism of Hofstadter, Boorstin, and Hartz

1. David M. Potter, *New York Review of Books,* 11 (December 5, 1968), 46, 48.
2. J. R. Pole, "Daniel J. Boorstin," 224.
3. Ibid., 224, 225, 228.
4. Ibid., 223–24.
5. Ibid., 235–36.
6. John P. Diggins, "Consciousness and Ideology in American History: The Burden of Daniel J. Boorstin," *American Historical Review,* 76 (February 1971), 100–101, 107.
7. Ibid., 101–102, 117.
8. Ibid., 104–107, 108n.
9. Ibid., 104.

10. Ibid., 105.
11. Ibid., 101, 107, 107n, 117. What amounts to a debate between Oscar Berland and Diggins over the relationship between Boorstin's writings and the thought of Hegel and Marx may be found in "Communications," *American Historical Review,* 76 (October 1971), 1245–54. I believe that Diggins more than holds his own in this exchange, but the reader should make his own judgment.
12. John P. Diggins, "Consciousness and Ideology in American History," 102.
13. Ibid., 111–12.
14. Ibid., 106.
15. Ibid., 105.
16. Ibid.
17. Ibid., 102–104.
18. Ibid., 105 (emphasis mine).
19. Ibid., 104–106, 109.
20. Kenneth McNaught, "American Progressives and the Great Society," *Journal of American History,* 52 (December 1966), 506–508, 511.
21. Marvin Meyers, "Louis Hartz, *The Liberal Tradition in America:* An Appraisal," *Comparative Studies in Society and History,* 5 (April 1963), 265–66.
22. Kenneth McNaught, "American Progressives and the Great Society," 506, 508–509, 516, 519. William M. Dick, *Labor and Socialism in America: The Gompers Era* (Port Washington, N.Y., 1972), 184, writes, "This work has argued that decisions taken by labor leaders on certain critical occasions determined this [nonsocialist] outcome."
23. Richard B. Morris, "Class Struggle and the American Revolution," *William and Mary Quarterly,* 19 (January 1962), 12.
24. Leonard Krieger, "The View from the Farther Shore," *Comparative Studies in Society and History,* 5 (April 1963), 269.
25. Marvin Meyers, "Louis Hartz; *The Liberal Tradition in America,*" 262, 265–66.
26. Thomas L. Hartshorne, *The Distorted Image: Changing Conceptions of the American Character since Turner* (Cleveland, 1968), 160.

Hartz's Fragmentation Theory

1. Louis Hartz, *The Liberal Tradition in America,* 20–21, 21n.
2. Edward Handler, editor, *The American Political Experience: What Is the Key?* (Lexington, Mass., 1968), 147.
3. Louis Hartz, "The Rise of the Democratic Idea," in Arthur M. Schlesinger, Jr., and Morton White, editors, *Paths of American Thought* (Boston, 1963), 37–51. Another brief essay is Hartz, "A Comparative Study of Fragment Cultures," in J. Rogers Hollingsworth, editor, *Nation and State Building in America: Comparative Historical Perspectives* (Boston, 1971), 10–26.
4. Louis Hartz, "The Rise of the Democratic Idea," 38–39, 41–42.
5. Ibid., 42–43.

6. Ibid., 39.
7. Ibid., 38–41.
8. Ibid., 38, 40–42.
9. Ibid., 43 (emphasis mine).
10. Ibid., 43–45.
11. Ibid., 45–46.
12. Ibid., 44–46, 50–51.
13. Louis Hartz, et al., *The Founding of New Societies: Studies in the History of the United States, Latin America, South Africa, Canada, and Australia* (New York, 1964), 24–48.
14. Edward Handler, editor, *The American Political Experience*, 4–7.
15. Ibid., 148.
16. Neal Riemer, "Two Conceptions of the Genius of American Politics," *Journal of Politics*, 20 (November 1958), 695–717; Riemer, *The Democratic Experiment* (Princeton, N.J., 1967).
17. Neal Riemer, "Two Conceptions of the Genius of American Politics," 697.
18. Ibid., 717.
19. Neal Riemer, *The Democratic Experiment*, 211.
20. Ibid., 3–4.
21. Ibid., 9, 216.
22. Ibid., 211–12
23. Ibid., 5–6, 137–45, 213.
24. Ibid., 218.

Criticism of Tocqueville

1. Edward Pessen, "The Egalitarian Myth and the American Social Reality: Wealth, Mobility, and Equality in the 'Era of the Common Man,'" *American Historical Review*, 76 (October 1971), 989.
2. Lee Benson, "Middle Period Historiography: What Is to Be Done?," in George Athan Billias and Gerald N. Grob, editors, *American History: Retrospect and Prospect* (New York, 1971), 174–90. Benson refers to Douglas T. Miller, *Jacksonian Aristocracy: Class and Democracy in New York 1830–1860* (New York, 1967), and Edward Pessen, *Jacksonian America: Society, Personality, and Politics* (Homewood, Ill., 1969).
3. Edward Pessen, "The Egalitarian Myth and the American Social Reality," 990.
4. Ibid., 1005–1006n. See also Pessen, *Jacksonian America*, 354–55, and Pessen, "Did Fortunes Rise and Fall Mercurially in Antebellum America? The Tale of Two Cities: Boston and New York," *Journal of Social History*, 4 (Summer 1971), 340n; Richard Herr, *Tocqueville and the Old Regime* (Princeton, N.J., 1962); Cushing Strout, "Tocqueville's Duality: Describing America and Thinking of Europe," *American Quarterly*, 21 (Spring 1969), 87–99; Gianfranco Poggi, *Images of Society: Essays on the Sociological Theories of Tocqueville, Marx, and Durkheim* (Stanford, Calif., 1972); Hugh Brogan, *De Tocqueville* (New York, 1973, Fontana Books edition); Irving

M. Zeitlin, *Liberty, Equality, and Revolution in Alexis De Tocqueville* (Boston, 1971); Lee Benson, "Group Cohesion and Social and Ideological Conflict: A Critique of Some Marxian and Tocquevillian Theories," *American Behavioral Scientist,* 16 (May–June 1973), 744–67.

5. Edward Pessen, "The Egalitarian Myth and the American Social Reality," 1005.

6. Edward Pessen, "Did Fortunes Rise and Fall Mercurially in Antebellum America?," 340n.

7. Edward Pessen, "The Egalitarian Myth and the American Social Reality," 1018.

8. Ibid., 995–96.

9. Ibid., 1021, Table 12; 1023, Table 14.

10. Edward Pessen, "Did Fortunes Rise and Fall Mercurially in Antebellum America?," 343.

11. Edward Pessen, "The Egalitarian Myth and the American Social Reality," 997–98.

12. Ibid., 999–1001, 1004.

13. Edward Pessen, "Did Fortunes Rise and Fall Mercurially in Antebellum America?," 343–44.

14. Edward Pessen, "The Egalitarian Myth and the American Social Reality," 1021.

15. Ibid., 1024–25.

16. Ibid., 1025; Edward Pessen, "A Social and Economic Portrait of Jacksonian Brooklyn: Inequality, Social Immobility, and Class Distinction in the Nation's Seventh City," *New York Historical Society Quarterly,* 55 (October 1971), 328, 331.

17. Edward Pessen, "The Egalitarian Myth and the American Social Reality," 1022–23.

18. Ibid., 1020, 1022, ; Edward Pessen, "A Social and Economic Portrait of Jacksonian Brooklyn," 333.

19. Edward Pessen, "The Egalitarian Myth and the American Social Reality," 990.

20. Ibid., 1028.

21. Edward Pessen, "Did Fortunes Rise and Fall Mercurially in Antebellum America?," 345–46.

22. Edward Pessen, "The Egalitarian Myth and the American Social Reality," 1012.

23. Edward Pessen, "Did Fortunes Rise and Fall Mercurially in Antebellum America?," 345, 350; Pessen, "A Social and Economic Portrait of Jacksonian America," 337.

24. Edward Pessen, "Did Fortunes Rise and Fall Mercurially in Antebellum America?," 345; Pessen, "The Egalitarian Myth and the American Social Reality," 1016.

25. Edward Pessen, "The Egalitarian Myth and the American Social Reality," 1016.

26. Ibid., 1029.

27. Ibid., 1004, 1015.
28. Edward Pessen, "Did Fortunes Rise and Fall Mercurially in Antebellum America?," 357.
29. Edward Pessen, "The Egalitarian Myth and the American Social Reality," 1012; Pessen, "A Social and Economic Portrait of Jacksonian Brooklyn," 337.
30. Edward Pessen, "The Egalitarian Myth and the American Social Reality," 1026, 1029–30; see also Lee Soltow, "Economic Inequality in the United States in the Period from 1790 to 1860," *Journal of Economic History,* 31 (December 1971), 822–39, which emphasizes conditions in the South.
31. Edward Pessen, "The Egalitarian Myth and the American Social Reality," 1014–15, 1020.
32. Ibid., 1019–20, 1022; Allan Kulikoff, "The Progress of Inequality in Revolutionary Boston," *William and Mary Quarterly,* 28 (July 1971), 375–412, depicts increasing social and economic stratification.
33. Edward Pessen, "The Egalitarian Myth and the American Social Reality," 1027.
34. Ibid., 1027–28; Pessen, "Did Fortunes Rise and Fall Mercurially in Antebellum America?," 353. That poverty was a problem is evident in the response to it described in Raymond A. Mohl, "Humanitarianism in the Preindustrial City: The New York Society for the Prevention of Pauperism, 1817–1823," *Journal of American History,* 57 (December 1970), 576–99.
35. Edward Pessen, "The Egalitarian Myth and the American Social Reality," 994.
36. Ibid., 1028.
37. Peter R. Knights, *The Plain People of Boston, 1830–1860: A Study in City Growth* (New York, 1971), 58.
38. Lowell E. Galloway and Richard K. Vedder, "Mobility of Native Americans," *Journal of Economic History,* 31 (September 1971), 646.
39. Lee Soltow, *Patterns of Wealthholding in Wisconsin since 1850* (Madison, Wis., 1971), 139, comments on this difference.
40. Peter Barnes, "How Wealth Is Distributed: The GNP Machine," *New Republic* (September 30, 1972), 18–19.
41. Edward Pessen, *Jacksonian America,* 348.
42. Edward Pessen, "The Egalitarian Myth and the American Social Reality," 1018, 1030.
43. Ibid., 1018.
44. Edward Pessen, "A Social and Economic Portrait of Jacksonian Brooklyn," 348–49.
45. Ibid., 350.
46. David Grimsted, "Rioting in Its Jacksonian Setting," *American Historical Review,* 77 (April 1972), 361–74, 389–97.
47. Herbert Ershkowitz and William G. Shade, "Consensus or Conflict? Political Behavior in the State Legislatures during the Jacksonian Era, *Journal of American History,* 58 (December 1971), 592n. See also Pessen, *Jacksonian America,* 350.

48. After the appearance of Pessen's articles, Frederic Cople Jaher published "Nineteenth-Century Elites in Boston and New York," *Journal of Social History,* 6 (Fall 1972), 32—77.

Chapter Three: Confinement of the Consensus View

The Critical Response to Consensus History

1. Arthur M. Schlesinger, Jr., "Liberalism in America: A Note for Europeans," *Perspectives USA* (Winter 1956), reprinted in Schlesinger, *The Politics of Hope* (Boston, 1963), 65.
2. Ibid., 65.
3. John Higham, "The Cult of the 'American Consensus': Homogenizing Our History," *Commentary,* 27 (February 1959), 93—100.
4. Arthur Mann, "The Progressive Tradition," in John Higham, editor, *The Reconstruction of American History* (New York, 1962), 171.
5. J. Rogers Hollingsworth, "Consensus and Continuity in Recent American Historical Writing," *South Atlantic Quarterly,* 61 (Winter 1962), 49.
6. Irving H. Bartlett, *The American Mind in the Mid-Nineteenth Century* (New York, 1967), 40.
7. Marvin Meyers, "Louis Hartz, *The Liberal Tradition in America:* An Appraisal," *Comparative Studies in Society and History,* 5 (April 1963), 267.
8. Frank Otto Gatell, "Beyond Jacksonian Consensus," in Herbert J. Bass, editor, *The State of American History* (Chicago, 1970), 353.
9. Dwight W. Hoover, "Some Comments on Recent United States Historiography," *American Quarterly,* 17 (Summer 1965, Part 2), 316—18.
10. Burl Noggle, "Variety and Ambiguity: The Recent Approach to Southern History," *Mississippi Quarterly,* 17 (Winter 1963—64), 21—23.
11. Samuel P. Hays, "The Social Analysis of American Political History, 1880—1920," *Political Science Quarterly,* 80. (September 1962), 393.
12. Richard Hofstadter, *The Progressive Historians: Turner, Beard, Parrington* (New York, 1968), 444n. Hofstadter also discusses the strengths and weaknesses of the consensus school in "The Importance of Comity in American History," *Columbia University Forum,* 13 (Winter 1970), 8—13.
13. Ibid., 445, 463.
14. Ibid., 442.
15. Ibid., 440, 444. Richard B. Sherman, "The Idea of Consensus in Recent Writing on American History," *Historisk Tidskrift,* 3 (1967), 395, notes that certain works which do not specifically mention "consensus" are identified with this approach.
16. Richard Hofstadter, *The Progressive Historians,* 452, 453.
17. Ibid., 456, 457.
18. Ibid., 459.
19. Ibid., 458. In "Political Parties," in C. Vann Woodward, editor, *The Comparative Approach to American History* (New York, 1968), 207, Hofstadter writes, "The relative blandness and the unpolarized character of Ameri-

can two-party politics need not blind us, however, to the fact that sharp conflict has been a recurrent fact of American political life, with a fairly severe crisis taking place about once in a generation." Hofstadter here echoes a statement by Robert A. Dahl, whose work he acknowledges.

20. Richard Hofstadter, *The Progressive Historians*, 462.
21. Ibid., 463.
22. John Higham, "Beyond Consensus: The Historian as Moral Critic," *American Historical Review*, 67 (April 1962), 618–22.

The Great Exception: The Civil War

1. Daniel J. Boorstin, *The Genius of American Politics* (Chicago, 1953, Phoenix Books edition), 124–32.
2. Louis Hartz, *The Liberal Tradition in America: An Interpretation of American Political Thought since the Revolution* (New York, 1955), 145–77.
3. Louis Hartz, "South Carolina vs. the United States," in Daniel Aaron, editor, *America in Crisis: Fourteen Crucial Episodes in American History* (New York, 1952), 75.
4. Harry V. Jaffa, "Conflicts within the Idea of the Liberal Tradition," *Comparative Studies in Society and History*, 5 (April 1963), 276, 277.
5. Daniel J. Boorstin, *The Genius of American Politics*, 121. In *Equality and Liberty* (New York, 1965), 3–41, 114–39, Jaffa comments on Boorstin's and others' consensus view of American politics.
6. Richard Hofstadter, *The Progressive Historians*, 457.
7. John P. Diggins, "The Perils of Naturalism: Some Reflections on Daniel J. Boorstin's Approach to American History," *American Quarterly*, 23 (May 1971), 171–72.
8. John P. Diggins, "The Perils of Naturalism," 177.
9. Ibid., 177.
10. Ibid., 172–73.
11. Ibid., 177.
12. John P. Diggins, "Consciousness and Ideology in American History: The Burden of Daniel J. Boorstin," *American Historical Review*, 76 (February 1971), 107–108, 110.
13. John Rosenberg, "Toward a New Civil War Revisionism," *American Scholar*, 38 (Spring 1969), 250–72.
14. Phillip S. Paludan, "The American Civil War Considered as a Crisis in Law and Order," *American Historical Review*, 77 (October 1972), 1013–14, 1016–19, 1021, 1023–27, 1030–33.

The Abstract Quality of the Consensus Formula: "Capitalism"

1. Harvey Wish, "The New Formalism versus Progressive Historians," *South Atlantic Quarterly*, 67 (Winter 1968), 93.
2. Harold W. Chase and Paul Dolan, *The Case for Democratic Capitalism* (New York, 1964), 122–43, deals with "The Marriage of Political and Economic Systems."

3. Frederic C. Lane et al., "Meanings of Capitalism," *Journal of Economic History,* 29 (March 1969), 5–12.

4. R. Joseph Monsen, Jr., *Modern Capitalism: Ideologies and Issues* (Boston, 1963), 16–47.

5. Robert L. Heilbroner, *The Worldly Philosophers: The Lives, Times, and Ideas of the Great Economic Thinkers* (New York, 1953), 267. See also C. Joseph Pusateri, "A Study in Misunderstanding: Franklin D. Roosevelt and the Business Community," *Social Studies,* 60 (October 1969), 204–11.

6. Richard J. Barber, "The New Partnership: Big Government and Big Business," *New Republic* (August 13, 1966), 20; David T. Bazelon, "Big Business and the Democrats," *Commentary,* 39 (May 1965), 39–46; John H. Bunzel, "The General Ideology of Small Business," *Political Science Quarterly,* 70 (March 1955), 87–102; R. Joseph Monsen, Jr., and Mark W. Cannon, *The Makers of Public Policy* (New York, 1965), 24–63, which emphasizes the distinction between "managerial" and "small business" ideology.

7. See, for example, David T. Bazelon, *The Paper Economy* (New York, 1963); Adolf A. Berle, Jr., *The 20th Century Capitalist Revolution* (New York, 1954); Berle, *Power without Property: A New Development in American Political Economy* (New York, 1959); Gardiner C. Means, *The Corporate Revolution in America: Economic Reality versus Economic Theory* (New York, 1962); Bernard D. Nossiter, *The Mythmakers: An Essay on Power and Wealth* (Boston, 1964); Michael D. Reagan, *The Managed Economy* (New York, 1963); Edward Ziegler, *The Vested Interests: Their Origins, Development, and Behavior* (New York, 1964).

8. Basil Rauch, *The History of the New Deal, 1933–1938* (New York, 1963, Capricorn Books edition), x–xi.

9. Oscar and Mary Handlin, *The Dimensions of Liberty* (New York, 1966, Atheneum edition), 103, 109.

10. Robert A. Lively, "The American System: A Review Article," *Business History Review,* 29 (March 1955), 86.

11. Ibid., 81, 94.

12. Mario Einaudi, *The Roosevelt Revolution* (New York, 1959), 179.

13. Arthur M. Johnson, "Continuity and Change in Government-Business Relations," in John Braeman et al., editors, *Change and Continuity in Twentieth-Century America* (Columbus, Ohio, 1964), 219, holds that the principal locus of business decision-making is still business.

14. Walter Gellhorn, *Individual Freedom and Governmental Restraints* (Baton Rouge, La., 1956).

15. John D. Hicks, *Republican Ascendancy 1921–1933* (New York, 1960), 67.

16. John Morton Blum, "The Public Image: Politics," in Robert E. Spiller and Eric Larrabee, editors, *American Perspectives: The National Self-Image in the Twentieth Century* (Cambridge, Mass., 1961), 13.

17. Rexford G. Tugwell, "A Planner's View of Agriculture's Future," *Journal of Farm Economics,* 31 (February 1949), 46.

18. Samuel P. Hays, *The Response to Industrialism 1885–1914* (Chicago, 1957),

32–37, 63–65, describes the shift in the labor movement's attitude toward the wage system from the pre- to the post-Civil War eras.

19. Rexford G. Tugwell, "After the New Deal: 'We Have Bought Ourselves Time to Think,' " *New Republic*, 99 (July 26, 1939), 323 (emphasis mine).

20. Bernard Sternsher, *Rexford Tugwell and the New Deal* (New Brunswick, N.J., 1964), 154–69.

21. Rexford G. Tugwell and E. C. Banfield, review, Philip Selznick, *TVA and the Grass Roots: A Study of the Sociology of Formal Organization* (Berkeley, Calif., 1949), in *Public Administration Review*, 10 (Winter 1950), 47–55.

22. Louis D. Brandeis, "Competition," *American Legal News* (January 1913), reprinted in Ervin H. Pollack, editor, *The Brandeis Reader* (New York, 1956), 154, 177.

23. Walter Adams and Horace Gray, *Monopoly in America: The Government as Promoter* (New York, 1955), v.

24. Ibid., vi.

25. Arthur A. Ekirch, Jr., *The Decline of American Liberalism* (New York, 1955).

26. Otis L. Graham, Jr., editor, *The New Deal: The Critical Issues* (Boston, 1971, 198–99. Graham cites Henry Kariel, *The Decline of American Pluralism* (Palo Alto, Calif., 1961), Grant McConnell, *Private Power and American Democracy* (New York, 1966), and Theodore Lowi, *The End of Liberalism: Ideology, Policy, and the Crisis of Public Authority* (New York, 1969). See also Daniel R. Fusfeld, "The Rise of the Corporate State in America," *Journal of Economic Issues*, 6 (March 1972), 1–22, and Louis Kohlmeier, *The Regulators: Watchdog Agencies and the Public Interest* (New York, 1969). The widely read book by Michael Harrington, *The Other America* (New York, 1962), repeatedly asserts that the New Deal aided primarily the middle third of American society.

27. Yale Brozen, "Is Government the Source of Monopoly?" *Intercollegiate Review*, 5 (Winter 1968–69), 67–78.

28. Herbert Kriedman, Letter to the Editor, *New York Times*, September 20, 1971.

29. Gaylord Shaw, *Toledo Blade*, August 1, 1971.

30. Richard J. Barber, *The American Corporation: Its Power, Its Money, Its Politics* (New York, 1970), 289.

31. David J. Rothman, *Politics and Power: The United States Senate, 1869–1901* (Cambridge, Mass., 1966).

32. Michael Reagan, "Reconstructing the Corporate System," in Irving Howe, editor, *The Radical Papers* (New York, 1966, Anchor Books edition), 178. David B. Truman, *The Govermental Process* (New York, 1960), is excellent on the role of organized interest groups in the formulation of legislation.

The Abstract Quality of the Consensus Formula: "Democracy"

1. Irving Kristol, "American Historians and the Democratic Idea," *American Scholar*, 39 (Winter 1969–70), 90–93.

2. Ibid., 94–100, 103–104.

3. Ibid., 101.
4. Ibid., 102.
5. Richard Hofstadter, *The Progressive Historians,* 453, 458.
6. Ibid., 454.
7. Charles Frankel, *The Democratic Prospect* (New York, 1956, Harper Colophon edition), 24–25.
8. Dan Nimmo and Thomas D. Ungs, *American Political Patterns: Conflict and Consensus* (Boston, 1967), 40, 42.
9. Ibid., 35–43, 71–72.
10. Samuel A. Stouffer, *Communism, Conformity, and Civil Liberties: A Cross-Section of the Nation Speaks Its Mind* (Garden City, N.Y., 1955), 26–57.
11. James W. Prothro and Charles M. Grigg, "Fundamental Principles of Democracy: Bases of Agreement and Disagreement," *Journal of Politics,* 22 (May 1960), 277.
12. Ibid., 282.
13. Ibid., 284.
14. Ibid., 282–83.
15. Ibid., 285.
16. Ibid., 286.
17. Ibid., 287–88, 291, 293.
18. Ibid., 293–94.
19. Herbert McClosky, "Consensus and Ideology in American Politics," *American Political Science Review,* 58 (June 1964), 364–65.
20. Ibid., 365–66.
21. Ibid., 366.
22. Ibid., 366–69.
23. Ibid., 368–71.
24. Ibid., 371–73.
25. Ibid., 372.
26. Ibid., 373.
27. Ibid., 373.
28. Ibid., 373–75.
29. Ibid., 376–77.
30. Ibid., 377.
31. Ibid., 377–79.
32. Ibid., 378.
33. Ibid., 378.
34. Ibid., 377.
35. Fred H. Willhoite, Jr., "Political Order and Consensus: A Continuing Problem," *Western Political Quarterly,* 16 (June 1963), 295–96.
36. Ibid., 298–300.
37. Ibid., 300–301.
38. Ibid., 301–303.
39. Ibid., 302–304.
40. Gerald Garvey, "The Theory of Party Equilibrium," *American Political Science Review,* 60 (March 1966), 29–30, 38.

41. *New York Times,* December 10, 1972.
42. Richard Strout, *Toledo Blade,* May 6, 1973.
43. Walter Dean Burnham, "The Changing Shape of the American Political Universe," *American Political Science Review,* 59 (March 1965), 27 – 28.
44. Louis Hartz, "Democracy: Image and Reality," in William N. Chambers and Robert H. Salisbury, editors, *Democracy in Mid-Twentieth Century America* (St. Louis, 1960), 13 – 29.
45. Ibid., 14.
46. Ibid., 13.
47. Ibid., 14.
48. Ibid., 14.
49. Ibid., 15.
50. Robert G. McCloskey, "The American Ideology," in Marian D. Irish, editor, *Continuing Crisis in American Politics* (Englewood Cliffs, N.J., 1963), 10 – 24.
51. See John H. Bunzel, *Anti-Politics in America* (New York, 1966); Roland DeLorme and Raymond G. McInnis, editors, *Antidemocratic Trends in Twentieth-Century America* (Reading, Mass., 1969); Murray Clark Havens, *The Challenge to Democracy: Consensus and Extremism in American Politics* (Austin, Texas, 1965); Seymour Lipset and Earl Raab, *The Politics of Unreason* (New York, 1970); David Spitz, *Patterns of Anti-Democratic Thought,* revised edition (New York, 1965).

Selectivity: "Givenness," Winners, and Ideology

1. Richard Hofstadter, *The Progressive Historians,* 457 – 58.
2. J. R. Pole, "Daniel J. Boorstin," in Marcus Cunliffe and Robin W. Winks, editors, *Pastmasters: Some Essays on American Historians* (New York, 1969), 220.
3. Ibid., 227 – 28, 236.
4. J. R. Pole, "Historians and the Problem of Early American Democracy," *American Historical Review,* 67 (April 1962), 628 – 46.
5. John B. Kirby, "Early American Politics—The Search for Ideology: An Historiographical Analysis and Critique of the Concept of 'Deference,' " *Journal of Politics,* 32 (November 1970), 831 – 32, 835 – 36.
6. J. R. Pole, "Daniel J. Boorstin," 227 – 29, 231. David Hackett Fischer, "John Beale Bodley, Daniel Boorstin, and the American Enlightenment," *Journal of Southern History,* 28 (August 1962), 327 – 42, rejects Boorstin's contrast between European and American culture, questioning both Boorstin's interpretation of the European Enlightenment and his assertion that there was no "special class of learners," familiar with European intellectual currents, in America.
7. J. R. Pole, "Daniel J. Boorstin," 225 – 26, 231 – 32.
8. Ibid., 223, 226 – 27.
9. Ibid., 230 – 32.
10. Ibid., 232; Pole, "The American Past: Is It Still Useable?," *Journal of American Studies,* 1 (April 1967), 75. Commenting on the first two volumes

of *The Americans,* David Hackett Fischer, *Historians' Fallacies: Toward a Logic of Historical Thought* (New York, 1970, Harper Torchbooks edition), 96, writes of "a history of American religion in which Jonathan Edwards is an unperson; a history of American politics in which political parties scarcely exist, and in which Hamilton and Jefferson do not have a serious difference of opinion; a history of American culture in which Herman Melville appears mainly as an unsuccessful lecturer."

11. J. R. Pole, "Daniel J. Boorstin," 223, 228–29, 233.
12. John P. Diggins, "Consciousness and Ideology in American History," 107–108, 110.
13. Ibid., 109–10.
14. Ibid., 110.
15. Ibid., 111–12, 112n.
16. Ibid., 102, 104, 111, 113, 116–17.
17. David Hackett Fischer, *Historians' Fallacies,* 155–57.
18. Thomas A. Kreuger, "American Labor Historiography, Old and New: A Review Essay," *Journal of Social History,* 4 (Spring 1971), 284.
19. Rudolph J. Vecoli, "Ethnicity: A Neglected Dimension of American History," in Herbert J. Bass, editor, *The State of American History* (Chicago, 1970), 70–88, is a useful commentary.
20. Martin T. Katzman, "Ethnic Geography and Regional Economies, 1880–1960," *Economic Geography,* 65 (January 1969), 45–52.
21. Michael Novak, *The Rise of the Unmeltable Ethnics: Politics and Culture in the Seventies* (New York, 1972). See also Mark R. Levy and Michael S. Kramer, *The Ethnic Factor: How America's Minorities Decide Elections* (New York, 1971): and Perry L. Weed, *The White Ethnic Movement and Ethnic Politics* (New York, 1973).
22. Milton M. Gordon, "Assimilation in America: Theory and Reality," *Daedalus,* 90 (Spring 1961), 263–85.
23. Edward O. Laumann and David R. Segal, "Status Inconsistency and Ethnoreligious Group Membership as Determinants of Social Participation and Political Attitudes," *American Journal of Sociology,* 77 (July 1971), 36–61. Segal distinguishes between socially visible and nonvisible lower status, in sets of inconsistent statuses, as sources of stress in "Status Inconsistency, Cross Pressures, and American Political Behavior," *American Sociological Review,* 34 (April 1969), 352–59.
24. I. A. Newby, "Historians and Negroes," *Journal of Negro History,* 54 (January 1969), 37, 45n., 46n.

Chapter Four: Conflict within Consensus: Party Politics

Abundance, Uniqueness, and Turning Outward

1. Howard Quint, "Socialism and Communism in Modern America," in Quint et al., editors, *Main Problems in American History* (Homewood, Ill., 1964), 2: 154. For a listing of histories of American socialism that judge its

rejection more or less inevitable in the light of the Lockean consensus, see Kenneth McNaught, "American Progressives and the Great Society," *Journal of American History,* 53 (December 1966), 506n. Excellent relevant essays are David A. Shannon, "Socialism and Labor," in C. Vann Woodward, editor, *The Comparative Approach to American History* (New York, 1968), 238–52, and D. H. Leon, "Whatever Happened to an American Socialist Party?: A Critical Survey of the Spectrum of Interpretations," *American Quarterly,* 23 (May 1971), 236–58.

2. Thomas C. Cochran, "The Legend of the Robber Barons," *Pennsylvania Magazine of History and Biography,* 74 (July 1950), 308; William N. Chambers, *Political Parties in a New Nation: The American Experience 1776–1809* (New York, 1963), foreword.

3. Samuel P. Huntington, *Political Order in Changing Societies* (New Haven and London, 1968). Unlike economists, political scientists, and sociologists, historians have done relatively little work in comparative development. For an introduction to the vast literature on this subject see Louis Hartz et al., *The Founding of New Societies: Studies in the History of the United States, South Africa, Canada, and Australia* (New York, 1964); C. E. Black, *The Dynamics of Modernization: A Study in Comparative History* (New York, 1966); Barrington Moore, Jr., *Social Origins of Dictatorship and Democracy: Lord and Peasant in the Making of the Modern World* (Boston, 1966); I. Robert Sinai, *In Search of the Modern World* (New York, 1967). In addition to the essay by the political sociologist Seymour Martin Lipset and Stein Rokkan cited in chapter 2, two comparative inquiries by Lipset should be mentioned: "Some Social Requisites for Democracy: Economic Development and Political Legitimacy," *American Political Science Review,* 52 (March 1959), 69–105; *The First New Nation: The United States in Comparative and Historical Perspective* (New York, 1963). Marvin E. Olsen, "Multivariate Analysis of National Political Development," *American Sociological Review,* 33 (October 1968), 699–712, is an expansion of some of Lipset's ideas. R. R. Palmer, *Age of Democratic Revolution* (Princeton, N.J., 1964), 2: 509–43, finds no parallel between the United States in the 1790s and today's new nations but cautions against overestimating America's uniqueness and places the American Revolution in a Western international setting. J. Rogers Hollingsworth, editor, *Nation and State Building in America: Comparative Historical Perspectives* (Boston, 1971), 279–88, has a valuable bibliography.

4. Lee Benson, *The Concept of Jacksonian Democracy: New York as a Test Case* (Princeton, N.J., 1961), 276.

5. Daniel J. Boorstin, *The Genius of American Politics* (Chicago, 1953, Phoenix Books edition), 1.

6. Ibid., 4.

7. Ibid., 34.

8. Richard Hofstadter, *The Progressive Historians: Turner, Beard, Parrington* (New York, 1968), 445, writes, "Boorstin is primarily concerned to affirm the unexportability of American ways." A useful anthology is Edward G. McGrath, editor, *Is American Democracy Exportable?* (Beverly Hills, Calif., 1968).

9. Carl N. Degler, "The American Past: An Unexpected Obstacle in Foreign Affairs," *American Scholar,* 32 (Spring 1963), 207.

10. Carl N. Degler, "The Irrelevance of American History in the 1960's," College of Arts and Sciences Lecture Series, Seton Hall University, May 10, 1967.

11. Louis Hartz, *The Liberal Tradition in America: An Interpretation of American Political Thought since the Revolution* (New York, 1955), 305.

12. Marvin Meyers, "Louis Hartz, *The Liberal Tradition in America:* An Appraisal," *Comparative Studies in Society and History,* 5 (April 1963), 265.

13. John Higham, *Writing American History: Essays on Modern Scholarship* (Bloomington, Ind., 1970), 165.

14. Kenneth Barkin, "A Case Study in Comparative History: Populism in Germany and America," in Herbert J. Bass, editor, *The State of American History* (Chicago, 1970), 372; See also Donald R. McCoy, "Some Underdeveloped Sources of Understanding in American History," *Journal of American History,* 54 (September 1967), 257—61; C. Vann Woodward, editor, *The Comparative Approach to American History,* 3—17; Carl N. Degler, "Comparative History: An Essay Review," *Journal of Southern History,* 34 (August 1968), 425—30, on the Woodward volume; Paul F. Bourke, essay review of the Woodward volume in *History and Theory: Studies in the Philosophy of History,* 9:1 (1970), 110—16; Hans R. Guggisberg, "The Uses of the European Past in American Historiography," *Journal of American Studies,* 4 (July 1970), 1—18, which emphasizes the wider perspective and the insights obtained by relating the history of the Old and New Worlds; Martin Ballard, editor, *New Movements in the Study and Teaching of History* (Bloomington, Ind., 1971), which presents articles that explore the internationalization of historical study; Rushton Coulborn, "A Paradigm for Comparative History?," *Journal of World History,* 12 (1970), 414—21; and Fritz Redlich, "Toward Comparative History: Background and Problems," *Kyklos: International Review for Social Sciences,* 11:3 (1958), 362—89, which begins with Herodotus.

15. See, for example, George Rude's pioneering comparative study, *The Crowd in History: A Study of Popular Disturbances in France and England, 1730—1848* (New York, 1964).

16. J. Rogers Hollingsworth, *Nation and State Building in America,* 1—2.

17. Kenneth Barkin, "A Case Study in Comparative History, 397. In addition to Barkin's study, I have found the following comparative items to be provocative: Val R. Lorwin, "Reflections on French and American Labor Movements," *Journal of Economic History,* 17 (March 1957), 25—44; Leonard Krieger, "The Idea of the Welfare State in Europe and the United States," *Journal of the History of Ideas,* 24 (October—December 1963), 553—68; C. L. Mowat, "Social Legislation in Britain and the United States in the Early Twentieth Century: A Problem in the History of Ideas," Irish Conference of Historians, *Historical Studies,* 7 (1969), 81—96; Samuel Mencher, *Poor Law and Poverty Program: Economic Security Policy in Britain and the United States* (Pittsburgh, 1967); Paul Dukes, *The Emergence of the Super-Powers: A Short Comparative History of the USA and the USSR* (New

York, 1970); W. H. Parker, *The Superpowers: The United States and the Soviet Union Compared* (New York, 1972). Robert S. Walters, *American and Soviet Aid: A Comparative Analysis* (Pittsburgh, 1970). See also David M. Kennedy and Paul A. Robinson, editors, *Social Thought in America and Europe: Readings in Comparative Intellecual History* (Boston, 1971). Comparative studies in the economics of the 1930s, the period of my special interest, are many; see, for example, Royal Institute of International Affairs, *Monetary Policy and the Depression* (London, 1933), *Unemployment, An International Problem* (London, 1935), *World Agriculture, An International Survey* (London 1932); W. Arthur Lewis, *Economic Survey 1919–1939* (London, 1939); and Bertil Ohlin, *The Course and Phases of the World Economic Depression: Report Presented to the Assembly of the League of Nations* (Geneva, 1931). Also available are many histories of individual nations such as Douglass Coplan, *Australia in the World Crisis 1929–1933* (New York, 1934), Arthur Montgomery, *How Sweden Overcame the Depression 1930–1933* (Stockholm, 1938), and several recent histories of Britain and Canada in the 1930s; articles on individual nations are gathered in an issue of the *Journal of Contemporary History,* 4 (October 1969); historians are just beginning to pursue genuinely comparative approaches: see John A. Garraty, "Radicalism in the Great Depression," in Leon Borden Blair, editor, *Essays on Radicalism in Contemporary America* (Austin, Texas, 1972); Garraty, "The New Deal, National Socialism, and the Great Depression," *American Historical Review,* 78 (October 1973), 907–44; William E. Leuchtenburg, "The Great Depression," in C. Vann Woodward, editor, *The Comparative Approach to American History,* 296–314; Charles P. Kindleberger, *The World in Depression, 1929–1939* (Berkeley, Calif., 1973); and Herman Van der Wee, editor, *The Great Depression Revisited: Essays on the Economics of the Thirties* (The Hague, 1972), which is broader in its coverage than its title suggests. Otis L. Graham, Jr., "The Age of the Great Depression, 1929–1940," in William H. Cartwright and Richard L. Watson, Jr., editors, *The Reinterpretation of American History and Culture* (Washington, D.C., 1973), 5o8n., lists five additional comparative studies of efforts to achieve recovery in the 1930s. The Revolution is probably the only field in American history with a tradition of comparative study, although there are indications that soon there may be one concerning slavery.

Socioeconomic Conditions, Politics, and Policies, 1914–1962

1. Robert E. Lane, "The Politics of Consensus in an Age of Affluence," *American Political Science Review,* 59 (December 1965), 876–77.
2. Heinz Eulau, "The Ecological Basis of Party Systems: The Case of Ohio," *Midwest Journal of Political Science,* 1 (August 1957), 125–35. Phillips Cutright, "Urbanization and Competitive Party Politics," *Journal of Politics,* 35 (August 1963), 552–64, agrees with Eulau.
3. David Gold and John R. Schmidhauser, "Urbanization and Party Competition: the Case of Iowa," *Midwest Journal of Political Science,* 4 (February 1962), 62–75; Charles M. Bonjean and Robert L. Lineberry, "The

Urbanization-Party Competition Hypothesis: A Comparison of All United States Counties," *Journal of Politics,* 32 (May 1970), 305 – 19. See also Philip Coulter and Glen Gordon, "Urbanization and Party Competition: Critique and Redirection of Theoretical Research," *Western Political Quarterly,* 21 (June 1968), 274 – 88, and Richard Zody and Norman R. Luttbeg, "An Evaluation of Various Measures of State Party Competition, ibid., 21 (December 1968), 723 – 24.

4. Richard E. Dawson, "Social Development, Party Competition, and Policy," in William Nisbet Chambers and Walter Dean Burnham, editors, *The American Party Systems: Stages of Party Development* (New York, 1967), 237. See also Dawson and James A. Robinson, "Inter-Party Competition, Economic Variables, and Welfare Policies in the American States," *Journal of Politics,* 25 (May 1963), 265 – 89. James R. Elliott, "A Comment on Inter-Party Competition, Economic Variables, and Welfare Policies in the United States," *Journal of Politics,* 27 (February 1965), 185 – 91, and Thomas R. Dye, *Politics, Economics, and the Public: Policy Outputs in the American States* (Chicago, 1968), as we shall see below, assign little or no causal weight to interparty competition.

5. Charles F. Knudde and Donald J. McCrone, "Party Competition and Welfare Policies in the American States," *American Political Science Review,* 63 (September 1969), 865.

6. Ira Sharkansky and Richard I. Hofferbert, "Dimensions of State Politics, Economics, and Public Policy," *American Political Science Review,* 63 (September 1969), 877 – 88.

7. John H. Fenton and Donald W. Chamberlayne, "The Literature Dealing with the Relationships between Political Processes, Socioeconomic Conditions, and Public Policies in the American States: A Bibliographical Essay," *Polity,* 1 (Spring 1969), 388 – 404.

8. Charles F. Knudde and Donald J. McCrone, "Party Competition and Welfare Policies in the American States," 865.

9. Thomas R. Dye, *Politics, Economics, and the Public,* 247.

10. Ira Sharkansky, *The Politics of Taxing and Spending* (Indianapolis, 1969), 124. Other studies by Sharkansky are *Spending in the American States* (Chicago, 1968), and *The Maligned States: Policy Accomplishments, Problems, and Opportunities* (New York, 1972).

11. Ira Sharkansky, *The Politics of Taxing and Spending,* 34, 152 – 61.

12. Ibid., 156 – 59, 161 – 62, 164 – 69.

13. Ibid., 143 – 44.

14. Thomas R. Dye, *Politics, Economics, and the Public,* Table 9-1, 244 – 45.

15. Ibid., Figure 3-1, 51.

16. Ibid., 250.

17. Ibid., 258.

18. Richard E. Dawson, "Social Development, Party Competition, and Policy," 206, 211.

19. Ibid., 237.

20. The source of election results is Paul T. David, *Party Strength in the United States 1872 – 1970* (Charlottesville, Va., 1972).

21. For lengths of terms and names of governors see Council of State Governments, *The Governors of the States 1900−1958* (Chicago, 1957), and Richard M. Scammon, compiler and editor, *America Votes: A Handbook of Contemporary American Election Statistics 1962* (Pittsburgh, 1964).

22. Richard E. Dawson, "Social Development, Party Competition, and Policy," table 2, 215−16; tables 4, 5, 6, 222−24; tables 11, 12, 13, 231−33. Paul T. David, *Party Strength in the United States 1872−1970*, 9−14, discusses various measurements of party strength.

23. Thomas R. Dye, *Politics, Economics, and the Public*, 253−54.

24. John Shelton Reed, *The Enduring South: Subcultural Persistence in Mass Society* (Lexington, Mass., 1972). See also Sheldon Hackney, "The South as a Counterculture," *American Scholar*, 42 (Spring 1973), 283−93.

25. James T. Patterson, *The New Deal and the States: Federalism in Transition* (Princeton, N.J., 1969), 161−66.

26. Paul T. David, *Party Strength in the United States 1872−1970*, 17.

27. Thomas R. Dye, *Politics, Economics, and the Public*, figure 2-1, 31--32.

28. Ibid., figure 3-1, 51.

29. Ibid., table 3-3, 54.

30. Ibid., 53.

31. Ibid., 54.

32. Ibid., 52−53.

33. The data from Dye is in ibid., figure 2-1, 31−32.

Democrats and Republicans

1. Clinton Rossiter, *Parties and Politics in America* (New York, 1964, Signet Books edition), 128n.

2. Ibid., table 10, 129.

3. Ibid., 128. A more sophisticated analysis covering the decade and a half after the New Deal is David R. Mayhew, *Party Loyalty among Congressmen: The Difference between Democrats and Republicans, 1947−1962* (Cambridge, Mass., 1966). Categorizing all congressional districts as "interested" or "indifferent" and 110 roll calls in the House of Representatives with reference to four kinds of issues—farm, city, labor, and Western—Mayhew finds, ibid., 146−68, that the Democrats tend to adopt an "inclusive" approach (several bills, no one of which commands majority support, all pass through mutual support of congressmen from various types of districts) while the Republicans are inclined to follow an "exclusive" approach (several bills attracting minority support all fail, with "indifferent" Republican congressmen displaying more cohesion than "interested" Republican congressmen). The Democrats' inclusive approach, Mayhew notes, harmonizes with their ideology of welfare liberalism—the basis for what he considers a conservative welfare state—but he points to the possibility that "inclusive" compromise may be the hallmark of a dominant rather than a welfarist party.

4. Herbert McClosky et al., "Issue Conflict and Consensus among Party Leaders and Followers," *American Political Science Review*, 54 (June 1960), 426.

5. Walter Dean Burnham, *Critical Elections and the Mainsprings of American Politics* (New York, 1970), 56.

6. Samuel Lubell, *The Future of American Politics,* Third Edition, Revised (New York, 1965, Harper Colophon Books), 57.

7. Ibid., 57.

8. Ibid., 57, 59.

9. Ibid., 63.

10. Ibid., 64.

11. William E. Leuchtenburg, "The Pattern of Modern American National Politics," in Stephen E. Ambrose, editor, *Institutions in Modern America: Innovations in Structure and Process* (Baltimore, 1967), 52–53.

12. Ibid., 52–53.

13. Richard Hofstadter, "Political Parties," in C. Vann Woodward, editor, *The Comparative Approach to American History,* 208.

14. William E. Leuchtenburg, "The Pattern of Modern American National Politics," 53–54.

15. Clinton Rossiter, *Parties and Politics in America,* 128n.

16. Daniel Nelson, *Unemployment Insurance: The American Experience, 1915–1935* (Madison, Wis., 1969), 192–219.

17. Walter Dean Burnham, "Party Systems and the Political Process," in William Nisbet Chambers and Burnham, editors, *The American Party Systems,* 289–304.

18. Philip Converse et al., "Stability and Change in 1960: A Reinstating Election," *American Political Science Review,* 55 (June 1961), 274. See also Angus Campbell, et al., *The American Voter* (New York, 1960). Lubell used the phrase "normal majority party" in *The Future of American Politics,* 57.

19. Philip Converse et al., "Stability and Change in 1960," 274.

20. Ibid., 272–73.

21. V. O. Key, Jr., *The Responsible Electorate: Rationality in Presidential Voting 1936–1960* (New York, 1968, Vintage Books edition), 16.

22. Gerald Pomper, "Classification of Presidential Elections," *Journal of Politics,* 29 (August 1967), 559.

23. Ibid., 536.

24. V. O. Key, Jr., *The Responsible Electorate,* 30.

25. Ira Sharkansky, *The Politics of Taxing and Spending,* 98.

26. Gerald Pomper, "Classification of Presidential Elections," 556–57.

27. V. O. Key, Jr., "Secular Realignment and the Party System," *Journal of Politics,* 21 (May 1959), 204–205, 208.

28. V. O. Key, Jr., and Frank Munger, "Social Determinism in Electoral Decision: The Case of Indiana," in Eugene Burdick and Arthur J. Brodbeck, editors, *American Voting Behavior* (Glencoe, Ill., 1959), 297.

29. V.O. Key, Jr., "Secular Realignment and the Party System," 204.

30. E. Jeffrey Ludwig, "Pennsylvania: The National Election of 1932," *Pennsylvania History,* 31 (July 1964), 336, 351.

31. Harold F. Gosnell and Norman N. Gill, "An Analysis of the 1932 Presidential Vote in Chicago," *American Political Science Review,* 29 (December 1935), 984; John M. Allswang, "The Chicago Negro Voter and the

Democratic Consensus: A Case Study, 1918–1936," *Journal of the Illinois State Historical Society*, 60 (Summer 1967), 145–75. Allswang's full-length study is *A House for All Peoples: Ethnic Politics in Chicago, 1890–1936* (Lexington, Ky., 1971). Arthur Mann, *La Guardia Comes to Power 1933* (Philidelphia, 1965), treats ethnocultural and socioeconomic factors in his analysis of voting behavior.

32. Clinton Rossiter, *Parties and Politics in America*, 134–35.
33. John Kenneth Galbraith, *Economics and the Art of Controversy* (New York, 1959, Vintage Books edition), 77.
34. Clinton Rossiter, *Parties and Politics in America*, 134.
35. Friedrich A. Hayek, *The Road to Serfdom* (Chicago, 1956, Phoenix Books edition), ix; Louis O. Kelso and Mortimer J. Adler, *The Capitalist Manifesto* (New York, 1958), 129–37; Adolf A. Berle, Jr., "Whose Socialism?, A Story of Pots and Kettles," *Reporter* (October 30, 1958), 12; Henry Hazlitt, "Whose Welfare State?," *Newsweek* (February 20, 1960), 89; on the acceptance of the New Deal by Americans in general, see Eric F. Goldman, *The Crucial Decade–and After: America, 1945–1960* (New York, 1961, Vintage Books edition), 292; on the unwitting acceptance of the New Deal by many of its critics, see John Kenneth Galbraith, *Economics and the Art of Controversy*, 54; on the acceptance of the New Deal by college students, including conservatives, see Andrew Hacker, "Economic Ideas of Undergraduates," *Challenge: The Magazine of Economic Affairs*, 11 (June 1963), 17. Alfred B. Rollins, Jr., editor, *Depression, Recovery, and War: 1929–1945* (New York, 1966), 173, entitles a selection "Consensus Established: Wendell Willkie Accepts the Accomplishments of the Decade, 1940."
36. Walter Dean Burnham, *Critical Elections and the Mainsprings of American Politics*, 91–134, 132–33.
37. William E. Leuchtenburg, "The Pattern of Modern American National Politics," 55–56, 59, 62, 64–65. On the conservative coalition see Charles H. Gray, "The Social Base of the Coalition of Southern Democrats and Northern Republicans," *Political Science*, 17 (1965), 26–36; Barbara Hinckley, "Coalitions in Congress: Size and Ideological Distance," *Midwest Journal of Political Science*, 16 (May 1972), 197–207; John Robert Moore, "The Conservative Coalition in the United States Senate, 1942–45," *Journal of Southern History*, 33 (August 1967), 369–76; Moore, "Senator Josiah W. Bailey and the 'Conservative Manifesto' of 1937," *Journal of Southern History*, 31 (February 1965), 21–39; James T. Patterson, *Congressional Conservatism and the New Deal: The Growth of the Conservative Coalition in Congress, 1933–1939* (Lexington, Ky., 1967); Patterson, "A Conservative Coalition Forms in Congress, 1933–1939," *Journal of American History*, 52 (March 1966), 757–72; W. Wayne Shannon, "The Revolt in Washington: The South in Congress," in William C. Havard, editor, *The Changing Politics of the South* (Baton Rouge, La., 1972). *Congressional Quarterly* reports that in 1971 the conservative coalition won 86 percent of Senate votes and 79 percent of House votes on which Republicans and conservative Democrats united. Quoted in George Jenks, *Toledo Blade*, February 13, 1972.

38. William E. Leuchtenburg, "The Pattern of Modern American National Politics," 53.

39. Herbert McClosky et al., "Issue Conflict and Consensus among Party Leaders and Followers," 407.

Party Strength and Internal Improvements, 1836−1852

1. David R. Mayhew, "Party Systems in American History," *Polity,* 1 (Fall 1968), 138.

2. W. Dean Burnham, *Presidential Ballots, 1836−1892* (Baltimore, 1955) 246−55, is the source of the voting statistics on which party percentages of the two-party vote are based.

3. Richard P. McCormick, *The Second American Party System: Party Formation in the Jacksonian Era* (Chapel Hill, N.C., 1966). 15, 353. Joseph A. Schlesinger, "A Two-Dimensional Scheme for Classifying the States According to Degree of Inter-Party Competition," *American Political Science Review,* 49 (December 1955), 1120−38, finds the relationship between voter behavior in gubernatorial elections and national elections in the period 1872−1948 different from that which obtained under the second party system.

4. Charles Sellers, "The Equilibrium Cycle in Two-Party Politics," *Public Opinion Quarterly,* 29 (Spring 1965), 33.

5. George Rogers Taylor, *The Transportation Revolution, 1815−1860* (New York, 1951), 372, 374, 377−78.

6. Richard P. McCormick, *The Second American Party System,* 14. See also Charles G. Sellers, "The Equilibrium Cycle in Two-Party Politics," 31−32.

7. If the vote of other parties is counted, in eight of the sixteen cases in which the winning party's percentage of the two-party vote was 61.0 or more, the winning party's percentage of the total popular vote fell below 61.0—to the 45.4−56.4 range in seven instances and to 60.8 in Alabama in the election of 1852.

8. George Rogers Taylor, *The Transportation Revolution,* 377.

9. Arthur M. Schlesinger, Jr., *The Age of Jackson* (Boston, 1945), 520.

10. Lee Benson, *The Concept of Jacksonian Democracy,* 109; William S. Hoffman, *Andrew Jackson and North Carolina Politics* (Chapel Hill, N.C., 1948), 100−101.

11. Glyndon G. Van Deusen, "Some Aspects of Whig Thought and Theory in the Jacksonian Period," *American Historical Review,* 63 (January 1958), 315.

12. Carl N. Degler, *Out of Our Past: The Forces That Shaped Modern America* (New York, 1958), 150−51.

13. Robert A. Lively, "The American System: A Review Article," *Business History Review,* 29 (March 1955), 82; Carter Goodrich, "Internal Improvements Reconsidered," *Journal of Economic History,* 30 (June 1970), 289−311, reviews literature appearing since the publication of Lively's article in 1955 and, while conceding some qualifications, reasserts the importance of public investment in internal improvements.

14. James Neal Prim, *Economic Policy in the Development of a Western State: Missouri, 1820−1860* (Cambridge, Mass., 1964), 125, 127. On the Mis-

souri Whigs, who also favored internal improvements, see John Vollmer
Mering, *The Whig Party in Missouri* (Columbia, Mo., 1967).

15. Quoted in Carter Goodrich, "The Virginia System of Mixed Enterprise: A
    Study of State Planning of Internal Improvements," *Political Science Quarterly,* 64 (September 1949), 355, 384, 386.

Democrats and Whigs

1. Alfred A. Cave, *Jacksonian Democracy and the Historians* (Gainesville, Fla.,
   1964), 54–86.
2. Ibid., 54–61.
3. Arthur M. Schlesinger, Jr., Letter to the Editor, *American Historical Review,* 54 (April 1949), 785–86.
4. Arthur M. Schlesinger, Jr., "Richard Hofstadter," in Marcus Cunliffe
   and Robin W. Winks, editors, *Pastmasters: Some Essays on American Historians* (New York, 1969), 289, 458n.
5. Marvin Meyers, *The Jacksonian Persuasion: Politics and Belief* (New York,
   1960, Vintage Books edition), vii, 8, 13.
6. Major L. Wilson, "Time and Political Dialogue in the United States,
   1818–48," *American Quarterly,* 19 (Winter 1967), 619–44.
7. Elliott R. Barkan, "The Emergence of a Whig Persuasion: Conservatism,
   Democratism, and the New York State Whigs," *New York History,* 52 (October 1971), 394.
8. Michael A. Lebowitz, "The Jacksonians: Paradox Lost?" in Barton J.
   Bernstein, editor, *Towards a New Past: Dissenting Essays in American History*
   (New York, 1969, Vintage Books edition), 83.
9. Henry Bamford Parkes, *The American Experience: An Interpretation of the
   History and Civilization of the American People* (New York, 1959, Vintage
   Books edition), 147–55.
10. Carl N. Degler, "The Loco Focos: Urban Agrarians," *Journal of Economic
    History,* 16 (September 1956), 322–33.
11. Richard T. Farrell, "Internal-Improvement Projects in Southwestern
    Ohio, 1815–1834," *Ohio History,* 80 (Winter 1971), 23.
12. Robert W. Johannsen, "The Sixty-Third Meeting of the Organization of
    American Historians," *Journal of American History,* 57 (September 1970),
    376–77.
13. Frank Otto Gatell, "Beyond Jacksonian Consensus," in Herbert J. Bass,
    editor, *The State of American History,* 350–53, 355–56.
14. Richard E. Ellis, *The Jeffersonian Crisis: Courts and Politics in the Young
    Republic* (New York, 1971), 274–75, 277–78.
15. Ibid., 279–83.
16. Marvin Meyers, *The Jacksonian Persuasion,* 237.
17. Frank Otto Gatell, "Beyond Jacksonian Consensus," 350–53, 356.
18. Ibid., 351–52, 354, 358–59.
19. Louis Hartz, *The Liberal Tradition in America,* 89, 94, 96, 99–101, 106.
20. Ibid., 124–28. See also, Hartz, "The Rise of the Democratic Idea," in
    Arthur M. Schlesinger, Jr., and Morton White, editors, *Paths of American
    Thought* (Boston, 1963), 47.

21. Louis Hartz, *Economic Policy and Democratic Thought: Pennsylvania, 1776–1860* (Cambridge, Mass., 1948).
22. Ronald P. Formisano, *The Birth of Mass Political Parties: Michigan, 1827–1861* (Princeton, N.J., 1971), 38.
23. Ibid., 46.
24. Michael A. Lebowitz, "The Jacksonians: Paradox Lost?" 74–82.
25. Arthur M. Schlesinger, Jr., "Richard Hofstadter," 289.
26. John M. McFaul, *The Politics of Jacksonian Finance* (Ithaca, N.Y., 1972), 211.
27. The relevant studies are discussed in Alfred A. Cave, *Jacksonian Democracy and the Historians,* 63–73, with the exception of Donald B.Cole, *Jacksonian Democracy in New Hampshire, 1800–1851* (Cambridge, Mass., 1970); and Max R. Williams, "The Foundations of the Whig Party in North Carolina: A Synthesis and a Modest Proposal," *North Carolina Historical Review,* 47 (April 1970), 115–29; Thomas B. Alexander et al., "Who Were the Alabama Whigs?," *Alabama Review,* 16 (January 1963), 5–19; and John Vollmer Mering, *The Whig Party in Missouri* (Columbia, Mo., 1967), especially 52–70.
28. Donald J. Ratcliffe, "The Role of Voters and Issues in Party Formation: Ohio, 1824," *Journal of American History,* 59 (March 1973), 847.
29. William G. Shade, "A Social Interpretation of Hard Money Politics in the West: The Case of Illinois," summarized in Robert W. Johannsen, "The Sixty-Third Meeting of the Organization of American Historians," 372.
30. James Rogers Sharp, *The Jacksonians versus the Banks: Politics in the States after the Panic of 1837* (New York, 1970), viii.
31. Ronald P. Formisano, *The Birth of Mass Political Parties,* 136–64, 165–94.
32. Ibid., 331.
33. William Gerald Shade, *Bank or No Banks: The Money Issue in Western Politics, 1832–1865* (Detroit, 1972), 18–19. Shade concludes that ethno-religious factors best explain voting behavior in "Pennsylvania Politics in the Jacksonian Period: A Case Study, Northampton County, 1824–1844," *Pennsylvania History,* 39 (July 1972), 313–33. In "Banks and Politics in Michigan, 1835–1845: A Reconsideration," *Michigan History,* 57 (Spring 1973), 50–52, Shade rejects Floyd Benjamin Streeter's socioeconomic explanation of partisanship in *Political Parties in Michigan, 1837–1860* (Lansing, Mich., 1918), and asserts the importance of the symbolic function of the bank issue in the cultural politics of the Jacksonian era.
34. John M. McFaul, *The Politics of Jacksonian Finance,* xiii–xiv, 211–12, 214–15. Peter Temin, *The Jacksonian Economy* (New York, 1969), expresses the econometrician's view which McFaul refers to.
35. Ibid., 212–13, 215.
36. Joel H. Silbey, review, Ronald P. Formisano, *The Birth of Mass Political Parties,* in *Journal of American History,* 59 (December 1972), 714.
37. Joel Silbey, *The Shrine of Party: Congressional Voting Behavior, 1841–1852* (Pittsburgh, 1967); Thomas B. Alexander, *Sectional Stress and Party Strength: A Study of Roll-Call Voting Patterns in the United States House of Representatives, 1836–1860* (Nashville, 1967).
38. David J. Russo, *The Major Political Issues of the Jacksonian Period and the*

Development of Party Loyalty in Congress, 1830–1840 (Philadelphia, 1972), 3, 4, 7, 47.

39. Ibid., 4.
40. Ibid., 8.
41. Ibid., 4, 8, 41.
42. Rodney O. Davis, "Partisanship in Jacksonian State Politics: Party Divisions in the Illinois Legislature, 1834–1841" in Robert P . Swieringa, editor, *Quantification in American History: Theory and Research* (New York, 1970), 150, 157–61.
43. Ibid., 155.
44. William Gerald Shade, *Banks or No Banks,* 137, 160; Herbert Ershkowitz, "The Origins of the Whig and Democratic Parties in New Jersey," *Proceedings of the Second Annual Symposium of the New Jersey Historical Commission* (Newark, 1971), 27–28. In subsequent research Davis has made a social analysis of county-level political activists in Illinois in the period 1831–1846, concluding that ethnocultural and sectional-religious factors may have been the bases of differences between Democratic and Whig leaders. Dewey Grantham, "The Sixty-Sixth Annual Meeting of the Organization of American Historians," *Journal of American History,* 60 (December 1973), 716.
45. Erling A. Erickson, *Banking on the Iowa Frontier 1836–1865* (Ames, Iowa, 1971), 14, 120.
46. Ibid., 119, 123–41.
47. George D. Green, "The Louisiana Bank Act of 1842: Policy Making during Financial Crisis," *Explorations in Entrepreneurial History,* 7 (Summer 1970), 404–405, describes an ideological spectrum running from staunch defenders of banks to advocates of hard money, with Whigs being somewhat more pro-bank than the Democrats, but notes the lack of adequate evidence on the party affiliation of the legislators for making a more precise delineation of party alignments.
48. James Rogers Sharp, *The Jacksonians versus the Banks,* 15–16, 218–19, 229–30, 233, 236–37, 266, 272, 323–27, 333–46.
49. Edward Pessen, "Jacksonian Quantification: On Asking the Right Questions," in Herbert J. Bass, editor, *The State of American History*, 366.
50. Harry R. Stevens, *The Early Jackson Party in Ohio* (Durham, N.C., 1957), 149, 160–63.
51. Otis L. Graham, Jr., *An Encore for Reform: The Old Progressives and the New Deal* (New York, 1967), 230, cites the relevant studies. See also David P. Thelen, "Social Tensions and the Origins of Progressivism," *Journal of American History,* 56 (September 1969), 323–41.
52. Harry R. Stevens, *The Early Jackson Party in Ohio,* 151.
53. Donald J. Ratcliffe, "The Role of Voters and Issues in Party Formation," 847–50, 865–67, 870. Jon L. Wakelyn, "Party Issues and Political Strategy of the Charleston Taylor Democrats of 1848," *South Carolina Historical Magazine,* 73 (April 1972), 72–86, is an excellent account of developments which foreshadowed the collapse of the second party system.

54. Donald J. Ratcliffe, "The Role of Voters and Issues in Party Formation," 850−63, 865, 868.

55. Ibid., 869−70. Norman Gasque Raiford, "South Carolina and the Second Bank of the United States: Conflict in Political Principle or Economic Interest?," *South Carolina Historical Magazine,* 72 (January 1971), 30−43, maintains that South Carolinians were opposed to internal improvements and favored the bank but supported Jackson on the latter issue in the hope that he would strike a blow at protective tariffs.

56. Ronald P. Formisano, *The Birth of Mass Political Parties,* 266−88.

57. Donald J. Ratcliffe, "The Role of Voters and Issues in Party Formation," 848n.

58. Ibid., 868.

59. Herbert Ershkowitz and William G. Shade, "Consensus or Conflict? Political Behavior in the State Legislatures during the Jacksonian Era," *Journal of American History,* 58 (December 1971), 591--611.

60. Ibid., 611.

61. Ibid., 613.

62. Ibid., 614−17.

63. Ibid., 617−18, 621.

64. Ibid., 621.

65. Lee Benson, *The Concept of Jacksonian Democracy*; Frank Otto Gatell, "Money and Party in Jacksonian America: A Quantitative Look at New York City's Men of Wealth," *Political Science Quarterly,* 82 (June 1967), 235−52; Edward Pessen, "The Wealthiest New Yorkers of the Jacksonian Era: A New List," *New York Historical Society Quarterly,* 54 (April 1970), 145−72; Pessen, "Moses Beach Revisited: A Critical Examination of His *Wealthy Citizens* Pamphlets," *Journal of American History,* 58 (September 1971), 415−26; Pessen, "The Occupations of the Ante-Bellum Rich: A Misleading Clue to the Sources and Extent of Their Wealth," *Historical Methods Newsletter,* 5 (March 1972), 49−52; Robert Rich, " 'A Wilderness of Whigs': The Wealthy Men of Boston," *Journal of Social History,* 3 (Spring 1971), 265−76.

66. Robert Rich, " 'A Wilderness of Whigs,' " 265.

67. Ibid., 276.

68. Edward Pessen, "Who Governed the Nation's Cities in the 'Era of the Common Man'?" *Political Science Quarterly,* 87 (December 1972), 600−609.

69. David J. Russo, *The Major Political Issues of the Jacksonian Period,* 28.

70. For an account of the political career of a senator who voted probank in 1832 but supported Jackson after the veto, see John M. Belohlavek, "Dallas, the Democracy, and the Bank War of 1832," *Pennsylvania Magazine of History and Biography,* 96 (July 1972), 377−90.

71. Jean Alexander Wilburn, *Biddle's Bank: The Crucial Years* (New York, 1967), 15−16, 16n.

72. John William Ward, *Andrew Jackson: Symbol for an Age* (New York, 1962, Galaxy Books edition), 210−12.

73. John M. McFaul, *The Politics of Jacksonian Finance,* xii.

74. Michael Fellman, "The Earthbound Eagle: Andrew Jackson and the American Pantheon," *American Studies*, 12 (Fall 1971), 68, 75.

75. James C. Davies, "Charisma in the 1952 Campaign," *American Political Science Review*, 48 (December 1954), 1083–1102; Heinz Eulau, "Neither Ideology Nor Utopia: The New Deal in Retrospect," *Antioch Review*, 19 (Winter 1959–60), 533.

76. Perry M. Goldman, "Political Virtue in the Age of Jackson," *Political Science Quarterly*, 87 (March 1972), 62.

77. Burton W. Folsom II, "The Politics of Elites: Prominence and Party in Davidson County, Tennessee, 1835–1861," *Journal of Southern History*, 39 (August 1973), 359–78. Joel H. Silbey, editor, *Political Ideology and Voting Behavior in the Age of Jackson* (Englewood Cliffs, N.J., 1973), 180–81, finds the socioeconomic analysis weak and the ethnocultural interpretation very impressive, although it rests on case studies as yet too few in number. Frank Otto Gatell, "The Jacksonian Era, 1824–1848," in William H. Cartwright and Richard L. Watson, Jr., editors, *The Reinterpretation of American History and Culture* (Washington, D.C., 1973), 319, concludes that "subsequent work in the period, though increasingly chary of the consensus-entrepreneurial beliefs, has not been unified to form a substitute overview."

78. Elliott R. Barkan, "The Emergence of a Whig Persuasion," 394, referring only to New York.

79. Arthur M. Schlesinger, Jr., *The Age of Jackson* (Boston, 1945), ix–x.

80. Edward Pessen, "Why the United States Has Never Had A Revolution—Only 'Revolutions,' " *South Atlantic Quarterly*, 72 (Winter 1973), 29–42.

Chapter Five: The Belated Recognition of Violence in Our Past

Beyond Political Economy

1. Walter Dean Burnham, "Party Systems and the Political Process," in William Nisbet Chambers and Burnham, editors, *The American Party Systems: Stages of Political Development* (New York, 1967), 282.

2. Michael Wallace, "The Uses of Violence in American History," *American Scholar*, 40 (Winter 1970–71), 90–91.

3. Ibid., 82–90, 94–96.

4. James P. Young, *The Politics of Affluence: Ideology in the United States since World War II* (San Francisco, 1968), 7, 204.

5. Allan G. Bogue, "United States: The 'New' Political History," *Journal of Contemporary History*, 3 (January 1968), 26.

6. Lee Benson, *The Concept of Jacksonian Democracy: New York as a Test Case* (New York, 1964, Atheneum edition), 273, 275.

7. Lawrence W. Levine, *Defender of the Faith–William Jennings Bryan: The Last Decade, 1915–1925* (New York, 1965), 180.

8. J. Joseph Huthmacher, *Massachusetts People and Politics 1919–1933* (New York, 1969, Atheneum edition), 190, 311.

9. Walter Dean Burnham, "Party Systems and the Political Process," 282–87, cites Hays's essay, "Political Parties and the Community-Society Con-

tinuum," in William Nisbet Chambers and Burnham, editors, *The American Party Systems,* 152–81, and Lee Benson, *The Concept of Jacksonian Democracy,* 165–207.

10. Robert K. Merton, "Patterns of Influence: Local and Cosmopolitan Influentials," in Merton, *Social Theory and Social Structure* (Glencoe, Ill., 1949), 387–420.

11. Samuel P. Hays, "Political Parties and the Community-Society Continuum," 153–54.

12. Richard Hofstadter, "Reflections on Violence in the United States," in Hofstadter and Michael Wallace, editors, *American Violence: A Documentary History* (New York, 1971, Vintage Books edition), 12.

Some Reasons for Historians' Neglect of Violence

1. Michael Wallace, "The Uses of Violence in American History," 81.

2. Ibid., 81–82.

3. Ibid., 82. Richard Hofstadter, "Reflections on Violence in the United States," 10, 25, 27, notes the non-antistate nature of American violence.

4. Michael Wallace, "The Uses of Violence in American History," 98–99.

5. Ibid., 96–97. Hofstadter, "Reflections on Violence in the United States," 7, refers to the "circumscribed character and the small scale of the typical violent incident."

6. Michael Wallace, "The Uses of Violence in American History," 98–99.

7. Ibid., 82. Hofstadter, "Reflections on Violence in the United States," 11, writes, "A high proportion of our violent actions has thus come from the top dogs or the middle dogs." See also ibid., 22, 37, 39.

8. Michael Wallace, "The Uses of Violence in American History," 91–94. Hofstadter, "Reflections on Violence in the United States," 39, uses the phrase "capital violence." See also ibid., 20, 37.

9. Michael Wallace, "The Uses of Violence in American History," 97.

10. Ibid., 97–98.

11. Ibid., 98.

12. Ibid., 98.

13. Ibid., 95.

14. Ibid., 99.

15. Ibid., 99–100.

Violence and Consensus

1. Stephan Thernstrom, "Urbanization, Migration, and Social Mobility in Late Nineteenth-Century America," in Barton J. Bernstein, editor, *Towards a New Past: Dissenting Essays in American History* (New York, 1969, Vintage Books edition), 168–69, 171–72.

2. This generalization is based in part on more than one hundred reports written from welfare case files for Lima, Ohio, 1927–1950, by students in my courses.

3. Robert Wiebe, "The Confinements of Consensus," *Northwestern Tri-Quarterly,* 6 (1966), 158. See also Robert H. Binstock and Katherine Ely,

   editors, *The Politics of the Powerless* (Cambridge, Mass., 1971).
4. David Brody, *Steelworkers in America: The Non-Union Era* (Cambridge, Mass., 1962).
5. Michael Wallace, "The Uses of Violence in American History," 101.
6. Bernard Sternsher, editor, *Hitting Home: The Great Depression in Town and Country* (Chicago, 1970), 6–14.
7. David Grimsted, "Rioting in Its Jacksonian Setting," *American Historical Review,* 57 (April 1972), 361n.
8. Bernard Sternsher, editor, *Hitting Home,* 27–35.
9. Aileen Kraditor, "American Radical Historians on Their Heritage," *Past and Present: A Journal of Historical Studies,* 56 (August 1972), 139.
10. Ibid., 141–42, 153.
11. George Rude, *The Crowd in History: A Study of Popular Disturbances in France and England, 1730–1848* (New York, 1964), 218; quoted in Bernard Sternsher, editor, *Hitting Home,* 13.
12. Gabriel Kolko, *The Roots of American Foreign Policy: An Analysis of Power and Purpose* (Boston, 1969), 9–12. On the recruitment process, see Dennis M. Ray, "Corporations and American Foreign Relations," *Annals of the American Academy of Political and Social Science,* 403 (September 1972), 80–92. Ray does not share Kolko's deterministic view.
13. Gabriel Kolko, *The Roots of American Foreign Policy,* 12.
14. James P. Young, editor, *Consensus and Conflict: Readings in American Politics* (New York, 1972), 2–3, 8–10.
15. George Rude, *The Crowd in History,* 264, 266; quoted in Bernard Sternsher, editor, *Hitting Home,* 16.
16. Gabriel Kolko, *The Roots of American Foreign Policy,* 12.
17. See, for example, Herbert R. Northrup, "Organized Labor and Negro Workers," *Journal of Political Economy,* 51 (June 1943), 206–21, and the titles listed in Bernard Sternsher, editor, *The Negro in Depression and War: Prelude to Revolution, 1930–1945* (Chicago, 1969), 324–26.
18. Murray B. Levin, *Political Hysteria in America: Democracy's Capacity for Repression* (New York, 1972). See also Alan Wolfe, *The Seamy Side of Democracy: Repression in America* (New York, 1973); and Richard E. Rubenstein, *Rebels in Eden: Mass Political Violence in the United States* (Boston, 1970).
19. Peter Davies, *The Truth about Kent State: A Challenge to the American Conscience* (New York, 1973); Nathan Lewin, "Kent State Revisited," *New Republic* (August 18 and 25, 1973), 16–19.
20. Herbert McClosky, "Consensus and Ideology in American Politics," *American Political Science Review,* 58 (June 1964), 376–77.

The Time of Recognition

1. Michael Wallace, "The Uses of Violence in American History," 82, 98n.
2. Harvey Wish, "The New Formalism versus the Progressive Historians," *South Atlantic Quarterly,* 67 (Winter 1968), 93.
3. Bernard Crick, "The Strange Death of the American Theory of Consensus," *Political Quarterly,* 43 (January–March 1972), 52.

4. Robert A. Dahl, "Cleavage," in Dahl, editor, *Political Oppositions in Western Democracies* (New Haven and London, 1966), 50, 53.
5. Michael Wallace, "The Uses of Violence in American History," 102.
6. C. Vann Woodward, "The Future of the Past," *American Historical Review*, 75 (February 1970), 715.
7. Michael O'Brien, "C. Vann Woodward and the Burden of Southern Liberalism," *American Historical Review*, 78 (June 1973), 601.
8. A highly theoretical expression of this methodological point is Ian Budge, "Consensus Hypotheses and Conflict of Interest: An Attempt at Theory Integration," *British Journal of Political Science*, 3 (January 1973), 73–98.

Chapter Six: Consensus and the Politics of Affluence

The Decline of the Conventional Dichotomy

Walter Dean Burnham, *Critical Elections and the Mainsprings of American Politics* (New York, 1970), 135.
2. Ibid., 135–36.
3. Ibid., 138–39.
4. Ibid., 137.
5. Ibid., 140–41.
6. Everett Carll Ladd, Jr., *Ideology in America: Change and Response in a City, a Suburb, and a Small Town* (Ithaca, N.Y., 1969), 41–52, 170, 343. See also Ladd, "Hometown, U.S.A.: The Rise of Ideology," *South Atlantic Quarterly*, 67 (Winter 1968), 23–39. *Ideology in America* deals with Hartford, Bloomfield, and Putnam, Connecticut. A study by two sociologists, Don Martindale and R. Galen Hanson, *Small Town and the Nation: The Conflict of Local and Translocal Forces* (Westport, Conn., 1969), includes some historical information on Benson, Minnesota; Ritchie Lowry, *Who's Running This Town?* (New York, 1965), is about Chico, California, and Herbert Gans, *The Levittowners* (New York, 1967), is about a New Jersey community. A historian deals brilliantly with the community-society continuum in Robert Wiebe, *The Search for Order 1877–1920* (New York, 1967).
7. Everett Carll Ladd, Jr., *Ideology in America*, 47.
8. James P. Young, *The Politics of Affluence: Ideology in the United States since World War II* (San Francisco, 1968), 204.
9. *Newsweek* (August 28, 1972), 18.
10. TRB, *New Republic* (September 16, 1972), 6.
11. Walter Dean Burnham, *Critical Elections and the Mainsprings of American Politics*, 140.
12. Samuel Lubell, *Toledo Blade*, November 12, 1972.
13. James Burnham, *National Review*, 24 (September 1, 1972), 942.
14. Thomas Senior Berry, *On Measuring the Response of American Voters to Changes in Economic Conditions, 1792–1972* (Richmond, Va., 1972).
15. James P. Young, *The Politics of Affluence*, 7.
16. Richard M. Scammon and Ben J. Wattenberg, *The Real Majority* (New York, 1971, Capricorn Books edition), 20, 32, 39–40.

17. William E. Leuchtenburg, *Franklin D. Roosevelt and the New Deal 1932–40* (New York, 1963), 332.
18. Paul Yon, Seminar Paper, Bowling Green State University, 1972.
19. Mike Feinsilber, UPI, *Bowling Green Sentinel-Tribune*, November 14, 1972; Robert Axelrod, "Where the Votes Come From: An Analysis of Electoral Coalitions, 1952–1968," *American Political Science Review*, 66 (March 1972), 14–15, 17–18.
20. David R. Segal and David Knoke, "Political Partisanship: Its Social and Economic Bases in the United States," *American Journal of Economics and Sociology*, 29 (July 1970), 256–61.
21. Ibid., 261–62.
22. Jerome M. Clubb and Howard W. Allen, "The Cities and the Election of 1928: Partisan Realignment?," *American Historical Review*, 74 (April 1969), 1205–20.

Realignment or Partyless Politics?

1. Walter Dean Burnham, *Critical Elections and the Mainsprings of American Politics*, 26–30, 142–43.
2. Ibid., 158.
3. Ibid., 166, 168–70, 173.
4. Samuel Lubell, *Toledo Blade*, September 18 and 19, 1972.
5. Walter DeVries and V. Lance Tarrance, *The Ticket-Splitter: A New Force in American Politics* (Grand Rapids, Mich., 1972), 143.
6. TRB, *New Republic* (December 2, 1972), 6.
7. *Toledo Blade*, November 15, 1972.
8. *National Review*, 24 (November 24, 1972), 1286.
9. *Toledo Blade*, December 3, 1972.
10. Paul R. Wieck, "Coalition Politics," *New Republic* (December 9, 1972), 15–16.
11. Walter Dean Burnham, *Critical Elections and the Mainsprings of American Politics*, 174.
12. TRB, *New Republic* (December 2, 1972), 6.
13. Walter Dean Burnham, *Critical Elections and the Mainsprings of American Politics*, 174. See also Burnham, "The End of American Party Politics," *Trans-Action*, 7 (December 1969), 12–23, and Burnham, "Crisis of American Political Legitimacy," *Society*, 10 (November–December 1972), 24–31.
14. James W. Lindeen, "Longitudinal Analysis of Republican Presidential Electoral Trends, 1896–1968," *Midwest Journal of Political Science*, 16 (February 1972), 122.
15. John Roos, "American Political Life in the 1960's: Change, Recurrence, and Revolution," *Review of Politics*, 34 (October 1972), 47–48.

Moods, Values, and Attitudes toward Change

1. David S. Broder, *The Party's Over: The Failure of Politics in America* (New York, 1972); Richard H. Rovere, "The Sixties: 'This Slum of a Decade,'"

New York Times Magazine, December 14, 1969, 25–27, 66, 71, 73, 76, 78; William L. O'Neill, *Coming Apart: An Informal History of America in the 1960's* (Chicago, 1971); Elbert W. Stewart, *The Troubled Land: Social Problems in Modern America* (New York, 1972); Vance Packard, *A Nation of Strangers* (New York, 1972); Stephen Barber, *America in Retreat* (London, 1970); Norman Macrae, *The Neurotic Trillionaire: A Survey of Mr. Nixon's America* (New York, 1970).

2. David Brudnoy, *National Review,* 24 (September 29, 1972), 1068.

3. Howard P. Chudacoff, *Mobile Americans: Residential and Social Mobility in Omaha, 1880–1920* (New York, 1972).

4. Rowland Berthoff, *An Unsettled People: Social Order and Disorder in American History* (New York, 1971), 457–79.

5. John R. Brooks, "A Clean Break with the Past," *American Heritage* (August 1970), 7, 68–71.

6. Ibid., 70, 72–74.

7. Bruce Cook, *The Beat Generation* (New York, 1971); Jack Newfield, *A Prophetic Minority* (New York, 1970, Signet Books edition), 25–34.

8. Richard King, *The Party of Eros: Radical Social Thought and the Realm of Freedom* (Chapel Hill, N.C., 1972); Penina Migdal Glazer, "From the Old Left to the New: Radical Criticism in the 1940's," *American Quarterly,* 24 (December 1972), 584–603.

9. Clyde Kluckhohn, "Have There Been Discernible Shifts in American Values during the Past Generation?" in Elting E. Morison, editor, *The American Style: Essays in Value and Performance* (New York, 1958), 180, 184.

10. Ibid., 184.

11. Thomas C. Cochran, "History and Cultural Crisis," *American Historical Review,* 78 (February 1973), 6. See also Paul Carter, *The Twenties in America* (New York, 1968), 27–31; Thomas J. Osborne, "The Puritan Ethic in Postwar America," *Colorado Quarterly,* 21 (Spring 1973), 473, where the author notes that during the early twentieth century the "symbiotic relationship between the Puritan ethic and the commercial society began to break down," and that the confusion of values which marked the transition from an agrarian to an industrial society was aggravated by the strain of the post–Second World War transition from an industrial to a technetronic society; and John M. Blum, "Exegesis of the Gospel of Work, Success, and Satisfaction in Recent American Culture," in Charles Morris, editor, *Trends in Modern American Society* (Philadelphia, 1962), 17–36.

12. *New York Times,* June 26, 1971, 1, 37. Thirty-eight percent thought unrest would "blow over"; 15 percent had no opinion. The complete report is Albert H. Cantril and Charles W. Roll, Jr., editors, *Hopes and Fears of the American People* (New York, 1971).

13. *New York Times,* November 26, 1971.

14. William Watts and Lloyd A. Free, editors, *State of the Nation* (New York, 1973), 19–32.

15. James J. Kilpatrick, *Toledo Blade,* December 2, 1972.

16. *New York Times,* November 5, 1972.

17. Arthur M. Schlesinger, Jr., "How McGovern Will Win," *New York Times*

Magazine, July 30, 1972, 11; Kevin Phillips, "How Nixon Will Win," *New York Times Magazine,* August 8, 1972, 8–9.

18. Mike Feinsilber, UPI, *Bowling Green Sentinel-Tribune,* November 14, 1972.
19. Summarized in Peter Lisagor, *Toledo Blade,* November 19, 1972.
20. Ibid.
21. Ibid.
22. *Toledo Blade,* December 17, 1972.
23. Clayton Fritchey, *Toledo Blade,* December 17, 1972; Stewart Alsop, *Newsweek* (December 4, 1972), 130.
24. Kevin Phillips, "The Future of American Politics," *National Review,* 24 (December 22, 1972), 1398.
25. Lloyd A. Free and Hadley Cantril, *The Political Beliefs of Americans: A Study of Public Opinion* (New Brunswick, N.J., 1967), 36.
26. William G. McLoughlin, "Pietism and the American Character," *American Quarterly,* 17 (Summer 1965), 176.
27. Marcus Cunliffe, review, Michael Kammen, *People of Paradox: An Inquiry Concerning the Origins of American Civilization* (New York, 1972), in *New York Times Book Review,* October 1, 1972, 4; Kammen, editor, *The Contrapuntal Civilization: Essays toward a New Understanding of the American Experience* (New York, 1971). June L. Tapp and Fred Krinsky, editors, *Ambivalent America: A Psycho-political Dialogue* (Beverly Hills, Calif., 1971), deals with the tension between freedom and authority.

The Breakdown of Consensus: Pessimism and Optimism

1. Walter Dean Burnham, *Critical Elections and the Mainsprings of American Politics,* 176.
2. Ibid., 177–81, 191.
3. Ibid., 186–89, 193.
4. Bernard Crick, "The Strange Death of the American Theory of Consensus," *Political Quarterly,* 43 (January–March 1972), 46–51.
5. Ibid., 50, 52–55.
6. Ibid., 55, 57, 59.
7. Ibid., 51–52, 57–59.
8. Ibid., 52, 55–59. See also Crick, "A Defense of Politics against Ideology," in Crick, *In Defense of Politics,* Second Edition (Chicago, 1972), 35–57.

Bad Times and Good Times: Change and Politics

1. Don S. Kirschner, *City and Country: Rural Responses to Urbanization in the 1920's* (Westport, Conn., 1970), xvi, 242.
2. Richard Jensen, *The Winning of the Midwest: Social and Political Conflict, 1888–1896* (Chicago, 1972); Paul Kleppner, *The Cross of Culture: A Social Analysis of Midwestern Politics, 1850–1900* (New York, 1970); Frederick C. Luebke, *Immigrants and Politics: The Germans of Nebraska* (Lincoln, Neb., 1969); Samuel T. McSeveney, *The Politics of Depression: Political Behavior in*

the *Northeast 1893–1896* (New York, 1972), a study of Connecticut, New York, and New Jersey; Don S. Kirschner, *City and Country*; Thomas P. Jahnige, "Critical Elections and Social Change: Towards a Dynamic Explanation of National Party Competition in the United States," *Polity*, 3 (Spring 1971), 465–500. See also Robert P. Swierenga, "Ethnocultural Political Analysis: A New Approach to American Ethnic Studies," *Journal of American Studies*, 5 (April 1971), 59–79; Richard A. Gabriel, "A New Theory of Ethnic Voting," *Polity*, 4 (Summer 1972), 405–28; James E. Wright, "The Ethnocultural Model of Voting: A Behavioral and Historical Critique," *American Behavioral Scientist*, 16 (May–June 1973), 653–74; and Abraham H. Miller, "Ethnicity and Political Behavior: A Review of Theories and an Attempt at Reformulation," *Western Political Quarterly*, 24 (September 1971), 483–500. Joel H. Silbey and Samuel T. McSeveney, editors, *Voters, Parties, and Elections: Quantitative Essays in the History of American Popular Voting* (Lexington, Mass., 1972), 430–33, has an excellent bibliography.

3. Don S. Kirschner, *City and Country*, 241–44.
4. Lester Atwell, *Life with Its Sorrow, Life with Its Tear* (New York, 1972, Pocket Books edition).
5. Robert Nisbet, "The 1930's: America's Major Nostalgia," *Key Reporter* (Autumn 1972), 4.
6. Warren Susman, editor, *Culture and Commitment 1929–1945* (New York, 1973), 11–12.
7. Eric F. Goldman, "Good-By to the 'Fifties and Good Riddance," *Harper's Magazine* (January 1960), 27–29. Don Hausdorff, "Topical Satire and the Temper of the Early 1930's," *South Atlantic Quarterly*, 65 (Winter 1966), 32, states, "With the possible exception of the renewed emphasis on economics . . . every one of the trends [in magazine humor] that had become so apparent by 1935 had been set in motion well before the depression."
8. Thomas P. Cochran, "History and Cultural Crisis," 9.
9. John A. Garraty, "Radicalism in the Great Depression," in Lee Borden Blair, editor, *Essays on Radicalism in Contemporary America* (Austin, Texas, 1972), 108.
10. Alfred Haworth Jones, "The Search for a Usable American Past in the New Deal Era," *American Quarterly*, 23 (December 1971), 710–24.
11. Andrew Bergman, *We're in the Money: Depression America and Its Films* (New York, 1971).
12. Charles C. Alexander, *Nationalism in American Thought, 1930–1945* (Chicago, 1969).
13. Phillip Eisenberg and Paul F. Lazarsfeld, "The Psychological Effects of Unemployment," *Psychological Bulletin*, 35 (June 1938), 358–90.
14. Daniel Yankelovich, *The Changing Values on Campus: Political and Personal Attitudes of Today's College Students* (New York, 1972); cited in Peter N. Carroll and David W. Noble, *The Restless Centuries: A History of the American People* (Minneapolis, 1973), 2:469.

15. Peter L. Berger and Brigette Berger, "The Blueing of America," *New Republic* (April 3, 1971), 20–23.
16. Jerrold K. Footlick, "On Campus: A Separate Peace," *Newsweek* (November 6, 1972), 108.
17. Ibid., 108, 113.
18. Lawrence E. Eichel et al., *The Harvard Strike* (Boston, 1970).
19. Nick Thimmesch, *Toledo Times,* March 22, 1973; Florence Mouckley of the Christian Science Monitor Service reports similar developments at Northwestern, Harvard, Columbia, New York University, Princeton, and the University of California at Berkeley in the *Toledo Blade,* May 26, 1973. Also compare James Simon Kunen, *The Strawberry Statement: Notes of a College Revolutionary* (New York, 1969), and Kunen, "The Rebels of '70: Confessions of a Middle-Class Drifter," *New York Times Magazine,* October 28, 1973, 22–23, 67, 69–70, 72, 74, 78–79.
20. Harold L. Sheppard and Neal Q. Herrick, *Where Have All the Robots Gone? Worker Dissatisfaction in the '70s* (New York, 1972); Arthur B. Shostak, *Blue-Collar Life* (New York, 1969); Irving Howe, editor, *The World of the Blue-Collar Worker* (New York, 1972); William Serrin, *The Company and the Union: The "Civilized" Relationship between the General Motors Corporation and the United Auto Workers* (New York, 1973); see also the titles cited in Herbert G. Gutman, "Work, Culture, and Society in Industrializing America, 1815–1919," *American Historical Review,* 78 (June 1973), 537n.
21. *New York Times,* December 10, 1972.
22. Daniel Snowman, *America since 1920* (New York, 1970, Perennial Library edition), 69.
23. Arthur M. Schlesinger, Jr., "Sources of the New Deal: Reflections on the Temper of a Time," *Columbia University Forum,* 2 (Fall 1959), 4–7.
24. Daniel Yankelovich, *The Changing Values on Campus,* cited in Peter N. Carroll and David W. Noble, *The Restless Centuries,* 469.
25. *New York Times,* February 18, 1973.
26. Walter T. K. Nugent, *Modern America* (Boston, 1973), 289.
27. Frederick G. Dutton, *Changing Sources of Power: American Politics in the 1970's* (New York, 1972, McGraw-Hill Paperback edition), 31.
28. Ibid., 67–71.
29. Mike Feinsilber, UPI, *Bowling Green Sentinel-Tribune,* November 14, 1972.
30. *New York Times,* September 30, 1970.
31. Stewart Alsop, "The Disappearing Monkeys," *Newsweek* (December 4, 1972), 130.
32. *Toledo Blade,* December 1, 1972.
33. Frederick G. Dutton, *The Changing Sources of Power,* 342.
34. Ibid., 219.
35. John C. Pierce, "Party Identification and the Changing Role of Ideology in American Politics," *Midwest Journal of Political Science,* 14 (February 1970), 31–33, 41. On competition for the middle-class vote since 1900, see John Morton Blum, "The Public Image: Politics," in Robert E. Spiller and Eric Larrabee, editors, *American Perspectives: The National Self-Image in the Twentieth Century* (Cambridge, Mass., 1961), 134–53.

36. William Watts and Lloyd A. Free, editors, *The State of the Nation,* 211.
37. Leonard J. Fein, "To Try to Dream Again," *New York Times,* February 11, 1973.
38. William Watts and Lloyd A. Free, editors, *The State of the Nation,* 21, find such a division in responses to a question on the state of the nation: "Moderates . . . were happier about the overall situation than those in-toward either side of the political spectrum." Paul A. Samuelson, "Road to 1984," *Newsweek* (August 13, 1973), 84, judges President Nixon as an "ideologue" who has wanted "to turn back the clock of history to the pre-New Deal days," while Richard J. Whalen, "Between the Idea and the Reality," *National Review,* 25 (January 19, 1973), 100, asserts that President Nixon "betrays the party's principles and blights its fortunes [by pursuing] continuity, more prudent management of prevailing assumptions, policies, and programs."
39. Richard Hofstadter, "Reflections on Violence in the United States," in Hofstadter and Michael Wallace, editors, *American Violence: A Documentary History* (New York, 1971, Vintage Books edition), 43.

Chapter Seven: Consensus and Losers: The New Left

America since the 1890s

1. Gerald N. Grob and George Athan Billias, editors, *Interpretations of American History: Patterns and Perspectives*, Second Edition (New York, 1972), 1:19.
2. Ibid., 21.
3. David Donald, "Radical Historians on the Move," *New York Times Book Review,* July 19, 1970, 1, 16.
4. Clifford Solway, "Turning History Upside Down," *Saturday Review* (June 20, 1970), 15, 62.
5. Ibid., 62.
6. Robert Allen Skotheim, editor, *The Historian and the Climate of Opinion* (Reading, Mass., 1969), 107; Irwin Unger, "The 'New Left' and American History: Some Recent Trends in United States Historiography," *American Historical Review,* 72 (July 1967), 1248.
7. Robert Allen Skotheim, editor, *The Historian and the Climate of Opinion,* entitles part 3 "A Dissenting Neo-Progressivism in the 1960's: The New Left Historians."
8. Clifford Solway, "Turning History Upside Down," 13.
9. Ibid., 13—15.
10. William H. Ferriss, "The Pragmatic Definition of History," *Southern Humanities Review*, 5 (Spring 1971), 182—95, discusses New Left historiography as a continuation of the tradition of Barnes, Beard, Becker, Robinson, and Turner.
11. Gene Wise, *American Historical Explanations: A Strategy for Grounded Inquiry* (Homewood, Ill., 1973), 85—86, 93—97, 107.
12. Letter, Lloyd C. Gardner to writer, October 6, 1970.
13. Clifford Solway, "Turning History Upside Down," 15.

14. Ibid., 62.
15. Ibid., 15, 62.
16. Ibid., 62–63. Irwin Unger, "The 'New Left' and American History," 1244–47, discusses Williams' *The Contours of American History* (Cleveland, 1968), and lists Williams' other major works, 1246–47n. Since the appearance of Unger's article, Williams has published *The Roots of Modern American Empire: A Study of the Growth and Shaping of Social Consciousness* (New York, 1969).
17. Clifford Solway, "Turning History Upside Down," 64.
18. Ibid., 13, 15, 64. Relevant articles on the historical profession are Joseph E. Illick, "Professionalism and Politics in the A.H.A.," *Antioch Review,* 29 (Fall 1969), especially 422–27, and J. Anthony Lukas, "Historians' Conference: The Radical Need for Jobs," *New York Times Magazine,* March 12, 1972, 38–40, 42–47. James B. Gilbert, "Scholarship or Commitment: A Hassle of Historians," *Nation* (January 20, 1969), and Ronald Radosh, "Annual Set-to: The Bare-Knuckled Historians," *Nation* (February 2, 1970), are reprinted in Blanche Wiesen Cook et al., editors, *Past Imperfect: Alternative Essays in American History* (New York, 1973), 2:335–41.

Present-Mindedness

1. Sydney E. Ahlstrom, "The Moral and Theological Revolution of the 1960's and Its Implications for American Religious History," in Herbert J. Bass, editor, *The State of American History* (Chicago, 1970), 111.
2. Clifford Solway, "Turning History Upside Down," 63.
3. Irwin Unger, "The 'New Left' and American History," 1243–44, 1261–62. Unger, review, Barton J. Bernstein, editor, *Towards a New Past: Dissenting Essays in American History* (New York, 1968), in *Journal of American History,* 55 (September 1968), 371, lauds some of the essays and welcomes the possibility that this book might trigger a vigorous dialogue.
4. Irwin Unger, "The 'New Left' and American History," 1242–43.
5. Clifford Solway, "Turning History Upside Down," 14.
6. Edmund S. Morgan, *The Birth of the Republic 1763–89* (Chicago, 1956), 51, 100.
7. Max Savelle, review, Edmund S. Morgan, *The Birth of the Republic,* in *William and Mary Quarterly,* 45 (October 1957), 618.
8. Jack P. Greene, "The Flight from Determinism: A Review of Recent Literature on the Coming of the American Revolution," *South Atlantic Quarterly,* 61 (Spring 1962), 258.
9. Merrill Jensen, "Historians and the Nature of the American Revolution," in Ray Allen Billington, editor, *The Reinterpretation of Early American History* (New York, 1968, Norton Library edition), 121.
10. Jack P. Greene, "The Flight from Determinism," 258–59.
11. Jesse Lemisch, "The American Revolution from the Bottom Up," in Barton J. Bernstein, editor, *Towards a New Past* (New York, 1969, Vintage Books edition), 16.
12. Ibid., 6, 19.

13. Eugene Genovese, quoted in Henry Fairlie, "Years of Intellectual Havoc," *Encounter* (September 1972), 54.
14. Gerald N. Grob and George Athan Billias, editors, *Interpretations of American History,* 1:1. J. H. Hexter, "The Historian and His Day," *Political Science Quarterly,* 69 (June 1954), 219 – 33, criticizes both the "present-minded" and the "history-minded" schools of historical thought.
15. Merton J. Dillon, "The Abolitionists: A Decade of Historiography, 1959 – 1969," *Journal of Southern History,* 35 (November 1969), 502.
16. Lawrence W. Levine, "The Historian and the Culture Gap," in L. P. Curtis, Jr., editor, *The Historian's Workshop: Original Essays by Sixteen Historians* (New York, 1970), 309.
17. Bertram Wyatt-Brown, "The New Left and the Abolitionists: Romantic Radicalism in America"; Gerald W. McFarland, "Inside Reform: Status and Other Evil Motives"; Stephen B. Oates, "Woe If It Comes with Storm and Blood and Fire"; Bertram Wyatt-Brown, "Response," *Soundings: An Interdisciplinary Journal,* 54 (Summer 1971), 147 – 90.

A Usable Past and a New American Dream

1. Robert Allen Skotheim, "Two Challenges to Historians," review, Howard Zinn, *The Politics of History* (Boston, 1970), and Martin Duberman, *The Uncompleted Past* (New York, 1969), in *Historian,* 33 (May 1971), 453.
2. Richard Hofstadter, *The Progressive Historians: Turner, Beard, Parrington* (New York, 1968), 451.
3. Robert Allen Skotheim, "Two Challenges to Historians," 455; Skotheim, *Totalitarianism and American Social Thought* (New York, 1971), 111.
4. Robert Allen Skotheim, *Totalitarianism and American Social Thought,* 112.
5. Ibid., 110.
6. Robert Allen Skotheim, "Two Challenges to Historians," 455.
7. Ibid.
8. Robert Allen Skotheim, *Totalitarianism and American Social Thought,* 109.
9. Warren I. Susman, "History and the American Intellectual: Uses of a Usable Past," afternote, in Hennig Cohen, editor, *The American Experience: Approaches to the Study of the United States* (Boston, 1968), 105.
10. Robert Allen Skotheim, editor, *The Historian and the Climate of Opinion,* 3.
11. Pardon E. Tillinghast, *The Specious Past: Historians and Others* (Reading, Mass., 1972), 22.
12. Ibid., 130.
13. Ibid., 178.
14. Gil Green, *The New Radicalism: Anarchist or Marxist?* (New York, 1971).
15. George E. Mowry, "The Progressive Movement," in John A. Garraty, editor, *Interpreting American History: Conversations with Historians* (New York, 1970), 2:119.
16. Douglas F. Dowd, "The Economic History of the United States in the Twentieth Century," in Herbert J. Bass, editor, *The State of American History*, 264 – 66. See also Melville J. Ulmer, "Economics on the New Left: More than Marxist," *New Republic* (December 26, 1970), 13 – 14; and Sumner M.

Rosen, "Keynes without Gadflies," in Theodore Roszak, editor, *The Dissenting Academy* (New York, 1968), 62—91.

17. Reed Whittemore, *New Republic* (July 17, 1971), 29.

18. Melville J. Ulmer, *New Republic* (April 15, 1972), 27.

19. Assar Lindbeck, *The Political Economy of the New Left: An Outsider's View* (New York, 1971, paperback); Robert L. Heilbroner, "Radical Economics: A Review Essay," *American Political Science Review,* 66 (September 1972), 1017—20. See also Richard C. Edwards et al., editors, *The Capitalist System: A Radical Analysis of American Society* (Englewood Cliffs, N.J., 1972); David M. Gordon, *Theories of Poverty and Unemployment: Orthodox, Radical, and Dual Labor Market Perspectives* (Lexington, Mass., 1972), especially 53—81; Charles Perrow, editor, *The Radical Attack on Business* (New York, 1972); and George Fischer, editor, *The Revival of American Socialism: Selected Papers of the Socialist Scholars Conference* (New York, 1971), especially 1:3—60.

20. Melville J. Ulmer, *New Republic* (April 15, 1972), 27.

21. Richard L. Strout, *Christian Science Monitor,* January 8, 1972.

22. Melville J. Ulmer, "The Collapse of Keynesianism," *New Republic* (May 5, 1973), 18—21.

23. Peter L. Berger and Brigette Berger, "The Blueing of America," *New Republic* (April 3, 1971), 23.

24. Eugene D. Genovese, "The Fortunes of the New Left," *National Review,* 22 (December 1, 1970), 1266.

25. Michael P. Lerner, *The New Socialist Revolution: An Introduction to Its Theory and Strategy* (New York, 1973).

26. Quoted in Robert Allen Skotheim, *Totalitarianism and American Social Thought,* 111.

27. Aileen S. Kraditor, "American Radical Historians on Their Heritage," *Past and Present: A Journal of Historical Studies,* 56 (August 1972), 150. For Lynd's views see "Historical Past and Existential Present," in Theodore Roszak, editor, *The Dissenting Academy,* 92—109.

28. Quoted in Aileen S. Kraditor, "American Radical Historians on Their Heritage," 151.

29. Ibid., 153.

The Reform Tradition

1. Robert Allen Skotheim, editor, *The Historian and the Climate of Opinion,* 5.

2. Barton J. Bernstein, editor, *Towards a New Past* (New York, 1969, Vintage Books edition), ix.

3. Richard Hofstadter, *The Age of Reform: From Bryan to F.D.R.* (New York, 1955), 60—93; Victor Ferkiss, "Populist Influences in American Fascism," *Western Political Quarterly,* 10 (June 1957), 350—73.

4. Norman Pollack, *The Populist Response to Industrial America: Midwestern Populist Thought* (New York, 1966, Norton Library edition); Walter T. K. Nugent, *The Tolerant Populists: Kansas Populism and Nativism* (Chicago, 1963); Michael Paul Rogin, *The Intellectuals and McCarthy: The Radical*

Specter (Cambridge, Mass., 1967).

5. Norman Pollack, *The Populist Response to Industrial America,* 11–12, 143.
6. Walter T.K. Nugent, *The Tolerant Populists,* 231–36.
7. Sheldon Hackney, *Populism to Progressivism in Alabama* (Princeton, N.J., 1969), 87, 326.
8. John L. Shover, "Populism in the Nineteen-Thirties: The Battle for the AAA," *Agricultural History,* 39 (January 1965), 17–24.
9. John L. Shover, "The Farm Holiday Movement in Nebraska," *Nebraska History,* 43 (March 1962), 54; Shover, "The Communist Party and the Midwest Farm Crisis of 1933," *Journal of American History,* 51 (September 1964), 265–66.
10. John L. Shover, "The Farm Holiday Movement in Nebraska," 54, 77; Shover, "The Communist Party and the Midwest Farm Crisis of 1933," 261–66.
11. Arthur Mann, "The Progressive Tradition," in John Higham, editor, *The Reconstruction of American History* (New York, 1962), 161.
12. Gabriel Kolko, *The Triumph of Conservatism: A Reinterpretation of American History, 1900–1916* (Glencoe, Ill. 1963); Kolko, *Railroads and Regulation, 1877–1916* (Princeton, N.J., 1965).
13. Gabriel Kolko, *The Triumph of Conservatism* (Chicago, 1967, Quadrangle Paperbacks edition), 58.
14. Fred Greenbaum, "The Progressive World of Gabriel Kolko," *Social Studies,* 60 (October 1969), 225–27.
15. Ibid., 227. Greenbaum refers to Robert H. Wiebe, "Business Disunity and the Progressive Movement, 1901–1914," *Mississippi Valley Historical Review,* 44 (March 1958), 664–85.
16. Ibid., 225.
17. Stanley P. Caine, *The Myth of a Progressive Reform: Railroad Regulation in Wisconsin, 1903–1910* (Madison, Wis., 1970), xii–xiii, 113, 202–203.
18. Theodore Lowi, *The End of Liberalism: Ideology, Policy, and the Crisis of Public Authority* (New York, 1969), 297–303.
19. Robert B. Carson, "Railroads and Regulation Revisited: A Note on Problems of Historiography and Ideology," *Historian,* 34 (May 1972), 439, 441–43, 445–46.
20. Gabriel Kolko, *The Triumph of Conservatism,* 294–300.
21. Philip Selznick, *TVA and the Grass Roots: A Study in the Sociology of Formal Organization* (New York, Harper Torchbooks edition, 1966), ix.
22. Howard Zinn, editor, *New Deal Thought* (Indianapolis, 1966); Paul K. Conkin, *The New Deal* (New York, 1967); Barton J. Bernstein, "The New Deal: The Conservative Achievements of Liberal Reform," in Bernstein, editor, *Towards a New Past,* 263–88. I have stressed the shortcomings of the New Deal in light of persisting poverty and racial discrimination in "The New Deal 'Revolution,' " *Social Studies,* 57 (April 1966), 157–62. For an early, succinct statement of the New Left view of the New Deal by a non-New Left historian, see Daniel Aaron, *Men of Good Hope: A Story of American Progressives* (New York, 1961, Galaxy Books edition), 293 (origi-

nally published in 1951). A popular expression of the New Left view of the New Deal is Charles A. Reich, *The Greening of America* (New York, 1971, Bantam Books edition), 42–61.

23. Otis L. Graham, Jr., editor, *The New Deal: The Critical Issues* (Boston, 1971), xiv–xvi, 171, 173–74. Jerold Auerbach, "New Deal, Old Deal, or Raw Deal: Some Thoughts on New Left Historiography," *Journal of Southern History*, 35 (February 1969), 18–30. John Braeman agrees with Auerbach in "The New Deal and the 'Broker State': A Review of the Recent Scholarly Literature," *Business History Review*, 46 (Winter 1972), 428–29.

24. Aileen S. Kraditor, "American Radical Historians on Their Heritage," 138–39, 143–46, 150.

25. Otis L. Graham, Jr., editor, *The New Deal,* 171–75, 177–78.

26. Ibid., 173–78.

Foreign Policy

1. See the reference to Williams' writings above, section entitled "America since the 1890's," note 14. The Open Door thesis is also expounded in Lloyd Gardner, *Economic Aspects of New Deal Diplomacy* (Madison, Wis., 1964); Jerry Israel, *Progressives and the Open Door: America and China, 1905–1921* (Pittsburgh, 1971); Walter La Feber, *The New Empire: An Interpretation of American Expansion, 1860–1898* (Ithaca, N.Y., 1963); Thomas J. McCormick, *China Market: America's Quest for Informal Empire, 1893–1901* (Chicago, 1967); and William Appleman Williams, editor, *From Colony to Empire: Essays in the History of American Foreign Relations* (New York, 1972). Anyone who is interested in the revisionist approach to the history of American foreign policy must consult the works of Gar Alperovitz, Gabriel Kolko, N. Gordon Levin, Jr., and Arno J. Mayer.

2. In his latest book, *The Roots of Modern American Empire,* Williams maintains that this mistaken belief was evident in the preindustrial era. Chapter 3 is entitled, "The Belief in the Necessity of Expanding the Marketplace and the Coming of the Civil War."

3. Eugene Genovese, "William Appleman Williams on Marx and America," *Studies on the Left,* 6 (January–February 1966), 70–86.

4. Robert W. Tucker, *The Radical Left and American Foreign Policy* (Baltimore, 1971), 16.

5. Stanley Coben, "Northeastern Business and Radical Reconstruction: A Re-examination," *Mississippi Valley Historical Review,* 46 (June 1959), 67–90.

6. Paul S. Holbo, "Economics, Emotion, and Expansion: An Emerging Foreign Policy," in H. Wayne Morgan, editor, *The Gilded Age,* Revised and Enlarged edition (Syracuse, N.Y., 1970), 201.

7. Joan Hoff Wilson, *American Business and Foreign Policy, 1920–1933* (Lexington, Ky., 1971).

8. Robert L. Heilbroner, "Phase II of the Capitalist System," *New York Times Magazine,* November 28, 1971, 87, 90.

9. Ibid., 87.

10. Robert W. Tucker, *The Radical Left and American Foreign Policy,* 140–45.
11. Robert Zevin, "An Interpretation of American Imperialism," *Journal of Economic History,* 32 (March 1972), 334–36.
12. Ibid., 338, 341–42.
13. Ibid., 343–45.
14. Ibid., 345–46.
15. Ibid., 342–43.
16. Ibid., 348, 353, 360.
17. Michael Harrington, *Toward a Democratic Left: A Radical Program for a New Majority* (Baltimore, 1969, Pelican Books edition), 189–90, 192, 195, 197–99, 203, 206.
18. Ibid., 186, 188, 196, 201, 213–16.
19. Paul S. Holbo, "Economics, Emotion, and Expansion," 207.
20. Ibid., 209.
21. Ibid., 211. See also David L.T. Knudson, "A Note on Walter La Feber, Captain Mahan, and the Use of Historical Sources," *Pacific Historical Review,* 40 (November 1971), 519–22.
22. Arthur M. Schlesinger, Jr., "America II," *Partisan Review,* 4 (1970), 509–10. See also J. A. Thompson, "William Appleman Williams and the 'American Empire,' " *Journal of American Studies,* 7 (April 1973), 99–100.
23. Charles S. Maier, "Revisionism and the Interpretation of Cold War Origins," in *Perspectives in American History,* 4 (1970); reprinted in Richard M. Abrams and Lawrence W. Levine, editors, *The Shaping of Twentieth–Century America: Interpretive Essays,* Second Edition (Boston, 1971), 594.
24. G. V. Plekhanov, *The Role of the Individual in History* (Moscow: Foreign Language Publishing House, 1944), 37–41.
25. Julius W. Pratt, *Expansionists of 1898: The Acquisition of Hawaii and the Spanish Islands* (Chicago, 1964, Quadrangle Paperbacks edition), 252.
26. Ibid., 278.
27. Walter La Feber, *The New Empire,* 390.
28. Ibid., 391, 404.
29. Walter La Feber, "That Splendid Little War in Historical Perspective," *Texas Quarterly* (Winter 1968), 89–98; reprinted in James M. Banner et al., editors, *Understanding the American Experience: Recent Interpretations* (New York, 1971), 2:155, 159–60.
30. Marilyn Blatt Young, "American Expansion, 1870–1900: The Far East," in Barton J. Bernstein, editor, *Towards a New Past,* 177, 181–83, 186, 189–90.
31. Ibid., 182.
32. Walter La Feber, *The New Empire,* 406.
33. Ibid., 416–17.
34. Edmund S. Morgan, *The Birth of the Republic 1763–89* (Chicago, 1956), 51–52.
35. Walter La Feber, *The New Empire,* 408.
36. Ibid., 390.
37. Ibid., 404.

38. Ibid., 417.
39. Paul Varg, "The Myth of the China Market, 1890–1914," *American Historical Review,* 73 (February 1968), 742–58.
40. Marilyn Blatt Young, "American Expansion, 1870–1900," 178–79.
41. Walter LaFeber, "That 'Splendid Little War' in Historical Perspective," 157.
42. Arthur M. Schlesinger, Jr., "America II," 507.
43. Ibid., 518–19.
44. Ernest R. May, "The Cold War," in C. Vann Woodward, editor, *The Comparative Approach to American History* (New York, 1968), 338–99.
45. Andrew Hacker, "On Original Sin and Conservatives," *New York Times Magazine,* February 25, 1973, 66.
46. Harrison E. Salisbury, review, Vera Vladimirovna Vishnyakova-Akimova, *Two Years in Revolutionary China 1925–1927* (Cambridge, Mass., 1971), and other books, in *New York Times Book Review,* September 19, 1971, 2.
47. George F. Kennan, "The Sources of Soviet Conduct," *Foreign Affairs,* 25 (July 1947), 566–82; Kennan, *Memoirs, 1925–1950* (Boston, 1967), 354–67.
48. Walter La Feber, "That 'Splendid Little War' in Historical Perspective," 153–54.
49. Ibid., 154–55.
50. Ibid., 154.
51. Ibid., 154, 160.
52. Daniel Snowman, *America since 1920* (New York, 1970, Perennial Library edition), 96–101.
53. Norman A. Graebner, "American Imperialism," in Howard H. Quint et al., editors, *Main Problems in American History* (Homewood, Ill., 1964), 2:114–15.
54. Ibid., 115–16.
55. *New York Times,* December 10, 1964.
56. Bill Moyers, *Listening to America: A Traveler Rediscovers His Country* (New York, 1972, Dell Books edition), 37.
57. Paul A. Samuelson, "Economic Postmortem," *Newsweek* (February 5, 1973), 78.
58. Walter La Feber, "That 'Splendid Little War' in Historical Perspective," 153.
59. Arthur M. Schlesinger, Jr., "America II," 517. For a similar assessment of businessmen's views in an earlier period see Alfred E. Eckes, Jr., "Open Door Expansionism Reconsidered," *Journal of American History,* 59 (March 1973), 911.
60. Gabriel Kolko, *The Roots of American Foreign Policy: An Analysis of Power and Purpose* (Boston, 1969), 11–12. Kolko is among the most doctrinaire revisionist historians of foreign policy. Gar Alperovitz, for example, argues that American imperialism which began as "dollar diplomacy" transcended its historical roots and became a moral mission. He also disagrees with Kolko on the role of public opinion. Gar Alperovitz, *Cold War Essays* (New York, 1970, Anchor Books edition), 87, 120–21. The economic

concerns of policymakers, as distinct from businessmen, are evident in a National Security Council Statement of Policy of early 1952, "United States Objectives and Courses of Action with Respect to Southeast Asia," which notes the importance of the area as "the principal world source of natural rubber and tin, and a producer of petroleum and other strategically important commodities." This statement also mentions non–Open Door economic considerations: the importance of the rice exports of Burma and Thailand to other nations in the area, and the economic and political impact the loss of Southeast Asia would have on Japan. Neil Sheehan et al., *The Pentagon Papers as Published by the New York Times* (New York, 1972, Bantam Books edition), 27–28.

61. William Appleman Williams, *The Great Evasion: An Essay on the Contemporary Relevance of Karl Marx and on the Wisdom of Admitting the Heretic into the Dialogue about America's Future* (Chicago, 1964).

Unfulfilled Promise

1. Gerald W. McFarland, "Notes on the New Left Historians," *Soundings: An Interdisciplinary Journal,* 53 (Winter 1970), 443.
2. William E. Leuchtenburg, "The Great Depression and the New Deal," in John A. Garraty, editor, *Interpreting American History,* 2:192.
3. David Donald, "Radical Historians on the Move," 25.
4. John Higham, *Writing American History: Essays on Modern Scholarship* (Bloomington, Ind., 1970), 168.
5. David Donald, review, Barton J. Bernstein, editor, *Towards a New Past,* in *American Historical Review,* 74 (December 1968), 531–33.
6. David Donald, "Radical Historians on the Move," 6.
7. John Higham, *Writing American History,* 167–68. The New Left preoccupation Higham refers to is evident in these titles: Marvin E. Gettleman and David Mermelstein, editors, *The Great Society Reader: The Failure of American Liberalism* (New York, 1967), Robert P. Wolff, *The Poverty of Liberalism* (Boston, 1968), and Norman D. Markowitz, *The Rise and Fall of the People's Century: Henry A. Wallace and American Liberalism 1941–1948* (New York, 1973), an indictment of post–New Deal liberalism. See also R.J. Wilson, "United States: The Reassessment of Liberalism," *Journal of Contemporary History,* 2 (January 1967), 93–105.
8. Henry Fairlie, "Years of Intellectual Havoc," 52–53, 55.
9. Christopher Lasch, "On Richard Hofstadter," *New York Review of Books* (March 8, 1973), 12–13.

Chapter Eight: Conflict and Consensus and Change

The Role of Ideas in History

1. Pardon E. Tillinghast, *The Specious Past: Historians and Others* (Reading, Mass., 1972), 13.
2. Carl G. Gustavson, *A Preface to History* (New York, 1955), 153.
3. Ibid., 162.

4. John William Ward, "Direction in American Intellectual History," *American Quarterly*, 18 (Winter 1966), 704.
5. Max Lerner, "Beard's 'Economic Interpretation of the Constitution,' " in Malcolm Cowley and Bernard Smith, editors, *Books That Changed Our Minds* (New York, 1939), 145–60; David W. Marcell, "Charles Beard: Civilization and the Revolt against Empiricism," *American Quarterly*, 21 (Spring 1960), 65–86.
6. Merle Curti, *The Growth of American Thought*, Third Edition (New York, 1964), xi, introduction to 1943 edition.
7. Carl G. Gustavson, *A Preface to History*, 155, 161–63.
8. Bernard Sternsher, *Rexford Tugwell and the New Deal* (New Brunswick, N.J., 1964).
9. John Maynard Keynes, "The United States and the Keynes Plan," *New Republic* (July 29, 1949), 159.

A Comparison of Boorstin and Hartz

1. Daniel J. Boorstin, *The Genius of American Politics* (Chicago, 1953, Phoenix Books edition), 36.
2. Ibid., 53.
3. Ibid., 65.
4. Ibid., 10.
5. Ibid., 16.
6. Ibid., 120.
7. Ibid., 108, 116.
8. Ibid., 125.
9. Ibid., 125.
10. Louis Hartz, *The Liberal Tradition in America: An Interpretation of American Political Thought since the Revolution* (New York, 1955), 85–86.
11. Ibid., 146–48, 150–51, 153, 155.
12. Ibid., 10.
13. Ibid., 283.
14. Walter Dean Burnham, *Critical Elections and the Mainsprings of American Politics* (New York, 1970), 179.

Hartz and His Critics

1. Louis Hartz, *The Liberal Tradition in America*, 23.
2. Louis Hartz et al., *The Founding of New Societies: Studies in the History of the United States, Latin America, South Africa, Canada, and Australia* (New York, 1964), 16–20; Hartz, "A Comparative Study of Fragment Cultures," in J. Rogers Hollingsworth, editor, *Nation and State Building in America: Comparative Historical Perspectives* (Boston, 1971), 23–26.
3. Louis Hartz et al., *The Founding of New Societies*, 4.
4. Louis Hartz, *The Liberal Tradition in America*, 283.
5. Ibid., 308–309.
6. Ibid., 3.

7. Ibid., 20.
8. Louis Hartz, "Comment," *Comparative Studies in Society and History,* 5 (April 1963), 282–84.

A False Dichotomy

1. Howard Zinn, *Postwar America: 1945–1971* (Indianapolis, 1973), xvi–xvii.
2. Louis Hartz, *The Liberal Tradition in America,* 14.
3. Aileen Kraditor, "American Radical Historians on Their Heritage," *Past and Present: A Journal of Historical Studies,* 56 (August 1972), 140.
4. Bernard A. Weisburger, *The New Industrial Society* (New York, 1969), 142; John B. Kirby, "Early American Politics—The Search for Ideology: An Historiographical Analysis and Critique of the Concept of 'Deference,' " *Journal of Politics,* 32 (November 1970), 819.
5. Benjamin F. Wright, *American Interpretations of Natural Law* (Cambridge, Mass., 1931).
6. Merle Curti, "The Great Mr. Locke: America's Philosopher, 1783–1861," *Huntington Library Bulletin,* 11 (April 1937), 107–51.
7. Fred Shannon, An Appraisal of Walter Prescott Webb's *The Great Plains: A Study in Institutions and Environment,* with comments by Walter Prescott Webb, a Panel Discussion, and a Commentary by Read Bain, Social Science Research Council, Critiques of Research in the Social Sciences, 3 (New York, 1940); J. H. Hexter, review, Walter Prescott Webb, *The Great Frontier* (Boston, 1952), in *American Historical Review,* 63 (July 1953), 963; David Potter, review, Webb, *The Great Frontier,* in *American Political Science Review,* 47 (September 1953), 871–74.
8. An exception is Jacob E. Cooke, "The Federalist Age: A Reappraisal," in George Athan Billias and Gerald N. Grob, editors, *American History: Retrospect and Prospect* (New York, 1971), 91–92n.
9. Allen F. Davis and Harold D. Woodman, editors, *Conflict and Consensus* in *Modern American History,* Third Edition (Lexington, Mass., 1972), viii. See also James P. Young, editor, *Conflict and Consensus: Readings in American Politics* (New York, 1972).
10. Cushing Strout, "The Sun Also Sets: A Note on Degler, Riesman, and Tocqueville," in Hennig Cohen, editor, *The American Experience: Approaches to the Study of the United States* (Boston, 1968), afterword, 37–38. See also Strout, *The American Image of the Old World* (New York, 1963), and Strout, *The Pragmatic Revolt in American History: Carl L. Becker and Charles A. Beard* (Ithaca, N.Y., 1966), preface for the Cornell Paperbacks edition, iii–iv.
11. Richard S. Kirkendall, "The New Deal as Watershed: The Recent Literature," *Journal of American History,* 54 (March 1968), 852.
12. Ibid.
13. Ibid., 839.
14. Gene Wise, "Implicit Irony in Perry Miller's *New England Mind,*" *Journal of the History of Ideas,* 29 (October–December 1968), 582.
15. Paul K. Conkin and Roland M. Stromberg, *The Heritage and Challenge of*

History (New York, 1971), 266, refer to quantitative history as a "recent fad."

16. See, for example, John M. Allswang, *A House for All Peoples: Ethnic Politics in Chicago 1890–1936* (Lexington, Ky., 1971).

17. Charles Tilly, *The Vendee* (Cambridge, Mass., 1964).

18. Herbert G. Gutman, "Work, Culture, and Society in Industrializing America, 1815–1919," *American Historical Review*, 78 (June 1972), 531–87.

19. Ibid., 540–43, 563.

20. J. G. A. Pocock, Announcement, The Conference for the Study of Political Thought, January, 1968, 2.

21. J. H. Plumb, review, Fernand Braudel, *The Mediterranean and the Mediterranean World in the Age of Phillip II* (New York, 1972), in *New York Times Book Review*, December 31, 1972, 8, 14. Plumb discusses the work of the Annales school.

22. Allan G. Bogue, "United States: The 'New' Political History," *Journal of Contemporary History*, 3 (January 1968), 22. The advantages and limitations of quantitative history are enumerated in J. H. Hexter, *Doing History* (Bloomington, Ind., 1971), 135–56, and Jean Marczewski, "Quantitative History," ibid., 3 (April 1968), 179–91.

23. Allan G. Bogue, "The 'New' Political History," 26.

24. J. Rogers Hollingsworth, editor, *Nation and State Building in America*, 252–53.

25. Irving Kristol, "American Historians and the Democratic Idea," *American Scholar*, 39 (Winter 1969–70), 104.

26. Gene Wise, "Implicit Irony in Perry Miller's *New England Mind*," 582.

27. Gene Wise, *American Historical Explanations: A Strategy for Grounded Inquiry* (Homewood, Ill., 1973).

28. Thomas H. Smith, "The Renascence of Local History," *Historian*, 35 (November 1972), 1–17.

29. Bernard Sternsher, editor, *Hitting Home: The Great Depression in Town and Country* (Chicago, 1970), 36–40.

30. Samuel P. Hays, "The Politics of Municipal Government in the Progressive Era," *Pacific Northwest Quarterly*, 55 (October 1964), 157–69.

31. John Higham, *Writing American History: Essays on Modern Scholarship* (Bloomington, Ind., 1970), 173. Howard V. Evans, "Current Trends in American and European Historiography," *Michigan Academician*, 4 (Fall 1971), 143–60, notes that historical writing since 1945 has become more comparative—as well as more analytic, quantitative, oral, psycholanlytical, and socio-economic.

32. Kenneth McNaught, "American Progressives and the Great Society," *Journal of American History*, 53 (December 1966), 511.

33. A. L. Burt, "If Turner Had Looked at Canada, Australia, and New Zealand When He Wrote about the West," in Walker D. Wyman and Clifton B. Kroeber, editors, *The Frontier in Perspective* (Madison, Wis., 1957), 75–77.

34. Kenneth D. McRae, "The Structure of Canadian History," in Louis Hartz et al., *The Founding of New Societies*, 219–74.

35. Seymour Martin Lipset, *New York Times Book Review,* December 12, 1965, 34.
36. Eugene R. Black, *Virginia Quarterly Review,* 41 (Winter 1965), 124–25.
37. J. Roland Pennock, *American Political Science Review,* 59 (September 1965), 698.
38. Dietrich Gerhard, "The Frontier in Comparative View," *Comparative Studies in Society and History,* 1 (March 1959), 207.
39. Ibid., 209–10.
40. Ibid., 211–13.
41. Ibid., 213–15. On the "metropolitan" interpretation see Marvin W. Mikesell, "Comparative Studies in Frontier History," *Annals of the Association of American Geographers,* 50 (March 1960), 71.
42. Dietrich Gerhard, "The Frontier in Comparative View," 215–17.
43. Ibid., 215–16.
44. Ibid., 219, 224, 226–28.
45. Ibid., 228–29.
46. John M. Murrin, review, Michael Kammen, *People of Paradox: An Inquiry Concerning the Origins of American Civilization* (New York, 1972), in *William and Mary Quarterly,* 30 (July 1973), 495.
47. Everett M. Kassalow, "U.S. Ideology and European Pragmatism," *Challenge: The Magazine of Economic Affairs,* 11 (July 1963), 22–25.
48. F. S. C. Northrup, "Ideological Man in His Relation to Scientifically Known Natural Man," in Northrup, editor, *Ideological Differences and World Order* (New Haven, Conn., 1949), 412.

Index